DATE LOANED

APR 1 4 1987			
DEC 1 1 1997			
GAYLORD 3563			PRINTED IN U.S.A.

THE
FEDERAL LANDS
REVISITED

THE FEDERAL LANDS REVISITED

Marion Clawson

Published by Resources for the Future, Washington, D.C.
Distributed by The Johns Hopkins University Press, Baltimore and London

Copyright © 1983 by Resources for the Future, Inc.
All rights reserved
Manufactured in the United States of America

Published by Resources for the Future, Inc., 1755 Massachusetts Avenue, N.W.,
Washington, D.C. 20036
Distributed by The Johns Hopkins University Press, Baltimore, Maryland 21218;
The Johns Hopkins Press, Ltd., London

Library of Congress Cataloging in Publication Data

Clawson, Marion, 1905–
  The federal lands revisited.

  (A comprehensive overview of the federally owned lands in the United States)
  Bibliography: p.
  Includes index.
  1. United States—Public lands. I. Title. II. Series.
HD216.C529 1983   333.1'0973   83-42904
ISBN 0-8018-3097-4 (hard)
ISBN 0-8018-3098-2 (pbk.)

Resources for the Future is a nonprofit organization for research and education in the development, conservation, and use of natural resources, including the quality of the environment. It was established in 1952 with the cooperation of the Ford Foundation. Grants for research are accepted from government and private sources only on the condition that RFF shall be solely responsible for the conduct of the research and free to make its results available to the public. Most of the work of Resources for the Future is carried out by its resident staff; part is supported by grants to universities and other nonprofit organizations. Unless otherwise stated, interpretations and conclusions in RFF publications are those of the authors; the organization takes responsibility for the selection of significant subjects for study, the competence of the researchers, and their freedom of inquiry.

This book is a product of RFF's Renewable Resources Division, Kenneth D. Frederick, director. Marion Clawson is senior fellow emeritus at Resources for the Future. The illustrations were drawn by Graham Associates, Inc. The index was prepared by Florence Robinson. The book was edited by Jo Hinkel and designed by Elsa B. Williams.

Contents

Foreword   xi

Preface   xv

Acknowledgments   xix

1   The Federal Lands—Their Role in U.S. Society
       and the Economy   1

2   The History of the Federal Lands   15

3   Federal Land Use, Planning, and Management Today   63

4   Federal Land Ownership—The Retentionists' Case   123

5   The Federal Lands—The Disposers' Case   149

6   The Federal Lands—Future Directions   170

7   Special Problems of Intermingled Federal–Private Land
       Ownership   230

8   Public Participation—By Whom, How, and When?   247

9   The Need for Further Research   261

A Chronological List of Publications Concerning
    the Public Lands   274

Appendix   279

Index   295

Tables and Figures

Tables

2-1.   Federal Land Grants to Groups of States, 1803 Through Fiscal
        1980   22
2-2.   Summary of Statistics on Origin, Disposal, and Present Status
        of Federal Lands   26
3-1.   Outer Continental Shelf Oil and Gas Lease Sales, for 1954–80   91
3-2.   Coal and Surface Ownership in the Major Coal-Producing
        States of the Western United States, for 1978   92
3-3.   Use of the Federal Lands, Circa 1980   106
3-4.   Approximate Capital Value of Federal Lands Administered by
        the Forest Service and by the Bureau of Land Management,
        for Selected Years   111
3-5.   Appropriations for Management and Gross Receipts of the
        National Forests and BLM Lands, for 1950, 1965, and 1980   119

6-1.   Legal Allocation of BLM Receipts, for Fiscal Year 1980   172

7-1.   Summary of Federal Agency Experience With Land Exchanges   240

A-1.   Grazing of Domestic Livestock on the National Forests, for
        1960–80   281
A-2.   Amount of Grazing, Grazing Receipts, and Grazing Fees in
        Grazing Districts, and Grazing by Big-Game Animals in the
        National Forests, for 1960–80   282
A-3.   Number of Timber Sales, Volume, Value, and Stumpage Price
        of Timber Cut and Sold from the National Forests for
        1960–80   283
A-4.   Number of Sales, Volume, Value, and Average Stumpage Price
        for Timber Sold from O & C Lands, for 1960–80   284
A-5.   Number and Acreage of Oil and Gas Leases Under USGS
        Supervision for the Public Domain and the Outer Continental
        Shelf, for 1960–80   285
A-6.   Oil, Gas, and Gasoline Production from the Public Domain,
        for 1960–80   286
A-7.   Production Value and Royalty Value for Oil, Gas, and Gasoline
        from the Public Domain, for 1960–80   287
A-8.   Oil, Gas, and Gasoline Production from the Outer Continental
        Shelf, for 1960–80   288
A-9.   Production Values and Royalty Values for Oil, Gas, and
        Gasoline from the Outer Continental Shelf, for 1960–80   289
A-10.   Coal Leases on Public Lands (Excluding Acquired and Indian
        Lands), for 1960–80   290
A-11.   Recreation on Forest Service Lands and All Lands Adminis-
        tered by the BLM, for 1960–80   291
A-12.   Receipts of the BLM, for 1960–80   292
A-13.   Forest Service Cash Receipts and Other Income, for 1960–80   293
A-14.   Expenditures of the Forest Service and the BLM, for
        1960–80   294

Figures

2-1.   Major eras in federal land ownership and land management
        in the United States between 1782 and 2000   16
2-2.   U.S. land acquisition between 1782 and 1867   18
3-1.   Grazing by domestic livestock on national forests and grazing
        districts and by big game on national forests for 1905 to 1980 66
3-2.   Grazing fees, in current dollars, forests and grazing districts
        from 1933 to 1980   70
3-3.   The volume of timber cut from the national forests, and timber
        sales from the O&C lands for 1905 to 1980   74
3-4.   Softwood lumber production, imports of softwood lumber,
        and softwood plywood production between 1920 and 1980   76
3-5.   Prices of timber sold from the national forests and O&C lands
        from 1905 to 1980   78
3-6.   Number and acreage of oil and gas leases on on-shore federal
        (public domain) lands, and number of wells started between
        1940 and 1980   86
3-7.   Oil and gas-equivalent production from the federal lands
        (public domain) and from the Outer Continental Shelf, and
        royalty values per barrel between 1954 and 1980   88
3-8.   Coal leases, mines, production, and royalties per ton on the
        public domain from 1950–1980   94
3-9   Outdoor recreation on the National Forest System, the National
        Park System, and BLM lands between 1920 and 1980   100
3-10.   Visits to the National Forest System and the National Park
        System, per 100 of total population, between 1950 and 1980   103

Foreword

Public land management and ownership have come under increasing scrutiny in recent years, partly because of the increased value of federal lands. Lands that no one seemed to want a half-century ago, when the federal government was still disposing of much of its territory, are now often highly prized for their timber, minerals, energy, and amenity outputs. Rising federal deficits and a general slowdown in economic growth have helped to focus attention on the costs and inefficiency of federal land management. In particular, management of the federal resource lands by the Bureau of Land Management and the Forest Service has been criticized as being both unduly costly and inefficient.

Despite the growing interest in selling off the public lands, private land management has not been exempt from criticism. Erosion and conversion of prime agricultural farmland to nonagricultural uses are cited as evidence that unconstrained private ownership and management practices are contributing to the long-term deterioration of our natural resource base and threaten the capacity of future generations to produce food and fiber. Moreover, there is concern that private owners neglect nonmarketable benefits of the lands such as watershed protection and wildlife habitat.

As yet, the nation has developed no clear rationale for the ownership and management of its lands. The absence of a consensus as to the nature and importance of the problems and the appropriate solutions is evident in the contradictions and inefficiencies that characterize existing arrangements and the frustrations that permeate efforts at reform. While government ownership and management are attacked, public intervention in the use of private lands is being extended. Private owners often are constrained in the use of their land by an array of federal, state, and local regulations. While each of these regulations may make sense from the perspective of the narrow policy objectives underlying its adoption, together they impose a bewildering and often conflicting set of constraints on landowners.

Consensus on land use policy may be an illusive goal. There is no agreement as to what is wanted and obtainable from the lands and what is the proper role of the government and private sectors in land use decisions. Despite these differences, society should expect more from its lands. But better policy is likely to depend on an improved understanding of both what is and what might be.

A major line of work pursued by RFF's Renewable Resources Division in recent years has been designed to provide the analysis and understanding needed to illuminate our policy options for managing both public and private lands. Our agenda has included national conferences to stimulate informed discussion of the issues and a research program that addresses a number of important issues.

Three interrelated studies in the area of land use and the spatial economy have been supported by the Richard King Mellon Foundation. One study examines the criteria for land use planning and control and seeks to provide suggestions for a more rational and systematic approach to land use control, distinguishing those areas best left to private decision from those appropriate for public intervention. A second analyzes the changing geographic structure of the U.S. economy and provides a basis for projecting future changes in the location of activity and for identifying urban policy issues. A third study looks at major migration shifts and their causes in order to illuminate regional policy and planning implications.

Agriculture and forestry are the two largest users of U.S. lands. Current land use and long-term land needs of these sectors have been the focus of major research efforts by the division. Agricultural research, supported in part by the Andrew W. Mellon and the Rockefeller Foundations, includes analysis of the long-term adequacy of agricultural lands and the impacts of erosion. A national conference on "The Adequacy of Agricultural Land—Future Problems and Policy Alternatives" was held in June 1980. RFF's forestry program, supported by the Forest Service and the Weyerhaeuser Company Foundation, includes research on multiple use of public lands, analysis of nonindustrial private forests, and long-term timber supply.

The division's most recent effort to illuminate land use issues focuses on the ownership and management of federal lands. With support of the Andrew W. Mellon Foundation and the Lincoln Institute, a national workshop on "Rethinking the Federal Lands" was held in Portland, Oregon, in September 1982. Occurring simultaneously with the planning of that workshop, Marion Clawson's own reconsideration of the federal lands became the subject of this book. As he documents in the Preface, Dr. Clawson has been active as either an analyst or administrator of the federal lands for nearly a half-century. Many of the insights and experiences gained during that period are captured in this volume. Indeed, the personal touch and wisdom of one of the nation's most prolific and thoughtful writers on land use issues ensure that this book will be a valuable addition to a literature to which Dr. Clawson already has made enormous contributions. But this book is much more than a rehash of other literature; it provides some fresh insights and suggests new approaches to a problem that has been with us for a long time. This research has been supported by RFF internal funds as well as by program funding from the Richard King Mellon Foundation and the Weyerhaeuser Company Foundation.

Washington, D.C.
June 1983   KENNETH D. FREDERICK, Director,
                                               Renewable Resources Division

                                               EMERY N. CASTLE, President,
                                               Resources for the Future

Preface

For forty-five years I have been professionally concerned with the federal lands of the United States—first as an economist in the Bureau of Agricultural Economics of the U.S. Department of Agriculture; then for six years as regional administrator and director of the Bureau of Land Management in the U.S. Department of the Interior; and, since 1955, as a member of the research staff of Resources for the Future (RFF). I was born and raised in Nevada, where nearly all the land is federally owned, and my father homesteaded there. Thus, my involvement in federal land matters is long, deep, and highly personal.

In writing books and articles for professional journals or contributing chapters in books edited by others, all concerned primarily with federal land, I scarcely could fail to have learned something about these lands (see page 274 for a chronological listing of these publications). In fact, I have acquired a great deal of knowledge, perhaps a little wisdom, and surely my fair share of biases and prejudices. As a result of this experience, today I am less willing than I was twenty or thirty years ago to make unconditional statements, sweeping generalizations, and unreserved recommendations. The history and present situation of the federal lands in the United States are highly complex; and almost any generalization must be modified by a footnote explaining that at some time, or in some resource situation, or under some law, the situation differs from the generality. Then, in turn, one often must modify the footnote, explaining that in still other situations these special relationships do not fully hold.

Nevertheless, a few generalizations can be made about the federal lands of the United States:

- Federal land ownership is an integral part of U.S. history, society, and economy.

- The United States has a mixed public-private economy as far as land and associated resources are concerned. The area of federal land is large, it contributes substantially to the output of natural resource raw materials, and its assets value and annual revenues are each large.
- The role of federal lands in the national life has changed greatly over the past 200 years, and further changes during the next several decades are highly likely.
- Some twenty years or more from now, the late 1970s and 1980s may appear as an important juncture in this evolving federal land history. In many important respects, times have changed in the United States in recent years, and it well may be argued that changes in federal land policy to meet these changing times only now are getting under way.
- The importance of the federal lands—however one wishes to measure "importance"—is increasing, and with their increased importance come increasing conflicts over these lands.
- As a result of the forgoing, I conclude that now is a propitious time for a reexamination of basic federal land policy—How much federal land should there be? How and by whom should it be used, and on what terms? While history is highly important, the future is more so. The future history of the federal lands obviously begins now, and it may significantly differ from the past.
- It is wholly possibly to invent new institutions and new arrangements for the use of the federal lands.

This book is primarily concerned with the federal lands administered by the Forest Service and the Bureau of Land Management (BLM). Only incidental consideration, particularly in chapter 2, is given to the National Park System, the federal wildlife refuges, the military lands, and other special kinds of federal lands. Under present laws, the Forest Service and BLM lands share many administrative similarities: They are managed for multiple uses; they have important commercial uses from which large revenues are obtained; and inevitable competition exists among possible uses, with each use having its own advocates. In addition, the two agencies manage by far the greater area of the total federal estate.

This book has been written for those interested in federal lands. I hope that foresters, range managers, mineral specialists, wildlife specialists, wilderness lovers, recreation managers, and other profes-

sionally specialized persons directly involved in federal land use and
management will gain some insights into specialties other than their
own, and that they will judge the book to be sound in their fields.
Nevertheless, it has not been written primarily for such specialists.
Many persons who are concerned today with the federal lands are
not as well informed as they wish to be. Therefore, I hope that
federal and state legislators and their staff will find it equally helpful.

This book has been written in serious but nontechnical language.
I have tried to explain terms, describe events, and discuss land uses
and management in terms understandable to anyone. The writing
style and organization permit a rapid skimming of those parts in
which the reader is less interested, while permitting a closer reading
where one's interest is greater.

This book is a research report in its use of concepts and empirical
data, but it also is more personal in tone than the usual research
volume from RFF. I cite sources where data exist and other research
is reliable, but I also assert as facts a number of matters for which
such references have not been published, and I make personal
judgments as well. I justify this, at least to myself, on the grounds
that my long experience with the federal lands has given me a body
of information, a basis for judgment, and a validity of opinion which
are valuable because of that experience. Others may not, of course,
be quite so convinced of the validity of statements based on personal
knowledge, but I ask them to evaluate what I say in light of my long
and close involvement with the federal lands.

Chapter 1 briefly introduces some of the major policy issues
concerning federal lands and sets forth the reasons why I think
changing times merit a new consideration of the federal lands. Chapter
2 is a history, drawn from the many published works on the subject,
bringing together those events that I consider most significant, seeking
to be insightful and significant rather than novel. I would argue that
one cannot possibly understand the present use and management of
federal lands without having at least a rudimentary knowledge of
their history; and while many persons are generally familiar with that
history, others are not. Further, I would argue that change, which
so dominates history, will continue to do so in the future even if we
cannot predict the nature of that change.

Chapter 3 considers present usage of the federal lands, including
specific data on usage trends since World War II. The data come
from official reports and other sources, but their assembly in convenient form is useful for any reader. The more important of these
data are included in a series of appendix tables. In chapter 3 I have

estimated the capital value of the federal lands at four periods since the mid-1920s. The great value of these lands is often overlooked: their present value is equal to about half of the national debt, as that debt is customarily reported, and the rate of their increase in value has been faster than that of the national debt. Though an immensely valuable resource, they have not been managed with a view to the most productive use of this great pool of capital.

In chapters 4 and 5 I depart from my role as an impartial economic analyst and, in turn, became a spokesman for the continued retention and for the large-scale disposal of the federal lands. Acting as a self-selected spokesman for viewpoints which I do not necessarily hold, I present the arguments as I think those who hold these views would do. To the greatest extent practical, I have buttressed these arguments with data and the quotations from those who espouse these views.

In chapter 6 five major alternatives for future federal lands policy are presented. I explore in some detail the potential of increased leasing of federal lands, under terms specified in law, and for all purposes (including wilderness). The novel feature of this chapter is the idea of pullback—a device whereby any other person or group may select as much as one-third of the area applied for in a lease or sale by any applicant, meeting the terms the first applicant must pay to the federal government. This can be done without consent of either the original applicant or the federal agency. Such a pullback provision would open up management of the federal lands to competition among rival applicants in the same way that the private market opens up economic issues for competition. Yet, at the same time, it would preserve the long-term federal ownership of the land.

In chapter 7 the special problems arising out of the intermingling of federal and nonfederal lands are discussed, based on current data. In chapter 8 the requirements and the problems of public participation in federal land management are considered. Chapter 9 considers the need for further research on federal lands and describes the type of study most needed.

I only can hope that this intellectual fare will interest and prove valuable to the reader. I have attempted to focus on the concerns that today have the most relevance and impact on future federal lands policy.

Washington, D.C.
June 1983

Marion Clawson
Senior Fellow Emeritus
Resources for the Future

Acknowledgments

I have had help from many persons in preparing this book. I am pleased to acknowledge their contributions while at the same time absolving them from responsibility for my conclusions. Here at RFF I have benefited greatly from the encouragement and counsel of Emery N. Castle and Kenneth D. Frederick, and from the written comments of three anonymous reviewers. Robert O. Day (then at RFF) and Christopher K. Leman offered helpful comments on an earlier draft. Catherine S. Tunis assembled the data for the appendix tables, thereby adding substantially to the information in this book and relieving me of much time-consuming data gathering. At least three secretaries have been very helpful as this manuscript emerged: Lorraine A. Van Dine, Maybelle Frashure, and Cynthia L. Stokes.

Among those outside of RFF, I wish to acknowledge John Baden, Richard W. Behan, Sandra L. Blackstone, Henry Clepper, Paul J. Culhane, Kenneth W. Erickson, Perry R. Hagenstein, Steve H. Hanke, William F. Hyde, Thomas M. Lenard, Robert H. Nelson, Jerry A. O'Callaghan, Dean N. Quinney, William. E. Shands, George Siehl, and Carl H. Stoltenberg. To all of them go my thanks.

I wish also to acknowledge my long-term debt to Horace Marden Albright—formerly director of the National Park Service, president of U.S. Potash, chairman of the board of RFF, as well as holder of many other positions, recipient of many awards, and, above all, counselor and friend. His particular input to this book has been limited, but his influence on me—as on scores of others of my generation—has been great.

I am also indebted to Jo Hinkel of RFF, whose gentle but firm editing of this manuscript has contributed greatly to its clarity and to whatever grace and charm it may have.

M. C.

1

The Federal Lands—Their Role in U.S. Society and the Economy

Extensive federal land ownership has been an integral part of U.S. society and economy throughout our national history. Since October 29, 1782, when the Confederation Congress accepted the donation of publicly owned lands outside the boundaries of the former British colony and newly independent State of New York, the federal government has owned substantial areas of land not required for its own activities. New York had proffered its land a year and a half earlier, to help resolve the controversies between the new states with claims to "western lands" (meaning Ohio and westward) and those states without such claims. Virginia, Massachusetts, Connecticut, South Carolina, North Carolina, and Georgia followed New York's example and, by 1802, the United States of America (under the Constitution adopted in 1789) had acquired by this means some 233 million acres of land—encompassing most of the territory westward from the original Thirteen Colonies to the Mississippi River. Federal land ownership thus antedates the Constitution, and some of the most significant legislation regarding these lands was passed during the period of Confederation.

Every government owns some land, for post offices or other government offices, for military forts and reservations, for lighthouses, and for scores of other public purposes. But this new federal ownership—the *public domain*—was generally expected to be transferred to private ownership for farms, forests, mines, cities, and other private land uses, and, indeed, much of it was. Although the original states donated to the national government those lands outside their

1

present boundaries, they retained the land they owned within those boundaries, and states later created out of the public domain (beginning with Ohio in 1802), or obtained by incorporation of previously independent countries (Texas in 1845, and Hawaii annexed in 1898), also had state lands.

Policy Issues

Throughout these 200 years of history, there have been several major policy issues. They may be broadly classified as follows:[1]

- How much land should the national government acquire by conquest, by treaty, or by purchase?
- Of the land acquired by the federal government, how much should be disposed of to private or to other governmental ownership, and how much should be retained more or less permanently in federal ownership?
- Assuming that at least some land will be disposed of, to whom should disposals be made? Should the disposals be permanent and complete—that is, in patent or fee simple? Should some parts of the bundle of land ownership rights, for example, mineral rights, be retained while other rights are disposed of? If the disposal is for a limited period only, to whom should it be made? And how can we assure the return of the use rights to the federal government at the end of the period?
- If permanent or temporary disposal is chosen, on what terms shall the federal lands be made available? If a price is to be paid, how shall it be determined—by specific prices in the law, by an administrator, or by public sale or auction? What terms (residency, maximum acreage, cultivation, and so on) other than price shall be imposed?
- If the decision is made to retain permanent title in the federal government for at least some land but also to permit private use, what conditions shall be imposed on such use? How shall one use be chosen over another? How shall one user be chosen in preference to another? By what means shall such decisions be enforced?
- How much effort and how many federal dollars shall be expended to conserve or preserve the federal lands against erosion, im-

pairment of plant cover, despoilation of aesthetic values, and the like? And how much should be spent on their management?

- What sort of relationship should exist between the federal, state, and local governments in the management of the federal lands and in the sharing of the revenues from them?
- How shall the planning for the use, management, disposal, retention, and other aspects of federal lands be carried on? What are the proper roles of interested users, other members of the public, elected officials in the legislative branches, elected or appointed officials in the executive branch, and the courts?

There have been scores, perhaps hundreds, of specific policy issues and struggles over the past two centuries, but most or all of them and all of the current issues can comfortably be fitted into this general schema of policy issues.

Wars and Armistices

The continued struggles between differing groups over these policy issues resemble a long-continued war among tribes or nations. With the actors sometimes allied one way, sometimes another, with no complete and lasting victory occurring at any time, these basic policy issues can never be settled permanently. Laws can be passed that seem to settle a policy issue, at least for the moment, but interpretation of the law is likely to renew the policy struggle and, for this reason, laws typically are amended with the passage of time.

A new law is an armistice which temporarily brings to a halt a long continuing political struggle. The armistice is agreed to when the parties involved realize, for the present, that complete victory is impossible and that continued fight will gain them less than a cessation. It provides time to care for the wounded, to bury the dead, to regroup forces, to bring up reinforcements, and to assemble new supplies. When the struggle is old and basic, there is little reason to expect that the armistice constitutes a final solution, though it may change the conditions for future struggle.[2]

The importance of each of these policy issues or of any combination of them has waxed and waned in public consciousness over the 200 years of federal land ownership. As I note in chapter 2, disposition of the public domain was a major national issue—indeed, at times the dominant national issue—throughout the nineteenth century. But interest in federal lands and in resource matters generally dropped off after World War I, perhaps reaching a low point through the 1920s.[3] In recent times, however, interest in federal lands has greatly revived. For reasons discussed below, times have changed—no less for the federal lands and the federal land-managing agencies than for many other aspects of national life.

The Private Economy

The United States is known throughout the world as one country where private enterprise and private ownership of property are dominant. How can this be reconciled with the extensive federal ownership of land—an ownership described as recently as 1970 as "one-third of the nation's land" and even now, after large chunks have been given to Alaska, one-fourth or more of the total land area?[4] This is a question which I have been asked many times, by professional workers in other countries who are uninformed about American land history, and it is not an unknown question within the United States.

The explanation for the continued and more or less permanent federal ownership of large areas of land in a country basically oriented toward private business and private property lies in the fact that private parties have had use of most of this large area. The government has used some areas for military reservations, for development of nuclear reactors, and for other special purposes; but in comparison with the total federal area, these have been limited. The vast majority of federal lands are used by ranchers, whose herds of cattle and bands of sheep graze the federal lands, and not by some vast federal livestock-owning enterprise. It is the private timber firm that cuts and processes the timber from the federal lands, not some government forest-processing bureau or corporation. It is the private miner and oil driller who extract the metals and the oil from the federal land, not some government enterprise. Private individuals make their own decisions about recreation on the federal lands. And one could go on. Public land agencies and private businesses have worked together to convert resources from the public lands into salable raw materials, a fact that belies the frequently expressed sterotype about the role of private enterprise in U.S. land management. It is precisely in this interface between public ownership and private use of the same lands that the conflicts with federal policy arise and persist.

National Versus Regional Interests

Natural resource use and development on both public and private lands in the United States always involves the federal government to some degree, whether its role is permissive (for example, to allow cutting, extraction, or use of resources on public lands), regulatory (for example, to order compliance with air and water quality laws), or financial (as in subsidies of many kinds). Given the complexity of the U.S. society, government, and the economy, it is no longer possible for the federal government to have a wholly noninvolved position. Anything it does or does not do in some way affects private natural resource use and development.

The development and use of natural resources, including the management and use of the federal lands, typically involves a disassociation of costs and benefits. One person or group gets the benefits, others (including the general taxpayer) bear the costs, in a disassociation between persons. But a disassociation also exists between time periods: costs are borne at one time, but benefits flow, it is hoped, for longer periods, and this too contributes to the disassociation among persons. At one extreme is the disassociation between generations: the investments made today may not pay off for us, but for our children or grandchildren; or the exploitation of resources today may have benefits now that undermine benefits for later generations. This typical disassociation of costs and benefits results in serious problems of efficiency and equity. How can one measure accurately the differences in costs and benefits over long periods of time, with the uncertainties inevitably present in such long-term calculations? Are the differences in costs and benefits among individuals "fair" in some sense of the word?

Natural resource use and development programs of every kind, but especially those with major direct federal financing, include substantial regional flows of capital and of income. The taxes are raised in some regions more often than in others and the federal investments or subsidies accrue more to some regions than to others. Some of these divergences are intended, as when the federal government carries on an irrigation development program in the West but not elsewhere. Some are not specifically planned to have major regional differences, but the nature of the resources and of the programs produces differential regional impacts, as, for instance, in the case of coastal zone legislation.

There is a natural divergence of interest between regions (or states) and the nation (or the federal government) in the development and use of natural resources, including federal lands, that causes a continuous tug-of-war between them. The regions naturally enough want to obtain the maximum gains but with minimum costs to themselves. They want help from the federal government when it is needed and—above all—they wish to avoid any but minimum interference from the federal government. The federal agencies, the president, and the Congress naturally enough want to know what they are getting for their money, or from their lands, and to a considerable degree want to control the natural resource uses financed by them.

These diverging interests are wholly natural in our political process, and we should expect and recognize them for what they are. Neither side can be wholly altruistic toward the other; and each naturally and properly emphasizes its own interests and role. This does not mean to imply that no common interests exist; in every symbiotic relationship, including parasitic ones, each party has an interest to see that the other party has the health or prosperity sufficient to enable its survival. Regions want a healthy nation, including a viable national economy. And for its part, the nation wants all its regions to be healthy.[5]

This divergence of interest between regions and the nation as a whole has gone on longer, and has been more violent, than we often realize. Many examples could be cited, but I will give only a few where violence, or at least threat of violence, was involved.

The "Whiskey Rebellion"

In 1794 farmers and others in western Pennsylvania not only refused to pay federal taxes on the whiskey distilled on their farms, but they met the federal tax collectors with force. This was the "Whiskey Rebellion." President George Washington personally led a contingent of troops to western Pennsylvania, taking action in some part against his old comrades-in-arms from the Revolutionary War. The ringleaders were captured, tried, and sentenced, but later were pardoned by Washington, who insisted that the national sovereignty be preserved against any local dissidents.

Secession of the lower Mississippi Valley states

In 1805 and 1806 Aaron Burr, who had been vice president under Thomas Jefferson, tried to promote secession of the lower Mississippi Valley states or land areas, with or without their ultimate union with Spain. He was arrested, tried for treason, and acquitted, and left the country in considerable disgrace. While his was not the only conspiracy for promoting secession of parts of the frontier in this general period of history, he was the most noted national figure. Although his efforts went further than others and the outcome was more decisive, once again the national interest had been preserved.

South Carolina's attempt at nullification

A vastly more serious threat to national sovereignty arose during 1828–32, when South Carolina asserted the right to "nullify" federal laws—that is, to decide for itself which federal laws it would obey. The specific issue was the collection of U.S. tariffs on goods imported through South Carolina's harbors. By force of arms, the state prevented federal employees from collecting import duties. The state assembled some thousands of volunteer troops to repel any federal action. President Andrew Jackson—himself a son of South Carolina who had spent most of his life in Tennessee—threatened to personally lead a large body of federal troops to put down the insurrection and to hang the governor and his chief fellow conspirators. After much inflammatory talk on both sides, a compromise was reached to somewhat reduce the tariffs and to postpone their collection. Each side claimed victory. As one biographer of Jackson has said, in historical retrospect it is unfortunate that Jackson did not carry out his threats, for had he done so, the next and by far most serious conflict in our national history might have been avoided.[6]

The Civil War

The most serious, by all odds, of the regional–national conflicts was the Civil War, lasting from 1861 to 1865. This extensive and bloody conflict arose over states' rights—the right of states to secede from the Union. Again, it was South Carolina where the issue erupted. As we know, the North (or the Union) won, and although the national unity was preserved, many consequent attitudes, programs, and problems originated with the conflict and its aftermath. The Civil War led to the abolition of slavery, and one may reasonably argue that the civil rights struggles and actions of the past two decades have their roots in both slavery and in the manner of its abolishment.

The "Sagebrush Rebellion"

Viewed against these major regional–national conflicts, the "Sagebrush Rebellion" of recent years has been, and I think will continue to be, a mild and gentlemanly conflict. Some western state legislatures have passed laws laying claims to federal lands within their borders; in other western states, similar legislative proposals were rejected outright or greatly diluted in their final form. Another version of this so-called rebellion asks for the large-scale transfer of federal lands to private ownership. We will consider this conflict in more detail in chapters 5 and 6. One can concede that the Sagebrush Rebellion reflects some deep-seated regional antagonisms. The legal contentions upon which the Sagebrush Rebellion is based seem worthless. And to this interested observer and nonparticipant in the current national political scene, the political basis of the Sagebrush Rebellion is weak indeed—even within the states that have passed laws supporting its principles. It remains a modernized and legalistic rebellion, one in which no western governor will be hanged or threatened with hanging, and no western city will be bombed or beseiged by ground troops.

Potential conflicts

There are, of course, many natural resource situations that pit one or more regions against the nation. For instance, there are problems in the leasing of federal lands in the West for coal development when the coal, or electricity generated from it, largely will be consumed elsewhere. Nearly all energy development programs embody actual or potential regional–national conflicts. The disposal of atomic wastes is another issue with major regional–national divergencies of interest. If atomic reactors are to be used for energy or other purposes, the wastes that are generated must be disposed of. Everyone agrees with this, but everyone also agrees that the wastes should be disposed of "somewhere else."

The issue of water rights—for example, federal versus state—also has major components for regional–national conflict. Even the issue of tribal versus community water rights may have a regional impact, if either party is more willing than the other to sell water outside of the region (as, for example, in the case of a coal-slurry pipeline). And the list could readily be extended.

In any consideration of regional versus national interests, the lobbying power of the regions at the national level cannot be ignored. The West has political power in the U.S. Senate wholly out of proportion to the size of its population. In the 1980 elections, control of the Senate shifted from Democrats to Republicans largely because of the shifts in the western states; but in California the Democrat won the Senate seat by a majority larger, in absolute numbers of votes, than the Republican majority in all the other western states combined. The West has never been unaware or indifferent to its political power in the Senate, nor bashful about using that power. Other regions, too, have their particular political strengths and know how to use them.

When exerting its political power, each region—as each other contestant in the political arena—must consider the necessity of making tradeoffs with other interest groups. This not infrequently requires that one regional interest be abandoned, as unattainable or too costly, in order to protect or gain another regional interest. And, of course, it is not unknown for regional interest groups knowingly to propose programs which cannot be implemented, but which they hope will give them some trading stock with interest groups from other regions, in order to achieve something which is both wanted and attainable.

The Changing Times

During the last decade of the nineteenth century and the first decade of the twentieth (see chapter 2 for a more detailed discussion of this period), the idea of allowing permanent federal ownership of some of the public domain was established. By World War I, a number of national parks had been created, each by specific congressional action, the national forests as a system of permanent federal lands had been authorized by congressional action and implemented by presidential decree, wildlife refuges had been established, preservation of antiquities on public domain lands had been directed by specific act; and in other ways the era of land disposal had been greatly modified. At the same time, the Forest Service and, to a lesser extent, other federal agencies had emerged as the fountainhead of conservationist wisdom and dedication, receiving substantial popular support and acclaim for their role.

By the end of World War I, conventional conservationist-liberal doctrine held that the remaining public lands should remain in federal ownership. About 1930, there was one half-hearted proposal for turning over the surface rights of the unappropriated and unreserved public domain lands to the states, but the latter rejected this proposal and it never was really pushed at the federal level. Passage of the Taylor Grazing Act in 1934 marked the closing of the public domain.[7]

In 1957 Held and I wrote:

> One assumption is basic to the entire study: that for an indefinite period
> into the future the acreage of land in federal ownership will show no
> major change from the present—377 million acres, excluding Indian
> lands which are not federally owned, and military reservations. [And
> also excluding Alaska, which was then not yet a state.] This assumption
> rests on the belief that the basic policy issue as to the role of the federal
> lands in our national economy and society has been settled, and that
> the people of the United States will not agree to major additions to
> federal land holdings nor to major disposition of them.[8]

This statement drew a little flak from the resource–development
groups dependent upon the federal lands, but surprisingly little from
others. While some may not have liked the implications of continued
federal land ownership, they recognized that our analysis of the
national will was reasonably accurate.

Thirteen years later the Public Land Law Commission recommended that "the policy of large-scale disposal of federal lands
reflected by the majority of the statutes in force today be revised and
that future disposal shall be of only those lands that will achieve
maximum benefit for the general public in non-federal ownership,
while retaining in federal ownership those whose values must be used
and enjoyed by all Americans."[9]

The wording is different, but the meaning is the same. This
statement by a large and diverse official commission that had been
created by special legislation clearly had far more policy significance
than the statement by two private researchers, however similar their
policy positions may have been. The end of one era and the beginning
of another seemed proclaimed.

Six years later many of the recommendations of the Public Land
Law Review Commission were translated into law in the Federal Land
Policy and Management Act of 1976. But a host of other legislation
as well (see chapter 2)—the Multiple Use Act of 1960, the Wilderness
Act of 1964, the Wild and Scenic Rivers Act of 1968, the National
Trails System Act of 1968, the Forest and Rangeland Renewable
Resources Act of 1974, the National Forest Management Act of 1976,
and others—seemed implicitly to assume continued permanent own-
ership of the present federal lands, although only the Federal Land
Policy and Management Act explicitly made this point. Some of the
other legislation seemed to expect further additions to federal land
ownership by purchases from states and individuals.

Since World War II, and especially since 1970—to the extent any
single year can ever measure the change from one historical period

to another—there have been major changes and developments in the use and management of the federal lands, in the attitudes of people generally toward these lands and toward the managing agencies, and thus to the problems the agencies inevitably face.[10] The most important of these changes are discussed in the paragraphs that follow.

Increased use of the federal lands for a variety of purposes. Since the mid-1920s timber sales have multiplied by a factor of nearly 10 (from about 1 billion to about 10 billion board-feet annually) on national forests; outdoor recreation on national forests has increased by a factor of about 40; and onshore minerals production (including oil and gas) has increased greatly, particularly from BLM land.

Perhaps more important than the actual increases—measured in terms of physical outputs or of visitors—has been the increased demand for all kinds and uses of resources, not always easily measured in statistical terms. For instance, demand for water in the West, where most of the federal lands are located, has increased greatly even though the flow of water from the federal lands has changed but little. The interest in wildlife has increased greatly, far more than the rather substantial increases in wildlife numbers. The demand for grazing has increased, even though there has been a decline in the amount of grazing permitted. Most impressive of all has been the enormous national interest in wilderness areas, far more than the very large increases in actual wilderness use. With increased demand from so many groups, competition among users and among specific uses has unavoidably intensified.

Increased revenues from the federal lands. Partly as a result of the increased outputs and partly as a result of higher average prices for timber, oil, and gas (and to a lesser extent for other outputs), revenues from the federal lands have increased rapidly indeed. The big revenue earner has been the offshore oil and gas leases, from federal "lands" whose existence was not included forty years ago. And onshore areas as well have shown vastly increased revenues. Both the Forest Service and the Bureau of Land Management would be on *Fortune's* list of the 500 largest corporations were they eligible for this type of classification—the BLM would fall within the top 50. These agencies are big business, in the modern American sense of the term, but never have they been managed primarily as business enterprises.

Federal lands as public capital. As a result of these use and income changes, the federal lands today represent a huge pool of public

capital. No comprehensive estimates, employing professionally recognized appraisal methods, have ever been made but the total value
of all federal land assets today must be measured in the hundreds of
billions of dollars (see table 3-3 for an estimate). This enormous pool
of capital has arisen without a conscious decision to accumulate such
public capital and without a public decision to invest so much public
capital in these natural resources. Economic change has suddenly
thrust the federal natural resource-managing agencies into the role
of great capitalists, as the small Arab oil sheikdoms have been thrust
into similar roles. However, it is doubtful that the federal agencies
have done as well in managing these great unexpected capital assets,
as have many of the oil exporters.

Increased public expertise. Whereas at one time most of the professional expertise in some natural resource-management fields was in
the federal land-managing agencies, today private corporations,
conservation groups, other special interest groups, and ordinary
citizens often have professional expertise as great as, or greater than,
the expertise found in the federal agencies. Relatively speaking, as
the demands upon their competence has risen, the agencies have lost
ground professionally; though today's agency personnel may be more
competent than their predecessors, the competence of those outside
the agencies has risen even more. Today there is vastly less public
willingness to accept federal expertise and pronouncements as deter-
minative.

Public challenges to agency policies. The extreme form of public
nonacceptance of federal agency omnipotence has been the lawsuit,
brought by citizen groups to compel the agencies to carry out
measures, authorized by law, that they otherwise would not have
done. Aided by new legislation and by changing attitudes of the
courts, dissatisfied citizen groups can and do sue federal agencies
frequently and with consequences undreamed of in 1950.

New attitudes toward conservation and exploitation. Virtually all private
user groups emphasize their concern for the environment and for
preservation of the long-run productive capacity of the federal lands.
It can be argued that some of the private users of federal lands
practice better planning and more effective management for their
long-run future productivity than do the federal agencies. Their
corporate ability to commit funds is greater than the agencies' capacity

to guarantee long-run appropriations. This fully offsets any greater devotion to the general welfare which agency personnel may have.

Legislative restraints on federal land-managing agencies. The federal land-managing agencies have been governed, helped, and restrained by a large body of legislation passed since 1960, as I have noted. While these various acts mostly preserve a degree of flexibility in operation and a degree of discretion to the federal agencies, they substantially direct and limit federal agency freedom. By and large, the political initiative for these acts came from the interest groups and from the Congress, not from the executive branch and the federal agencies.

Dissatisfaction with federal land management. Less easily measured but, I think, highly significant is a general discontent with federal land management as it has been practiced both in the past and today. The laws and lawsuits are one evidence of such dissatisfaction—if there were perfect acceptance of federal land management, there would be no need for new laws or for litigation. The political pressures exerted by industries seeking greater mineral development or larger timber sales, by preservationists seeking the formal designation of additional wilderness areas, and by other specific interest groups are evidence that such groups are not wholly satisfied with federal land management as it has been practiced, or as they think it would be practiced in the absence of their efforts. The public reaction to proposed regulations and plans for specific areas are another evidence of dissatisfaction. The dissatisfactions with present federal land management are diverse, as are the proposals for change.

More complex management issues. As a result of the combined effects of the developments of the past thirty years, the federal land-managing agencies today face a complexity of management issues that are orders-of-magnitude greater than was the case earlier in the development of the federal land-managing system. The responsibilities of the agencies have increased enormously, as have the conflicting pressures on them. Though the problems and the responsibilities have changed, the basic *modus operandi* of federal land management continues to be bureaucratic measurement of facts and planning with interest group participation on the federal level, agency confrontation of applicants and agency decision making based on interest group applications, and agency field administration.

While the combined effect of these changes has been enormous, the various changes have occurred incrementally, even when the size of the increments was large. The agencies have been forced to make many changes in personnel, in methods of internal operation, and in dealing with interest groups—while at the same time preserving the basic operating structure and methods intact.

At no time during these past thirty years has there been a major reconsideration of the whole concept of public land ownership, nor a major challenge to its continuation, nor a major change in the relationship of federal land users to the agencies and to the general public. Perpetuation of federal land ownership, modified in administration only to the degree forced by changing socioeconomic forces, has been an article of faith for the dedicated conservationists. Perhaps the time has come to think the unthinkable, or at least to consider wholly different alternatives to the present situation.

Notes

1. Marion Clawson, "The Federal Land Policy and Management Act of 1976 in a Broad Historical Perspective," *Arizona Law Review* vol. 21, no. 2, 1979.

2. Ibid., p. 585.

3. Donald Swain, *Federal Conservation Policy, 1921–33* (Berkeley, University of California Press, 1963).

4. Public Land Law Review Commission, *One-Third of the Nation's Land* (Washington, D.C., Government Printing Office, 1970).

5. See Kent A. Price, ed., *Regional Conflict and National Policy* (Washington, D.C., Resources for the Future, 1982).

6. Marquis James, *The Life of Andrew Jackson* (New York, Bobbs-Merrill, 1938). A one-volume edition of two parts published earlier by same author and publisher.

7. E. Louise Peffer, *The Closing of the Public Domain, Disposal and Reservation Policies 1900–50* (Stanford, Calif., Stanford University Press, 1951).

8. Marion Clawson and Burnell Held, *The Federal Lands: Their Use and Management* (Baltimore, Md., The Johns Hopkins University Press for Resources for the Future, 1957) p. 5.

9. Public Land Law Review Commission, *One-Third*, p. 1.

10. Emery N. Castle, "Land, People, and Policy: A National View," and Norman Wengert, "Land, People, and Policy: A Western View," both in the *Journal of Soil and Water Conservation* vol. 37, no. 1 (January–February) 1982.

2

The History of the Federal Lands

No one can really understand the present situation with respect to federal lands or make reasonable projections about their future without knowledge of their history. Federal land history is complex, with scores of special laws, unique situations, and other aspects which are not easily summarized. This chapter presents only the briefest discussion of the history necessary for the reader's understanding of the chapters that follow.[1]

The Period from 1782 to 1960

The history of the federal lands from 1782 to 1960 consists of five distinct but somewhat overlapping eras or phases: acquisition, disposal, reservation, custodial management, and intensive management (figure 2-1).[2] A sixth era ensued after 1960, which I have designated as a period of consultation and confrontation.

Acquisition

The first step in the acquisition of federal lands was the cessation of claims held by the original states to "western lands," meaning mostly those from Ohio to the Mississippi River. The next big acquisition, the Louisiana Purchase, occurred in 1803 when President

15

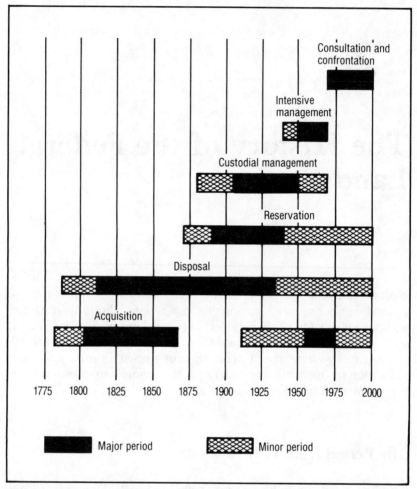

Figure 2-1. Major eras in federal landownership and land management in the United States between 1782 and 2000.

Jefferson, without specific authorization from the Congress, agreed to pay $15 million to France for a huge area—generally, the drainage of the Missouri River and some adjacent lands, a remote, unexplored, and unknown region. If a modern president bought Antarctica for $300 billion from the nations claiming it, without advance congressional approval, it would be roughly comparable to Jefferson's action. Ultimately it turned out to be a splendid real estate coup, and what is more important, it gave the new nation control of the Mississippi

River to its mouth, and removed the French from the North American continent, at least for the moment (figure 2-2). It nearly doubled total U.S. territory and more than tripled the existing public domain lands.

In 1819 the United States bought Florida from Spain for about $7 million, thereby clearing up some messy border disputes, moving Spain out of the country, and securing Spain's relinquishment of its claims to the Pacific Northwest. Americans who had migrated to Texas (then a part of Mexico) rebelled in 1836 and set up an independent country, which was annexed by mutual agreement in 1845. There was some doubt about the exact boundaries of Texas, and in 1850 the new state ceded to the United States a substantial area of land outside of the present boundaries of the state. The land within today's state boundaries remained the property of Texas, and over the years it largely has been disposed of to private owners. A war with Mexico—provoked by the United States, as most Mexicans and many independent observers agree—led to a treaty in 1848, whereby all the Southwest, including parts of New Mexico and Colorado, and all of Nevada, Utah, and California, and nearly all of Arizona, were added to the country and to the public domain. In 1846 a compromise with Great Britain had given to the United States the western states of Oregon, Washington, Idaho, and some neighboring territory. In a treaty with Mexico, the United States made the Gadsden Purchase, along the present border, in 1853. The last great expansion was the purchase of Alaska from Russia, in 1867, for about $7 million—again, a purchase that enabled the United States to evict a foreign power from an area to which Americans had a real claim— and in time a territory that proved to be a good real estate bargain. These, plus a few odds and ends covered by special treaties, constitute the expansion process of the United States, whereby in less than a century the colonies along the Atlantic Coast became the nation who owned the entire mid-continent of North America.

Private claims to land in some of these areas—as in Louisiana, New Mexico, California, and elsewhere—which had originated earlier, were always acknowledged and accepted in the treaties or purchases of acquisition. However, because generally poor land records had been kept, there were many frauds depriving the U.S. government of land which was rightly hers, as well as numerous and, at times, pathetic instances when parties who honestly believed they owned land could not provide legal proof of such ownership.

Far more important was the fact that all this territory had been occupied by American Indians prior to European and Mexican

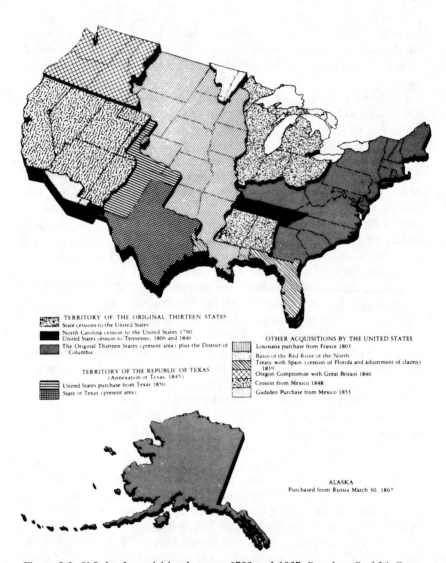

TERRITORY OF THE ORIGINAL THIRTEEN STATES
State cessions to the United States
North Carolina cession to the United States 1790
United States cession to Tennessee, 1806 and 1846
The Original Thirteen States (present area) plus the District of
Columbia

TERRITORY OF THE REPUBLIC OF TEXAS
(Annexation of Texas, 1845)
United States purchase from Texas 1850
State of Texas (present area)

OTHER ACQUISITIONS BY THE UNITED STATES
Louisiana purchase from France 1803
Basin of the Red River of the North
Treaty with Spain (cession of Florida and adjustment of claims)
1819
Oregon Compromise with Great Britain 1846
Cession from Mexico 1848
Gadsden Purchase from Mexico 1853

ALASKA
Purchased from Russia March 30, 1867

Figure 2-2. U.S. land acquisition between 1782 and 1867. Based on Paul W. Gates,
History of Public Land Law Development (Washington, D.C., Government Printing Office,
1968) p. 76.

settlement. Our history of dealing with Native Americans is a confused
and generally disgraceful one. Their concept of land differed from
the settlers'; they had no understanding of what the government
meant by land ownership. Sometimes with the aid of whiskey and
the threat of arms, treaties were negotiated, which the native signers
did not really understand. The treaties were violated repeatedly by

white settlers and others on the frontier. The Indians were pushed back—"cleared"—at first toward the western lands that were occupied by other Indian peoples; and later they were relegated to reservations. We deal with Native American claims in more recent decades by financial remuneration or by giving some land in payment for the extensive areas taken many decades ago.

With the exception of the recognized private claims and the acknowledged Indian claims to land within the territories obtained by the processes just described, all the land became public domain, eligible under existent law for disposal to private individuals or to states.

There were some relatively small federal land acquisitions between 1911 and 1960, as well as some major acquisitions after the mid-1950s, which will be considered on page 41. The Weeks Act, passed in 1911, enabled the Forest Service to acquire land which became a major part of the national forests in the eastern half of the United States—the sole base for such forests in states that never had been part of the public domain.

Another land transaction—better described as a repossession than as an acquisition—has become very important for the federal land management policies of today. This was the O & C area in western Oregon.[3] In 1869 a grant of land was made to the Oregon and California railroad (hence the name, O & C), which later was taken over by the Southern Pacific railroad. The grant specified that "the land granted . . . shall be sold to actual settlers only, in quantities not greater than one quarter section to one purchaser, and for a price not exceeding two dollars and fifty cents per acre." When it became apparent that these terms of the grant had been violated, the government sued for repossession of the land, and, in 1916, the U.S. Supreme Court held that these lands were to be "revested and reconveyed" to the United States, and that the railroad company was to receive a sum equal to $2.50 per acre for the area that would have been included in the grant. The Coos Bay wagon road grant lands had a somewhat similar history of grant and reconveyance and management. These lands are a highly valuable forested area, whose administration will be considered in some detail later. Although part of this grant was within the boundaries of national forests and all the rest of the grant area was relatively close to national forest boundaries, administration of the O & C lands was placed in the General Land Office (now the Bureau of Land Management), not in the Forest Service. A controversy between the two agencies ensued regarding the administration of that part of the O & C which lay within national forest boundaries. This controversy was not settled until 1954 by legislation which confirmed the disputed lands as O & C and perpetuated the generous distribution of their revenues to the counties, but put their actual administration in the hands of the Forest Service. By far the greater part of the O & C lands, however, always have been managed by the Bureau of Land Management or its predecessor.

Disposal

Even before the cessations from the states with western land claims were completed, the disposal process began. Beginning slowly, as figure 2-1 shows, it continued unabated, often at breakneck speed, until 1934, when President Roosevelt withdrew from private entry all the remaining public domain after passage of the Taylor Grazing Act. These lands were withdrawn from entry to forestall a flood of grazing homestead entries by ranchers and others who correctly saw the end of wholesale disposal of the public domain.[4] Disposal was a particularly complex process, governed by literally thousands of laws whose administration in the field often deviated greatly from the provisions of the law. What follows below is the briefest possible account of the disposal process. For more detailed accounts, the reader should consult the books cited in note 1 at the end of this chapter.

Preliminary to actual disposal of the public domain, the lands were surveyed. There was a great deal of debate and experimentation, especially in Ohio, where there were no less than nine major survey systems tried, as well as some minor variants.[5] In this matter, as in so many others, Thomas Jefferson played a major role. At his suggestion, a *rectangular* cadastral survey was adopted and applied to the entire United States from Ohio westward, with the result that today even a casual observer can see the straight north-south east-west lines dividing the country into largish blocks or "sections," 1-mile long on each side and containing 640 acres each; into smaller blocks of 160 acres ("quarter sections") a half-mile long on each side; "40s" a quarter-mile long on a side; or into still smaller units in some areas. A cadastral survey marks and measures land properties as a basis for land titles; and although it does not have to be rectangular, ours was. The difficult problems of intermingled private-public ownership (described in chapter 7) are sometimes attributed to the rectangular cadastral surveys but, in fact, they are more fairly charged to other aspects of the disposal process. In the end, the survey process left an enduring and indelible mark upon most of the American landscape, as farms, roads, streets, and cities have all conformed in large measure to the survey pattern established.

The new federal government was eager to dispose of its land, for it badly needed cash. But sales were slow, in part because the states had large areas of more or less equally good land, located closer to established markets, which they wished to sell. Some public domain was given to war veterans, or they were given scrip which could be used to buy public land. Most of them sold the scrip to land speculators, for a small fraction of its face value. For a long time there was a struggle between actual or would-be settlers on the frontier, who wanted the public lands sold in farm-sized tracts and at offices near the frontier, and land developers and speculators, who wanted to buy land in large blocks at the national capital. A particularly nettlesome issue concerned the rights, if any, of the settler who entered (strictly speaking, illegally) on the public domain in advance of cadastral survey and who demanded preferential treatment ("preemption") when the land was finally put up for sale—with the preemptor arguing, accurately enough, that he and his family had risked their lives and had erected an effective screen between the Indians and the older settlements. As time passed, the balance of land acquisition shifted more toward the settler and away from the large land dealer or developer.[6]

Land sales were supposed to occur by public auction. In a few cases, land did sell at prices substantially above the legal minimum; Rohrbaugh relates how sales in Alabama in the mid-1830s were actually quite competitive, with higher bids than economic returns justified.[7] But for the most part, nearly everywhere, exactly the opposite situation existed; "claim associations," made up of settlers, speculators, and hangers-on, decided who should be allowed to bid the minimum legal price on each tract when it was put up for sale, and others were prevented or threatened with severe harm if they ventured to bid.[8] In the end, the cash sale process disposed of about a fourth of the federal land. This process of cash sales continued until 1891, long after the next major system of disposal to private individuals had begun.

A politically popular drive for free land from the federal government began fairly early.[9] Congress, in 1842, passed an act granting free land to settlers on the frontier in western Florida, thus encouraging a buffer against Indian attacks. In 1850 free land was provided on a larger scale to settlers in Oregon and, in 1853, to settlers in Washington. Similar legislation was enacted in New Mexico. In all, nearly 10,000 claims for about 3 million acres of land were made under these special acts.

Beginning in 1844, a national drive was begun for free homesteads anywhere on public domain. Horace Greeley played a major role in this proposal, and, by 1858, the idea was adopted by the new

TABLE 2-1. FEDERAL LAND GRANTS TO GROUPS OF STATES, 1803 THROUGH FISCAL 1980
(in millions of acres)

			Purpose of grant			
Group of states	Common schools	Other schools	Railroads, wagon roads, canals and rivers[a]	Swamp reclamation	Other	Total
Eighteen states not formed from public domain[b]	0	5.2	0	0	—	5.2
Nineteen states formed from public domain, outside of West[c]	26.2	6.8	43.9	62.4	7.8	147.2
Eleven western states[d]	51.3	4.6	2.7	2.5	10.4	71.5
Alaska	0.1	0.1	0	0	104.4	104.6
TOTAL	77.6	16.7	46.6	64.9	122.6	328.4

Note: Items may not add exactly to totals, due to rounding.

Source: Department of the Interior, Bureau of Land Management, *Public Land Statistics, 1980* (Washington, D.C., GPO, 1980), tab. 4, pp. 6–7.

[a] This does not include the 94 million acres granted directly to railroad corporations.

[b] Connecticut, Delaware, Kentucky, Maine, Maryland, Massachusetts, New Hampshire, New Jersey, New York, North Carolina, Pennsylvania, Rhode Island, South Carolina, Tennessee, Texas, Vermont, Virginia, and West Virginia.

[c] Alabama, Arkansas, Florida, Georgia, Illinois, Indiana, Iowa, Kansas, Louisiana, Michigan, Minnesota, Mississippi, Missouri, Nebraska, North Dakota, Ohio, Oklahoma, South Dakota, and Wisconsin.

[d] Arizona, California, Colorado, Idaho, Montana, Nevada, New Mexico, Oregon, Utah, Washington, and Wyoming.

Republican party.[10] After much political maneuvering, a homestead bill passed in 1860, but was vetoed by President Buchanan. Southern senators and congressmen had opposed such legislation, fearing that free land settlement would prevent the extension of slavery to southern states west of the Mississippi. With these men out of the Congress during the Civil War, the original Homestead Act was passed in 1862. For a nominal fee, a citizen could acquire as much as 160 acres of public domain, on condition that he reside on and cultivate the land. For farmers in the central part of the country 160 acres was a good-sized farm, but for farmers in the areas of the western Corn Belt, Great Plains, and westward, a 160-acre farm was not an economic proposition.[11] The area available under the Homestead Act was enlarged in 1909 to 320 acres, and to 640 acres in the Stock-Raising Homestead Act of 1916. These acreages were too small and came too late to meet the needs of ranchers trying to acquire native rangeland. The basic Homestead Act was extended in several other ways—the Timber Culture Act, Desert Land Act, Timber and Stone Act, and others—each aimed at making it easy for individuals, and sometimes corporations, to obtain particular areas of the public domain for special uses. Eventually, more than one-fourth of the public domain was disposed of under the Homestead Act and subsequent laws.

Since the first grant of federal lands to Ohio in 1802, a total of 328 million acres has been granted to the states (table 2-1). This equals more than 14 percent of the total U.S. land area, more than 18 percent of the total land *ever* in the public domain, and more than 28 percent of the total public domain disposed of. Clearly, grants to the states have been an important channel for the transfer of public domain out of federal ownership. A detailed account of these grants can be found in chapter 6, where the possibility of large further grants to the states is also considered.[12]

In return for these grants of public domain, all the new states explicitly, in the acts creating them, waived all claims to additional federal land. These waivers have assumed new importance in light of today's Sagebrush Rebellion. In addition to the common school grants, all states (even the non-public domain states, which got scrip instead of land) were given a grant for an agricultural college—hence the term *land-grant college*. Moreover, all public domain states got additional grants for such things as mental institutions, hospitals, and the like. A substantial part of their grants were "swamp and overflowed" lands, on the theory that the federal government could not or would not drain or otherwise improve them and that possibly the states might. These latter grants included a good share of Florida, and were widely abused in such areas as the Sacramento and San Joaquin Valleys of California and in the Mississippi Delta, which today are some of the finest farming lands in the country. In all, more than one-fifth of the public domain was given to the states by these means.

Grants of public domain were also made to subsidize transportation, chiefly railroads but some canals and wagon roads as well. The railroad grants typically consisted of alternating sections of land for some specified distance (often 10 miles, sometimes 20) on either side of the completed railroad. If these sections were already taken by private parties or included as part of prior grants to others, "in lieu" selections, also of alternating sections, could be made up to some greater distance (often twice as far) from the rail line. The price of the intervening checkerboard public lands was then doubled when they were sold. It was thought that the building of the railroad would increase the value of the public lands and that the buyer would get twice the price per acre with a railroad. It was also thought that by granting alternating sections, the railroads would get a reasonable share of both the best and the poorer public lands. Later, when the national forests were created, the railroads were permitted to select other land for their original grant lands incorporated into the forests. As can be imagined, fraud was involved in some of these in-lieu selections.[13]

By the time the western states were admitted to the Union, most grants to aid the railroads were being made directly to the railroad corporations, so the grants to western states for this purpose were relatively small. They would have been much larger if grants made directly to the railroads in the West had followed the procedure established in the Midwest and the South, where direct grants to states could, in turn, be granted to railroads.

Some concern had been expressed over the constitutionality of land grants made directly to private corporations, but by the time the major transcontinental railroads were being built, the grants of public domain land were made directly to the railroad corporations. The earliest such transcontinental railroads crossed land not located in any state, but in territories.

The data in table 2-1 are for lands whose title has actually passed from the federal government to the states. Dragoo notes, "In addition to those grant lands that have passed title to the states, large acreages of public domain are still outstanding to several states. Many of the state entitlements still owing are in-lieu selections to replace lands which were never received by the states due to federal withdrawal or third party withdrawal pursuant to public land laws in effect at the time of statehood grant."[14] In 1970 the Public Land Law Review Commission noted that 900,000 acres were still owed to the states.[15] Dragoo notes that, in 1975, 200,000 acres were still owed to Utah and 180,000 acres to Arizona, the two states with the largest area of unsatisfied grants. In any alternative program for future administration of the federal lands, provision must be made for satisfaction of these grants, which had been promised to the states at the time of their admission to the Union or shortly thereafter.

Of the total U.S. area of 2,312 million acres, 475 million were never public domain (the original states and those formed out of them, and Hawaii and Texas). Or, to put it another way, 1,838 million acres were once public domain (including Alaska); and of these, nearly 1,144 million acres had been disposed of by 1980 (table 2-2). Some of this land was purchased subsequently by federal, state, or local governments, so that one cannot precisely classify this area as the privately and state-owned land of the United States, but it comes close to it. For the vast majority of the private land which was once public domain, the first link in the chain of today's legal title was its conveyance from public to private ownership.

The process of land disposal was a lusty affair—a headlong, even precipitous process, full of frauds and deceits, but one which transformed a great deal of land into valuable private property—and one which built a nation. Historians, political scientists, conservationists, and others have frequently criticized the speed, disorder, fraud, and other undesirable features of the long disposal process. If the process had been slower, with more opportunity to learn from experience, some mistakes possibly could have been avoided. But would even worse consequences have ensued?

Consider, for example, that as late as 1840 Russia had a "permanent" settlement on the northern California coast, which was abandoned because it was thought that the sea otter population, sought for its valuable fur, had been exhausted to the point of unprofitable further exploitation. Had Russia hung on for another decade until after gold was discovered in California, or had the American settlements of California been delayed for several decades, Russia might never have relinquished its territory. Are we better pleased today to have our country in our own hands, a little scarred from its rapid pioneer exploitation, or would we now prefer a less scarred countryside in the hands of another nation?

Cameron, speaking explicitly about forestlands, but in terms which could equally well be applied to all land, puts it very graphically:

TABLE 2-2. SUMMARY OF STATISTICS ON ORIGIN, DISPOSAL, AND PRESENT STATUS OF FEDERAL LANDS
(millions of acres)

Origin	No. of acres	Disposal	No. of acres	Present federal land ownership, by agency[d]	Public domain (no. of acres)	Acquired (no. of acres)[e]	Total (no. of acres)
Never public domain	475	Disposal to states	328	Forest Service	160	28	188
Original states[a]	305	Schools of all kinds[c]	94	Other USDA agencies	f	f	f
Texas	170	Swamp reclamation	65	Bureau of Land Management	395	2	398
Public domain	1,838	Other	169	National Park Service	62	7	68
State cessions[b]	237	Granted or sold to homesteaders	288	Fish & Wildlife Service	39	4	43
Louisiana Purchase	530			Other Department of Interior agencies	4	3	7
Red River Basin	30	Granted to veterans as military bounties	61	All Other	17	16	34
Cession from Spain	46	Granted to railroad corporations	94				
Oregon Compromise	184	All other	374				
Mexican cession	339						
Purchase from Texas	79						
Gadsden Purchase	19						
Alaska Purchase	375						
Total U.S.	2,313	Total	1,114	Total federal land ownership	678	60	738

Note: Included as federal lands are inland water areas. Totals may not add, due to rounding.
[a]Marion Clawson and Burnell Held, *The Federal Lands: Their Use and Management* (Baltimore, Md., Johns Hopkins University Press for Resources for the Future, 1957) p. 21.
[b]Bureau of Land Management, *Public Land Statistics 1980*, p. 3.
[c]Ibid., p. 5.
[d]Bureau of Land Management, *Public Land Statistics 1980*, pp. 10–12.
[e]Much of this was once public domain; disposed of, it later was repurchased.
[f]Less than 500,000 acres.

Assuredly America's forests were plundered—by the American people. Pioneer thought, the point of view of the spirit of adventure, had to run its appointed course. That it ran somewhat beyond that course and played the devil with certain material things of great value is cause for deplorement [sic], to be sure. But it is not cause for putting the blame on the other fellow and giving way to despair. The American people squandered their patrimony. The American people alone are to blame. But at that did they not come pretty close to getting value received? Has, after all, their typical Anglo-Saxon muddling with their forest been so expensive?

There is in truth another side to the doleful tale of denudation, devastation, plunderation [sic]. It is possible for a man to squander a fortune and win a greater in the process. Or to lose in gold and gain in character. Seldom, however, does a spendthrift beat the game spiritually as well as materially. But is it not that after all what America has done in the course of her woodland wasting? Measured by the dollar yardstick does the billion or so in timber that has been wasted or stolen begin to compare with the tens of billions of solid values represented by the empire that the spirit of the Borderers has made an accomplished fact since 1850?[16]

Reservation

It was the excesses of the disposal process that led to the permanent reservation in federal ownership of some of the public domain. There had been some land reservations early in our national history; Cameron details, and Ise and Hibbard briefly mention, one now-forgotten episode of American forest history, when an attempt was made to reserve for the building of warships the oaks along the southern Atlantic Coast, because ships made of oak were believed to be superior in battle to those made of any other wood.[17] That effort failed, largely because the federal government was unwilling to spend money to protect this forest resource from trespass and theft. In any event, ships made of iron and steel shortly rendered wooden warships obsolete. Hot springs, salt springs, and some other areas considered vital for general public use were reserved by special laws from disposition to private ownership. For instance, the area now known as Hot Springs National Park in Arkansas was set aside as early as 1831.

Commissioners of the General Land Office and secretaries of the interior complained repeatedly, but to no avail, of their inability to enforce the land laws as written, to search out and strike down fraud, and to protect the public domain against trespass, but Congress was unwilling to appropriate the sums required or to take decisive, but often unpleasant, actions. By the last quarter of the nineteenth century, there arose a great deal of sentiment among the eastern "establishment" for a drastically different handling of the public domain, including the permanent reservation of part of it.[18] One instance—but at that time an isolated event rather than a reversal of national policy—was the establishment, in 1872, of Yellowstone National Park, widely hailed in more recent years as the first national park in the world. Ise has well described its establishment:

> The establishment of Yellowstone was, of course, due partly to the efforts of few of these idealists, several of them men of influence. Reservation was possible because most private interests were not looking so far west at this early date, for there were no railroads within hundreds of miles of Yellowstone. Lumbermen had moved into the Lake States and were too busy slashing the pine forests there to reach out for timber lands in this inaccessible region; the hunters and trappers were here, but were not an important political force; the cattlemen, who have been in recent years so powerful an influence against some conservation legislation, were not yet invading the Far West in large numbers; the water-power interests that have been among the most serious threats to a few later national parks were not interested here. With Indians still a lurking danger, the "poor settlers" had not ventured into this region in great numbers and were not calling for Congressional consideration.[19]

The first *system* of permanent federal land reservation was the forest reserves (now national forests) created by the Forest Reserve Act of 1891. In the decade or two preceding it there had been a series of committees and commissions, and important actions taken by the American Forestry Association and by the American Association for the Advancement of Science—all of interest to students of this matter, but too complicated to be recounted here. There had been bills introduced in Congress and some committee discussions took place, but no decisive action was taken until 1891. In a bill for a general revision of the land laws, a Section 24 was added at the last-minute conference, without ever having been considered by either the House or Senate. It was passed in the very last hours of the closing congressional session. Dana has described this event in his usual succinct and informative fashion:

> The report of the conference committee reached Congress on February 28, 1891, four days before the date for final adjournment. In the Senate, which had ordinarily been hostile to measures of this sort, Senator Plumb of Kansas insisted on speedy consideration, and the bill passed with little comment. In the House, Representative McRae of Arkansas objected to Section 24 on the ground that it gave the President too much power and that no one could foresee its consequences. . . .The

bill did not come before the House again until the closing hours of the session on March 2, when it was passed without debate. It was signed by the President on March 3. . . .The section authorizing the President to set aside the forest reserves, which was attached to the bill in violation of the rule forbidding the inclusion of any new material in a conference-committee report, appears to have been added at the insistence of Secretary (of the Interior) Noble. He had been well educated by Bowers, Fernow, and others and is reported to have told the committee that he would get the President to veto the bill unless this particular section were included. That it was prepared in considerable haste is indicated by the fact that it is not even a complete sentence. . . .[20]

Ise, noting that the bill was considered in the House simply on a verbal presentation, because it had not been printed, goes on to say:

Thus the passage of the Forest Reserve Act, the first important conservation measure in the history of our national forest policy, cannot be credited to congressional initiative, but to a long chain of peculiar circumstances which made it impossible for congress to act directly on the question. If the conference committee, like most public land committees, had included a majority of men hostile to conservation; if the forest reserve provision had been attached to anything but a conference bill; if the question had come up at the beginning instead of the close of the sesssion; if there had been less of a public demand for revision of the land laws; if the bill had been a short one, with only a few clauses; if Congress had been a little less familiar with the general provisions of the omnibus bill under discussion and so more careful to scrutinize them, or if members had realized what important results were to follow; if any one of a score of possible contingencies had prevailed, the passage of a general forest reserve measure at this time would probably have been impossible. Congress was not yet fully converted to the principle of forest reservation, as later developments clearly show.[21]

Successive presidents withdrew from the public domain nearly 40 million acres for inclusion in the Forest Reserves by 1897, despite the fact that there was no provision in law for the management or use of these withdrawn lands. President Theodore Roosevelt withdrew a vast amount of the public domain, bringing the gross acreage of the national forests up to nearly their present level; however, some eliminations and some additions have been made to these earlier withdrawals to arrive at the present acreages and boundaries. Roosevelt withdrew some of these lands after Congress had passed a bill limiting his authority to do so in several western states without its consent; after which exercise he signed the bill into law.

During 1909 to 1934 there were a number of other withdrawals of public domain, for the mining of phosphate, coal, and other minerals for Naval Petroleum Reserves, for power sites, for the establishment of national monuments, parks, and wildlife refuges, and for several users. During much of this time a running battle ensued between the National Park Service and the Forest Service, as the former sought to have new national parks created out of national forests, and the latter resisted the raids upon its territory. The Weeks Act of 1911 provided for the purchase of private lands for incorporation into national forests; and while not, strictly speaking, a reservation of public domain, it had a similar purpose. Weeks Act purchases made the federal government a land manager in states where it had never been, and reinstated it in states from which it had withdrawn. During this period the Forest Service, by administrative action, established wilderness and wild areas. The former areas encompassed 100,000 acres or more, the latter were smaller but otherwise similar. During this quarter-century there occurred individually small but collectively important measures that affected the public domain and its continued permanent ownership by the U.S. government.

The next far-reaching event in the reservation of the public domain was the passage of the Taylor Grazing Act in 1934. Until then, the public domain had been a grazing commons. Grazing under these conditions had a deleterious effect on the land, although concerned stockmen on their own or with state help were able to achieve some degree of control over grazing on the public domain. Gifford Pinchot, during his directorship of the Forest Service, had sought to persuade stockmen—especially those in the Great Plains where unplowed native grassland was extensive—to accept some sort of federal grazing control, under his supervision, of course. He made a considerable number of converts among the cattlemen, but the sheepmen totally opposed him.[22]

By the 1920s, the grazing situation on the remaining public domain was growing steadily more serious. Despite the efforts of the states and of many conservation-minded ranchers to achieve some sort of control over grazing on the federal lands within their borders, overuse of the range and its consequent deterioration were rampant. One major disturbing factor was the advent of the "tramp sheepmen," who owned little or no private land but grazed their animals wherever they could on a year-long basis—right up to the edge of small towns, in the middle of the public range that an established cattleman considered to be "his," and on any other available rangeland. To check this practice, a number of bills were introduced, many resolutions were passed, and proposals for control of grazing increased during this general period. The Forest Service backed the Colton Bill that passed the House in 1932 but was not reported out of committee in the Senate. With the coming of President Roosevelt's New Deal, Secretary of the Interior Harold L. Ickes instituted a new drive in a different direction. But convincing Rep. Edward T. Taylor of western Colorado of the need for federal legislation, and his subsequent drive and ability in pushing his bill through the Congress, were perhaps the decisive elements. The bill passed the House on a recorded vote, and the Senate by an unrecorded voice vote. Apparently this was done because many western senators who saw the need for the act were reluctant to be placed on public record, fearing that they later might be attacked by special interest groups in their state.[23]

The Taylor Grazing Act placed administration of the grazing districts and leases in the Department of the Interior, where shortly a new Division of Grazing—later known as the Grazing Service—was created. It was merged in 1946 with the venerable General Land Office to form the Bureau of Land Management. The original act provided for inclusion of only 80 million acres in the new grazing districts, or about half the remaining unappropriated and unreserved public domain in the forty-eight contiguous states. This was increased to 142 million acres in 1936, which was essentially all the public domain conveniently located in such blocks as to be readily included in grazing districts. Grazing within districts initially was authorized under short-term licenses and later under longer-term permits. No limit is placed on the acreage that might be included in grazing leases outside of districts, as long as the lands are "not suitable" for inclusion in grazing districts.

The preamble of the Taylor Grazing Act refers to the "pending final disposal" of the public domain, a phrase which has created no end of debate and argument. Does it mean that the Taylor Grazing Act is merely an interim measure, to be replaced at a later date by something else? Or does it mean, as I always have contended, that the establishment of a grazing district was in itself "final disposal?" Or is this merely political language, but otherwise largely without meaning, that was deemed necessary to enable some western senators and representatives to vote for the act? In any event, the significance of this phrase no longer matters, now that the Federal Land Policy and Management Act of 1976 has been passed, a matter to which I shall revert later in this chapter.

Custodial management

The management of the national forests, the grazing districts, and other more or less permanently reserved federal land beginning from the date of their first reservation may reasonably be described as "custodial." Some of that management later (after about 1950, but before 1960) became "intensive" (see page 37). The developments since 1960 will be considered on page 39.

As noted earlier, the passage of the Forest Reserve Act in 1891 made no provision for any private use of the reserved lands. In 1897 President Cleveland withdrew an additional 21 million acres, more than doubling the total forest reserve area. This action touched off a storm of protest, and, in an unusual legislative manuever, a forest management law was attached to an appropriations act. This hasty, more or less expedient, and very determined action on the part of the Congress is similar to the passage of the National Forest Management Act in 1976.[24]

This legislation was generally cited as the basic authority for Forest Service timber sales for more than seventy-five years, until it was overturned in the *Monongahela* court decision of 1973–74, to be replaced by the 1976 Act (see page 49). Although the *Monongahela* decision applied to one timber sale only, the Forest Service (properly in my judgment) applied it to all sales within the region of the court's jurisdiction. It was generally thought by conservationists and the forest industry alike that the same strictures would soon be applied to all national forest timber sales. The Forest Service and the forest industry felt that this jeopardized all such sales.

With the passage of the 1897 Act, authority to manage the Forest Reserves was created but there was neither men, money, competence, nor—it sadly must be conceded—will to manage them constructively and effectively. Their management, such as it was, from 1891 to 1905 was in the hands of the General Land Office. Pinchot, hardly a fair or impartial critic, denounced that management in his customary florid style:

> In practice, thanks to lax, stupid, and wrongheaded administration by the Interior Department, the land laws were easily twisted to the advantage of the big fellows, and western opinion was satisfied to have it so.. . .The management was awful. Division P of the General Land Office at Washington, to which the Department had given the Reserves in charge, knew literally nothing about them or what ought to be done with them. At that time (1899) not one man in Division P had ever set foot in a Forest Reserve or had even seen one Forest Reserve tree, unless perhaps from a Pullman car window. The abysmal ignorance of the Washington office about conditions on the ground was outrageous, pathetic, or comic, whichever you like. Division P ordered one supervisor to buy a rake for himself and another for his ranger and rake up the dead wood on the Washington Forest reserve—a front yard of a mere three and a half million acres, where the fallen trees were often longer than a city block and too thick for a man to see over.[25]

Pinchot describes in detail the flagrant political favoritism in the appointment of men in the General Land Office. His stories are, as far as I know, accurate; but he also could have, with equal truth, reported many instances of courageous, dedicated, and competent service by the same organization, as have Clepper and others.[26]

During one of the several commission studies of the public domain, Pinchot had been briefly employed by the General Land Office. Convinced by his experience there that the organization was hopeless, he went to the Department of Agriculture, where he was named head of its tiny Division of Forestry in 1898. From this position he launched one of the most explicit, determined, and successful bureaucratic empire-building campaigns that Washingon—even with its long experience in such manuevers—has ever seen. It culminated in the establishment of the Forest Service and the transfer to it of the forest reserves, renamed the "national forests," in 1905. If Pinchot had chosen instead to reform the General land Office, and if his efforts had been successful—two enormous "ifs"—the management of national forests, grazing districts, and associated federal lands all would have been in one agency, and the whole history of bureaucratic rivalry over federal land administration would have been different. It should be added that a major reason Pinchot was so successful as an empire-builder was that he developed and cultivated a close friendship with President Theodore Roosevelt. With Roosevelt no longer in the White House, Pinchot's towering Napoleonic complex soon led him to challenge publicly President Taft, and Pinchot was out.

For the times, Pinchot created a magnificent federal agency, which quickly brought a wholly new level of management to the national forests. He recruited many able, intelligent, dedicated young graduates from the newly established forestry schools, but he also recruited many equally able and dedicated, if not so formally well-trained, men from private industry. For instance, Alfred F. Potter and Will C. Barnes, who had been ranchers in Arizona, rose to top positions in the Forest Service. Pinchot created a decentralized, on-the-ground type of operation, with the ranger authorized to take actions within defined limits and according to specified policies and procedures. The ranger was guided by a "Use Book," which Pinchot specified must be small enough to fit in a hip pocket—quite different from the Manual and the regulations of today!

The new agency had to establish at the field level the boundaries of the forests as specified in the proclamations, to suppress trespass and illegal taking of timber, and to fight fires. It had to develop techniques for all these tasks. Early on it was established that the Forest Service had the authority to regulate grazing on the national

forests. The controversy over grazing fees began as early as 1907—
and has continued, waxing and waning at intervals, to the present.
The new Forest Service aroused a great deal of antagonism on the
part of ranchers and others who challenged anyone who sought to
restrain their actions in any way. As one old Forest Service hand,
who lived through those years, once said to me privately in the late
1930s as we were discussing some of the regulatory problems the
new Grazing Service was encountering, "The ranchers challenge the
actions of these Grazing Service guys, but they challenged our very
right to live." And indeed, violence was directed at some Forest
Service personnel. The challenge was not directed to the specifics of
Forest Service action but to any and all forms of federal control over
federal lands.

The level of activity on the national forests from 1905 to about
1950 was low, judged by present-day experience. Up until 1922, the
volume of timber sold was less than 1 billion board-feet annually; it
then rose, during the building boom of the 1920s, to nearly 1.5 billion
board-feet for about a decade, falling again sharply in the Great
Depression. Although it rose again during World War II, it did not
exceed 3 billion board-feet until 1944. So much more accessible
private timber was waiting for harvest that the demand for national
forest timber was low; during the 1930s, national forest timber sales
were intentionally held low to reduce the pressure on stumpage prices
in order to force even faster liquidation of the private timber, much
of which was being held under conditions of financial distress.

Pinchot scarcely recognized the existence of outdoor recreation,
and it was not until 1924 that the Forest Service regularly collected
any statistics about the extent of this activity. At that time, total annual
recreation visits made to national forests were less than 5 million,
compared with about 200 million visitor-days today. While these
measures may not be precisely comparable, the vast increase in
recreation is real enough.

The first efforts at wilderness establishment occurred around 1920,
by administrative action of the Forest Service, rather than legislation—
and with virtually no notice being taken by the Congress.

Some attention was paid to wildlife and watershed management,
but it was minimal by present-day standards. Roads, cars, vacations,
recreation equipment, and all the rest of it were at a relatively
primitive level, hence the low level of outdoor recreation. It was the
combination of all these factors which made national forest management primarily custodial. It was important to protect the resources
for some future day when they really would be needed. Unfortunately,

it seems to me, this philosophy of protection at low output levels has persisted to the present when circumstances are very different.

Although our primary concern here is with management of the national forests, it is necessary to mention briefly that the Forest Service developed two additional activities—research and cooperation with states, the latter especially in the prevention and suppression of forest fires. A federal agency with the reputation and the competence of the Forest Service is a national asset at all times, and the nation will from time to time require its services for functions outside its primary mission, for example, its shelter-belt tree-planting program in the Great Plains in the 1930s.

The management of the unappropriated and unreserved public domain from 1900 was in the hands of the General Land Office until 1934. Established in 1812, the General Land Office antedated its own department, and for decades had performed vital services in the disposal of the public domain. During its early decades, the commissioner of the General Land Office was as prestigious a position as a Cabinet office; senators resigned to assume the office, and Abraham Lincoln was an unsuccessful candidate for the position. In later decades, the agency became more legalistic, more politics-ridden, and less inclined to adopt new ideas and practices. Though Pinchot's earlier comments are not fairly balanced, his general disparagement is basically correct. What Pinchot did with the Forest Reserves, a lively commissioner of the Land Office might have done; but none tried anything so daring. One old employee of BLM told me in 1948 that he had known but one commissioner who either knew or cared what the work of the agency was all about.

Its management of the public domain from 1900 to 1934 may be characterized as custodial, even as magisterial. It allowed (and disallowed, for legal and not for conservationist reasons) original homestead, enlarged homestead, stock-raising homestead, and other forms of entry. It also acted slowly on land exchanges, many of which were instituted by the Forest Service, whereby public domain outside of a national forest was traded for private land within a forest, thus increasing the latter. The area of public domain included in these and other forms of entry exceeded 10 million acres every year up to 1922, and ran as high as 5 million acres as late as 1931.[27] A common myth exists that the day of homesteading ended with the disappearance of the frontier in 1890 or shortly thereafter; nothing is further from the truth, for land disposal continued actively up to the passage of the Taylor Grazing Act and the presidential land withdrawals made to effectuate it. Time necessarily elapsed between original entry and final entry (or proof), and some entries never made it. Final entries ran on at a fairly high rate for some years after 1934 when original entries were, to all intents, cut off. These disposal activities were important, especially to the land claimants, but, at the most, they were custodial management.

The General Land Office also issued mineral leases. For a few years after oil was first discovered on the public domain, the oil-bearing land was disposed of under the placer mining provisions of the mining law, which dated from 1872. But this led to so much confusion and struggle, including armed disputes among rival claimants, that these lands were withdrawn from oil and gas entry about 1910. In 1920 Congress passed a Mineral Leasing Act, which opened the unreserved public domain to oil and gas leasing. Legislation also provided for leasing of the public domain for coal, potash, phosphate, and other minerals, but the actual volume of such leases was small during this period.

When the Taylor Grazing Act was passed, its administration was not assigned to the General Land Office but to a new agency, the Division of Grazing. I never have seen any evidence that Secretary of the Interior Ickes or any of his advisors drew, what seems to me, the obvious lesson from the establishment of the Forest Reserves under the General Land Office a generation earlier, namely, that you must have an agency capable of carrying out the law or you will lose the opportunity to do so. But the lack of interest, competence, and vision for conservation management of the grazing lands within the General Land Office was so evident to all observers that the new agency was established. It was headed in its early years by a most remarkable person, a lawyer-rancher from western Colorado, Farrington Carpenter, a product of Princeton and Harvard, but also a cattleman, who was recognized as such by western ranchers.

The problems of bringing the grazing operations of nearly 25,000 ranchers under the terms of the Taylor Act were very great indeed. Many of the ranchers lacked good documentation of their land ownership, fences frequently were not on legal property lines, and written records of grazing on the public domain were nonexistent although ranchers often had personal knowledge of where and when they and their neighbors had grazed livestock. Carpenter established little more than a skeletal organization, decentralized to field operations and decisions. Regulations had to be written to take cognizance of the highly varied grazing resource situations in the West. Extensive use was made of advisory boards of livestock raisers—a necessary step, in view of the lack of data from other sources, but one which continually drew criticism from many persons. Rather quickly the truly tramp sheepmen were eliminated—as the act clearly intended—and the pressure on the grazing lands was reduced.

The Grazing Service encountered many difficulties, at least some of which were of its own making, and in 1946 it was substantially dismantled before being combined with the General Land Office to form the Bureau of Land Management.[28] The story of attacks on it by Congress is an involved and somewhat confused one, with conservationists generally interpreting it as political interference with a highly principled resource management agency. My own view differs, but a full exploration of this subject would involve more detail than that strictly necessary for our purposes here. The rebuilding of the grazing administration, or the building of the BLM, will be discussed below.

The Grazing Division, the Forest Service, the National Park Service, and other federal agencies during the Depression years of the 1930s made extensive use of various forms of manpower not in the established wage market. In particular, the Civilian Conservation Corps ("the 3 Cs") provided numbers of mostly young men, who were able to do a great deal of highly practical and worthwhile work on the land; the Works Progress Administration recruited its workers, some of whom were highly skilled, from the welfare rolls, and many fine things were accomplished by them. In addition, other programs were available and used by these agencies.

Intensive management

The period of intensive management lasted from about 1950 to about 1960. The post-1960 period has been marked by so many new laws and developments that it will be treated separately. It is also the most recent period, and because of this is of greatest interest. The 1950 date is, in some respects, an arbitrary one; the process of intensification of management on national forests, grazing districts, and other related federal lands was a gradual one, and the selection of any date within a span of years may be either criticized or defended. I have chosen 1950 because the fiscal year 1951 (beginning then on July 1, 1950) was the first year in modern times that the federal lands as a whole produced greater gross revenues than their total expenditures, including investment expenditures.[29] In the fifties the national forests produced larger gross revenues than expenditures on current management; in most years, they produced a surplus above investment and operating expenses combined, and for the decade as a whole there was surplus above all outlays of more than $20 million. In our naivete, Held and I thought the day had come when the national forests of the country could and would produce a continuing surplus for the taxpayers of the country.[30] Little did we reckon with the Forest Service's ability to turn surplus into deficit and to persuade a new Kennedy administration that larger appropriations for the Forest Service were synonymous with conservation. The surpluses of the 1950s turned to large net deficits in the 1960s, remaining so until today when the gross expenditures are nearly double the receipts— and both are at a much higher level than that of twenty years ago. The public domain under the BLM has always produced a net balance of receipts over expenditures because of large mineral lease receipts; but operations on its lands also became more intensified during the late 1940s and the 1950s.

The volume of timber cut from national forests rose from less than 4 billion board-feet in 1950 to more than 9 billion board-feet by 1960; the number of outdoor recreation visits increased from fewer than 30 million to more than 90 million in the same period; the amount of forage made available to game animals increased more than 50 percent; the forage available for domestic livestock, however, declined by about 10 percent; and in many other ways, the use or output of the national forests rose during this decade. Both annual operating expenditures and annual investments on the national forests rose greatly also (in current dollars, but these were years of much lower inflation than recent ones). Since the land area of the national forests changed but a little in these years, these measures of input and output all point toward intensification management.

The volume of timber sold from O & C lands rose from about 400 million board-feet at the beginning of this decade to about 1 billion board-feet annually by the end of it; the number of both domestic and game animals in the grazing districts changed relatively little; the number of oil and gas leases rose from fewer than 30,000 to nearly 140,000, and the acreage under lease rose from fewer than 25 million acres to well over 100 million. The number of actively producing oil and gas wells more than doubled; potash and phosphate production from leased lands rose greatly, but coal production did not (coal is a special situation and will be discussed in more detail later). The BLM kept no records of outdoor recreation in those days, but there is good reason to believe that the tremendous upsurge in recreational use of both national forests and national parks extended to the BLM lands also. Total receipts from grazing, oil and gas, recreation, minerals, and coal (excluding the revenues from Outer

Continental Shelf leasing) rose nearly four times during the decade, as did total expenditures, but the latter amounted to only about one-fifth of the former.

Thus, by every test, intensity of national forest, grazing district, and related land management rose greatly during the 1950s. Obviously this put more severe pressures on Forest Service and BLM personnel—more timber sales, more mineral leases, more people to deal with in campgrounds, and the like.

By no means do I wish to downgrade the importance of the work of these two agencies in those years; indeed, as a participant part of the time, I found the experience exciting, rewarding, and satisfying, for I felt we were doing useful service for the country. But, in retrospect, these were also rather quiet years—more a continuation of what had gone before than an illuminating experience for what was to come later. There were some new laws enacted in this decade, but nothing like what came in the 1960s and 1970s; there were interactions with many publics, but, again, nothing like what was to come. We must therefore turn to the more recent federal land history.

The Period Since 1960

Figure 2-1 shows a sixth major era of federal land management, which I call "consultation and confrontation," that began in 1960. Although figure 2-1 may suggest that intensive management of the federal lands ended in 1960, in fact, it is an integral part of the present era. This new era ended the custodial management, but, as did its predecessor, it overlapped to some degree acquisition, disposal, and reservation eras. Clearly, in this case, as in all other analyses of historic changes, the change was not sudden, nor could a precise date be given for its advent. Rather it evolved over time and 1960 seems to be the date that is most acceptable.

Culhane also recognizes six major eras of federal land management.[31] His analysis is in agreement with that shown in figure 2-1, except that for the sixth era he uses the name "extensive preservation," and he dates it to 1964. He, too, considers that intensive management has continued up to the present and also emphasizes the overlapping of the various major eras.

By whatever name one chooses to describe the present management of the federal lands, and from whatever date one thinks the present era began, it is fairly clear to any informed observer that the past twenty years as a whole differ substantially from the earlier years.

Some of the same forces which shaped federal land management earlier still continue, but major new forces are now operative.

Continuation of past trends

Although the years since 1960 have been greatly different for the federal lands than those that went before, some more or less obvious trends remain from the past. Acquisition, disposal, reservation, and management continued, although on a somewhat different scale and with different problems and opportunities.

Major "land" acquisition occurred during the 1960s and 1970s. The so-called Tidelands issue was settled in 1953, when federal legislation previously vetoed by President Truman was signed by President Eisenhower. It gave the states title to areas of the ocean three miles seaward of the line of their true tidelands, whose title had always been theirs. At the time, it was believed that this three-mile belt contained all the oil and gas which could ever be exploited economically, but new technologies for drilling in deeper water, out to where the depth is 600 feet or more, soon extended the boundaries of the areas open for exploitation. For example, the area off the Atlantic, Gulf, and Pacific coasts out to 600-feet depth is something on the order of 200 to 250 million acres. There are additional areas off the Pacific, Bering, and Arctic coasts of Alaska, and still larger areas to be exploited should the boundary for U.S. mineral exploitation be pushed seaward 200 miles from the U.S. coast. as has been done for fisheries exploitation.[32] By asserting its claim to adjacent ocean, the United States acquired a new area of federal "land" that about equals the cessions of the original states. Areas of the earth's underwater surface, which thirty years ago seemed as remote as the moon, have become part of the sovereign United States and one would be foolhardy indeed to draw any lines with confidence that mineral development would never proceed beyond them.

Persons primarily interested in timber, grass, and outdoor recreation on federal lands often are inclined to push aside any consideration of these Outer Continental Shelf (OCS) areas, on the grounds that such areas have no meaning for their special interests. This is a very shortsighted viewpoint. True enough, neither trees nor grass grow where the water is deep, but neither does much grow in some of the harsher deserts; the minerals taken from the ocean bed enter into the same channels of commerce as do the minerals taken from the dry land, and to that extent the development of the OCS areas inevitably affects the mineral development of dryland public lands, and this, in turn, has affected the production and use of trees and grass.

Since 1960, some federal acquisition of dryland areas has taken place. The 1911 Weeks Act had been the basis for the acquisition of considerable areas of national forest land over the years, especially in the establishment of the eastern national forests. The New Deal years had seen the acquisition of areas for wildlife refuges, but it was not until 1960 that the federal government bought national parkland. Prior to that date land for national parks had come from existing federal holdings (much of it from national forests), or had been donated by private citizens (as were Grand Teton, Acadia, and Shenandoah National Parks). In 1961 a precedent was set when the federal government set out to acquire land for the Cape Cod National Seashore. Since then land has been acquired for several national parks or recreation areas, including the Redwoods National Park and the Santa Monica Mountains Recreation Area—large and expensive acquisitions, whether measured in terms of total monetary cost, cost per acre, or cost per visitor-hour. The Land and Water Conservation Fund, established in 1964, provides the funds for considerable federal acquisition of areas primarily valuable for outdoor recreation, especially in the national forests and parks. These acquisitions were relatively small when compared with the vast land area of the United States or with the area already in federal ownership; but in local terms they have often been highly important.

Some federal lands in the "lower 48" states, having a smaller total acreage but an often significant impact on local situations, have been disposed of. Disposals of federal lands in Alaska to that state and recognition of native claims to land in that state removed huge areas from federal ownership there. The leasing of federal lands, or disposal of some rights to the land, have been more important. The number and acreage of unexplored oil and gas leases rose greatly during speculative frenzies of the 1950s, peaking at nearly 140,000 leases and well over 100 million acres by 1960. Both numbers of leases and acreage receded somewhat but have since stabilized at about 100,000 leases and about 80 million acres.[33] The vast majority of such lands are never drilled, and after a period of years without exploration the land reverts to the federal government; therefore, an approximate stability of numbers of leases and of acreage means that about as much land is leased each year as reverts out of lease. The land speculation of the 1950s has not abated but now is better controlled by the BLM. When leases expire or are relinquished by the lessee or are canceled by the BLM, such areas are reopened for lease, and applications are received for a simultaneous filing period. Filing fees are charged (on a profit-making basis), and lottery drawings are held in a vast, federally sanctioned and conducted national lottery that may not be faultless, but at least it bears very little resemblance to the process followed for minerals development.[34] Many of the lands included in the new lease applications have at one time been leased, have reverted to government ownership, and been leased again. Like the Irish Sweepstakes, winners are few but a small number do strike it rich if an oil company with funds and competence decides that the land is worth drilling. Lands not previously leased continue to be available for lease on a first-come-first-served basis.

The leasing of federal land for coal mining or extraction of federally owned minerals under land whose surface rights are owned by private individuals is a vastly different affair, which will be explored more fully in chapter 3. To a large extent, the oil and gas companies have always dealt with a leasebroker—a person who serves as the intermediary between the leaseholder and the wildcat oil driller. The wildcatter has preferred this, because it enables him to assemble a large acreage within which any oil or gas deposit is likely to be confined, without tipping his hand as to what he was doing, which would have run up the leasing costs greatly and encouraged a few landowners to hold out in the hope of a greater gain. The coal companies have sought instead to deal more directly with the federal government, although they too have used leasebrokers for private lands. It takes many years and a goodly amount of capital to develop an operating coal mine, whether by deep or surface mining. The number of coal leases in effect—comparatively small during the 1950s—rose considerably by 1970, but was still less than 600 during the 1970s. Production from these coal leases lagged greatly; the major companies interested in coal development simply acquired reserve deposits for the great increase in coal demand that they foresaw and which, in fact, developed by the early 1970s. Today this concern continues, and they have reserve deposits under lease to provide for any future increases in demand.

The number and acreage for other mineral leases also rose during the 1960s and 1970s. Some of these leases, although small in total acreage, as compared with the vast federal holdings, were of great importance in local situations.

The volume of timber sold from the national forests rose from somewhat more than 9 billion board-feet in 1960 to a peak of somewhat over 12 billion board-feet in 1973, but since then it has declined to about 9 or 10 billion board-feet annually. The number of livestock grazed on both national forests and grazing districts has declined slightly since 1960.

The 1960s and 1970s saw substantial designation of federal land in national forests and grazing districts for wilderness purposes, and additional lands were under study as potential wilderness areas. These were, in effect, withdrawals within withdrawals—that is, virtually none of this federal land had been open to private ownership except under the mining laws, and it continued to be open for this purpose within wilderness areas during the study period and through 1983. The withdrawals stopped timber sales and road building in these areas.

All of the forgoing—plus the large increases in expenditures by the agencies, greater revenues from timber sales and mineral leases particularly, and the accompanying great expansion in agency personnel—might have been seen simply as a continuation of the era of intensive federal land management. That is, to a considerable extent the events I have described in this section might have been considered merely more of the same.

However, since 1960 there have been three truly major events or situations which, in my judgment, warrant calling this a new era. These are (1) the passage of a number of major new laws; (2) increased knowledge of resource matters by the public, new popular attitudes toward the agencies and toward the federal lands, and new abilities on the part of the general public to influence the federal land management agencies; and (3) a new role for the courts.

A flood of new laws

The legislation regarding federal lands in the 1960s and 1970s— as with that on other subjects in the same period—must be considered in the light of major social, political, ideological, and economic trends. These were the decades of increased federal activity generally— antidiscrimination laws, increased welfare programs, the "war on poverty," and others. There was a marked tendency to look to the federal government for a solution of social problems. At the same time, the 1960s in particular were a period of social protest (including civil disorders and demonstrations), in part exacerbated by the Vietnam war. The age structure was also changing, with far more young people, often political activists, involved than previously. To a substantial extent, these decades were a time of change. The federal land laws passed in this period would not have been passed, had it not been for this social and political milieu.[35]

There are, of course, a great many laws enacted by the Congress and signed by the president in any twenty-year period.[36] In what follows, I have chosen for brief discussion eight "major" laws directly relating to the federal lands and others, perhaps equally important in their total impact, but less directed to the federal lands. I have intentionally omitted the Alaska land legislation of 1980, since the whole focus of this book is on the "lower 48" states. There have also been important amendments to older acts, such as the coal leasing acts, which also have been omitted.

The Multiple Use–Sustained Yield Act. In 1960 the Multiple Use–Sustained Yield Act provided a firm legislative foundation for the multiple-use management of the national forests, which had long been a Forest Service practice. The agency sought the legislation, fearing (and as events proved, rightly so) that without such a mandate it might be under legal and political attack for its multiple-use management. No significant popular demand existed for the legislation, although it was of concern to some interest groups. The act referred to "the combination (of uses) that will best meet the needs of the American people; making the most judicious use of the land . . .without impairment of the productivity of the land. . .and not necessarily the combination of uses that will give the greatest dollar return or the greatest unit output."

Multiple use is a term that has great conceptual, ideological, and emotional values for many persons; its very ambiguity enables each to interpret the term as desired. Only when attempts are made to put the general idea into practice is the wide disagreement in meaning evident. The act gave the Forest Service a mandate for multiple use of forestlands but no specific guidance on policy issues and still less guidance for actual forest management in the field.

The Wilderness Act of 1964. This act and its administration have been one of the most important, most controversial, and most bitterly—even emotionally—defended and criticized of all the legislation passed in the last two decades. As Fairfax reports: "Nine years of deliberation saw sixty-five different bills introduced, twenty of which passed in one house at one time or another."[37]

There had been two main policy issues, as well as some of lesser importance: (1) "What areas would be included initially in the system, and who would be authorized to modify or add to that system?" and (2) "What uses are allowed in the wilderness areas."[38]

On the first point, advocates of wilderness had envisioned a large system, with the president empowered to add new areas to the existing system. Under previously enacted legislation, the president had been empowered to designate national monuments. The act as passed included automatically all the national forest wilderness areas, designated by the Forest Service; and it ordered the Forest Service to study primitive areas and potential wilderness areas in national forests. The secretary could make recommendations to the president, who could alter them but final action was to be taken only by the Congress. The act prohibited the building of roads and the harvest of timber; already established motorboat and aircraft use was allowed to continue; mineral exploration could continue to the end of 1983, but patents issued under the mining law would convey title only to the minerals, not to the surface of the land. Domestic livestock grazing could continue under permit.

The opposition to the act had focused on the "locking up" of important mineral, timber, and other resources. Senators Clinton Anderson, Frank Church, Wayne Morse, Philip Hart, Thomas Kuchel, James Murray, Hubert Humphrey, Paul Douglas, and Richard Neuberger, and Rep. John Saylor—all strong supporters of the bill and spokesmen for the wilderness interests—sought to assure its opponents that the act would not take out of commercial production any land not already designated by the administrative action of the Forest Service.[39] Senator Church, speaking for the Committee on Interior and Insular Affairs, said:

> Inclusion of the wild, wilderness, primitive, park, and wildlife areas in the wilderness preservation system will cause little or no disruption of individual, communities, or economic patterns. The areas have been withdrawn for years. There have been no timber sales from the forest lands involved. . .we undertake to confine the proposed wilderness system to those areas of public land that have already been set aside for recreational use. Thus, the system could only include areas already designated as wild areas, wilderness areas, canoe areas, primitive areas in national forests, primitive-type areas in national parks and in national monuments, and such areas in wildlife refuges and game ranges. That is the maximum possible scope of the wilderness system to be established by the bill.[40]

Other statements in the debates referred to 15 million acres to be designated as wilderness.

Fairfax has described what has happened since the act was passed:

> . . .Although the Wilderness Act itself affected only specified areas of the national forests managed since 1940 as wilderness, the act's coverage

has been greatly expanded by agency action and judicial interpretation. It is frequently asserted by wilderness opponents that these interpretations went far beyond the Wilderness Act's original purpose. There does not seem to be much question that neither the bill's sponsors nor its opponents envisioned this expansive reading of the act. However, in assessing the complaints about the "stretching" of the 1964 legislation, a number of factors must be considered. First, Congress can and frequently does ignore the procedures and limitations it established in the act by adding wilderness areas to the system entirely on its own, irrespective of the former status of the land.[41]

Though Fairfax is quite right in citing the prerogatives Congress extends to itself, the opponents of the wilderness system—after having muted their opposition to the act upon receiving assurances from responsible senators as to its ultimate coverage—felt they had been double-crossed. The expansion of the act has caused its critics to question the integrity of the wilderness advocates. The latter, of course, have similar doubts about their opponents. One consequence of prolonged controversy on any issue is often the deep mistrust it develops on each side; each can feel that it is only "getting even" with its opponents, no matter what it does.

By 1972, more than 50 million acres in national forests, national parks, and federal wildlife areas (but excluding BLM areas) were under review by the agency or by the Congress for possible addition to the wilderness system.[42] At that time, the Forest Service had under review some 55 million acres of roadless lands, for possible addition to the wilderness system. In 1971 the Forest Service undertook the Roadless Area Review and Evaluation (RARE I). And in 1977 the new Carter administration undertook RARE II, the results of the first review not being considered satisfactory by the proponents of wilderness or to the courts which had ruled on suits brought by wilderness advocates. At one time as much as 62 million acres of the total 192 million acres of the national forests were temporarily withdrawn from multiple-use management pending their review and appraisal, as agreed to in a court suit brought by conservation groups.[43]

In addition, very large areas of the BLM lands, including lands in Alaska, were also under review for possible inclusion as wilderness. The RARE II report recommended that 15 million acres be included in wilderness within national forests, that 36 million acres be released from further consideration, and that 10 million acres be reserved for further study. Of the areas under BLM management, 23 million acres were recommended for further study and the rest were recommended for release from further consideration. However, none of these agency recommendations is conclusive or binding until Congress has acted.

By court orders, these areas under review are closed to the same uses that would be excluded if the land is later placed in a wilderness. From the viewpoint of the wilderness opponents, therefore, the study of any area for inclusion in the wilderness system is, at least for the present, as restrictive as if it actually had been designated as wilderness. From the viewpoint of the wilderness advocates, the areas are set aside but not fully protected. The resultant situation is hardly one to quiet fears on either side. One can safely assert that controversy over wilderness will not soon end.

The Classification and Multiple Use Act.   In 1964 the Bureau of Land Management received specific authority in the Classification and Multiple Use Act and in its companion, the Public Land Sale Act, to examine and classify public domain for retention or for disposal, and it obtained new authority for methods of land disposal. In 1963 there were seven days of hearings before a subcommittee of the House Committee on Interior and Insular Affairs on three bills which had been introduced by congressmen and on one bill which had originated in the Department of the Interior.[44] In the summer of 1964 there were two days of hearings before a subcommittee of the Senate Committee on Interior and Insular Affairs on the two bills which had been passed by the House (out of the four listed above) and on a bill to establish the Public Land Law Review Commission.[45] What started in the House as an effort to provide the BLM with more authority to sell the public domain for industrial, urban, and related purposes (subject to a classification of the land as suitable and needed for such uses) was transformed into acts in which the land-classification authority emerged as the primary purpose and the land-disposal authority was of secondary importance. The multiple-use bill became another act. Debated separately in the House, but during the same hearings in the Senate, the bill to establish the Public Land Law Review Commission (PLLRC) was considered. Although this bill had originated in the Congress, it had administration support. The classification and sale authorities of these acts were limited to a period ending six months after the PLLRC report was due, on the assumption that it would recommend permanent legislation to supplant these temporary acts. As it turned out, congressional action on the PLLRC report was delayed until the passage of the Federal Land Policy and Management Act of 1976, and the BLM continued to act under the 1964 Acts.

These bills drew considerable support at the hearings from conservation groups, ranchers, and local governments. There was some concern that the authority to sell land would be the opening wedge in a program of wholesale disposal of the public domain, but those raising this point were reassured by the departmental spokesmen. It was pointed out that Section 7 of the Taylor Grazing Act had provided land-classification authority and that the new authority was both a reaffirmation and, to some extent, an extension of that classification. The Department of Interior asserted, and no one disputed its statement, that the BLM had for some years been practicing multiple-use management of the federal lands under its administration, and that the new act simply gave congressional approval and support to what the agency had been doing. Thus, for the BLM, the 1964 Classification and Multiple Use Act was in many ways similar to the 1960 Multiple Use Act for the Forest Service—it was more an expression of current congressional attitude than an instrument designed to increase the agency's power.

The Trans-Alaska Pipeline Act.   In 1973 Congress passed the Trans-Alaska Pipeline Act, a law representing a significant feeling on the part of Congress that the pipeline had been delayed long enough for environmental considerations. Oil had been discovered on the North Slope of Alaska in 1968 and almost immediately proposals were made to construct a pipeline over federal lands to the open seaport of Valdez. The oil companies paid more than $900 million as bonuses (in addition to continued royalties) to the state of Alaska for the oil leases. Clearly, the impetus for the act came from the industry and not from the federal agencies.

The Forest and Rangeland Renewable Resource Planning Act.   In 1974 Congress passed the Forest and Rangeland Renewable Resources Planning Act (RPA), moving to do so within about six months from the time a bill to this end was first introduced—a very quick response on the part of Congress for such an important piece of legislation. Impetus for the act came primarily from the Congress, particularly from Sen. Hubert Humphrey; whereas the Forest Service and the administration were more reactive than active. John McGuire, who was chief of the Forest Service when both the 1974 and 1976 Acts were passed, has said, "Although the Forest Service had engaged in program planning at intervals since World War II, the 1974 Act originated in Congress, and not in the executive branch. It came about because of senatorial dissatisfaction with the annual budget presentations for the Forest Service."[46]

The 1974 Act was the first one signed by Gerald Ford after he assumed the presidency; and it is generally believed it would have been vetoed, because of its provisions about financing national forest management, except that the president did not wish to start his administration with a veto. The act is complicated and has some provisions that seem incompatible with others.[47] It is, above all, a planning act, requiring that an assessment of all renewable resources be made every ten years, and that a program for the national forests be submitted every five years. The latter includes effectuating budgets, and the president—if his budget is in disagreement with the proposal—must explain his rejection of the monetary proposals of the planning program. This requirement, an attempt on the part of Congress to force the president to implement the planning of the act, was the feature to which President Ford objected strongly. The act clearly intends that national forests be forced into more economic management. The act also provides for public participation, for timber sales, for reforestation, and many other functions. The Forest Service (technically, the secretary of agriculture) presented its first assessment and program to the Congress in early 1976. These received little attention from the Congress, which was overwhelmed at the time by more pressing matters concerning the national forests. These initial reports were extensively criticized by professional resource workers, and it soon became apparent that the Forest Service was ill-prepared to make the analyses and write the reports.

The National Forest Management Act.   Technically the 1976 National Forest Management Act (NFMA) was an amendment to the RPA, but it so extensively amended the 1974 Act that it was, in effect, a wholly new piece of legislation. The NFMA was enacted largely because the final court decision in the 1975 *Monongehela* case was judged by both its supporters and opponents to forbid the sale of timber from national forests as it typically had been practiced by the Forest Service. While the decision was technically concerned with the 1897 Act, (described on page 32), basically the lobbying by conservation organizations concentrated on outlawing the clear-cutting of timber. The 1974 Act—although strengthened and made more specific in numerous ways by the 1976 Act—remains primarily a planning act, that places its greatest emphasis on more economic management of the national forests.

The 1976 Act, perhaps more than most legislation, represented a compromise among competing viewpoints. When it was finally passed, expressions of approval came from many diverse groups. As John F. Hall of the National Forest Products Association said, "In reviewing the National Forest Management Act, several people have commented that it sets the stage for forest management for the next seventy-five years. I must add that it also sets the stage for litigation and judicial involvement in forest management for the next ten years at least. I caution you, when the chief of the Forest Service, the Sierra Club's Washington, D.C., representative, and I say that that 1976 Act is a reasonable and workable statute—and we have each made such statements—each of us may be reading a different act."[48]

How this act has worked in practice will be considered in chapter 3. As is usual, regulations had to be written under the act, but the act had an innovative provision in this regard. It provides for the creation of a committee of scientists who are not only to advise the secretary but also are directed to make their report public. This provision has been carried out, and the regulations have been widely criticized by industry, by conservation groups, and by professional associations.[49] Revised regulations were circulated for comment in early 1982 and adopted later in that year.

The full implications of the act are not yet apparent. Obviously, it provides more guidelines for the Forest Service than had been given previously, but the Congress rejected the conservationists' proposals to reduce the Forest Service's freedom to make professional judgments regarding specific resource situations.[50] Based on my own experience in federal land administration, I judge that the act presents great opportunities to an agency prepared to take advantage of them, but that it cannot compel the Forest Service to operate in ways it does not choose.

The Federal Land Policy and Management Act. The Federal Land Policy and Management Act (FLPMA), passed in 1976, repealed much of the detailed legislation that had burdened the BLM for decades, replacing it with new and more general legislation, that gave the BLM significant additional powers.[51] The act embraces the idea of permanent federal ownership of all federal lands except when— as a result of land use planning—a determination is made that disposal of a specific parcel would serve the national interest. Some provisions of the act apply to the national forests, the result of congressional determination to bring all the federal lands under more nearly similar laws. This act, like the NFMA, is basically a planning act. It endorses multiple use—and who does not, in general terms? There is greater recognition of environmental concerns; and BLM lands are clearly brought under consideration for wilderness reservation. There is provision for public participation—as there is in the NFMA. The secretary of the interior has new and significant authority to enforce his regulations on the federal lands. The BLM, anxious to have this legislation, initiated efforts in that direction. Much of the act flowed out of the reports of the Public Land Law Review Commission of six years earlier. The administration proposals were critically examined and considerably modified by the Congress. Like the NFMA, the full implications of this act will be evident only after it has been in force for some time.

When it comes to important legislation primarily concerned with other matters that affects federal land use and management, one is faced with an embarassment of riches—there are so many laws that could have been included here, but because of space limitations I must single out only a few.

The National Wild and Scenic Rivers Act and the Trails System Act. Both these acts were passed in the same week of 1968. The general purpose of each is suggested by their titles. Each involves federal lands but nonfederal lands as well, hence they are borderline for my characterization as "major" federal land acts.

The National Environmental Policy Act. On January 1, 1970, President Nixon signed the National Environmental Policy Act of 1969 into law. The bill had aroused little public interest during its passage through Congress. Except for one feature that was added more or less off-handedly, the act was more an expression of congressional concern than a positive program for environmental protection.[52] The unique feature of the act was its requirement that analyses of environmental impacts had to accompany all proposals for "major federal action significantly affecting the quality of the human environment." When the act was passed, no one knew what an Environmental Impact Statement (EIS) should contain, or what constituted a significant action requiring such a statement. The courts soon broadened the definitions of each, almost certainly beyond anything the act's sponsors had intended and certainly far beyond what potential opponents of the act had dreamed of. Today, as one cynical federal administrator said, agency personnel can hardly flush the toilet without previously filing an Environmental Impact Statement. The willingness of the courts to insist upon complete, more revealing, and extensive Environmental Impact Statements, and to accept conservationists' criticisms that the terms of the act have not been complied with, have totally revolutionized federal land management. Partly as a defense against possible legal actions, the federal agencies have made the Environmental Impact Statements so long, so filled with

more or less meaningless figures, and so costly to prepare that even
the Council on Environmental Quality has sought to shorten and
simplify them. However, a governmental process once begun can
rarely be completely stopped or fully reversed.

The Endangered Species Act. Passed in 1973, the Endangered Species
Act seeks to prevent the extinction of endangered species of plants
and animals on both federal and private lands. Large social values
are attributed to the preservation of every species of life, and critical
habitats must be identified and protected if possible. In general terms,
such a viewpoint commands great public support but, as in so many
other instances, problems arise when attempts are made to translate
general ideas into specific actions. That the law has teeth is evident
from the fact that protection of the snail darter stopped work on the
almost completed Tellico Dam in the Tennessee Valley area. When
it was subsequently discovered that this fish also existed in areas not
threatened by the dam, the ruling was overturned by an act of
Congress and the dam was completed. The Endangered Species Act,
if taken literally, could threaten every other use of federal land. The
possibility exists that a team of really imaginative biologists can almost
surely find an endangered plant, animal, reptile, insect, bird, or fish
species in every area. The potential effects of the act frightened even
its supporters so that in 1978 amendments provided for a Cabinet-
level committee to weigh the costs and benefits of applying the law
in specific locations.

Other legislation. In 1977 what was technically considered to be an
amendment to the Clean Air Act of 1955 and its 1963 and 1970
Amendments was signed into law. Clearly, the changes in the 1977
Amendments practically constituted a new act. Closely allied to this
were the Federal Water Pollution Control Act of 1972 and the Clean
Water Act of 1977. All this legislation was concerned with air and
water everywhere, and most of the use and controversy over these
laws has been concentrated in urban areas. However, each applies to
forest and range operations as well, and each to some extent has
affected the management of the federal lands.

Students of natural resource and environmental law will protest
that the foregoing discussion has omitted many significant laws.
Intentionally, I have passed over those laws relating primarily to
parks and wildlife and omitted laws applicable only to Alaska. Since
1970, numerous laws have been enacted that in some degree affect
federal land use and management: the Solid Waste Disposal Act, the

Geothermal Resources Act, the Alaska Native Claims Settlement Act, the Wild and Free Roaming Horse and Burro Act, the Coastal Zone Management Act, the Federal Environmental Pesticide Control Act, the Noise Control Act, and the Bald and Golden Eagle Protection Act. There are still others of less than general applicability, or ones which pertain to less-important subjects, or amendments to appropriation acts which apply to specific situations. Additionally, there are literally thousands of bills which have not been passed—some quite important ones, such as those to create a national land use planning program.

One may say, as something of an understatement, that the 1970s particularly, and the 1960s to some extent, were an era of copious federal land legislation. The laws were important; but still more significant were the public attitudes that led to these laws, a subject to which we now turn. It should be noted, as we leave the matter of legislation, that there was a rather noticeable trend away from federal agency leadership and toward congressional initiative, that was spurred on in many cases by special interest groups. The difference between the Multiple Use Act of 1960, which the Forest Service initiated and strongly pushed, and the 1974 and 1976 National Forest Acts, which the Congress initiated and the Forest Service reacted to, is illustrative of this trend.

Public participation

The flood of laws described in the forgoing section was possible only because the public attitudes toward federal lands in the 1960s and 1970s differed from those held in 1950s and earlier. Generally, this increased interest occurred, in part, because so many more of the general public became users of federal lands, primarily through outdoor recreation activities. In addition, the growing conservationist-environmentalist movement, which found expression in such happenings as Earth Day, aroused interest in federal lands as well as in other natural resources. The controversies, described in the following subsection, also drew public attention to natural resource issues generally and to federal lands more specifically. Journalists as well suddenly discovered natural resources and federal lands. Some of their concerns and interests were absurdly naive but did reflect popular interest. If people were interested enough to read about resource and environmental issues, or to watch television programs about them, then naturally enough journalists gave the public the information it was interested in.

Much of the new legislation—the RPA, NFMA, and FLPMA particularly—called for public participation in the planning and the management of the federal lands. Generally speaking, these and other laws called for public participation at every stage in planning, from the initial consideration of a problem to the promulgation of the final regulations, the drafting of an effectuating bill, or the preparation of an effectuating appropriation. Laws and court decisions increasingly called for formal public hearings, with many of the trappings of a formal legal procedure, as part of the final planning process.

Almost everyone endorses the idea of public participation in public business—which, after all, is what the management of the federal lands is. As in so many other aspects of federal land management, the problems arise not at the general level but when attempts are made to translate general ideas into specific actions. (The problems of public participation are described further in chapter 8.)

But it is timely to point out that the public—really, "the publics"— who are concerned with the federal lands today differ greatly from the public of a generation ago. The ordinary user of the federal lands—recreationist, rancher, logger, oil driller, and others—is today vastly better educated than were his parents, has a higher income, and is more likely to have traveled and to have used federal lands in some other state or region. The modern user of the federal lands generally accepts as desirable federal agency administration, but he or she is less inhibited about speaking out and asserting rights and opinions than was the user of a generation ago. Today's user is far less deferential to the federal agencies, knowing that he or she is as likely to have as much expertise as the federal employee. It is simply a different public world for the federal agency personnel today.

For a time, in the late 1960s and early 1970s, the word "public" was almost synonymous with "conservationists." The conservationists overwhelmed the public meetings, sent volumes of mail to agencies and to their congressmen in support of their positions, and were the persons to whom the journalists turned for interviews. The conservationists also initiated lawsuits.

To some extent, this situation changed in the late 1970s and the early 1980s. Whipping up a show of public attitude is a game that two can play. Industry and other special interest groups opposed to specific wilderness proposals have been able to generate as much, sometimes even more mail than wilderness supporters, and have developed their own legal action groups as well.[53]

Confrontation

The ultimate in public participation, when friendly cooperation and negotiation break down or come to an impasse, is confrontation, or more specifically, the lawsuit. A generation ago, citizen lawsuits against federal agencies were almost unknown—personally I do not recall any being initiated during the five years that I was director of the BLM (1948–53). Today, lawsuits are so commonplace that a federal administrator who has had none in a month begins to wonder if he is slipping.

Several things have happened to bring about this radical shift:

- First, some of the new legislation has provided openings for litigation. Particularly, as it has worked out, the National Environmental Policy Act of 1969, with its requirement for Environmental Impact Statements, opened the door to many suits.[54] The courts as a whole have taken a "generous" view of this act and of these statements, responding to the pleas of environmental groups that such statements as written by federal agencies were inadequate, and that actions could not proceed until satisfactory statements had been prepared.

- Second, the courts generally have taken more generous attitudes toward letting interest groups and even individuals sue in the name of larger groups. While there have been some variations among courts, generally many persons or groups today are able to sue when similar persons or groups would not have been so empowered a generation ago. The statutes have explicitly or implicitly encouraged this attitude on the part of the courts.

- Third, the judiciary of the United States as a whole is far more activist today than it was many years ago. This is clearly a legacy of the Warren Court, which took action on civil rights, voting representation, and other matters which the U.S. Supreme Court previously had refused to consider. This activism permeates lower levels of the judiciary also so that courts in recent years have pronounced judgments on natural resource issues, including federal land issues, with a frequency unknown heretofore.

- Fourth, but perhaps the more important factor has been the changing attitudes of the public, or at least of large sectors of it. With the new laws on the books, conservation groups hire lawyers and devote substantial sums to legal action. Law has become a key area of expertise for environmentalists, on a par with their expertise in natural sciences. Today many conservationists and other special interest groups will enter into litigation despite the costs or their possible defeat, when once they never would have considered such a step. While lawsuit and conservationist went hand in hand in the 1960s and early 1970s, today they have been joined in the courts by industry. It is entirely possible that the pendulum of judicial activism will swing back in the next decade.

It is impossible to list all the lawsuits brought over federal lands. The major cases are listed by Dana and Fairfax, and the interested reader is referred to their account.[55] Their review demonstrates a few vital points regarding the federal lands: (1) the courts have been very active, during the past decade, on natural resource matters generally and on federal land matters specifically; (2) court decisions vitally affect federal land management; and (3) federal land management agencies can no longer ignore the possibility of adverse legal action. Some courts have asserted more expertise in land management than resource specialists would have accorded them, and the indirect effect of some of their decisions may be far reaching. Land-administering agencies must be much more careful in the actions they take, in view of the possibility of adverse court action. The direct costs of legal action are great to the parties involved, but the money costs to the agencies may be quite overshadowed by the costs in time and money imposed by such delay. Those who oppose certain kinds of actions on federal land have found legal action or the threat of legal action a prime delaying tactic.

Some Observations on the History of Federal Lands

Contemplating the 200 years of federal land history as it has been sketched in this chapter leads to several major generalizations, which may be applicable to the future as well as to the past:

- The passage of federal land laws and, to some extent, the administration of those laws have always been in the hands of persons who were often ill-informed and physically remote from the lands. Federal land was a frontier matter for more than a century, and for the past 100 years it has been primarily a western matter. Complaints about the role of distant legislators and administrators have been made continuously throughout this long history, by the persons most affected by the laws.

It may be argued that whatever the basis for criticism of their land use decisions, legislators and administrators today are better informed than their predecessors about the federal lands. But the vast majority of the Congress is neither informed nor much interested in federal lands, but these persons still vote on federal land matters.

There is another and socially more responsible side to this matter of legislation enacted primarily by nonresidents of the region. As I have noted in chapter 1, there is almost always a national-regional divergence on the topic of federal land management. Local citizens may be both more informed and more directly interested, but they are also more likely to emphasize their local economic interests rather than the national interest in any federal land matter. The more distant legislator may lack something in local knowledge, but this may be more than offset by a broader and more detached social outlook.

• Laws relating to federal lands frequently have been enacted as a direct response to an acute situation. Sometimes, as in the Mining Law of 1866, the legislation has simply legitimized situations which had grown up in actual land use. In fact, delay is not limited to federal land law; Congress and the state legislatures respond primarily to clearly evident, existent, perceived problems. The passage of the National Forest Management Act of 1976 in response to a court decision is a dramatic recent example. One might argue that federal land legislation has nearly always been "too late"—that is, what would have been farsighted and creative twenty or thirty years earlier is already largely outdated and even irrelevant by the time it is passed. The general Preemption Act of 1841, enacted thirty years after the fact of preemption, was generally effective; the Homestead Act of 1862 was passed after most of the suitable land had been disposed of; the Enlarged Homestead Act of 1909 and the Stock-Raising Homestead Act of 1916 each were enacted far too late to achieve their purpose; the Taylor Grazing Act of 1934 would have been far more appropriate thirty years earlier; the Wilderness Act of 1964 came more than forty years after the idea of wilderness reservation was initiated by the Forest Service; the Federal Land Policy and Management Act of 1976 would have been really constructive if passed in 1934 (when the Taylor Grazing Act went into effect); and one could go on.

Admittedly, there are great difficulties in foreseeing future needs, and, of course, hindsight always is more accurate than foresight. But the tendency of the legislative process to respond only to evident problems or crises does have serious implications for future federal land management. Some analogies come to mind: fire prevention is neglected, in favor of fire fighting; or health care is neglected, in favor of hospital emergency care. If the necessary response occurs after situations have become acute, then purposeful and economic management of the federal lands is more difficult, if not impossible, to achieve.

• Operation of federal land laws in the field always differs from what the lawmakers intended. Naturally enough, the local citizenery has sought to interpret federal land laws to their advantage, or to ignore or prevent their application, or to modify laws and the regulations. To a considerable extent, this is desirable; the United States is a big and diverse country, and what works well in one region may not work so well elsewhere. But when local people take the interpretation of federal laws into their own hands, much of the rationale for federal land ownership is lost.

Earlier in this chapter I cited some illustrations of those at the local level modifying land law to local interests. Malone has described how the early settlers along the Maine coast thwarted the laws of the King of England regarding timber harvest, and Gould has described how the frontiersmen in Maryland thwarted the landed proprietor, Lord Baltimore.[56] With the growth of the federal land-managing bureaucracy and the location of federal employees in closer proximity to the land they administer, outright disregard of federal law is less likely to go unnoticed than it was during much of the great settlement period of the nineteenth century. However, it is still a mistake to think that mere passage of a law changes operations on the land.

• Federal land legislation typically has been imprecise in its language, often because the compromises necessary to pass the legislation were made only because the results were stated in vague terms. Not all of this has occurred in the past; for example, we have seen how this applies to the 1976 National Forest Management Act. Congress passes a bill and the president signs it into law, leaving to the federal agencies the task of trying to make the compromises work in the field and to the courts the task of trying to decide what the legislators really meant when they enacted the legislation. This vagueness and the compromise out of which legislation arises are a necessary part of democratic political process, and it can be argued that this is a socially more desirable method of governing than any other that can be devised. But it does make difficult the economic and efficient management of the federal lands for any purpose or for any output.

• Finally, it should be noted that when the self-interest of federal land users does not lead them to act as the law intended or as the administrators think desirable, then it is necessary to devise administrative controls over private actions in order to achieve the desired result. Government at all levels and in all activities has grown more complex over the years, and this is certainly the case in federal land management. The difference between the Forest Service Use Book of Pinchot's day, and the 26-foot shelf of Forest Service regulations today fully symbolizes the changes that have occurred in government. Today, when action on the land does not fit the law or the present regulations, the typical action is to extend the regulations. Perhaps this is both inevitable and unavoidable, but it also discourages the more efficient management of the federal lands. The possibility that the self-interest of federal land users can be harnessed to socially desired ends will be considered in later chapters.

Notes

1. There is an extensive professional literature and an immense popular and semipopular literature about federal land history, which it is impossible to enumerate completely, much less to summarize fully. There are three classic books which deal with federal lands from their beginning up to the date the books were written, and which consider such lands for all their uses (as far as these were evident at the time). They are listed below in the order in which they appeared:

B. H. Hibbard, *A History of Public Land Policies* (New York, Macmillan, 1924).

Roy M. Robbins, *Our Landed Heritage: The Public Domain 1776–1936* (1 ed., Princeton, N.J., Princeton University Press, 1941); and *Our Landed Heritage: the Public Domain, 1776–1970* (2 ed., Lincoln, University of Nebraska Press, 1976).

Paul W. Gates, *History of Public Land Law Development*, written for the Public Land Law Review Commission (Washington, D.C., Government Printing Office, November 1968).

In addition, there are several books which I regard as topflight but which deal only with certain periods in federal land history, with certain uses of the land, or otherwise are less than complete in their coverage. They are listed below in alphabetical order:

Jenks Cameron, *The Development of Governmental Forest Control in the United States* (Baltimore, Md., Johns Hopkins University Press, 1928).

Vernon Carstensen, ed., *The Public Lands—Studies in the History of the Public Domain* (Madison, University of Wisconsin Press, 1963).

Samuel T. Dana, *Forest and Range Policy—Its Development in the United States* (New York, McGraw-Hill, 1956).

Samuel T. Dana and Sally K. Fairfax, *Forest and Range Policy* (rev. ed., New York, McGraw-Hill 1979). The first edition has much more detail, including legal citations to laws which are missing from the revised edition; the latter has a detailed and highly useful account of legislation since 1956.

Samuel P. Hays, *Conservation and the Gospel of Efficiency—The Progressive Conservation Movement, 1890–1920* (Cambridge, Mass., Harvard University Press, 1959).

John Ise, *The United States Forest Policy* (New Haven, Conn., Yale University Press, 1920); and *Our National Park Policy: A Critical History* (Baltimore, Md., Johns Hopkins University Press for Resources for the Future, 1961).

E. Louise Peffer, *The Closing of the Public Domain—Disposal and Reservation Policies, 1900–1950* (Stanford, Calif., Stanford University Press, 1951).

Malcolm Rohrbough, *The Land Office Business—The Settlement and Administration of American Public Lands, 1789–1837* (New York, Oxford University Press, 1978).

Harold K. Steen, *The U.S. Forest Service—A History* (Seattle, University of Washington Press, 1976).

There are, of course, scores if not hundreds of excellent books which deal somewhat, sometimes only peripherally, with the federal lands.

2. Marion Clawson and Burnell Held, *The Federal Lands—Their Use and Management* (Baltimore, Md., Johns Hopkins University Press for Resources for the Future, 1957).

3. Gates, *History of Public Lands;* and also Elmo Richardson, *BLM's Billion-Dollar Checkerboard: Management of the O & C Lands* (Santa Cruz, Calif., Forest History Society, 1980). This book may be obtained from the U.S. Government Printing Office in Washington, D.C.

4. Jerry O'Callaghan is currently writing a history of the Bureau of Land Management in which he describes this presidential action very well.

5. William E. Peters, *Ohio Lands and Their History* (New York, Arno Press, 1979); see especially chap. 4. See also Lowell O. Stewart, *Public Land Surveys* (New York, Arno Press, 1979). This is an earlier account of problems of land surveyors written in 1935, and reprinted in 1979). See also Earl G. Harrington, "Cadastral Surveys for the Public Lands of the United States," in Vernon Carstensen, ed., *The Public Lands—Studies in the History of the Public Domain.*

6. See, for instance, Henry Tatter, *The Preferential Treatment of the Actual Settler in the Primary Disposition of the Vacant Lands in the United States to 1841* (New York, Arno Press, 1979); and Charles Judah Bayard, *The Development of Public Land Policy 1783–1820, With Special Reference to Indiana* (New York, Arno Press, 1979).

7. Rohrbough, *The Land Office*, especially chap. 11.

8. See Dana, *Forest and Range Policy;* and Ise, *The United States Forest Policy.* Also see Benjamin F. Shambaugh, *Constitution and Records of the Claim Association of Johnson County, Iowa* (New York, Arno Press, 1979); and Allan G. Bogue, "The Iowa Claim Clubs: Symbol and Substance," in Vernon Carstensen, ed., *The Public Lands.*

9. Gates, *History of Public lands,* pp. 388–399.

10. Robbins, *Our Landed Heritage,* pp. 174–182.

11. Paul W. Gates, "The Homestead Law in an Incongruous Land System," *American Historical Review,* vol. 41 (July) 1936.

12. Gates, *History of Public Lands,* pp. 310–311.

13. See, for instance, S. A. D. Puter, *Looters of the Public Domain* (Portland, Ore., Portland Printing House, 1908).

14. Denise A. Dragoo, "The Impact of the Federal Land Policy Management Act

Upon Statehood Grants and Indemnity Land Selections," *Arizona Law Review* vol. 21, no. 2 (1979) p. 395.

15. Public Land Law Review Commission, *One Third of the Nation's Land* (Washington, D.C., Government Printing Office, 1970) p. 246.

16. Cameron, *The Development*, pp. 116–117.

17. Ibid.; and Ise, *Forest Policy*; and Hibbard, *A History*.

18. Samuel P. Hays, in *Conservation*, makes this point very well.

19. John Ise, *Our National Park Policy*, pp. 17–18.

20. Dana, *Forest and Range Policy*, pp. 100–101.

21. Ise, *Forest Policy*, pp. 117–118.

22. Peffer, *The Closing*; and Hays, *Conservation*.

23. I am indebted to Jerry O'Callaghan for this information.

24. Dana, in *Forest and Range Policy*, pp. 104–109, has an excellent account of this event.

25. Gifford Pinchot, *Breaking New Ground* (New York, Harcourt, Brace, 1947) pp. 161–162.

26. Henry Clepper, *Professional Forestry in the United States* (Baltimore, Md., Johns Hopkins University Press for Resources for the Future, 1971). Hays, in *Conservation*, gives a fair and insightful discussion of this period.

27. Clawson and Held, *The Federal Lands*, p. 429.

28. Marion Clawson, *The Bureau of Land Management* (New York, Praeger, 1971).

29. Marion Clawson, *The Federal Lands Since 1956—Recent Trends in Use and Management* (Washington, D.C., Resources for the Future, 1967) pp. 112–113.

30. Clawson and Held, *The Federal Lands*, p. 102.

31. Paul J. Culhane, *Public Land Politics: Interest Group Influence on the Forest Service and the Bureau of Land Management* (Baltimore, Johns Hopkins University Press for Resources for the Future, 1981) p. 41.

32. Clawson and Held, *The Federal Lands*, p. 102.

33. The detailed basic data on this subject for each year are found in *Public Land Statistics* published annually by the BLM. A source more convenient for many readers, where good summary statistics for several years are presented, is the *Statistical Abstract of the United States*, published each year by the Bureau of the Census.

34. I have received advertising from a firm in Connecticut which solicits participation through it, of course, in the BLM drawings. "Many of these leases are immediately salable for huge sums of money. . .and many provide you with continuous 'royalty payments.' " "Your passport to a fortune provided to you by the U.S. Government." "You can win $100,000 or more!" Other firms regularly advertise in national magazines such as *Fortune*.

35. Marion Clawson, "The Federal Land Policy and Management Act of 1976 in a Broad Historical Perspective," *Arizona Law Review* vol. 21, no. 2, 1979.

36. Dana and Fairfax in *Forest and Range Policy*, rev. ed., are extremely helpful in this regard. Their volume serves as the basis for most of the rest of this section.

37. Ibid., p. 217*ff.*

38. Ibid., p. 218.

39. John T. Keane, in "The Wilderness Act as Congress Intended," *American Forests* (February) 1971, gives an excellent account, comprised largely of extensive quotes from the committee report and from congressional debates on the bill.

40. Ibid.

41. Dana and Fairfax, *Forest and Range Policy*, rev. ed., pp. 221–222.

42. *Report of the President's Advisory Panel on Timber and the Environment* (Washington, Government Printing Office, 1972). See p. 521.

43. I am indebted to my RFF colleague, John V. Krutilla, for the information in the rest of this paragraph.

44. U.S. Congress. House. Hearings before the Subcommittee on Public Lands of the Committee on Interior and Insular Affairs. 88th Cong. 1st sess.: on H.R. 106, To provide that certain public lands of the United States shall be disposed of for their highest and best use, and for other purposes; on H.R. 255, To provide for the orderly classification and disposal of public lands not required for any federal purpose; on H.R. 5498, To promote the sale and beneficial use of public lands by amending Sec. 2455 of the revised statutes, as amended (43 U.S.C.1171), and for other purposes; and on H.R. 5159, To authorize and direct that certain lands exclusively administered by the Secretary of the Interior be managed under principles of multiple use and to produce a sustained yield of products and services, and for other purposes. Serial No. 11, Pt. I, Use and Disposal of Public Lands (Washington, D.C., Government Printing Office, 1963).

45. U.S. Congress. Senate. Hearings before the Subcommittee on Public Lands of the Committee on Interior and Insular Affairs, 88th Cong., 2nd sess.: on H.R. 5159, An Act to authorize and direct that certain lands exclusively administered by the Secretary of the Interior be classified in order to provide for their disposal or interim management under principles of multiple use and to produce a sustained yield of products and services, and for other purposes; on H.R. 5498, An Act to provide temporary authority for the sale of certain public lands; and Hearings on H.R. 8070, An Act for the establishment of a Public Land Law Review Commission to study existing laws and procedures relating to the administration of the public lands of the United States, and for other purposes (Washington, D.C., Government Printing Office, 1964).

46. John R. McGuire, "The National Forests: An Experiment in Land Management," *Journal of Forest History* vol. 26, no. 2, (April) 1982, p. 91.

47. *Implementation of Resources Planning Act,* Hearings before the Subcommittee on Forests of the House Committee on Agriculture, 95th Cong., 1st sess., Serial No. 95-II. My own testimony appears on pp. 83–132.

48. John F. Hall, "National Forest Timber Obligations," *The Crisis in Federal Forest Land Management* (Washington, D.C., Society of American Foresters, 1977).

49. Society of American Foresters, *The Forest and Rangeland Renewable Resources Planning Act: The RPA Process—1980,* Report of the Task Force on RPA Implementation, (Washington, D. C., April 1981).

50. John R. McGuire, "National Forest Policy and the 94th Congress," *Journal of Forestry* vol. 74, no. 12 (December 1976).

51. The *Arizona Law Review,* vol. 21, no. 2 (Summer) 1979, includes sixteen articles on the Federal Land Policy and Management Act of 1976 by various specialists and informed persons.

52. Dana and Fairfax, *Forest and Range Policy,* rev. ed., pp. 209 and 237.

53. Prior to his selection as Secretary of the Interior, James G. Watt headed the Mountain States Legal Foundation, an organization formed for this purpose.

54. Frederick R. Anderson, assisted by Robert H. Daniels, *NEPA in the Courts: A Legal Analysis of the National Environmental Policy Act* (Baltimore, Md., Johns Hopkins University Press for Resources for the Future, 1973.)

55. Dana and Fairfax, *Forest and Range Policy,* rev. ed., pp. 411–424.

56. Joseph J. Malone, *Pine Trees and Politics: The Naval Stores and Forest Policy in Colonial New England, 1691–1775* (New York, Arno Press, 1979); and Clarence P. Gould, *The Land System in Maryland, 1720–1765* (New York, Arno Press, 1979).

3

Federal Land Use, Planning, and Management Today

Uses of Federal Lands

As noted in chapter 1, the most basic and dominant fact about federal lands is that they are used by private persons, groups, and corporations. In the pages that follow I will discuss the primary uses of the U.S. federal lands—grazing, timber harvesting, the extraction of coal and nonfuel minerals, as well as outdoor recreation and other activities.

Grazing

Prior to 1934. The grazing of domestic livestock—the oldest major use of federal land—involves the largest acreage of any use and has important political, social, and economical ramifications. From the earliest colonial days a private grazing economy on public lands existed at the frontier of the settled areas. This use of the public lands, serving as a buffer between the settlements and the Indians, expanded somewhat in peaceful times and contracted during hostilities with the Indians.

During the Civil War the normal channels of trade had been cut off, and the foraging cattle bred, unrestrained by good animal husbandry practices, especially in parts of Texas. Following the war, the nature of grazing economy on public lands suddenly changed drastically. Throughout the period between 1870–90, large-scale cattle drives took place, with the cattle overwintering on the northern plains.

The winter cold served a beneficial purpose: it killed the ticks that carried fever so that by the following year cattle could be shipped to midwestern and eastern markets without spreading the disease. By 1890, grazing of cattle and sheep had spread to virtually all of the western range, most of it on federal lands. This was also the year in which the Bureau of the Census said it was unable to identify a frontier between settled and unsettled areas.

In most parts of the West, the fur trappers and the miners came earlier than the ranchers, but the trappers used the federal lands only slightly before moving on. However, as soon as the miners discovered minerals, they sought title to lands that had been previously under federal jurisdiction.

Cattle ranching in the West involved a relationship between privately owned land (to produce hay for winter feeding in the North and as a water source in the South) and the public rangelands which typically were used seasonally. Ranches were developed, investments were made, and ranch values arose on the basis of the use of the federal and the private lands in combination. The ranchers using the federal lands had no clear legal right to do so. They were trespassers in a sense, although the federal government never took effective action to prevent their livestock from grazing on the federal lands. Some illegal fencing of the federal land on the part of the livestock owners occurred throughout the ranching history of the West, and spasmodically the federal government undertook to have the fences removed, only to see them reappear. From the earliest ranching days, homesteading existed in one of its forms in the ranching country. Not infrequently the homesteader was someone who planned to sell the land to an established rancher, thus transferring its title from public to private hands. From 1870 onward, "tramp" sheepmen grazed their flocks year-round on federal lands, but, since much grazing was limited to certain seasons, many sheepmen came to own key tracts of seasonal range, and thus in some degree were in control of federal lands.

Although the national forests were not established until the years between 1891 and 1910, their lands previously had been used fully— in fact, in the case of grazing, were often severely overused. When the Forest Reserves were under its jurisdiction, the General Land Office was greatly disturbed by the problems of grazing management.[1] The grazing of domestic livestock was an early concern of Pinchot's when the Forest Service took over management of the newly designated national forests in 1905.[2] For one thing, it was by no means clear that the 1897 Act, which authorized timber sales from the forest reserves, empowered the government to manage grazing on them as well. By careful bureaucratic maneuvering, Pinchot obtained a legal decision from the attorney general confirming his power to issue regulations on another matter, not then in dispute, but one which readily could be extended to control and manage grazing. The legal power of the Forest Service to do so was upheld by the Supreme Court in 1911.

The relationship that exists between private and federal lands is closer for grazing than for any other major land use, largely because of the seasonal nature of that use. The rancher must have the capacity to care for the animals at seasons when they are not on the federal land—that is, to have "commensurability." With rare exceptions, the grazing use of federal lands is not decided by competitive bidding among possible applicants. Outside of the fact that this would be difficult in some cases, the basic reason for this is that when federal management of grazing lands began for both national forests and grazing districts, private uses already had been established. The agencies can control the season of grazing use, the amount or intensity of use, and various livestock practices on the range, but they must deal with established ranchers who have held grazing privileges on the federal land. Today there is no place for the newcomer on the federal range; someone may buy an established ranch and take over its grazing, but to establish a wholly new grazing use is virtually impossible today.

As figure 3-1 shows, in 1910 the permitted grazing on the national forests approximated 15 million animal-unit-months (AUMs).[3] The whole concept of range carrying capacity had to be developed by the Forest Service, primarily through the medium of range surveys to measure estimated amounts of forage and future trends in range conditions.

During World War I, permitted grazing use on national forests rose by one-third. There is some difference of opinion as to the degree to which this increase was motivated by political considerations and a "win the war" philosophy. At any rate, it was a most unfortunate development, for it quickly became apparent that the capacity to sustain so many animals simply did not exist, at least on the ranges as they then were. Reductions in grazing use were required by the Forest Service and, by the late 1920s, permitted use was below the prewar level. Under pressures from the ranchers, ten-year permits were issued about this time, which stabilized grazing use on the national forests for a few years. By the mid-1930s, the Forest Service again began to reduce permitted grazing and, by the early 1950s,

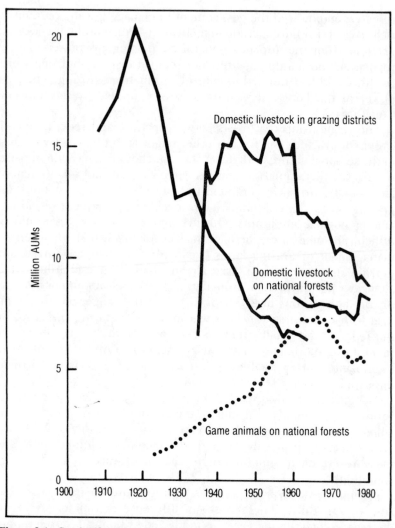

Figure 3-1. Grazing by domestic livestock on national forests and grazing districts and by big game on national forests for 1905 to 1980. Data for grazing districts up to 1960, and for national forests up to 1964, are taken from Marion Clawson, *The Federal Lands Since 1956* (Washington, D.C., Resources for the Future, 1967) pp. 58 and 67. Data for grazing districts, from 1961 to 1980, and for the national forests, from 1965 to 1980, are from tables A-1 and A-2.

grazing use nearly had been cut in half from the 1930 level. Incremental reductions continued until 1964. More recently, the Forest Service has reported the grazing data differently; and as a consequence, a higher line of grazing use from 1960 to 1980 is shown in figure 3-1. Broadly speaking, one can say that grazing use of the national forests has stabilized since about 1950. Although there clearly have been reductions in some areas and perhaps increases in others, the major trends, which were apparent earlier, have now flattened out.

From 1923, when data first became available, until the early 1960s, the period when large-scale reductions in grazing of domestic livestock on the national forests were under way, the amount of forage taken by game animals on the national forests rose greatly, from a relatively unimportant amount in the early 1920s to a significant amount by the early 1950s. In 1957 Held and I pointed out that a continuation of past trends would mean more forage taken by game animals than by domestic livestock before 1960, and, in fact, this did occur in 1961.[4] From a situation of relatively stable trends in grazing by big-game animals in the 1960s, there has been some decline to the present, and forage taken by big-game animals today is about two-thirds as large as that taken by domestic livestock.

Not all of the increases in grazing by big game animals came at the expense of domestic livestock. Some of the increase occurred in areas (such as the southern national forests) where grazing of domestic livestock was not important, or where the game took forage plants not usually grazed by cattle and sheep. But it is difficult to believe that there was no direct replacement of domestic livestock by game animals. To the extent that big-game animals increased in numbers, to consume the forage left ungrazed by the reduced number of the domestic livestock, the conservation objective of the Forest Service in reducing permitted numbers of livestock was thwarted.

From 1934 to present. Upon passage of the Taylor Grazing Act (1934), grazing districts were fully stocked with domestic livestock—indeed, generally they were seriously overstocked. This, in fact, was the reason that support for the act existed in the West. The amount of permitted grazing rose rapidly from 1934 to 1941, as more grazing districts were established, and then hit something of a plateau from 1941 to about 1959. During these years substantial range improvements—such as water development to enable grazing on previously unusable areas, or fences to control livestock so as to permit a more even use of the forage, or range reseeding to introduce new stands of grasses to replace the native species that had been eliminated by earlier overgrazing, and other measures—enabled the grazing of essentially the same number of livestock within essentially the same districts, but with less environmental damage.

Since the mid-1950s, the Bureau of Land Management has reduced the numbers of domestic livestock permitted on grazing districts, so that the trend has turned definitely and rather regularly downward, until it has reached only two-thirds its peak level. The downward trend on grazing districts during this period is similar to that shown for the national forests some twenty years earlier. To an unknown, but probably significant, extent it is the same ranchers (or their descendents) who have experienced the decline in grazing districts, as they earlier had experienced it on the national forests.

The reductions required by the Forest Service and BLM reflected their concern at protecting the production capacity of the federal lands. These reductions, occurring at a time when nearly every other use showed an upward trend, combined with the serious uncertainties and disturbances to traditional relationships resulting from the application of the Environmental Policy Act to the federal ranges, is surely one of the basic causes of the Sagebrush Rebellion. Ranchers saw themselves losing out seriously at a time when most or all other user groups were gaining increased access to the federal lands, and naturally enough they were disturbed and angry. This is not, of course, to argue that there would have been no controversy had grazing continued undiminished, nor is it evidence that the grazing reductions were unnecessary for conservation purposes.

Grazing fees. There has been virtually continuous controversy over grazing fees on federal land since 1906, when they were first imposed by Pinchot and the Forest Service.[5] There have been numerous investigations into the question, perhaps a dozen major studies have been undertaken. The difficulties in estimating the value or price of grazing as if a perfectly competitive market existed—when, in fact, there is no such a market—are apparent. The basic problem, however, stems from the fact that there is no agreement on the goal or principle by which fees should be established. Pinchot, the Forest Service, conservationists in general, and, in recent years, the Congress have all argued for fees which would represent the full market value of the grazing—if a market value could be estimated. The ranchers and their spokesmen in Congress have consistently sought something less, in part basing their contentions on the undeniable fact that the ranching investments were made on the basis of lower (or zero) grazing fees. Partly to win political support for the Taylor Grazing Act, Secretary of the Interior Harold Ickes disavowed any intent to make the act a revenue raiser, promising to set fees at the cost of administration, which he grossly underestimated. Until the mid-1960s, these lower-than-real costs were the basis for fees in the grazing districts.

The fees actually charged have risen substantially during the past fifty years (figure 3-2). For many years, the fee in grazing districts remained fixed for several years at a time and moved upward by discrete steps, but more recently it usually has varied from year to year. The fee in the national forests has been more variable from year to year, in part because each year the fee has been geared to the price of livestock products in the preceding year. The grazing fee on national forests was higher than that in grazing districts, by varying amounts and percentages, until about 1970, but during the past decade both fees have changed similarly, with the grazing districts fee actually higher than the national forest fee in some years. About 1960 the grazing fee per animal-unit-month in grazing districts was similar to the farm price per pound of all beef cattle, with the grazing fee on national forests at about double this level. Today, despite very large increases in the farm price of beef cattle, each grazing fee per animal-unit-month is about double the farm price per pound of beef cattle.

The Public Rangelands Improvement Act of 1978 established the present grazing fee formula for use by the BLM and the Forest Service. That formula defines fair market value for public grazing as the $1.23 base established by a 1966 Western Livestock Grazing Survey, multiplied by the result of the Forage Value Index (computed annually from data supplied by the Economic Research Service) and added to the combined Index (Beef Cattle Price Index in the preceding year minus the Price Paid Index) and divided by 100. The equation is:

$$\text{Annual Grazing Fee} = \$1.23 \times \frac{\text{Forage Value Index} + \text{Beef Cattle Price Index} - \text{Price Paid Index}}{100}$$

Annual decreases or increases are limited in any year to not more than a 25 percent change from the previous year. Under this formula grazing fees can go down as well as up, and, in fact, fees as announced

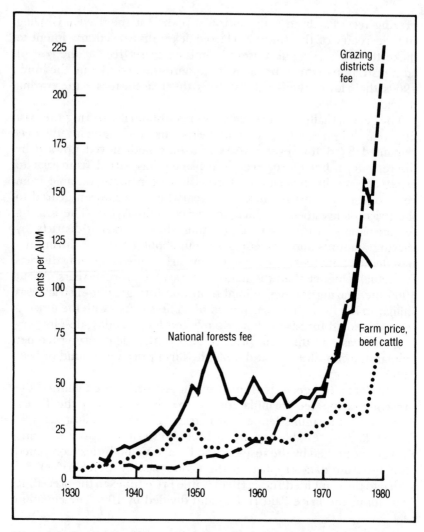

Figure 3-2. Grazing fees, in current dollars, for forests and grazing districts from 1933 to 1980. The fees are calculated by dividing grazing receipts by the total reported animal-unit-months of grazing. Data are taken from tables A-1 and A-2.

for 1982 were lower than fees in 1981 because beef cattle prices in 1981 were lower than in 1980. Fees in 1983 are still lower, because cattle prices dropped in 1982.

The level of grazing fees in national forests and grazing districts has been an issue of intense ideology on the part of many conservationists and their organizations. Emotionally they have resented the fact that ranchers were allowed to graze their livestock at fees often lower than those the ranchers were paying to rent private grazing land. These same people have shown no comparable concern for the fact that outdoor recreation generally, wilderness use in particular, wildlife grazing on federal lands, metals taken under the mining law, and water flowing from federal lands have each provided valuable goods and services at prices still lower, in relation to market value, than the ranchers have paid for grazing. Not surprisingly, no outrage has been expressed for these low prices. It seems to depend on who is getting the federal gravy, as to how sinful it may be. On a purely fiscal basis, grazing fees are petty stuff. They could be doubled, or multiplied by 5 or 10, and they still would be a drop in the bucket when compared with timber or mineral leasing receipts.

Grazing permits. Grazing permits on federal lands involve comparatively few people *directly*. At their peak, both the grazing districts and the national forests had about 25,000 permittees. In many cases ranchers held permits for both national forests and grazing districts. Moreover, some ranchers held permits on more than one national forest and grazing district, but each permit was counted as a separate entity. Since 1940, the number of ranches in the West has declined substantially, as has the number of farms in other regions, and from the same basic cause—technological change which enables one person to farm a larger area of cropland or to care for a greater number of livestock. Today, permittees number probably about half that of the peak years.

But counting numbers of permittees or making any economic calculations on the value added by the livestock-grazing industry seriously underestimates the sociopolitical significance of ranching in the West, including ranching based on public land use. Ranches and ranching are deeply embedded in the ethos of the West,[6] with many of the leaders in the region having family roots and emotional ties in the ranching industry. Others, lacking a family history of ranching, nevertheless are eager to obtain a ranch as a mark of social status. Many persons making money elsewhere have chosen to spend some of it in establishing a life-style which includes a ranch—and this is not always based on economic incentives. It is interesting how many commercial products—leading cigarette brands, for instance—seek to identify themselves with ranching in their national advertising.

At the same time, there has been much liberal–conservationist rhetoric directed against ranchers and range livestock. John Muir referred to sheep as "hoofed locusts," Bernard De Voto directed a great many of his columns against the ranchers, William Voigt has discussed them in disparaging terms, and there have been other critics as well.[7]

In my judgment, the problems of permanent use of grazing lands has not been fully solved anywhere in the world today. I say this with the full knowledge that grazing of domestic livestock has continued in some parts of the Middle East for 4,000 years or longer. But how to make the maximum economic use of grazing resources for the longer pull—which means preserving their basic productive capacity—and to have the flexibility to meet an occasional severe drought are problems affecting graziers the world-round.

At any rate, one can fairly confidently predict that the policy issues with respect to grazing on federal lands in the United States have not all been solved, but rather will recur over time.

Timber

In chapter 2 I pointed out that the basic reason for establishment of the Forest Reserves in 1891 as the first *system* of permanent federal lands was to ensure a future timber supply. The wording of Section 24 of the 1891 Act clearly implies a concern for timber supply. In the last quarter of the nineteenth century, many conservationists, including Gifford Pinchot, were greatly disturbed by the trends in forestry and with the availability of timber.[8] Many alarmist statements were made, including those by Pinchot and President Theodore Roosevelt, prophesying a coming "timber famine."[9] Conservationists were greatly impressed by the destructive timber-harvesting practices of the forest industry of that period and by the poor forest regeneration following such harvesting. The cutover areas were repeatedly burned, often with large and destructive fires, many of which were set by loggers, with the intent and the result that forest regeneration was prevented. At that time and for several decades later, foresters greatly underestimated the natural regenerative capacity of American forests.[10]

The illegal harvesting of timber from the public lands had begun long before Independence; for example, Malone traces it in Maine from the late seventeenth century up to the time of independence.[11] Extensive timber trespass on federal lands had taken place in the Lake States and other regions where few national forest reserves were established, primarily because by the time the national forests were established little public domain was left in those regions. The largest national forests were in the Rocky Mountains and to the west. Much of the best and most accessible forestland in these regions was already in private ownership by the time the national forests were established. Some had been included in railroad land grants, and the rest of it had moved from federal to private ownership by the statutes then in force. But a great deal of forested land was still under federal ownership, simply because it was located where, given the demand for timber and the methods of transportation, the land was valueless, or at least not worth the modest costs of acquiring it for private ownership. Pinchot and the Forest Service naturally enough took for national forests the best forestland then in the public domain. In its way, this reservation process was as selective as had been the process of alienation to private ownership in the preceding decades. This double selectivity—first of private, then of national forest—dominates the location and the character of western forests today.

Pinchot eagerly sought to apply to national forests the concepts of forest management which he had developed on private lands in the years before the Forest Service acquired control over the national forests. For the most part, these consisted of fire prevention and control, of slash disposal when harvest did occur, and of harvest by approved methods, primarily selective cutting. But sales from the new national forests were slow for many years: there was simply too much equally good or better timber, more accessibly located, in private hands. Timber harvest from the national forests did not reach 2 billion board-feet in any year prior to 1930 (figure 3-3).

When the Great Depression hit in 1930, demand for lumber and other forest products fell off severely. Zivnuska has pointed out how many larger forest firms acquired extensive timber holdings in the period between 1900 and 1920. They had been influenced in some degree by Pinchot's rhetoric about the coming timber famine and by their own observations of local exhaustion of accessible timber. Based on the assumption that timber prices would rise, some of this forest acquisition was financed by borrowings, including the issuance of timber bonds.[12]

Timber sales. Timber is sold from national forests in sales held at specified times throughout the year. Timber sold at a sale is harvested over a period of years following the sale; some harvest may take place in the same year, some in the following year, some in the second year following the sale, and some in still later years. Volumes sold and volumes harvested are equal over a period of years except for very small relinquishments of sales made by timber purchasers; but in any one year, they may differ considerably. In the timing of their national forest timber purchases, buyers have always sought the maximum flexibility allowed by the Forest Service in order to time harvests to

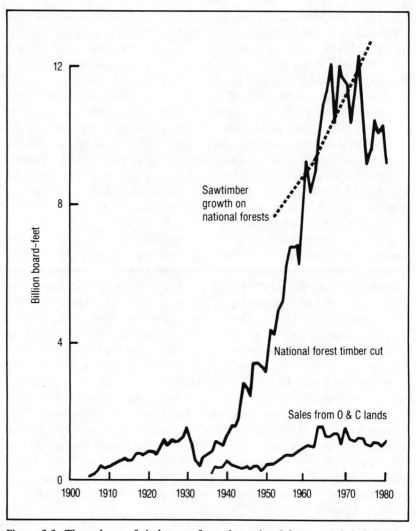

Figure 3-3. The volume of timber cut from the national forests, and timber sales from the O&C lands for 1905 to 1980. Data for the years through 1965 are taken from Marion Clawson, *The Federal Lands Since 1965* (Washington, D.C., Resources for the Future, 1967). For later years, data are from tables A-3 and A-4.

meet market conditions. Thus, the overall trends for sales and harvests will be about the same.

Although stumpage prices did rise somewhat until the Depression, the rise had not been great enough or the liquidation rate of private timber had not been fast enough to offset the full force of the Depression, which found many forest owners with volumes of timber and of debts which they could not continue to carry. They were under severe financial pressure to liquidate their holdings, regardless of prices. During this period a great effort was made to organize the forest industry, under the New Deal's National Recovery Act, in order to stabilize lumber prices and the rate of forest liquidation.[13] Although this effort at price stabilization collapsed, the Forest Service limited its sales during the 1930s so as not to add to the liquidation pressure.

From World War II through the mid-1960s, timber sales from the national forests rose rapidly and rather steadily, from about 2 billion board-feet annually to about 12 billion board-feet, with an average annual increase of about 400 million board-feet. For a very short period in the 1960s, sales of sawlogs actually exceeded growth of sawtimber, partly because growth was so far below its potential; but the annual growth of growing stock each year considerably exceeded the sale of timber measured in the same way. A purely economic timber-management plan would have resulted in sales of sawtimber vastly exceeding growth, so that the old mature and overmature timber would be harvested and replaced by younger growing stock. From the mid-1960s until 1980, the volume of timber sold from national forests declined by approximately one-fourth.

The decline in volume of timber sold after the mid-1960s is all the more striking when it is compared with changes taking place in total timber harvest and utilization (figure 3-4). Total domestic production of softwood lumber (national forest timber is predominantly softwood) remained roughly constant from 1950 to 1980. This fact, easily ascertainable from readily available statistics, has confused many observers—including many economists—who have not looked beyond it. U.S. imports of softwood lumber, predominantly from British Columbia, have increased considerably and far more striking has been the major increase in softwood plywood manufacture.

In this connection it is necessary to distinguish between a fiber-conversion ratio and an economic conversion ratio, for comparison of plywood with lumber. A board-foot of lumber once measured 12-inches square and 1-inch thick; today, as a result of customary planing, it is likely to be but 3/4-inch thick. Plywood is usually measured in a 3/8-inch thickness or its equivalent for thicker sheets. Thus, on a fiber-equivalent base, a square foot of plywood is equal to about half a board-foot of lumber, perhaps a little less; but on an economic base, a square foot of plywood often substitutes fully for a board-foot of lumber. The very substantial substitution of plywood for lumber in construction and in finished houses is due less to this economy of fiber use than it is to savings in labor. Figure 3-4 shows equivalent plywood and lumber production.

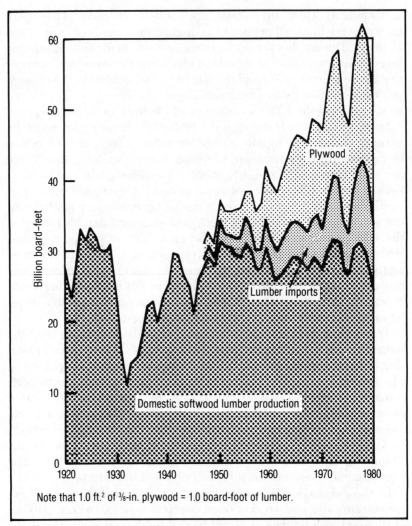

Figure 3-4. Softwood lumber production, imports of softwood lumber, and softwood plywood production between 1920 and 1980. From Marion Clawson, "Shelter in America: Costs, Supply Constraints, and the Role of Forests," Draft Manuscript (Washington, D.C., Resources for the Future, 1982).

Many of the better logs from national forests have been used for plywood manufacture, hence timber sales from national forests must be compared with total lumber and plywood manufacture. On this basis, it is evident that sales of timber from national forests have not kept pace with the increasing demand for wood-fiber forest products (excluding paper).

For many years, the O & C timber in western Oregon under BLM management was located in more remote areas than was national forest timber in other regions, including western Washington; but within Oregon, O & C timber is generally more accessible to transportation than is national forest timber. Timber sales from O & C lands were very slow until about 1940, partly because legislation for the management of these lands was lacking and partly because demand for all Oregon timber was low at that time.[14] From 1940 until the mid-1950s, timber sales from O & C lands were relatively constant, at a rate only slightly less than was then judged to be their sustained-yield capacity. After the mid-1950s there was some rise, then a leveling off of timber sales from O & C lands. As figure 3-3 clearly shows, the volume of timber from O & C lands is small as compared with the volume sold from national forests as a whole; but in western Oregon, O & C lands are approximately as important a source as the national forests.

Timber prices. The price at which timber from federal lands is sold reflects the demand for timber as well as the Forest Service's timber sale policy (figure 3-5). Earliest records of timber sales from national forests or from O & C lands up until World War II show that the annual average price of stumpage never reached $3 per 1,000 board-feet. In the late 1940s, prices began to rise a little as it became apparent that the end of the old-growth harvest was in sight—even with the Forest Service's policies of sustained yield and slow harvest of the old-growth timber. The severe economic costs of holding too much timber in a period when stumpage prices were rising slowly had adversely affected many firms who had acquired timber after 1900. Many such firms developed a policy of not owning much, if any, stumpage, relying instead on buying privately held timber which was in ample supply then.

Following World War II, timber processers realized that the supply of privately owned stumpage readily available for purchase was rapidly dwindling, and a scramble ensued to purchase timber and land. Prices for stumpage sold from national forests then began to rise sharply, from the $10 to $15 level of the 1950s and early 1960s to prices in excess of $100 by the late 1970s. Stumpage prices always reflect a consensus on the part of buyers as to future stumpage prices; that is, if dominant buyers expect stumpage prices to rise next year, prices are promptly bid up this year. A rising market thus feeds upon itself, to a substantial degree. This type of speculation is common for all durable assets, of course. But at any given date it may result in prices

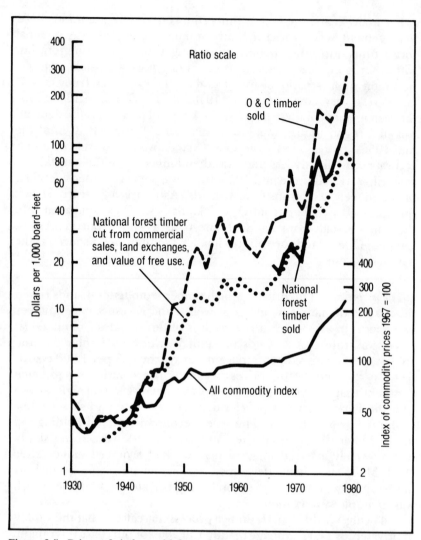

Figure 3-5. Prices of timber sold from the national forests and O&C lands from 1930 to 1980. Stumpage prices are taken from tables A-3 and A-4 and are calculated from data in Marion Clawson, *The Federal Lands Since 1956* (Washington, D.C., Resources for the Future, 1967); the all-commodity index is taken from *Statistical Abstracts* for various years.

which are seriously out of line with demand and supply conditions at that moment, as it did for stumpage prices.

The very rapid rise in stumpage prices for O & C timber in the early 1950s was followed by a period of generally declining prices until the mid-1960s. Since that time the really rapid rises in stumpage prices began for O & C timber, reaching $250 or more by the late 1970s. Prices of national forest timber rose more slowly than did prices of O & C timber in the 1950s, largely because prices of national forest timber were affected by timber sales in regions where the demand for stumpage rose more slowly than it did in western Oregon. A disparity between O & C and national forest stumpage prices has continued, although both moved up strikingly until 1980—at a much faster rate than has the index of all commodity prices, even though the latter includes the price of oil, the increases in price of which have attracted so much public attention. The severe decline in housing construction, beginning in 1979, and continuing through 1982, resulted in a sharp fall in prices of stumpage from federal forests, especially in 1981 and 1982. If the rate of housing construction rises in 1983, stumpage prices will firm up and then rise, but it is most unlikely that they will reach the peaks shown in figure 3-5.

A most interesting feature shown in figure 3-5 is the disparity between the price at which national forest timber sold from 1973 to 1980 and the average price paid by timber harvesters for the national forest timber actually cut each year. In a period of rapidly rising stumpage prices, as the past decades have been, the difference between what is paid for new purchases and what was paid two years ago or more, and is only now being harvested, is very large indeed. If stumpage prices declined over a period of years (as O & C timber did from the mid-1950s to the mid-1960s), then the lag between purchase and harvest would work the other way, and harvesters would be paying a lot more for cut timber than for newly purchased timber. In 1981–83, many purchasers of national forest timber, especially in the West, have had large volumes of timber under contract, at stumpage prices which will make profitable conversion of this timber to lumber and plywood impossible unless the prices of these commodities rise sharply.

Those forest industry firms who had bought national forest stumpage at very high prices, gambling on future increases resulting from continuing inflation, have sought some relief from the Forest Service. At the same time, other firms have objected to this, contending that those firms who have paid more than the timber proved to be worth should pay the penalty for their overbidding. In early 1982 the Forest

Service extended the contract period within which the timber could be harvested, which may prove to be a significant relief, depending on the future course of inflation. At the same time, the Forest Service proposed a system of rewards and penalties to encourage prompt harvesting of timber purchased from the national forests. Various legislative proposals to give relief to buyers of national forest timber were advanced in 1982, but, by early 1983, none had been enacted. It seems likely that the terms of timber sale from national forests will be a significant policy issue in the next several years.

Timber is sold from national forests and from O & C lands by so-called competitive sale. The agency publicly offers for sale the timber from a tract of its land, and either a sealed bidding process or an oral auction takes place at a designated date. The agencies engage in varying degrees of consultation with prospective timber purchasers, ranging from highly informal talks to receipt of formal proposals from interested firms. Sale of federal timber involves a considerable expenditure of time, effort, and money, and there is little purpose in offering a lot of timber for sale unless there is a reasonable prospect that there will be an interested bidder. The agency defines and marks the boundaries within which the harvest is to take place, marks or describes the trees to be cut, specifies the method of timber harvest (that is, clear-cutting, shelterwood, selective cutting, or other), estimates the volume of the timber offered, and makes an elaborate estimate of the value of the timber. Sales are advertised in appropriate ways. Prospective buyers are free, indeed, are encouraged, to inspect the site and make their own estimates of volume, quality, and harvest cost.

Timber appraisal process. The process of timber appraisal by both the Forest Service and the BLM has grown increasingly complex and costly over the years, in part because stumpage prices have risen so much. Errors in estimating value are more costly now than when prices were lower, and could expose the agencies to the possibility of adverse public comments. Some of the increased complexity of appraisal is a result of normal bureaucratic processes and tendencies. Beginning at the mill, an estimate is made of the value that the trees—when cut, transported, and processed—will yield. From this value are deducted processing, harvesting, necessary road-building, and other costs. At each stage, costs include normal profits, sufficient to keep the processor in business for possible future purchases. In addition, conversion factors must be estimated for every stage.

Road-building costs are often large, and road specifications must be made. The stumpage price is a residual figure, after all costs have been deducted from product values. As a residual, it is subject to errors inherent in the estimating process. Indeed, if there was truly active competition in the economist's sense of the term, then the appraisal process would be unnecessary.

In fact, something quite different than classic economic competition exists for federal timber.[15] The number of bidders is often small; in an earlier time (and even today in some localities) the agency would be lucky to receive a single bid at or above the appraised price. At the most there will be several bidders, but not the large number that economic theory postulates for pure competition. And it should be noted that each buyer is as much concerned with and influenced by his rivals' actions as he is by the characteristics of the timber itself. Collusion among potential buyers has often been suspected and has been proved in a few cases—although it is typically very difficult to prove. When one processor repeatedly bids for timber in one federal area but not in an adjacent one, and his possible rival repeatedly bids for timber in a second area but not in the first, suspicions of collusion naturally arise. But there may not be outright collusion in the legal sense; there may simply be an "understanding"—that is, if you'll keep out of my area, I'll keep out of yours.

In part because of speculative buying in anticipation of continued rapid inflation, recent prices bid in the localities of most active demand for federal timber generally have been far above the appraised value of the timber. Naturally this has raised major questions about the accuracy or the utility of the appraisal process. If buyers are willing to pay far more than the appraised value—for whatever reason— what has been gained by making the time-consuming and expensive appraisal? Even today in localities where demand is not so active, the appraised value puts a floor under the bidding. Retention of the appraisal process today, where and when conditions are so different, may simply be a bureaucratic lag in adjustment to changing times. The federal agencies have the legal power to reject any and all bids on each sale. Without detailed appraisal and without advertising of an appraised price, timber can be offered for sale; if bids were lower than the agency thought reasonable, all could be rejected and the large costs of appraisal thus eliminated.

Far more important than deficiencies in the competitive process is the fact that the price at which the federal timber can be sold is a function of the volume of timber offered. The federal agencies simply cannot accept the "market price"; they make the market price by their timber sales policy.[16] If they sell more timber, the price will be lower than it will be if they sell less.

If, during 1974–80, the Forest Service had offered 5 billion board-feet *more* timber annually, stumpage prices would have risen far less. But exactly by how much less? This, of course, involves some estimate of the price elasticity for stumpage generally and for federal stumpage in particular. For our present discussion, there is no need to estimate precise dollar effects; but no one can deny that they would have been considerable, and the policy decision on how much timber to sell dominated prices far more than any conditions of timber sale. Had the Forest Service sold a lot more stumpage than it did, and had the terms of sale (for example, down payments and interest charges on value of uncut timber) been less favorable to speculative stumpage purchase, federal stumpage prices would not have risen so sharply from 1974 to 1980 or fallen so sharply after 1980, and the difficult situation would not have arisen of uncut timber at prices impossible of being sustained by timber manufacture.

Misled by the fact that stumpage prices are expressed in dollars and result from what is described as "competitive bidding," economists who should know better have been led into believing that such prices are actually the competitive market prices of economic theory. They have then contrasted these prices with the administratively determined prices (often zero) on outdoor recreation and wilderness use, in an effort to describe the basic differences between the two kinds of prices. In fact, each price is administratively determined, and neither is a fully competitive economic price. More careful attention to the characteristics of each price is called for here.

Economic effects of Forest Service timber policy. The Forest Service has been widely criticized by the forest products industry, by some conservationists, by many economists, by some of the western states, and by others for its very slow rate of harvesting old-growth timber.[17] Their criticism is based on several conditions: a slow harvest means great loss of timber volume from mortality; high investment in standing timber and an associated low rate of return; low or even negative rates of net timber growth, which would be possible by new second-growth timber; and it unavoidably puts pressures on private timber, actually contributing to community instability rather than promoting it. The Office of Management and Budget (OMB) and the General Accounting Office (GAO) have repeatedly pressured the

Forest Service into making larger timber sales in order to accelerate the rate of harvest of the old-growth timber. It is also true that many conservationists would like to reduce or eliminate timber harvest on the national forests, and they will employ any tactics, including lawsuits, to that end. Thus, the Forest Service is often caught in the middle, between opposing interest groups.

At one point, President Carter announced that the Forest Service would sell 2 billion board-feet more timber annually as a price control measure; later that same day the Chief of the Forest Service announced that it would take the Forest Service three years to accelerate timber sales to this degree. The Forest Service thus far successfully has resisted the criticisms from outside the agency and the efforts to make it sell more timber, citing the National Forest Management Act as its primary defense. That act endorses not only sustained-yield management but also evenflow of timber. Critics of the Forest Service have argued that the act provides flexibility for greater sales and that the real reason for the agency's foot-dragging is its own policy commitments. John B. Crowell, the current assistant secretary of agriculture under whose direction the Forest Service falls, has announced his policy of increasing timber sales from the national forests over the next several years; it will be extremely interesting to see if he succeeds where others have failed.

If the Forest Service had been a profit-maximizing oligopsonist from 1905 to date, it would have followed essentially the same sales practices as actually have been employed: that is, the use of modest annual sales to more or less meet annual operating costs (which a private firm probably would have kept lower), and the hoarding of its immense timber resource for a future rise in price.[18] Most of the Forest Service officers would not have understood, and surely would have rejected, the profit-maximizing oligopsonist rationale, but the results would have been the same, or closely similar. This policy might have been profitable for a private firm; but its social wisdom is more problematical.

Peak timber sales of timber from the federal lands were about one-fifth of the total U.S. timber supply. They are always a larger proportion of softwood timber supply, because the national forests and the O & C lands are mostly softwood forests; they are more significant in the West than nationally; and in some localities they dominate the forest situation. For instance, in some parts of the Rocky Mountains national forest timber is just about all the timber there is. In other regions, especially in the South, national forest timber is not a major part of the total supply.

The Forest Service sales policy affects the volume of timber sold from national forests, which, in turn, affects the price of that timber; this, then, affects the price of lumber and other forest products. These prices affect housing costs, and the latter are included in the Consumer Price Index, to which many wages and retirement payments are linked. While the direct effect of timber prices seems small, it is magnified greatly by its secondary effects. Thus, Forest Service timber sales policy gets translated into general inflationary pressures; this is, of course, the primary reason that the OMB, GAO, and the president have been concerned with the level of national forest timber sales. In the complex economy and society of the United States today, the managment of timber on federal lands cannot be examined in isolation from the total economy.

Oil and gas

Oil and gas bring in the largest revenues among all the uses of the federal lands, including the offshore "lands," and as such they deserve special notice. The oil and gas from onshore and Outer Continental Shelf (OCS) areas also makes up a significant part of the nation's supply.

Mining Laws of 1866 and 1872. The Mining Laws of 1866 and 1872 were designed to provide a means for individuals to obtain title and to extract valuable metals from the public domain; at the time of their passage, the idea of oil and gas development from the federal lands was undreamed of—it had been only a very few years earlier that the first oil well had ever been dug (and it had been dug, not drilled) and there was no reason to believe that some day large deposits of oil and gas would be found on the federal lands.

For many decades there was no practical legal method of obtaining oil and gas from the federal lands. Shortly after 1900, some oil developments took place under the claim that the oil and gas were "placer" deposits. Mining laws required a discovery on each 20-acre claim—an area far too small for an oil pool. Title was both expensive and uncertain until a discovery was actually made. In particular, a wildcat oil driller was not protected after he made a "discovery" until he could get the claim recorded in the county recorder's office. There were serious conflicts—sometime violent—among rival applicants and between discoverers and claim jumpers.

Pickett Act (1910). In 1909 President Taft withdrew from entry and disposal about 3 million acres of potential oil lands in California and Wyoming.[19] Presidents had made withdrawals of public domain by proclamation for many years, without having an explicit legal authority to do so. Taft was reluctant to use authority not explicitly granted, but he was convinced that the situation was sufficiently serious to require immediate action. Unbothered by such legal niceties, his predecessor, President Theodore Roosevelt, had made withdrawals frequently. Taft sought, and obtained through the Pickett Act of 1910, the general legal authority to make withdrawals of the public domain, for various public purposes. Although his specific withdrawals were denounced in Congress, the act was passed.

In 1915 the legal authority of the president to make withdrawals of the public domain, even prior to the passage of the Pickett Act, was upheld by the Supreme Court in *United States* v. *Midwest Oil Company*.[20] The Court affirmed the executive withdrawals "in light of the legal consequences flowing from a long continued practice to make orders like the one here involved." In this case, the Court took the position that the Congress, knowing what the president was doing and not trying to stop him, had acquiesced in his power to make such withdrawals. This is interesting and in sharp contrast to the actions of lower courts in the 1970s who rejected the same arguments about Forest Service timber sales under the 1897 Act. The power of the president to make withdrawals of federal land is apparently sharply defined and somewhat limited by the Federal Land Policy and Management Act of 1976, but it would be a serious mistake to conclude that all the controversies over withdrawals thereby have been settled.

Mineral Leasing Act. Before 1910, the placer provisions of the Mining Law had provided a poor means for obtaining oil or gas from the public domain. For ten years after that date, because of the withdrawals, no means existed until the Mineral Leasing Act was passed in 1920. It applied to oil and gas, oil shale, coal, phosphate, and sodium, and a few years later was amended to apply to potash and sulfur also, each for onshore public domain. The act is long and complicated and has been amended many times; a virtual army of lawyers make their living from its interpretation and their efforts to interpret it to the their clients' advantage. A full consideration of the law is unnecessary for the purposes of this book.

The 1920 Act provides for competitive and noncompetitive leases on onshore federal lands. The statute strictly limits competitive leases to federal lands that the U.S. Geological Survey (now the Mineral Management Service) has determined to be within the known geologic structure of a producing oil or gas field. According to the statute,

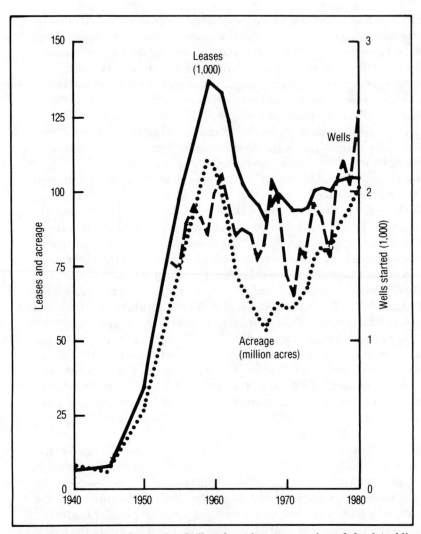

Figure 3-6. Number and acreage of oil and gas leases on onshore federal (public domain) lands, and number of wells started between 1940 and 1980. Data for 1940–59 are taken from *Federal and Indian Oil and Gas Production, Royalty Income, and Related Statistics* (Washington, D.C., U.S. Department of the Interior, Conservation Division, Geological Survey, June 1981); and data for 1960–80 are from table A-5 through table A-9.

lands not within such structures are leased noncompetitively to the first qualified applicant. In 1959 the BLM interpreted this "first in time" applicant clause, by regulation, to mean that for certain lands whose previous lease had expired, the first applicant could be chosen by a drawing from among those who had applied during an open filing period. This approach reduced conflict and legal challenge among first applicants. The first such drawing was held in 1960.

Noncompetitive leases are issued without payment of an initial bonus bid. Noncompetitive leases require the lessee to pay 12.5 percent royalty on any oil or gas produced, while competitive lessees pay a bonus bid plus *not less than* 12.5 percent. Competitive leases are issued for a period of five years, and noncompetitive leases for ten years, with each lessee having the privilege of two-year lease extensions, if drilling is in progress, or under certain other circumstances. According to the BLM, each type of lease continues in force so long as oil or gas are produced in paying quantities.

Filing fees are charged to applicants for oil and gas leases. For a long time, the fee was $10 per application; but in 1980 it was raised, first to $25 and then to $75 per application. Higher application fees obviously discourage speculative filings. While a higher fee is obviously a greater cost to a serious wildcat oil driller, even the present fees are but a tiny fraction of the costs entailed during exploration.

During the 1920s and 1930s, there was some oil and gas leasing of public domain under the 1920 Act, including some leases in California which later proved to be highly valuable. But the number of leases and the acreage affected were comparatively small—as late as 1940, fewer than 7,000 leases and less than 8 million acres were involved (figure 3-6). Leasing held at about this level through World War II, after which it boomed. Almost all the new leases were noncompetitive. This period was marked by a highly developed industry of lease dealers and brokers, who encouraged ordinary citizens, who had no idea of what was involved, to apply for leases in the hopes of a windfall, while at the same time they assembled acreage for serious wildcat drillers. This kind of leasing reached a peak about 1960, with more than 130,000 leases and over 110 million acres under lease. Both leases and acreage declined in the early 1960s, the leases leveling off at about 100,000 and the acreage falling to less than half its peak, from which it has since recovered almost to its earlier peak. A revision of the act in 1960 increased the annual rentals considerably.

As noted, leases were awarded for definite periods of time unless oil was discovered. If no discovery was made (or no drilling attempted), the land reverted to public domain status and was available for leasing

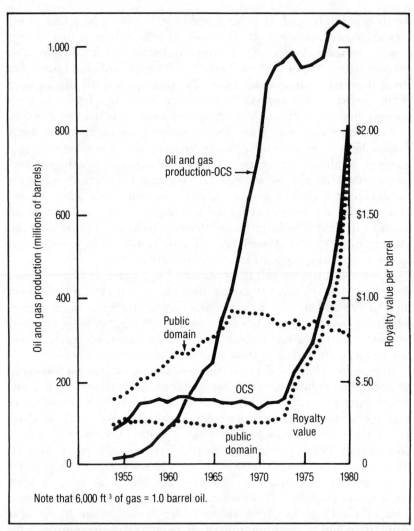

Figure 3-7. Oil- and gas-equivalent production from the federal lands (public domain) and from the Outer Continental Shelf (OCS), and royalty values per barrel between 1954 and 1980. Data for 1954–1959 are taken from *Federal and Indian Lands Oil and Gas Production, Royalty Income, and Related Statistics* (Washington, D.C., U.S. Department of the Interior, Conservation Division, Geological Survey, June 1981); and data for 1960–80 are from table A-6 through table A-9.

to some new party. Thus, the relatively constant number of leases in the last fifteen years has been possible only by the reversion of some lands and the issuance of new leases. The BLM in 1960 abandoned the old first-come-first-served basis for lands whose leases had expired, and a new system entailing simultaneous filing period and a lottery for awarding of the lease was substituted. As noted earlier, the result is a federally sanctioned and operated national lottery which bears only limited resemblance to mineral development. However, it must be noted that some of the leasing is responsible and serious because the prospects for oil and gas discoveries are good. As figure 3-6 shows, the yearly number of new wells has about doubled in the past ten years.[21]

The production of oil and gas (on an oil equivalent basis) from the onshore public lands rose steadily from 1940 to 1967, but has shown a slight downward trend since then (figure 3-7). The royalty value per barrel reflects the percentage royalty (mostly 12.5 percent), the makeup of the output, and the price of oil and gas. Until 1972, the royalty payment per barrel for oil and gas from onshore public domain was very close to 25 cents. Then, as oil prices rose sharply internationally, the royalty value also rose to about $2.00 per barrel by 1980. Until 1954, oil and gas from the public domain constituted about 75 percent of the BLM's total revenues, and these in turn were about equal to total revenues from the national forests. Throughout the period of record, some of the oil and gas has come from leases on national forests and is included in the total; in earlier years this was small in dollar terms and still is small as a percentage of the total.

Oil and gas from the Outer Continental Shelf. The Outer Continental Shelf (OCS) enters the picture in 1954. (We have briefly noted the history of these "lands" in chapter 2.) On the OCS, oil and gas leases are awarded on the basis of competitive bid. For most of the lease sales, the royalty rate is 16 2/3 percent and the bid is of an initial cash bonus. On a few sales, the bids have been in terms of a percentage royalty. The Department of Interior chooses the tracts offered for bid only but after consideration of tracts that have been nominated by industry or in which an interest has been expressed. Although the tracts offered have been studied as carefully as possible prior to drilling, and are always considered to be likely prospects for oil and gas, the whole operation remains highly speculative. Moreover, it is very costly—hundreds of millions of dollars are bid as cash bonuses for some leases, and drilling costs are very great indeed. Only the largest oil companies can afford to invest the sums required, and in order to share the risk even they have frequently entered into short-term or limited partnerships with other oil companies for specific tracts. The sums paid in bonuses have been very large, indicating that the companies thought the prospects of profitable oil and gas development were very good. It remains to be seen whether they may have paid more than was justified, considering the risks involved, or whether they have made highly profitable finds.

Although each lease includes an "acreage" or area, and each lease sale results in the issuing of a number of leases, a more meaningful indication of how important each lease sale is can be seen in the total amount of bonuses paid by the successful bidders. Table 3-1 shows the total bonuses paid for major OCS oil and gas lease sales during 1954–80.

One noteworthy characteristic of this bonus record is the highly variable and intermittent nature of the bonus revenue to the federal government. Although the amount of bonuses paid is not constant from year to year, a marked upward trend is apparent and is expected to continue. The royalty income, which can be inferred from the data shown in figure 3-7, is relatively regular from year to year. The bonus income obviously depends on the number and acreage of lease offerings, and also on how interested in bidding large oil firms are.

Oil and gas production from the OCS began in 1954 at a very low level; in 1966 it exceeded production from the onshore areas, and by 1980 was more than three times as high. The rate of annual increase in output was very great, for the years between 1954 and 1971, but since then it has been more modest in percentage terms. From 1954 to 1970, oil and gas from the OCS (in oil-equivalent terms, 6,000 cubic feet equals 1.0 barrel) were about equal; by 1980, the amount of gas was more than three times as large as oil.

From 1954 to 1970, the royalty value per barrel for oil and gas from the OCS was about 1.5 times the royalty value from onshore areas. Since then, the gap gradually closed until, by 1980, the onshore areas produced a higher royalty value per barrel of oil and of gas equivalent than had the OCS areas. By the late 1970s, the OCS was producing about 15 to 20 percent of all U.S. oil and 20 to 30 percent of all U.S. gas. Thus, the OCS is important today, and high hopes are held by many knowledgeable people that future production will be very much greater. OCS oil and gas development requires large sums of capital, the risks of loss and possibility of gain are great, and the environmental risks are disturbing to many people. The lead times for development are long. In some instances—as for example, in ice-bound areas off the Arctic coast of Alaska—leases must be

TABLE 3-1. OUTER CONTINENTAL SHELF OIL AND GAS LEASE SALES, FOR 1954–80

Year	No. of sales	No. of acres leased	Total bonus paid for leased tracts (millions $)	Average bonus paid per acre ($)
1954	3	486,870	141.0	289.52
1955	1	402,567	108.5	269.59
1956	—	—	—	—
1957	—	—	—	—
1958	—	—	—	—
1959	2	171,300	89.7	523.92
1960	2	707,026	247.0	349.34
1961	—	—	—	—
1962	3	1,929,177	489.5	253.72
1963	1	312,945	12.8	40.93
1964	2	613,524	95.9	156.27
1965	1	72,000	33.7	468.62
1966	3	141,768	209.2	1,475.32
1967	2	746,951	510.1	682.88
1968	3	934,164	1,346.5	1,441.33
1969	3	114,282	111.7	976.91
1970	2	598,540	945.1	1,579.06
1971	1	37,222	96.3	2,587.29
1972	2	826,195	2,251.3	2,724.94
1973	2	1,032,570	3,082.5	2,985.15
1974	5	1,762,158	5,022.9	2,350.34
1975	4	1,679,877	1,088.1	647.74
1976	4	1,277,937	2,242.9	1,755.14
1977	2	1,100,734	1,568.6	1,425.06
1978	4	1,297,274	1,767.0	1,362.09
1979	6	1,767,443	5,078.9	2,873.63
1980	3	1,134,238	4,204.6	3,707.14

Note: Dashes (—) indicate that no leases were sold.

Source: Division of Offshore Resources, Bureau of Land Management, Department of the Interior, Washington, D.C.

issued first, after which the successful company can develop the necessary techniques for oil exploration, which may take several years.

Since the late sixties, the OCS has produced about two-thirds of the BLM's receipts, completely overwhelming the onshore oil and gas, the timber, and especially the grazing receipts. The production from one good OCS lease well may yield more money to the federal government than all the grass in Nevada.

In addition to its oil and gas reserves, the OCS has produced a little sulfur, but so far no other minerals have been exploited.

Coal

Mineral Leasing Act (1920). The Mineral Leasing Act of 1920 included coal as one of the minerals to which the act applied. The management of all federal lands for every use encounters problems because of the intermingled nature of federal and nonfederal land (most are owned by the state), including the boundary problems associated with intermingled ownership. (These matters, the subject of chapter 7, will not be explored in detail here.) But these problems are perhaps more serious for coal development than for any other use of the federal land. The problems of intermingled ownership are exacerbated by the separation of title to surface and subsurface resources, which is especially common for coal. The ownership situation for western coal resources is quite complex (table 3-2). The federal government owns the coal on more than 11 million acres, but on two-thirds of this land someone else holds the surface rights. Even this comparison greatly understates the complexity of the problem. It is conceivable that the ownership categories could be for large areas, within each of which one ownership pattern exists, and thus

TABLE 3-2. COAL AND SURFACE OWNERSHIP IN THE MAJOR COAL-PRODUCING STATES OF THE WESTERN UNITED STATES, FOR 1978 (1,000 acres)

Ownership	Thousands of acres
Public domain surface	
Federal coal	3,751
Nonfederal coal	43
Private surface	
Federal coal	6,005
Nonfederal coal	4,689
State surface	
Federal coal	99
Nonfederal coal	951
Forest Service surface	
Federal coal	943
Nonfederal coal	13
Other surface	
Federal coal	638
Nonfederal coal	194
Total	17,356

Sources: National Academy of Science–National Research Council, *Surface Mining: Soil, Coal, and Society* (Washington, D.C., Government Printing Office, 1981); and U.S. Department of Interior data based on known recoverable coal resource areas, as defined by the U.S. Geological Survey.

that the boundary problems would be minimal. In fact, however, the ownership units are small compared with the area required for an economic coal-mining development. As the national Research Council reports:

Most laws for transferral of land from public to private ownership and most of the private transactions for coal-bearing land have been for units of land smaller than are optimal or efficient for coal mining. A great deal of the public domain was transferred to private individuals in tracts of 160 acres or less. The railroad grants were large in total acreage, but were usually divided into tracts of 640 acres or less. The sizes of the tracts were, of course, a response to economic and technological conditions at the time they were created.[22]

The number of leases awarded for coal extraction on the federal lands remained low from 1920 until the early 1970s (figure 3-8). The total outstanding leases numbered less than 500 until 1960, the number of producible mines declined steadily, and continued to do so until recently, and despite lease requirements for diligent development—the volume of coal mined remained low until the early 1970s.[23] Local and regional markets for coal were relatively small, there was no production of western coal for the national market, and mines on private land filled most of the demand for coal.

This situation began to change in the 1960s, as coal companies and others in the energy sector saw that the coming demands for energy were almost certainly going to create a large demand for western coal. The number of leases began to rise by 1960, and by the early 1970s nearly had doubled. Actual coal production lagged, beginning to rise only in 1973. The approximately 70 million tons of coal mined from federal lands in 1980 is but a small part (roughly 10 percent) of total U.S. coal production, but most analysts expect western coal, and more particularly coal mined on federal lands, to become a much larger part of the total U.S. energy supply in the next several years. Royalties per ton were low and relatively constant until nearly 1975 but have mounted sharply in the last few years.

The Department of the Interior has vacillated with respect to the leasing of federal coal. Until about 1970, this leasing was largely neglected at policymaking levels within the department. The requirements of the leases were not strictly enforced, and the potential values of western federal coal were apparently unappreciated. By the early 1970s, public criticism increased over the great numbers of leases and the acreage they encompassed; the low production levels of the existing leases; the low royalties paid; the possibility of monopolization of federal coal, by oil companies and others not primarily in the business of coal mining; the environmental consequences of surface

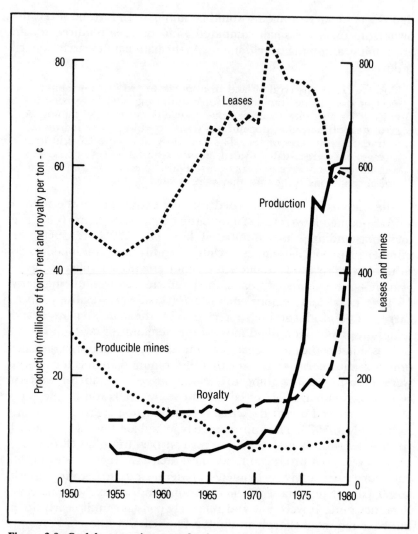

Figure 3-8. Coal leases, mines, production, and royalties per ton on the public domain from 1950–80. Data for 1950–68 are taken from *Federal and Indian Lands Coal, Phosphate, Potash, Sodium, and Other Mineral Production, Royalty Income, and Related Statistics* (Washington, D.C., U.S. Department of the Interior, Conservation Division, Geological Survey, June 1981); and data for 1960–80 are from table A-10.

mining; and associated policy issues. The low rentals and royalties on the coal leases may have been reasonable enough when the leases were issued, given the low level of demand for federal coal at one time, but no provision has been made for updating the terms of the leases as economic conditions changed. Lack of provision for updating fees or charges when prices change is by no means limited to coal bases, for example, see repayment clauses in federal irrigation contracts and land prices in mining law.

Coal Leasing Amendments Act (1976). The Coal Leasing Amendments Act was passed in 1976, partly to promote competitive coal leases on the federal lands. The Department of the Interior had declared a moratorium on issuing new leases in 1971. Extensive debates took place within the department, as to the degree to which coal leasing should be based on consultation with coal companies and others, the extent of the federal controls over leasing, and related matters. There was a good deal of criticism over the leasing of large areas which remained undeveloped, and over the way in which leases had been transacted or assigned; but such policies were defended by others as being essential so that coal producers could work out long-range development plans. There is an inevitable divergence of interest between the coal companies, who want large acreages under lease for development at the economically optimum time, and the government and other resource managers who advocate diligent development on leased acreages.

Surface Mining Control and Reclamation Act (1977). In 1977 the Surface Mining Control and Reclamation Act was passed, affecting both private and public lands. In general, it prohibited development in certain kinds of situations (for example, in alluvial valleys) and required restoration of the surface in mined areas. States were expected to assume major responsibility for enforcement of the act, and the federal government was authorized to step in where states failed or were unwilling to take this responsibility. There have been substantial controversies over definitions of terms used in the act, over the methods of restoration required, and over terms of the act generally; also, there have been substantial controversies over the respective roles of federal and state governments. The 1977 Act required the coal developer to obtain the consent of the owner of the surface rights, thereby injecting a powerful new bargaining element into the whole matter.

In addition to this, several of the western states have imposed severance taxes on coal mined from federal land, which substantially reduces the profitability of such mining. All methods of western coal development on federal lands require water, some far more water than others. Water is generally fully appropriated—often overappropriated—in the West, hence any new water requirements for coal development will have to come out of current supplies. This can only lead to further conflicts among users, which will be exacerbated by the unsettled questions regarding federal versus Indian water rights.

Almost every scenario of future energy production and use for the United States includes a larger role for federally leased western coal. The problems will almost certainly increase in difficulty and the policy conflicts become more intense.

Other leasable minerals

The Mineral Leasing Act of 1920 and its amendments cover several minerals (for example, phosphate and potash) in addition to oil, gas, and coal. The development of some of these minerals on federal lands is highly important nationally (for example, potash), to the locality where the development takes place, or for the industry based on such minerals. In 1976 the leasable onshore minerals other than oil, gas, and coal produced a total of about $17 million in rents and royalties to the federal government, out of total onshore rents and royalties of about $330 million. These figures give some idea of the importance of these minerals in the total picture of federal land management.

Exploration for mining

Mining Laws of 1866 and 1872.   Mining was one of the earliest uses of the public domain in the United States. After unsuccessful attempts to lease lead deposits in Missouri in the first half of the nineteenth century, all federal laws relating specifically to mining use of public domain were repealed. The California Gold Rush and other early western mining development took place under local laws that had been devised and enforced by local associations of miners. These various western local laws became federal statutes under the Mining Laws of 1866 and 1872.

Under those federal laws, mining on the public domain enjoyed a preferential status. Anyone could search for minerals anywhere on the public domain and was urged to do so. A miner or a would-be miner could file a claim (usually about 20 acres in area) anywhere, and acquire some exclusive right to search for minerals on it, as long as the search was diligent and the miner was working constantly on the claim.[24] The claim was "valid" only with a discovery of minerals sufficient to warrant a "prudent man" investing time and effort in their development. As long as the claimant complied with the not particularly onerous requirements, the claim could be held indefinitely and extraction of any minerals could occur, without payment of any royalty or fee. If the claimant wanted full title to the land, by compliance with other (and not very onerous) requirements, a patent to the claim could be obtained, after which it was private property subject to the laws of the state or territory in which it was located. Between the date of location and the date of patent the claimant had some, but not complete, rights to the land, but the federal government also had some rights. The latter almost never sought to assert its rights during the nineteenth century or until recent times, unless the land was needed for some clear public purpose such as, for example, a military base.

Materials Disposal Act (1955). For some decades the mining industry has strongly resisted any significant modification of the 1872 Law. The terms of the law (annual assessment work of $100, $500 in improvements for patent, a price per acre of $2.50 when the patent is issued, and other criteria) were established in 1872 and may have been quite reasonable and necessary then. They have not been changed over the years, despite changes in the purchasing power of the dollar or other economic changes. One major change in the law occurred in 1955 when the Materials Disposal Act was amended to place pumice, pumicite, ordinary sand and gravel, and cinders under this act and to remove them as locatable minerals under the mining law.[25] That act also provided for federal sale of timber on all new claims, prior to their going to patent. There have been many proposals for major changes in the mining laws from the conservationists generally, as well as from the Departments of the Interior and Agriculture, the Public Land Law Review Commission, and others.

Federal Land Policy and Management Act (1976). However, in 1976, the Federal Land Policy and Management Act made some significant changes in the mining law, while at the same time preserving many of its essential features. Claims thereafter had to be filed in the appropriate BLM office as well as in county or state offices as required by state law.[26] The search for minerals in wilderness areas or those considered for designation as wilderness was modified.[27] However, the same basic system of claims, the same acreage per claim, the absence of royalties, and many other features of the law remained unchanged.

As noted in chapter 2, substantial amounts of federal land have been withdrawn at one time or another, for one purpose or another, so that they are no longer available for new mining claims. All withdrawals have to recognize, of course, any valid existing claims at the date of withdrawal. Conservationists both inside and outside the federal government, thwarted in their efforts to include recognition of alternative uses of the federal land in the mining law and to improve some conservation or environmental restraints on mining, have effectively modified it by getting large areas of federal land removed from mining development. Valid claims in wilderness areas remain so and additional claims may be filed until a date specified in the Wilderness Act—currently by the end of 1983. But restrictions on access to claims and requirements for surface protection or reclamation, as well as limitations on searches within areas under study for possible wilderness designation, have severely restricted mineral development in wilderness areas. One only has to listen to the wails of the mining industry to realize that significant changes have occurred.

The availability of federal lands for mineral exploration and development promises to be a continuing policy issue for the federal lands. The issue is often drawn as a contest between the mining industry and the public and private conservationists; but it is rather more than this, because all of us have a real stake in both an adequate supply of minerals and in conservation of the federal lands.

Outdoor recreation and related activities

Included here are (1) all forms of outdoor recreation—camping, picnicking, fishing, hunting, hiking, and any others, including all visits to wilderness areas; (2) wildlife, for hunting and for photographing and observing, but with a considerable value (at least to many people) for its own sake; and (3) watershed values. Clearly, there are great differences among these activities, even among those grouped under a single heading as, for instance, outdoor recreation. But some common features among these activities do exist.

Common features. First, each is a valuable use of natural resources, although typically the use of the area for the service rendered is not sold in a competitive market, not sold for a money price, or both. Charges for recreation—the only service in this group for which charges are often made—are primarily for the service provided the user, as in the case of fees, ski lift, rather than for the natural resource itself. This differs significantly from the other uses of federal land, even though the extent of this difference is typically exaggerated. The "market" prices for grazing, timber, and minerals are far from perfect by the economists' standards of the competitive market. This is especially true for timber, where the price is greatly affected by the decisions of the Forest Service as to the volume of timber to offer for sale.

Second, these services must be consumed on the spot, whereas timber can be harvested and used hundreds or thousands of miles away, or minerals may be extracted and transported to distant markets. Outdoor recreation must be consumed on the spot—even though recollection of the experience may be one of the most valuable aspects of the recreational activity.[28] The user comes to the resource, for this group of outputs—the resource is not transported to the user.

Third, the landowners supplying these services or goods—whether public agency or private owner—typically get little or no revenues from the use of the land. The earlier "commercial" uses return varying amounts of revenue to the landowners—more, in the case of oil, gas, and timber, but little or nothing in the case of minerals. While fees or charges may bring in some revenues from outdoor recreation (as, for instance, permission to hunt on private lands), typically the services and goods under consideration here bring in no revenue for use of the land; and when some is produced, it is unlikely to equal the costs of collection or of land management. These are, in general, the free-riders on the federal land.

Measuring recreation visits. It is difficult to measure outdoor recreation in accurate and meaningful ways. Some users go on the land, whether public or private, without permission or without detection or measurement—hunters walking through the woods, for instance, may cross a property line.

A more serious problem is to define what is being measured. At one time, the federal agencies counted "visits" to their areas; each person entering a park or forest was counted as one visitor, regardless of how long the visitor stayed or regardless of the activities carried on. To meet this matter of varying time periods for a visit, the data were compiled on the basis of "user-days"—the person entering and staying two days was counted as two visitor-days. More recently, these data have been somewhat standardized by conversion to visitor-days of twelve hours each, so that the visitor who picnicked for only an hour is counted as less than the overnight camper. None of these measures of numbers of frequency and length of visits really get at

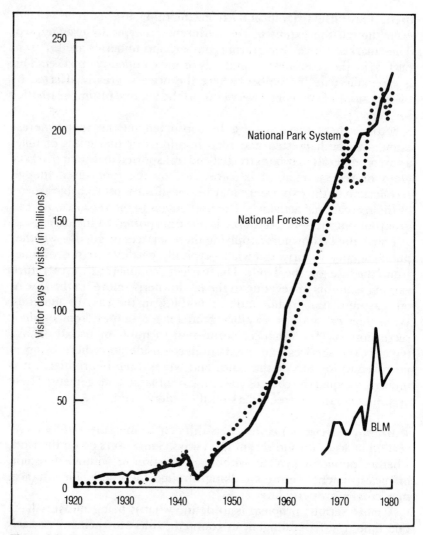

Figure 3-9. Outdoor recreation on the National Forest System, the National Park System, and BLM lands between 1920 and 1980. Data for all years through 1964 are based on the number of visits; those for 1965–80 are based on the number of visitor-days. Data for the National Park System and national forests for 1925–59 are taken from Marion Clawson, *The Federal Lands Since 1956* (Washington, D.C., Resources for the Future, 1967); data for the National Park System for 1960–80 are from the National Park Service; and other data are from annual reports of the chief of the Forest Service and from *Public Land Statistics.*

the matter of what the visitor got out of the visit—the quality dimension, as it were. Thus they do not measure how much recreationists might have been willing to pay for the privilege of using the land. However, data on numbers of visits or numbers of visitor-days do tell an important story, especially because recreational use of federal lands has changed so much over the past several decades.

In 1980 there were 220 million visitor-days on units of the National Park System, 233 million visitor-days on the national forests, and 65 million visitor-days on BLM lands (see figure 3-9 and table A-11). These figures should be compared with about 500 million visitor-days on all U.S. state parks. For a population of 228 million people in 1980, these figures mean that the hypothetical average person spent one visitor-day in a national forest, spent a similar amount of time in a unit of the National Park System, spent about one-quarter of a visitor-day on BLM land, and about two visitor-days in a state park. In fact, of course, a large part of the total population never got to any of them, so that the numbers of visits per person actually visiting any of them was substantially higher—but to an unknown degree. While there are differences among these various areas, there are also great similarities among them, as far as outdoor recreation is concerned. The closely similar trends on the National Park System and on the national forests is striking. Clearly, attendance at each was affected by generally common factors.

From 1910 to 1970 and later, the recreation usage on each of these areas rose nearly 10 percent annually.[29] The greater the use each year, the greater the demand, and the larger the increase in use (in absolute numbers) from one year to the next. These increases slowed down a little in severe Depression years such as the early 1930s, but some increases were experienced even then. The only period of real contraction in use was World War II when gasoline and tire rationing sharply curtailed all travel. Does this have a lesson for the future, if all forms of travel are inhibited by high energy prices? The great increases in usage of these federal and state areas was caused by the combined effect of more people, higher average real incomes per capita, more leisure (including more years in retirement for older people and older ages before youths entered the labor force), and better means of transportation. Clearly a 10 percent annual increase (or, for that matter, any other constant percentage increase) cannot go on forever, because it leads in time to impossible figures—people in time would be forced to spend more than 365 days a year in outdoor recreation.

The rate of increase in outdoor recreation on federal lands may be slowing down and surely must slow down at some future date. Even the most avid users of such areas may be approaching satiety; many areas have become so crowded that the users of a generation or even a decade ago are turned off by the crowds; and the rising cost of transportation has clearly dampened the demand for some users.

When the recreation visitation data are reduced to a constant population (per 100 population, as shown in figure 3-10), such a slowdown in the rate of increase seems to have occurred already. The rapid increases in rate per 100 total population of the 1950s has gradually given way to a slower rate of increase, especially for the years since 1970. Recreation visits in 1981 and 1982 were down somewhat, in large part because of the depressed economic conditions, but the major slowdown in the growth rate took place well before this. If recreation visits per 100 of total population, to the national forests and the National Park System, have indeed hit a plateau, then future increase in total visitation will be proportional to population growth.

Camping. The available data suggest that 20 to 30 percent of the total population camps sometime during the year in developed camping areas (some may be private, but most are public); an approximately equal percentage camps sometime during the year in comparatively undeveloped areas (most of which are publicly owned); and approximately similar percentages hunt and backpack during the year.[30] Somewhat larger numbers go fishing, or picnic, or go sight-seeing, or drive for pleasure in outdoor settings. There is an unknown but obviously large degree of overlap among these groups and activities.

Even today in many locations, federal lands are open to outdoor recreation on a first-come-first-served basis. Sometimes access is limited by the capacity of the campground, but often it is limited by nothing more than the tolerance of the visitors for crowding. Today the usage is more strictly based on the capacity of the area to provide the kind of service sought—access to a wilderness area may be rationed, for instance. Recreationists on federal lands have typically paid little or nothing for access to the areas, though fees may be charged for special services such as camping or boat-launching. The National Park Service has generally spent twenty times as much each year as it has collected in revenues from all sources. It is not easy to make similar comparisons for recreation services provided by the

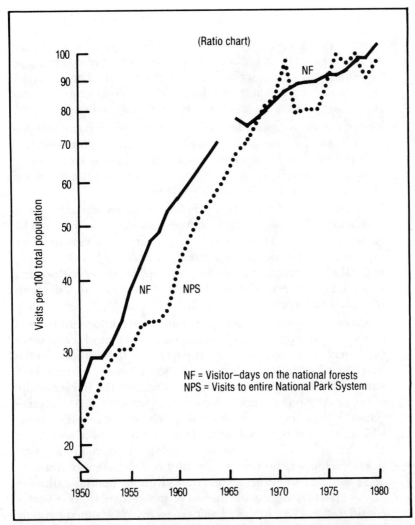

Figure 3-10. Visits to the National Forest System and the National Park System, per 100 of the total population, between 1950 and 1980.

Forest Service and BLM, in part because expenditures for many services—roads and fire control, for example—benefit many users, including recreationists but also others. But there seems little doubt that the expenditures of public funds on these areas for the provision of outdoor recreation substantially exceed the revenues obtained from this use of the federal land.

Wilderness.   Wilderness areas present special characteristics:

- Some commercial uses of the land, such as timber harvest, are
  excluded entirely and others, such as mineral development, are
  permitted but circumscribed in important ways. These restrictions on use apply, at least for the present, to areas under serious
  review for possible inclusion in the wilderness system.
- The presently designated wilderness areas include many millions
  of acres and the areas under study are even larger. These contrast
  with the relatively small areas used for developed recreation—
  campgrounds and the like—but are smaller than the extensive
  federal areas open to hunting or hiking.
- The value of the wilderness areas for the wilderness experience
  is threatened by overuse as wilderness, as well as by invasion of
  commercial uses. This has led to rationing of access to some
  wilderness areas under National Park Service, Forest Service,
  and BLM management; and it seems highly probable that
  rationing will be extended in the future to other areas, if demand
  continues to increase.
- And last, "wilderness" has a large emotional component to both
  supporters and opponents—an emotional content which it sometimes seems to me is out of proportion to the realities.[31] One
  advocate of wilderness refers to it as "sacred space,"[32] and others
  stress the unique character of such areas and the irreversibility
  of the development process that destroys wilderness. At the same
  time they support the wilderness designation of eastern areas
  which were once highly developed but have reverted to something
  like the original state and see nothing incongruous in their
  positions. Opponents will picture the dire consequences of setting
  areas aside as wilderness, sometimes without realistic estimates
  of the effects of such withdrawals of the particular areas under
  consideration. The values of wilderness are proclaimed strongly
  by supporters but the existence or the size of such values have
  rarely been put to the test of willingness to pay for the areas
  concerned.

Outdoor recreation of all kinds on federal land, including wilderness
use, has economic importance not only to the users of such areas but
to those who provide supplies and services to users. This is obvious
to anyone who has visited the trade centers near the federal lands;
there is no need to argue the point here, nor to try to present
quantitative figures.

The federal lands are an important home for many kinds of wildlife, as earlier subsections have pointed out. The value of much of this wildlife finds expression in the data on outdoor recreation, as hunting, photographing, and observation are the basis for much outdoor recreation. But to many people, wildlife has values (ideological, emotional, or whatever you wish to call them) beyond those reflected in the user statistics. In this respect, wildlife has many similarities to wilderness. Wildlife is the particular concern of several federal agencies and the Forest Service and BLM are clearly directly concerned. The major legislation requiring planning on these lands, discussed later, directly requires attention to the wildlife resources and values.

The federal land clearly has great value as watershed. The role of management for the watersheds is often exaggerated. Poor management can impair water quality, while good management cannot increase water quality above the original no-management condition. Watershed management can affect water volume within some limits, primarily by manipulation of vegetation, but this is often neither easy nor cheap. Much of the water value is largely irrespective of watershed management. As noted, the landowner usually gets no reward from any watershed management he may practice.

Water, as a natural resource, is assuming greater importance and likely will be the subject of increasing controversy, especially in the West. The federal *land* agencies are less directly involved in some of those impending controversies than are some of the other federal agencies. But the possibility of managing federal land primarily for water yield is likely to emerge as one major policy issue, and this would, of course, directly involve the Forest Service and BLM.

Summary

The federal lands today are used for many purposes and by many user groups (table 3-3). Oil and gas are the big money producers, bringing in 81 percent of the total revenue from the federal lands including offshore areas. The 1982 and future figures will be much larger, both in absolute numbers and as a percentage of the total. If each person or organization using the federal lands, whether as a single recreationist or as a large leaseholder, is counted as one, and if each recreation visit is counted as one person, then outdoor recreation involves by far the largest number of users, about 99 percent. If data on visitor-days could be reduced to actual numbers of persons involved, this number and this percentage would be far

TABLE 3-3. USE OF THE FEDERAL LANDS, CIRCA 1980

Activity	Federal land administered under	Approximate number of users (in thousands)	Approximate area available for use (millions of acres)	Payment to federal government (millions of $)	Basis of payment[a]	Terms for obtaining use and governing use
Grazing	FS	16	(100)	11[b]	Administrative action	Application by user; terms set by agency
	BLM	14	156	16[c]	Administrative action	Sale offering by agency; competitive bid
Timber	FS	89	92	730		
	BLM	1.8[d]	5[e]	303[f]		
Oil and gas, onshore:[g]						
Noncompetitive	BLM	} 105		} 605[h]	In law	Application and lottery; 12½% royalty
Competitive	BLM				In law	Advertised by agency; competitive bid; 12½% royalty
Oil and gas, OCS	BLM	2.2	10.7[i]	4,101	In law	Advertised by agency; competitive bid; 16⅔% royalty

Coal[g]	BLM	.5		32	Administrative action	Application; royalty fixed by agency
Other leasable minerals[g]	BLM		1.0[j]	17	Administrative action	Application; royalty fixed by agency
Mining exploration	FS, BLM	Unknown		0	None	User chooses any open areas
Recreation	FS[k]	238,549	172	18	Administrative action	Decision by users
	BLM[k]	64,706	447			
Total payments				5,833[l]		

Note: Numbers in parentheses are estimates by the author.

Source: As far as possible, data are based on appendix tables, supplemented where necessary by data from other official reports and by the author's estimates.

[a] All payments are generally authorized by law, but in some cases the precise payment is specified in the law. These are the ones here listed as "in law."

[b] 1978.

[c] 1979.

[d] O & C only.

[e] Excludes Alaska.

[f] O & C only; 1979.

[g] National forests and acquired lands have been included in BLM.

[h] Public domain only; excludes acquired lands.

[i] Area under lease; total area of OCS, over 200 million acres.

[j] Area under lease; potential area, more than 11 million acres.

[k] Visitor-days, not visitors; includes wilderness areas. Based on 1979 figures for BLM.

[l] Not shown separately.

smaller but still the most numerous user group. If consideration is given to employees of timber harvesters, oil developers, and other purchasers or leaseholders (which would be extremely difficult to do, and has not been attempted here), then recreation would show up as relatively less but still dominant as to numbers of users. But recreation, including wilderness, returns less than 1 percent of the total revenue. No attempt has been made in table 3-3 to estimate the contribution of any use to the national or regional economy; these are strictly revenue to the federal Treasury. Timber is important, both in numbers and in revenue. Many persons will be surprised to see how large a timber revenue the BLM receives, compared with that of the Forest Service. In part, this is due to the much higher average price received for O&C timber sold than the average price received for all national forest timber.

The terms of using the federal lands are highly varied. Oil development on the Outer Continental Shelf is wholly by competitive bidding; mining and recreation involve very low or zero costs for use of the resource (each, of course, involves large "extraction" costs). One can explain these differences by describing their history, but the rationale of the great differences is more difficult to discern. Table 3-3 is accurate as a *general summary* but there are numerous details, exceptions, and amendments necessary to afford a complete account of present day uses of the federal lands.

Monetary Values of Federal Lands

It is generally agreed by all interested and informed persons that the federal lands are highly valuable. The controversies over their use and management are indirect but powerful evidence of their value— if they were worthless or nearly so, there would be no point in fighting about them. But no comprehensive evaluation of the full economic value of the federal lands (including the Outer Continental Shelf) has ever been made. It is obvious that the acquisition cost is meaningless—if the Louisiana Purchase cost something like 15 cents per acre in the early nineteenth century, that is scarcely a realistic present-day value for the best coal deposits on federal land in the northern Great Plains.

The value of the federal lands, including the offshore areas, might be estimated by a real estate appraisal process, similarly to the way this process is used for private land. It often would be difficult but not impossible to find actual transactions in sale and purchase of reasonably comparable land, which is a necessary part of the real estate appraisal process. This limitation would be especially severe for national parks and wildlife refuges but these are not under consideration here. However, sufficient information and experience exists for competent real estate appraisers to place a reasonably accurate value on federal lands. Appraisals of the total value of real estate do not assume, of course, that all the land would be sold in any given time period. In spite of problems, a total appraised value of all federal real estate could be estimated, in the same way that a total appraised value of all private property in some city or county is estimated. But it would be costly to do and it has never been attempted.

An alternative approach is to estimate present value by the capitalization of estimated future net income from the land. This requires some estimate of the amount and the timing of the future income stream, to which is applied an appropriate interest rate to calculate present value. There are some technical problems in use of this apparently simple process, as a considerable body of professional literature attests. In theory, a different formula is applied to an income stream from renewable resources, which might continue forever, as compared with nonrenewable resources which are expected to be exhausted after a period of time. In practice, the differences may not be great, as far as estimated present value is concerned. Many coal, oil, and other mineral deposits are expected to have exploitation periods of twenty to fifty years or more, and the present discounted value of an income stream from a renewable resource which begins only twenty to fifty years in the future, even if thereafter it continues forever, is not very large, especially when interest rates are high.

Like so much of economics, a procedure to apply discount rates to a future net income stream in order to estimate present values is easy to state and hard to apply in practice. What is an appropriate discount rate—3 percent, as representing a long-term low-risk rate, or 15 percent as representing a short-term high-risk rate? Choice of the discount rate largely determines the present value. Major uncertainity exists as to the probable future income stream; one has only to look at the changes which have occurred in income from federal lands in the past three decades or so, to see how difficult this would have been in the past, and there is little reason to think that the future is any more clearly discernible. It is not only that the volume of output has risen so much, and that prices have advanced so rapidly and so far, for each of the measurable outputs from the federal land; new discoveries of minerals may be made or new uses of federal lands may be developed, which are unknown and perhaps unknowable today.

In theory, it is the *net* income from the land which should be capitalized into a present value. This presents an added complication to estimating values of federal land. For much federal land, net revenue is a minus number—costs exceed revenues. Yet obviously the land and its resources have value. In view of the major uncertainties about future income streams and in view of lack of consensus among economists as to appropriate discount rates, refined and elaborate analyses seem inappropriate. Nevertheless, even crude estimates of the value of the federal lands are helpful (see table 3-4). The details of the calculations of these estimates are indicated in the footnotes to the table. The process is a simplified discounting of gross revenues to present value of income at each time period. The land, as sheer space has value—one need only read in the newspapers the controversies over the proposed use of some of the Great Basin for the MX missiles, or read the advertisements of land dealers who hope to gull uninformed city people into buying unimproved "wide open spaces," to realize that space, as space, is valuable. The grazing, recreation, wildlife, and watershed values of the federal land are considerable; in table 3-4, these values have been lumped into a land value figure for the BLM and into the timber value for the national forests.

These estimates are unquestionably crude and, therefore, imprecise, and possibly may be somewhat in error. My judgment is that they are accurate within a factor of two—that is, that the true figure is more than half but less than twice as large as shown. They are fully adequate to support the analysis which follows. The reader may cut any figure in half or double any figure in the table without significantly changing the conclusions which follow.

Table 3-4 shows the enormous rise in the value of the federal lands over the past fifty or sixty years, from $4 billion in the 1920s to nearly $500 billion at present, when measured in current dollars. When allowance is made for the changing general price level, the increase is less but still very great—more than 20-fold in less than sixty years. The rise has been especially rapid in the past decade. This great increase in capital value of the federal lands has not been due to any investment made by the federal management agencies nor to any management action undertaken by them, nor to anything the federal government as a whole has done, but rather stems from the general reevaluation of all natural resources currently under way throughout the world. There has never been a conscious political or social decision

TABLE 3-4. APPROXIMATE CAPITAL VALUE OF FEDERAL LANDS ADMIN-
ISTERED BY THE FOREST SERVICE AND BY THE BUREAU OF LAND
MANAGEMENT, FOR SELECTED YEARS

Lands administered by	Mid-1920s	1950	Circa 1974	FS (1980) and BLM (1981)
Values in current prices (billion $)				
Forest Service	2	16	42	350
Bureau of Land Management	2	5	58	130
Total	4	21	100	480
Implicit price deflators				
GNP (1972 = 100)	(33)[a]	53.8	116.0	178.9
Total value (billion 1980$)	21.7	63	154	480

Note: BLM lands: $5 per acre in mid-1920s, $10 per acre in 1950, and $20 per acre in 1974 and 1981; plus 10 times annual income from mineral leases from onshore land and from the Outer Continental Shelf; plus 20 times annual income from timber sales; with no allowance for any other values.

Sources: Data on Forest Service lands for 1974 taken from Marion Clawson, Economics of National Forest Management, (Washington, D.C., Resources for the Future, June 1976); other years, approximate volume of standing timber times average price received for timber sales from national forests, divided by two to reflect present liquidation value of timber, multiplied by two to reflect land and other values in addition to timber.

[a] Estimated.

to accumulate this enormous pool of capital. It is, incidentally, today about half as large as the entire reported national debt and also about half as large as the entire residential mortgage debt of the country. The pool of capital in the federal lands today does not represent "saving" in the sense that a part of the income stream was diverted from consumption to capital accumulation. The pool of capital in the federal lands is a significant sum by any standards; its importance has been rather generally overlooked by economists, by resource specialists, and by legislators and other government officials. Capital of this magnitude in this form should earn substantial annual income; it surely could be invested elsewhere to earn a great deal of current income.

The federal lands have never been managed as being primarily a capital asset. Their managers have been conservationists, foresters, range management specialists, wildlife specialists, geologists, engineers, and the like, but never bankers or financial managers. How much different would the management of the federal lands be, if efficiency in the use of capital was the dominant guide to management?

This question has rarely been raised. But it seems fairly clear that the answer today is probably a good deal different than the answer would have been in the 1920s. The amount of capital in the federal lands today is too large for the matter of its efficient use to be neglected.

Planning by the Forest Service and the BLM

Every individual, every private organization, and every public agency plans in the sense that he, she, or it has goals or purposes in mind, has at least some capacity to move toward these goals, and makes some effort to do so. The plans may be formal, written, quantitative, and sophisticated; or they may be tentative, unwritten, imprecise, and based on folk wisdom rather than highly professional insights. But there is no reason to conclude that the latter type are less accurate, less reliable, or less likely to be effective in action than the former. Merely because there exists no document labeled "plan," there is no reason to believe that no effective plan exists. Complexity should not be confused with competence, when plans are considered.

The Forest Service

The Forest Service long has had written plans at ranger district, national forest, regional office, and national headquarters levels. Such plans have been part of the budgetary and administrative process. It was necessary that such plans be written because of the agency's policy of frequent transfers of personnel, especially at the local level. If the new ranger was to know what the old ranger had done, past reports had to be available; and if the new ranger was to advance operations in a meaningful fashion, there had to be a plan to which he or she could refer. These plans were often the basis for public relations efforts and for information to the public—"I and E," information and education, in the old terminology. This differed considerably from today's kind of public involvement, as will be discussed in chapter 8. Although the plans of the Forest Service in an earlier day were developed internally without public input, they nonetheless were important and effective.

The extensive legislation of the 1960s and early 1970s (the Multiple Use Act, the Wilderness Act, and several others) implied but did not specify planning by the Forest Service. That is, if the general objectives of the Multiple Use Act were to be met, the Forest Service obviously had to have some kind of a plan—at every level, whether formal or informal.

The Bureau of Land Management

Planning within the BLM was, for many years, far less developed, and much less formal, and the plans, based on intuitive judgments, were largely unwritten. My personal experience in the BLM from 1948 to 1953 showed that the agency had definite ideas of what it wanted to accomplish and how it proposed to do it, given the resources available, but that it had few, if any, documents labeled "plans." By the early 1960s, the BLM began to develop more formal plans.

As Hagenstein reports, "Despite the lack of legislative direction for planning prior to FLPMA, the BLM had previously developed a planning process and had prepared first generation management framework plans for a substantial part of the public lands. Although the main thrust of the management framework plans was limited by the perception of the BLM's role as one of responding to applicants for the use of public lands, the plans themselves met reasonable standards of professional competence."[33]

Leman, who has considered the planning of BLM, especially at field levels, summarizes his views as follows:

> The effectiveness of the formal comprehensive land use planning system implemented in the Bureau of Land Management in the 1970s varied a great deal from place to place. And although the system was improved with experience, generally it encountered some practical and conceptual difficulties with data, specificity, currency and adaptability, and the need to focus on key issues, time horizons, and geographic areas. At the same time, the real planning of the agency was often being conducted through a *de facto* multiple-use system combining many separate planning efforts, not all of them recognized as such. The segmented or incremental nature of this *de facto* system was not as much of a drawback as might be expected, because even at best, the formal system, despite its comprehensive aspirations, cannot alone do the job.[34]

Legislation of the mid-1970s

The legislation of the middle 1970s (the Renewal Resources Planning Act of 1974, the National Forest Management Act of 1976, and the Federal Land Policy and Management Act of 1976) drastically changed planning by the Forest Service and the BLM. Achterman and Fairfax report, "The lynch-pin (*sic*) of the FLPMA is land use planning."[35] A similar statement could be made about each of the other two acts. While there are important differences among these acts, they share great similarities and common features:

- Each act is a specific directive from the Congress to the agency, to engage in land use and other resource planning. Such planning will no longer be at the initiative and discretion of the agency with the tacit consent of the Congress, instead the agency has been directed by law to do so. Many of the directives are quite specific though not always consistent; in some ways the agencies are given general directives and are required to work out the specifics by themselves. To one with several decades of experience in natural resource planning and management, the faith of the Congress in the efficacy of planning to solve problems seems touchingly naive. I personally endorse planning, but I expect the planning process to solve few policy issues. Nevertheless, plans must be, and will be, made under any circumstances and a more formal planning process has much to commend itself.

- Each act places a great emphasis on resource inventory. Certainly, the best available data about resources should be used in any planning process. But inventories always suffer from at least two handicaps: (1) they cost money—and time; and (2) they are always somewhat out-of-date and always somewhat inadequate to meet the desires, if not the needs, of the planner. Moreover, no amount of data will resolve policy issues. Emphasis on accumulation of better data is often an excuse for poor planning, if indeed not a soporific to calm agency fears that the planning is inadequate. The agencies and the user public must, however, be pleased that the Congress has recognized the importance of inventory data—especially if that recognition gets translated into appropriations.

- Each act includes a large measure of economic balancing of benefits and costs. As Krutilla and Haigh say:

> There appears to be little doubt that Congress has charged the Forest Service to manage forest and rangeland resources in an economically efficient manner. . . . this directive prescribes a methodology and decision criteria which are intended to maximize the benefits of multiple-use sustained-yield management. . . . there are nevertheless three apparent internal inconsistencies. One, the culmination of mean annual increment as a harvest criterion. . . . Two, the limitation on timber removal. . . could interfere with the

realization of maximum benefits. . . . The third apparent inconsistency relates to the provisions in legislation calling for public involvement or citizen participation.[36]

I would describe all three acts as requiring considerable but not complete reliance on economic analysis and economic criteria. I think it doubtful that any of the parties to public land controversies is willing to accept the results of economic analysis when the conclusions run against his chosen policy position. Such reluctance may be founded partly on a justifiable distrust of the reliability of some of the economic analyses made, but some of it goes deeper than that.

- Each act includes a high consideration for protection and, if possible, improvement of the environment. The acts are not mere reaffirmations of the Environmental Policy Act of 1969 but positively state the case for environmental protection.
- Each act requires that the planning be interdisciplinary. Professional personnel of different training and backgrounds are required to work as teams, with the apparent expectation that this somehow will produce a more comprehensive and inclusive analysis of the resource situation and the resulting plans than would be forthcoming by persons of more limited background.
- Each act requires that the planning must involve the public. This subject will be explored in some detail in chapter 8, but a few general comments may be made here. Public involvement must take place at all stages in the planning process, from the earliest to the final consideration, and the acts are rather specific about how this involvement is to be encouraged. Some of the advocates of public participation would apparently like to see public involvement carried into the actual management of the resources, but this is not provided for in the laws. There are clearly problems, risks, and even dangers in public participation which seem not to be fully recognized in these laws. The role of interest groups and of the courts is implicit rather than explicit, but surely activities by both interest groups and courts are to be expected.
- Each act, but especially the two relating to national forests, tries to tie together the planning process and the appropriation process. The Congress sought in each to push the president into submitting budgets which conformed to the plans; and the presidents thus far have been, and confidently can be expected

in the future to be, opposed to these efforts by the Congress to dictate the level of appropriations for these federal lands.

- Each of the acts contains specific provisions for the updating of plans prepared pursuant to the acts.

Forest Service planning under the 1974 and 1976 Acts has been widely and sharply criticized and also warmly defended. These criticisms and defenses were developed rather fully at a conference on forest land use conducted by Resources for the Future in March 1981. As John L. Walker stated, "The NFMA planning process [that] I see emerging slowly, painfully and expensively is badly flawed by a traditional mindset that leads to the imposition of management constraints on forest land use programs with little or no concern over the resultant benefits or costs to society. It is the lack of rational economic objectives."[37] He goes on to give a detailed critique of the Forest Service planning process. At the same conference, Douglas R. Leisz, associate chief of the Forest Service, while acknowledging some problems, naturally enough strongly defended his agency's planning:

> The comprehensive planning process established by the Resources Planning Act and National Forest Management Act has prompted a number of significant changes which make a great difference in Forest Service management and planning. The impacts of these two laws are still evolving, however, and are interacting with the provisions of other laws. Therefore, it is still too early to fully assess the extensive impacts of this planning process. However, my preliminary assessment is that these laws have been a great help in allowing us to compete for funds within an austere federal budget. Our experience in carrying out this planning process has provided a "shakedown" period, which has revealed several areas where the efficiency and effectiveness of the process can be improved. We remain optimistic that the process is workable.[38]

It is interesting and probably significant that Leisz used the effect of this planning process upon the appropriations for the agency as his measure of the effectiveness of the process. I have heard other Forest Service personnel defend their planning on the same ground, and there seems little doubt that the Forest Service has obtained larger appropriations during the period while this planning was going on and that such larger appropriations probably can be "credited" to the planning process. The effect upon appropriations may be a rational bureaucratic test for the effectiveness of planning; it can hardly be accepted by independent analysts, legislators, or the public at large as a sufficient test or even as an accurate measure. Good planning, in the social sense, might as well reduce unneeded and unproductive appropriations as to increase them. The true test is the economic efficiency with which available funds are used with and without planning.

At the same conference, Krutilla and his associates took a somewhat intermediate position, but one much nearer that of Leisz than that of Walker:

> From our perspective we feel that the process initiated by the Renewable Resources Planning Act and the National Forest Management Act pursuant to multiple-uses of forest and range land is progressing, not only in the right direction, but also with admirable accomplishment given the monumental size of the task in relation to the time and budget constraints. The level of intense effort necessary to launch a Forest System wide forest planning exercise is doubtless the most demanding the first time around, but the achievements speak well for the effort.[39]

A few weeks later at a meeting of western forest economists at Wemme, Oregon, Richard Behan, Carl Newport, John Baden, and Richard Stroup among others, sharply criticized the national forest planning at that date, as they saw it.[40] The unanimity of sharp criticism was impressive; so was the lack of any strong defense of that planning. In terms of the differences of opinion expressed at the RFF conference in March, these speakers at Wemme were far more critical of Forest Service planning than Walker had been.

In April 1981 the Society of American Foresters issued a position paper on the Resources Planning Act process.[41] While it dealt with the implementation of the act in general, rather than focusing explicitly on planning, it did touch upon the planning efforts under the act. Generally speaking, this statement was highly critical of the agency's planning processes.

It is readily apparent that in one major respect the Forest Service and the U.S. Department of Agriculture have not followed the planning procedure of these acts, particularly as they apply to RARE I and RARE II. Wilderness planning was singled out for special and separate attention, not in conformity with the general planning provisions of these acts, and without regard for the possible multiple uses of the areas considered for inclusion in the wilderness system.

These three acts have clearly imposed new and heavy burdens on the Forest Service and the BLM—burdens with which each agency is struggling to meet. Whether one defends or criticizes the planning to date in either agency, it is apparent that each agency's planning process is in a state of flux. It would require a major effort by a team of researchers to ascertain how planning in each agency was actually operating in the field at any given time, as contrasted to the way the headquarters of each agency believe it is operating. Moreover, if such a study could be made, it would be out-of-date before the report could be published, because procedures are changing so that results differ as time goes on. Within a few years, we will be able to tell how the planning processes actually work in each agency, but even then the picture may well be clouded by other developments. However, it is evident in 1982 that each agency is struggling with a planning process which has not yet produced workable plans at a reasonable cost in time and money, at all levels in each organization.

Levels of Management in Forest Service and BLM

The acreage of national forests and of onshore BLM lands have changed very little for a good many years; the BLM has had added to its responsibilities the substantial, and as yet not completely defined, Outer Continental Shelf areas. The enormous expansion in expenditures from these two agencies is therefore the best possible measure of the intensity of their management, including the intensity of their planning and of their environmental impact analysis (table 3-5). Increased expenditures mean more personnel and other inputs into the management process. Because expenditures and receipt data are complicated, there is grave danger that the same sums are counted twice (or more) as funds are shifted from agency to agency or account to account. Table 3-5 seeks to avoid this danger: the sums shown in it are all in current dollars, and any attempt to deflate them to constant dollars would be difficult indeed. The ideal measure would be the salaries of employees actually doing the same work at different dates—not merely the salaries of employees in the same grade—but no such measure is available.

But even if the numbers for 1950 were multiplied by ten and the numbers for 1965 were multiplied by three—and these are intended as extreme values, with the likely true value considerably lower—it is apparent that expenditures today are on a much higher level than formerly, if measured in dollar terms and also for the Forest Service if measured in comparison with gross receipts. Two major factors are involved in the greater costs: (1) an increased level of environmental concern, which means more employees working directly and, because of the typical delays, more employees working indirectly for the same outputs; and (2) greater public participation in federal land

TABLE 3-5. APPROPRIATIONS FOR MANAGEMENT AND GROSS RECEIPTS OF THE NATIONAL FORESTS AND BLM LANDS, FOR 1950, 1965, AND 1980
(millions of current $)

Appropriations and gross receipts	1950	1965	1980
Appropriations for management (excluding investments)			
National forests	49	203	1,700
BLM lands	9	60	350
Gross receipts			
National forests[a]	35	149	655
BLM lands[b]	36	225	5,079

Sources: The 1950 and 1965 data are from Marion Clawson, *The Federal Lands Since 1956—Recent Trends in Use and Management* (Washington, D.C., Resources for the Future, 1967) pp. 109 and 111; national forest data for 1980 are from *Report of the Forest Service, Fiscal Year 1980 Highlights,* FS-364 (Washington, D.C., USDA Forest Service, July 1981); BLM data for 1980 are from materials presented by Associate Director Ed Hastie to meeting of Natural Resources Council, 1981.

[a]Excludes mineral receipts from national forests, which are credited to the BLM.

[b]Includes mineral leasing receipts on national forests, acquired lands, and other miscellaneous amounts.

planning, which also means more costs and more delay. By attributing the higher costs to these two factors, no judgment is expressed as to whether the higher costs are worthwhile from a national viewpoint or whether the processes of government are more or less efficient today than formerly. Whatever the explanation, the fact remains that costs have risen greatly.

The staffing of the Forest Service and BLM is different today than formerly, particularly in regard to the professional skills of the newer staff members. Many of the new employees of the Forest Service are not foresters but have other professional backgrounds. Many diverse skills are found among BLM staff these days—landscape architecture, archeology, and many others, once unknown to agency personnel.

The receipts from these lands are also up sharply in current dollars. In figure 3-5 there is a line representing the index of all commodity prices. If that line is used for correction of the numbers to constant dollar terms, the receipts shown in table 3-5 show a very great increase from 1950 to 1980. The rise is most marked for oil and gas receipts—which naturally enough are following (with some lag) the upward trend in world oil prices—and for timber, where the rise in receipts results from the much higher prices but also from the larger volumes sold annually since 1950.

The Forest Service spends more than it collects, mostly by a ratio of 2 to 1, except for a few years in the fifties when receipts equaled or exceeded expenditures. The BLM always collects far more than it spends, but only because of its large mineral leasing receipts. It then (under law) disburses most of the revenue from onshore sources to states and counties, so that the net amount remaining in the Treasury is much smaller than the gross revenues.

Notes

1. Samuel T. Dana, *Forest and Range Policy—Its Development in the United States* (1 ed., New York, McGraw–Hill).

2. Ibid.; also see Gifford Pinchot, *Breaking New Ground* (New York, Harcourt Brace, 1974).

3. Measurement of the output of natural grazing lands is always difficult and inexact to a degree. At best, numbers of livestock actually grazing can be measured, including the time grazed on a specific area, although there is sometimes some uncertainty as to the numbers on the federal land; but livestock vary in size, nutritive requirements and forage preferences, as well as in other ways. There is no certainty as to the amount or kinds of feed the livestock are actually receiving from the land. For instance, at times animals will gain in weight, at other times merely hold their own or even lose weight, which suggests that the feed actually taken from the land differs with the seasons. The usual conversion ratio between sheep and goats in one group and cattle and horses in another is that five animals of the first two species are equal to one of the latter two species. Efforts at refined adjustment can be made by conversion of animals of different ages in each species to an adult equivalent, generally based on average weight per animal of the age class. The Forest Service, in 1977, decided that its previous estimates of animal-unit-months of grazing were too low and applied a correction factor of 1.2 to all animal-unit-month numbers thereafter. In table A-1 and figure 3-1, we have estimated grazing use since 1960, with the correction factor applied throughout in order to present an accurate picture of grazing trends. Although the Forest Service shows numbers of swine in the data on animals grazed, it does not count them into the numbers of animal-unit-months of grazing on the ground that the swine feed differently than the other classes of livestock.

Estimates of grazing by big-game animals are particularly difficult and particularly likely to be in error. First, there is considerable uncertainty as to numbers of each species; several species (especially deer, the most numerous species in many areas) are seasonally migratory, and there may be some doubt as to when they entered and when they left a particular area of federal land. These difficulties in measuring grazing output are inherent in the situation; the federal agency personnel have done the best job that could be done, in most cases.

4. Marion Clawson and Burnell Held, *The Federal Lands—Their Use and Management* (Baltimore, Md., Johns Hopkins University Press for Resources for the Future, 1957).

5. For a brief but reasonably inclusive account of the early controversies, see Marion Clawson, *The Western Range Livestock Industry* (New York, McGraw–Hill 1950).

6. Clawson, *The Western Range Livestock Industry.*

7. Dana, *Forest and Range Policy;* De Voto, for years a columnist for *Harpers* magazine, frequently attacked the western ranchers. See also William Voigt, Jr., *Public Grazing Lands: Use and Misuse by Government and Industry* (New Brunswick, N.J., Rutgers University Press, 1976).

A number of writers have cited Muir's use of the term "hoofed locusts." For example, John Ise, *Our National Park Policy—A Critical History* (Baltimore, Md., Johns Hopkins

University Press, 1961) p. 59; Joseph M. Petulla, *American Environmental History—The Exploitation and Conservation of Natural Resources* (San Francisco, Calif., Boyd and Fraser, 1977) p. 232; and Roderick Nash, *Wilderness and the American Mind* (New Haven, Conn., Yale University Press, 1967) p. 130. Nash cites Muir's book, *My First Summer in the Sierra*, as one such source.

8. Dana, *Forest and Range Policy.*

9. The term was used explicitly by Roosevelt in one message to the Congress and at the Governor's Conference in 1908, and the same idea but not the same words were used by other speakers at that conference. See Dana, *Forest and Range Policy*, pp. 159–161; also Henry Clepper, *Professional Forestry in the United States* (Baltimore, Md., Johns Hopkins University Press for Resources for the Future, 1971) chap. 4.

10. Marion Clawson, "Forests in the Long Sweep of American History," *Science*, vol. 204, no. 4398 (June 15, 1979); this is also RFF Reprint 164.

11. Joseph J. Malone, *Pine Trees and Politics: The Naval Stores and Forest Policy in Colonial New England, 1691–1775* (New York, Arno Press, 1979).

12. John A. Zivnuska, *Business Cycles, Building Cycles, and Commercial Forestry* (New York, Institute of Public Administration, 1952) (Processed).

13. Dana, *Forest and Range Policy;* see also William G. Robbins, "The Lumber Industry and the National Recovery Administration," *Journal of Forest History* vol. 25, no. 3 (July 1981).

14. Elmo Richardson, *BLM's Billion-Dollar Checkerboard—Managing the O & C Lands* (Santa Cruz, Calif., Forest History Society, 1980).

15. Walter J. Mead, *Competition and Oligopsony in the Douglas Fir Lumber Industry* (Berkeley, University of California Press, 1966). Also see Walter J. Mead, "Pricing Policy for Timber Products from Forest Lands—Resource Allocation and Income Distribution Effects," in Marion Clawson, ed., *Research in Forest Economics and Forest Policy* (Washington, D.C., Resources for the Future, 1977). The latter includes a number of relevant references.

16. *Report of the President's Advisory Panel on Timber and the Environment* (Washington, D.C., Government Printing Office, April 1973).

17. Ibid.; also see Marion Clawson, *The Economics of National Forest Management* (Washington, D.C., Resources for the Future, June 1976); and Thomas M. Lenard, "Wasting Our National Forests," *Regulation* (July/August 1981). The Lenard article cites several other references. See also Oregon State Forestry Department, *Forestry in Oregon: 1980 Oregon Timber Supply Assessment* (Salem, Oregon State Forestry Department, December 1980).

18. Marion Clawson, *Decision Making in Timber Production, Harvest, and Marketing* (Washington, D.C., Resources for the Future, 1977).

19. Dana, *Forest and Range Policy;* also see Charles F. Wheatley, Jr., "Withdrawals Under the Federal Land Policy Management Act of 1976," *Arizona Law Review* vol.21, no. 2 (1979).

20. Wheatley, "Withdrawals," p. 314.

21. Two references which consider federal lands in general for energy development are Stephen L. McDonald, *The Leasing of Federal Lands for Fossil Fuels Production* (Baltimore, Md., Johns Hopkins University Press for Resources for the Future, 1979); and U.S. Department of Energy, *The Use of Federal Lands for Energy Development*, DOE/EIA–0201/8 (Washington, D.C., March 1980).

22. Committee on Soil as a Resource in Relation to Surface Mining of Coal, *Surface Mining: Soil, Coal, and Society*, Final Draft Report, (Washington, D.C., National Research Council, Oct. 24, 1980) pp. 3–15.

23. In the preparation of this subsection I have been greatly aided by reference to an unpublished manuscript by Robert H. Nelson, "The Socialist Experiment in America:

The Management of Federally Owned Coal," (April 1981). He is, of course, not responsible for my interpretations of his material. A revision of his manuscript, entitled "Federal Coal Policy" has been accepted for publication by Duke University Press and is scheduled for publication in 1983. An extremely useful document, publicly available, and with an extensive bibliography, is Richard L. Gordon's, *Federal Coal Leasing Policy: Competition in the Energy Industries* (Washington, D.C., American Enterprise Institute for Public Policy Research, 1981).

24. This is the doctrine of *possessio pedis,* briefly described by Robert W. Swenson, in Paul W. Gates, *History of Public Land Law Development* (Washington, D.C., Government Printing Office, November 1968) p. 732.

25. Dana, *Forest and Range Policy.*

26. Cheryl Outerbridge and Don H. Sherwood, "Recordation and Filing of Unpatented Mining Claims and Sites with the Federal Government," *Arizona Law Review* vol. 21, no. 2 (1979).

27. Craig P. Hall, "Mineral Exploration and Development in Bureau of Land Management Wilderness Study Areas," *Arizona Law Review,* vol. 21, no. 2, (1979).

28. Marion Clawson and Jack L. Knetsch, *The Economics of Outdoor Recreation* (Baltimore, Md., Johns Hopkins University Press for Resources for the Future, 1967).

29. Clawson and Knetsch, *The Economics.*

30. Bureau of the Census, Department of Commerce, *Statistical Abstract 1980* (Washington, D.C., 1980) p. 245.

31. Marion Clawson, "Wilderness as One of Many Land Uses," *Idaho Law Review* vol. 16, 1980.

32. Linda H. Graber, *Wilderness as Sacred Space,* Monograph 38, (Washington, D.C., Association of American Geographers, 1976).

33. Perry R. Hagenstein, "Public Lands and Environmental Concerns," *Arizona Law Review* vol. 21, no. 2 (1979) p. 456.

34. Christopher K. Leman, *Formal Vs. De Facto Systems of Multiple Use Planning in the Bureau of Land Management: Integrating Comprehensive and Focused Approaches,* Discussion Paper D-89 (Washington, D.C., Resources for the Future, January 1982).

35. Gail L. Achterman and Sally K. Fairfax, "The Public Participation Requirements of the Federal Land Policy and Management Act," *Arizona Law Review* vol.21, no. 2 (1979) p. 526.

36. John V. Krutilla and John A. Haigh, "An Integrated Approach to National Forest Management," *Environmental Law* vol. 8, no. 2 (Winter 1978) p. 413. This is also RFF Reprint 156. John Baden and Richard Stroup presented a critique of the Krutilla–Haigh paper in the same journal.

37. John L. Walker, "National Forest Planning: An Economic Critique," in Roger A. Sedjo, ed., *Governmental Interventions, Social Needs, and the Management of U.S. Forests* (Washington, D.C., Resources for the Future, 1983).

38. Douglas R. Leisz, "The Impacts of the RPA/NFMA Process upon Management and Planning in the Forest Service," in Sedjo, ibid.

39. John V. Krutilla, Michael D. Bowes, and Elizabeth A. Wilman, "National Forest System Planning and Management: An Analytical Review and Suggested Approach," in Sedjo, ed., ibid.

40. See Richard Behan, "RRA/NFMA—Time to Punt," *Journal of Forestry* (December 1981); John Baden and Richard Stroup, "Timber Beasts, Tree Haggers, and the Old Folks at Home," in *Natural Resources: Myths and Management* (Cambridge, Mass., Ballinger, In press). Carl Newport's discussion is unpublished.

41. Task Force on RPA Implementation, *The RPA Process—1980* (Washington, D.C., Society of American Foresters, April 1981).

4

Federal Land Ownership— The Retentionists' Case

If changing times call for a fundamental reconsideration of the role of federal lands in the national economy, then one major policy issue is whether they should be retained in federal ownership or be disposed of to the private sector.

The case for retention in federal ownership of extensive areas of land has developed in three rather distinct, but somewhat overlapping, periods: first, the rejection of unrestricted disposal of federal land; next, public acceptance of more or less permanent reservation of land in federal ownership, but without a clear idea as to what would be done with it; and finally, the development of concepts of use and management of the reserved lands, including multiple use of these lands.

In this chapter I will present the retentionists' case for continued federal land ownership, and in chapter 5 I will do the same for the transfer of federal lands to private ownership. Each argument has its supporters, and I have attempted to present each case as strongly as possible.

Even though my own position is not necessarily theirs, and each side may claim that I have failed to present its case as strongly as I should, I have selected the arguments which I think are the strongest and most telling ones. And for each case I have sought to present ideas that directly challenge the position of the opposition.

The retentionists point to the deficiencies of private land ownership while the advocates of disposal cite the deficiencies of public land management. Each side is perhaps stronger in its criticisms of the other than it is in stating its own positive case.

There is much to be said in favor of allowing the proponents to speak for themselves, but this procedure is not as practical as one might hope. Although there are some instances where the issue of federal versus private land ownership has been faced directly, with opposing arguments clearly stated, perhaps even in quotable terms, far more often the stated positions have been incidental to an account devoted primarily to other subjects. Whenever possible, I have used direct references, but most of what follows is necessarily my interpretation of someone else's implied position.

Historical Development of the Case Against Wholesale Disposal

The retentionists base their case against disposal on three major arguments: (1) public outrage over widespread fraud and mismanagement that resulted from disposal of the the federal lands; (2) concern over the destruction of natural resources as a result of land disposal; and (3) concern over the social aspects of the land disposal process. In the pages that follow I will trace the historical development of the case against disposal and the arguments underlying permanent retention of these lands by the federal government, and will attempt to put the retentionists' case in perspective.

Outrage at fraud and trespass

Fraud in disposal of federal lands and trespass on, or illegal use of, federal lands was widespread from the beginning of federal land ownership. I have noted this generally in chapter 2, but here it is essential to develop this subject in more detail. Fraud and trespass had been widespread in colonial days—pine timber was taken illegally from Crown lands in Maine,[1] land was occupied in trespass in the proprietorship colony of Maryland,[2] and settlers repeatedly violated treaties with Indians by trespassing on their lands.[3] Such actions were inevitable, given distant governments with only a minimal presence on the land, the immensity of the land and forest resources (as measured against the needs and abilities of the settler to use them), and the qualities of self-reliance and independence which characterized the people on the frontier, and a widespread disrespect for governmental authority when it interfered with use of natural resources readily at hand.

Some trespassers entered the lands for the purpose of harvesting timber. Dana reports on such instances in the Southeast in the period between 1830 and 1850, and in the Lake States during 1850 to 1875.[4] Clepper also has described very graphically the courageous (but generally unsuccessful) efforts of General Land Office fieldmen to stop trespass in the Lake States in the face of actual violence from trespassers and their local sympathizers.[5]

Working within the system, an unscrupulous lumberman would buy, at auction, a 40-acre tract of federal timberland, which could legally be harvested. Then he would instruct the timber crew to cut both that tract and the land around it. Such operations were later termed *round 40s*.

Particularly outrageous examples of fraud occurred in situations where the settler was required to make improvements and to reside on the land, as mandated under the Homestead Act of 1862, or where disposal was limited to certain kinds of land, such as the swamp and overflowed lands granted to the states. Robbins relates how settlers would swear they had constructed a 12-by-18 house in compliance with the residence and improvement requirements of the law, neglecting to say that it was a dollhouse measured in inches, not a human habitation measured in feet.[6] Agents of states which had agreed to sell land to land dealers and speculators, after receiving title from the federal government, would swear that they had crossed the swampland by boat—neglecting to mention that the boat had been mounted on a wagon and was pulled by horses over perfectly dry land.

The Homestead Act permitted an applicant, after only a few months' residence, to acquire title by buying the land (for only $1.25 per acre, which was cheap in those days) rather than serving out the five years of residence required by the 1862 Law. With the shortened residence requirements, often entries were made by persons not at all interested in using the land themselves; and others made entries in the names of nonexistent persons. Later these tracts were resold to an individual or corporation. In this way a great deal of excellent forestland was transferred from federal to private ownership. Gates reports that lively markets developed: "Relinquishments were bought and sold at every land office and land brokers' notices such as the following were openly displayed: 'Relinquishments always on hand,' 'We have deeded land and relinquishments so cheap it will make you smile,' 'Relinquishments bought and sold.' "[7]

Another provision of the laws establishing national forests allowed persons who had valid land claims within national forests to relinquish these claims for which they could receive an equal number of acres in a location of their choosing. Homestead and other land claims were filed for land on bare mountain tops above the timberline in some national forests. Later, these nonproductive acres were relinquished in return for an equal acreage of highly productive forest elsewhere. Dana recounts in some detail a particularly voracious example of such land fraud in Oregon that occurred around 1900.[8] While incarcerated, one of the participants, angered because his erstwhile cronies had abandoned him when he was convicted and jailed, wrote a lengthy book, *Looters of the Public Domain,* in which he detailed how he had organized these frauds.[9] As a result of this episode, one of Oregon's senators was convicted and sentenced to jail (he never served his sentence because he died shortly thereafter), and a representative was federally indicted for fraud and bribery.

Several of the principals in the Oregon case, including persons employed by the General Land Office, had been bribed to make false statements (in some cases, under oath), or to take other improper and illegal actions on these land cases. Puter relates one delightful (from the perspective of history!) incident in which two men, employed as special agents by the Land Office, were bribed by land claimants to make false reports on the extent of the improvement on some mountain top claims. Unaware that the other also had been bribed, each went to considerable lengths to report on what he had seen without the other being able directly to contradict him. Only later did each learn that the other had also been bribed, and that all their efforts at deception had been unnecessary. By no means the only such incident, the Oregon land frauds were some of the more outrageous and more fully exposed of the many frauds that took place.

Many historians have related the various attempts of General Land Office commissioners and the secretaries of the Department of the Interior to get Congress to take some effective measures, such as legislation to enable the agencies to haul violators more promptly into court or funding to provide adequate staff to uncover and prosecute trespasses and frauds. There is no need to present a detailed account of these efforts; they occurred almost continuously from about 1840 until 1900 or later. Almost all were total failures; small and poorly financed steps were taken at intervals but nothing really effective was accomplished. The plain truth was that Congress did not want to stop such actions. Gates has commented on the attitude of westerners, saying, "They favored transferring public lands to private ownership as rapidly as possible and were not very squeamish as to how that alienation was achieved."[10] The commissioners and secretaries repeatedly called attention to the fact that the Homestead Act and many other laws were ill-adapted to the transfer of either forest or grazing land from public to private ownership in units of reasonable economic size and on terms appropriate to the land use. The cultivation requirement of the original Homestead Act was meaningless when not followed, or pernicious if cultivation were actually attempted on much of the plains and mountain land.

There were a number of special inquiries made by government bodies and by private groups. An especially effective Public Land Commission, established in 1879, issued a good report, and other useful documents were written by its members or other staff. A Forest Commission was established in 1896, and a second Public Lands Commission in 1903. These commissions assembled a great deal of information, more than previously had been available, and they helped to inform the general public and the Congress; but relatively little in the form of curative legislation resulted from any of them. For our purposes it is enough to point out that (1) frauds and trespass were widespread; and (2) this aroused indignation on the part of a relatively small portion of the general public and concerned public officials, but their efforts proved relatively ineffective in stopping either the fraud or the trespass. This last fact helped to set the stage for withdrawal of federal lands from disposal, as will be described later.

However, these frauds in public land disposal greatly have influenced the thinking of more recent writers on federal lands, as the following passages demonstrate.

Ise, in *The United States Forest Policy*, says:

Forces unfavorable to conservation had on the other hand attained formidable power. Swamp land grants, grants for education, military bounties, and the whole hydra-headed system of grants and concessions to the railroads had provided for the alienation of several hundred million acres of land—some of it timber land. The Preemption, Commutation Homestead, Desert Land, Public Sale, and Private Entry laws were available to timbermen for the acquisition of remaining tracts; and there was no reason to expect that any of these laws would soon be repealed. The Free Timber and Timber and Stone acts completed the category of iniquitous statutes. . . . [T]hese various factors operated to accomplish the destruction or alienation of most of the valuable public timber during the following years, and . . . conservation forces finally saved to the American public a frazzled remnant of their original magnificent heritage. . . .[11]

Pinchot, who discusses this problem at some length, briefly summarizes the situation: "Thus the natural resources, with whose
conservation and wise distribution and use the whole future of the
Nation was bound up, were passing under the control of men who
developed and destroyed them with one and only one object in
mind—their own personal profit. And to all intents and purposes the
Government of all the people did nothing about it."[12]

Robinson, in much more recent times, briefly has expressed a
similar sentiment:

> The first century of American independence passed without any general
> forest land legislation being enacted. Land was an asset to be converted
> to cash. Forests were plentiful and were regarded as an obstacle to
> progress. Land had to be cleared for settlements, farms, and the raising
> of livestock. Through most of the nineteenth century the public forests
> were plundered. Settlers, commercial enterprises, railroads, and river-
> boats all contributed to the plunder. A number of acts were passed to
> protect public lands against extensive trespass. These were generally
> ineffective in that they were poorly enforced and easily evaded. In part
> this resulted from public apathy toward conservation, but it was also
> attributable to Congressional failure to provide for the disposition of
> such timber.[13]

And Voigt notes, "This began as a simple account of how an
aggressive clique of public land-using stockmen in the West attempted
a colossal grab of public domain and national forest grazing areas,
only to be countered by a straggly but determined aggregation of
conservationists who didn't admit they were outgunned and fought
back to at least a temporary victory."[14]

Concern over resource depletion

The second major reason for rejection of continued wholesale
disposal of federal lands was the public's rising concern over natural
resource depletion. This concern was not as widespread, acute, and
insistent during the nineteenth century when the disposal process
was proceeding at headlong speed as it was to become later. Although
Marsh wrote his classic book *Man and Nature* in 1865, he was far in
advance of professional or popular thinking of the time.[15] The word
conservation was not used commonly in connection with natural
resources until the turn of the century, when President Theodore
Roosevelt, in particular, adopted it.

Probably this stemmed from the fact that up until the nineteenth century the supply of natural resources seemed so great that little thought and less action were devoted to their conservation for future generations. This was particularly true for the forests—so vast they seemed endless, they were so full of timber that early lumbermen could not visualize a day when it would be scarce. For many of these forests, the standing trees were worthless—the land without trees was more valuable than the land with trees. Clearing the standing timber, selling some if there were a market, using some for construction and fuel on the farm, and burning the rest was not only profitable for the farmer but socially productive as well. Where the trees had positive value, the economic thing to do was to harvest them and thus convert their capital into a more liquid and productive form. There was little or no concern about forest regeneration; on the contrary, fires were repeatedly set to prevent regrowth of seedlings.

Something of the same situation existed on the plains and other grazing areas. The sea of grass seemed so infinite that the early livestockmen could not envisualize its exhaustion. The earliest livestock development on the fringes of settlement and across the West after the Civil War also encountered the classic common property problem. The land belonged to the federal government, which throughout the nineteenth century never exerted any positive control or management of the grazing resource. Livestock could roam at will or could be driven over the land unhindered by fences except where livestockmen illegally erected them. If one stockman kept his cattle from close grazing, another was likely to graze his livestock there to consume the remaining forage. Such overgrazing on the public domain eventually affected popular attitudes toward natural resource conservation.

A diligent search of newspapers, magazine articles, speeches, and other public materials written during the period of greatest federal land disposal would reveal some criticism of natural resource exploitation. Robbins quotes the secretary of the interior saying, in 1897, "The timber growth in most or many of the older states has been ruthlessly laid waste, and in some sections the settlers are realizing its scarcity, its cost for domestic uses growing greater from year to year."[16] Some writers have assembled information on the results of the natural resource exploitation accompanying the land disposal process while others merely have asserted such exploitation existed. Lillard, for instance, has graphically described the appearance of logged-over forested areas, especially in the Lake States, after logging ceased—soils were eroded, streams were silted up, and the whole landscape was changed drastically.[17] And Hays well summarizes forest exploitation as he saw it:

> The lumber industry provided a dramatic example of resource exploitation in the last half of the nineteenth century. Low prices for forest land and the meager amount of capital required encouraged many enterprising Americans to enter the field. The industry was highly mobile; lumbermen rapidly cut and abandoned lands, and moved on to new areas. Facing the uncertainties of a high degree of competition, timber operators could not, with profit, utilize fully their resources. Few cut more than the most valuable trees; they left second-grade timber as waste. Lumbermen showed little concern for fire and disease damage, the destruction of trees during logging, or provisions for adequate reproduction. By the latter part of the nineteenth century the obvious waste from these practices prompted a few leaders in both public and private forestry to demand that the country give more attention to a program of scientific management.[18]

In 1933 the Forest Service prepared its classic report, *A National Plan for American Forestry*. A few quotes from this voluminous study will provide the flavor of the agency's view at that time regarding private ownership of forestland—an ownership which had resulted from the wholesale disposal processes of the nineteenth and early twentieth centuries:

> That practically all of the major problems of American forestry center [are] in, or have grown out of, private ownership [p. v].
>
> The most fundamental and underlying cause for the delinquency and abandonment of much cutover land is that it was acquired by [the] lumberman owner not as property to be cropped in perpetuity, but rather merely for its virgin timber values. After these were taken off, the naked land by itself was of no interest to him. The tradition of the American lumber industry has been "to cut out and get out"—an outgrowth of the once prevalent impression that the virgin timber supplies of the country were inexhaustible and of the very low prices at which virgin stumpage could be bought. The public land laws and the early policies of the States and Nation made easy this practice of stripping off the virgin timber in one region and moving on to another. The unwisdom of this, not only from the point of view of the public but from that of the private owner who might have benefitted in the long run by a sustained-yield policy of management, is becoming more and more apparent. A question raised very sharply by this breakdown in private ownership is whether the whole conception of transferring to private ownership so much forest land was not in error [p. 881].
>
> In the United States today, as a result of logging, forest fires and the unwise selection and improper use of agricultural land, there are at least 135 million acres not long ago fertile and productive that are now

denuded and unproductive. The idleness of this great acreage is not, however, its worst feature. Far more harmful in terms of public welfare is the capacity inherent in such lands for rapid deterioration or for causing damage to other lands and waters through erosion [p. 1485].[19]

Hays describes the situation on the public domain grazing areas as he saw it, "Amid this turmoil the public range rapidly deteriorated. Originally plentiful and lush, the forage supply was subjected to intense pressure by increasing use."[20] Robbins has described the situation on the public domain grazing areas thusly: "Not only did these cattle interests use the land, but much of the land they used was ruined by overgrazing. This was even more true of the sheep grazers of Utah."[21]

In 1936 the Forest Service presented a comprehensive analysis of the western rangelands in its report entitled *The Western Range*. According to the report, the agency's view of private rangeland ownership and use was as follows:

Forage depletion for the entire range area averages more than half; the result of a few decades of livestock grazing [p. vii].

The sum total of the effects of past land policy on range lands has been: . . . The passage to private ownership of an enormous area of land, the size of which is not yet accurately known, that is either submarginal even for range use by private operators because of low productivity, etc., or has high public values such as watershed protection which are difficult or impossible for private owners to maintain [pp. 12–13].

Widespread, continuous, and exhaustive use of the forage has changed the whole character of the virgin range. The outstanding changes have been (1) the passage of much of the land from federal ownership to other forms of control, (2) a reduction in the area available for range use, (3) a tremendous decrease in the quantity and quality of the forage, and (4) a deterioration of the basic resource, the soil itself [p. 81].

By far the most significant departure from the virgin range conditions is the change in the plant cover. Although varying in density under different forms of management, the plant cover in every range type is depleted to an alarming degree. Many valuable forage species have disappeared entirely. Palatable plants are being replaced by unpalatable ones. Worthless and obnoxious weeds from foreign countries are invading every type [p. 83].[22]

Concern over social aspects of disposal

The third general ground for criticism of wholesale and rapid disposal of the federal lands was the social aspect of such disposal.

The Jeffersonian ideal has been that of the yeoman farmer, economically and politically independent and free, tilling his own plot of
land. This ideal was the moral underpinning of the free soil and free
land movements of the mid-nineteenth century. The 1880 Census of
Agriculture for the first time collected information on farm ownership
and farm tenancy, and the results were highly disturbing to those
deeply committed to the family-owned farm.[23] More than a quarter
of the farms and of the farm acreage were operated by tenants, not
by owners; and many of the owners were heavily in debt, so that
their continued possession of the farm was by no means certain.
Various defenses of farm tenancy were offered, among them: that it
was often a step toward farm ownership (what was later termed the
agricultural ladder concept), or that tenancy on a farm of adequate
size was economically preferable to ownership of a substandard farm.
Much of this defense ignored the racial aspects of tenancy—that
black farmers in the South were nearly all tenants, and that a significant
proportion of all tenants were these black Southerners. At the very
least, the agricultural conditions revealed by the 1880 Census made
one skeptical of the public domain disposal process: obviously it had
not produced the results Jefferson had sought.

A later study dealt with the concentration of forest land ownership.
By far the most detailed and careful study of forests in the United
States up to that date, the Bureau of Corporations' final report, was
issued in 1913–14. This study had been undertaken in response to
congressional resolutions. Dana says that "the Bureau of Corporations
found that in the investigation area 195 holders, many interrelated,
controlled half of the privately owned timber. . . . Vast speculative
purchases had, in the judgment of the Bureau, led to dominating
control of the standing timber by a comparatively few large holders.
There had been an enormous increase in the value of stumpage
'which the holder neither created nor substantially enhances' and
which promised the fortunate owners still greater profits than those
already realized."[24]

Hays shows how the concern over concentration of forest and other
land ownership was part of the active, emotional, and political crusade
against monopoly that occurred around the turn of the century in
which President Theodore Roosevelt played a major role.[25]

Some of these criticisms regarding the social costs of rapid wholesale
disposal of the public domain became more effective as the momentum
grew for reservation and continued federal ownership of these lands.

Summary of the retentionists' case against unrestricted disposal

The retentionists base their case against further transfers of public land to private ownership on the considerations that follow.

Private ownership of land and its natural resources has led to exploitation, not to conservation, in every period of U.S. land history. It is claimed by the retentionists that the primary goal of the individual landowner or firm is private profit and that they have little or no concern for the public welfare. According to the retentionists, the historical record is incontrovertible in this regard. Tracing the history of fraud and trespass on the U.S. federal lands, the literature cited in this chapter explicitly reinforces their argument.

In its concern for profits today, private exploitation of natural resources is particularly dangerous and undesirable. Soil is eroded, timber is cut, and grass is overgrazed, all for present gain. The retentionists, who fear that the search for current profits may lead to the impoverishment of future generations, ask, "How can a society be so indifferent to its own viability?"

Private ownership of the land and its associated natural resources exploits the marketable resources and values and, at the same time, neglects the nonmarketable values. Advocates of retention cite such examples as timber harvesting, mining, and grazing which occur without regard for watershed or wildlife values; timber harvesting and the mining of minerals with little concern for wilderness values; and real estate subdivisions that destroy the land's amenity values, including one's right to privacy. According to the retentionist, the profit motive operates to secure profits for the exploiter but disregards those values to society that do not appear in market transactions, even though the social values often constitute the real rewards to the national life.

Development of the Case for Permanent Retention

As mentioned earlier, the development of the case for permanent retention of the federal lands evolved over a long period. Advocates for retention joined together, effectively ending the wholesale disposal of the public domain. Later, they endorsed the principle of multiple use on the federal lands and claimed that only under federal management could economic and socially optimal values be achieved.

Reservation: A reaction against disposal

The third major era in federal land history was that of reservation (see chapter 2). While it ultimately led to positive programs for management of the lands reserved "permanently" in federal ownership, it initially was simply a reaction against continued wholesale or unhindered disposal of the public domain.

Yellowstone National Park is generally cited as the first major permanent reservation of federal land although previously other smaller reservations had been designated (see page 27). The reservation of Yellowstone was most unusual and was made possible only because there was no interest in private ownership of the land at that time. Sponsors of the park were concerned lest it pass into an exploitive type of private ownership, but neither they nor the Congress knew exactly what national park status entailed.

This attitude on the part of the Congress was most strikingly apparent in its lack of appropriations for the park. Ise reports on the beginnings of Yellowstone:

> As a fitting recognition of his work in exploration, Nathaniel P. Langford was appointed Superintendent of the park, without salary and without any appropriations for five years. He faced an imposing array of difficulties and impossibilities, aside from the difficulty of living on his private income. It was assumed at the time the park was established that it would be self-supporting, that concessioners would pay as rents enough to provide for administration and protection, and that there would be no need for Congressional appropriations. Hayden had given assurances on this point to get the park established, and Langford also believed that the park would be self-supporting, although he thought that an appropriation would be necessary at first to mark the boundaries and protect the game and natural formations which were being destroyed by visitors. Langford, like Congress, had the theory that only private enterprise could do things efficiently, and suggested that it might be well to lease the important points of interest to concessioners, who would be authorized to protect them, and grant leases for toll roads, which would be self-supporting.[26]

Congress was very chary with appropriations for Yellowstone Park for many years. The Corps of Engineers built roads in the park; and from 1887 to 1901 the army, who had full charge of the park, provided some protection services. Only gradually did the idea of continued management—in the positive sense of the term—emerge, but even at that only minimum appropriations were made.

The first system of permanent federal land reservations began in 1891. While often referred to as the Forest Reserve Act, the actual reservation authority in the act was hidden away in one small, somewhat incomplete, and mostly unnoticed section of a long and complex general law for revising statutes relating to disposal of the public domain. We have traced its history in chapter 2; and, as I noted there, no legal authority for the use of the resources of the reserved lands existed until 1897, when provisions for such administration were added to a pending appropriations bill. Although some persons lobbied for reservation of forest and other lands in the last decade of the nineteenth century, they had little say in how the reserved lands should be managed and used.

In fact, both before and after passage of the 1897 Act, there was substantial opposition to any commercial use of the reserved areas. If he had been able to do so, John Muir would have closed the forest reserves to commercial use, much as the national parks were closed. Even after the passage of the 1897 Act, which explicitly authorized timber sales (under conditions which ultimately were to prove onerous), the Department of the Interior refused to authorize grazing use in the forest reserves until public opinion in the West forced it to do so.[27] Under laws and regulations of the forest reserves—from 1897 until they were transferred to the new Forest Service in 1905—some commercial uses were permitted, but the extent of that use was not great and was, on the whole, grudgingly conceded.

Pinchot, on the other hand, strongly believed in the use and development of federally owned resources—land, forests, minerals, and water power.[28] As head of his small Bureau of Forestry in the Department of Agriculture, he sought, mostly in vain, more positive management of the forest reserves. Because of his friendship with the president, he was able to initiate several highly unusual administrative arrangements, such as *de facto* serving as the legal counsel for the Department of the Interior while also acting as bureau chief in another department. On the whole, his efforts to change the Department of the Interior and its General Land Office were unproductive, but he did get the forest reserves transferred from the Department of the Interior to the Department of Agriculture, where they were placed under the direction of a new Forest Service, which he directed. When this was accomplished in 1905, Pinchot was then in a position to begin positive and active management of the national forests, as well as to exert a considerable influence on other aspects of the administration's resource policy. He undertook the major job of "educating" the Congress and the general public, as to what management really entailed. Much opposition to development remained, which materialized in a bitter and emotional battle between Muir and Pinchot over the development of the power resources at the Hetch Hetchy dam site in a national forest in California.

Multiple use: A defense for federal land ownership

All land in the United States produces more than one kind of goods and services. Some rain or snow falls everywhere, even on the driest parts of Death Valley, hence all land is watershed, though the amounts of water received and the value of the water may differ greatly. There is some form of wildlife everywhere, including on the severest deserts, though the variety of wildlife differs greatly from area to area. All land offers scenic or amenity values to someone. Most land is used to some degree for outdoor recreation by someone. A great part of the United States is covered with forests which produce wood for a wide variety of uses; and other large areas have grass or other native vegetation which provides the basis for an extensive range livestock industry. The volume and the kinds of outputs and their mix is to some degree subject to human control or influence; but many kinds and quantities of outputs will be forthcoming without input from humans or despite efforts to control or eliminate such outputs.

Out of these basic biological facts has grown the concept of multiple land use—the deliberate attempt to secure more than one kind of output from an area. The term *multiple use* has extremely wide appeal, in considerable part because the concept is loosely defined, or at least loosely used; hence any user can decide what he or she wishes it to mean. If all kinds of outputs are expected from the same acre at the same time, conflicts are inevitable and complete success is impossible. If consideration is given to different kinds of outputs at different times, or to different outputs from closely intermingled tracts operated under single management, or to several but not necessarily all possible outputs, then the possibilities of multiple use become much greater. As it has turned out, multiple use has become one of the major arguments for continued federal land ownership and management.

As I have noted, Pinchot strongly believed in use and development of the national forests. In the letter of instructions from the secretary of agriculture to Pinchot when the latter took charge of the national forests in 1905—a letter which Pinchot himself wrote—reference is made to water, wood, and forage, and to agricultural, lumbering, mining, and livestock interests.[29] Pinchot emphasized mineral and water power development on the national forests rather more than do most modern foresters. Although an avid outdoorsman himself, he made scant mention of outdoor recreation in his writings—the subject is not listed in the index to his book and does not, I believe, appear anywhere in the text. He makes no mention of wilderness, as we now use that term, and given his pro-development bias, he probably would be opposed to setting aside large areas of national forests as wilderness. That usage of the national forests was formalized only after 1920, when Aldo Leopold and Arthur Carhart urged that some national forest areas be kept in as near pristine condition as possible. Their concept of wilderness differed somewhat from that of today; Leopold felt that a wilderness should be an area large enough to require two days' travel by pack train to reach its center, and when the Forest Service first established wilderness areas by executive order they were 100,000 acres or more in extent.[30] Today, relatively natural areas in any ownership of less than 100 acres which are accessible by easy auto travel qualify as wilderness in the popular mind. Hays has described how Pinchot's ideas about national forest management fitted into his ideas and those of others about natural resource use, development, and conservation in general.[31]

Although Pinchot had the idea of multiple land use strongly in mind, he did not, as far as I can find, use that term. I cannot, in fact, discover when the term (as distinguished from the idea) first was used. From personal knowledge, I think that the idea and the term were fairly well entrenched in Forest Service thinking by the late 1920s or the early 1930s, but Clepper claims that the earliest official definition of the term he can find in Forest Service documents dates from 1944.[32] Nonetheless, it is certain that the term was widely used by the end of World War II and was sanctioned, if not precisely defined, in the Multiple Use and Sustained Yield Act for the national forests in 1960 and in the Multiple Use Act of 1964 for the BLM. The meaning implied by those acts and in today's popular usage expresses a desire for a kind of management that is defined in the minds of the users rather than in specific instructions to the agencies. Almost everyone supports the general idea; it is its translation into practice that produces controversies.

In 1947, long after the idea of multiple use became widely accepted, the economic rational for multiple use of federal lands was well developed by Kelso.[33] The economic value of all outputs from a land area may be maximized by a program of management which does not seek to obtain the greatest value of any single output; by sacrifice of the output of one good or service, other goods or services may be produced in volume that makes the value of the whole greater than that achievable by any other way.

Because the production of some goods and services from land produce values which are not ordinarily captured in the market place and because some of the consequences (good and bad) of management on one site affect lands outside of that site or persons not involved in the decision-making process, it is often argued that only public ownership will produce the optimum social output from a given area of land. Clearly, few, if any, private owners could afford a wilderness of a few thousand acres or larger; private owners rarely gain anything from watershed management, though they may be constrained by law to avoid unduly damaging the water quality; landowners often are unable to capture wildlife or recreation values on their land, except for their personal consumption; and the esthetic or amenity values which others see in a tract of forest or range rarely produce any income to the landowner. Thus, if all these kinds of values are to be produced to an economically or socially optimum extent, then public ownership is necessary.

Rise of conceptual support for retention

From 1905 onward as the Forest Service—first under Pinchot's leadership and then under that of others—continued to manage the national forests with competence, dedication, and integrity, the popular and political support for continued federal ownership of these lands gradually grew. There is a long history of public land management, including controversies of these decades, which need not be reviewed again here. The Taylor Grazing Act in 1934 was a compromise between those wishing the public domain to be available for disposition and those desirous of permanent reservation of these lands in federal ownership, but at least it marked the end of the era of wholesale unrestricted disposal.

All of the writings cited thus far in this chapter are, to a degree, supportive of the positive case for retention in federal ownership of the lands now so owned. In addition, some others are more explicit to this point. For instance, the volume edited by Darling and Milton, and more particularly the essay by Brinser, rather clearly support continued federal land ownership.[34] Ise, in his book on national parks, is most positive about the case for federal ownership of the national parks; while he does not explicitly deal with federal lands outside of the parks, those of us who knew him can confidently assert that he would have applied some of the same logic to the lands outside of the parks, had he considered them in detail.[35] In their book on the eastern national forests, Shands and Healy explicitly accept continued federal ownership of these lands.[36] At the symposium on Federal Lands Forest Policy in 1978, organized by the Lewis and Clark Law School–Northwestern School of Law, most of the speakers seemed implicitly to accept the idea of continued federal land ownership.[37] The same was true of most of the writers in the *Arizona Law Review* who evaluated the Federal Land Policy and Management Act.[38] None of these sources has as explicit and forthright defense of continued federal land ownership as one would like, for an exposition of the retentionists' case; but this absence of explicit statement is in itself significant, because it means that continued federal land ownership is implicitly accepted, as something not worth arguing about—at least, not currently.

Conservation organizations such as the Sierra Club, the Wilderness Society, the Izaak Walton League, the Audubon Society, the National Wildlife Federation, the Natural Resources Defense Council, and others of the generally "liberal" conservation orientation also implicitly assume continued federal ownership of the present federal lands, focusing their attention on how these lands should be managed, not upon whether they should remain federal. The somewhat more conservative professional organizations, such as the American Forestry Association, the Society for Range Management, and the Society of American Foresters also implicitly accept continued federal ownership of these lands while also arguing, but in a different manner than the first-named group, about the way in which the federal lands should be managed. And many of the "Nader's Raiders"-type organizations would also argue positively for retention of federal lands in federal ownership.

In considerable part, this tacit acceptance of continued federal ownership of the federal lands arises out of a general feeling that the ownership issue has been settled. As I pointed out in chapter 1, that indeed seemed to be the situation in the 1950s and 1960s; the possibility of large-scale transfer of federal lands to private ownership was not raised for serious debate in those decades, hence there was little reason for any organization to expend much effort in defending this policy position—its efforts could better be spent on influencing how these lands were administered.

Much of the value of certain natural resources arises out of option demand. Krutilla has described and defended option demand as follows: "This demand is characterized as a willingness to pay for retaining an option to use an area or facility that would be difficult or impossible to replace and for which no close substitute is available. Moreover, such a demand may exist even though there is no current intention to use the area or facility in question and the option may never be exercised. If an option value exists for rare or unique occurrences of nature, but there is no means by which a private resource owner can appropriate this value, the resulting resource allocation may be questioned."[39]

The option demand for some types of land—for example, wilderness—will not be met if the land is privately owned. Public, and preferably federal, ownership of the land is therefore necessary.

Popular support for wilderness has been one major impetus for continued federal ownership and management of large areas of federal land for several decades. Wilderness advocates repeatedly cite Thoreau's statement: "In wilderness is the preservation of the world."[40] Howard Zahniser, long-time executive officer of the Wilderness Society, has stated the case at greater length and with more specificity: "It is a bold thing for a human being who lives on the earth but a few score years at most to presume upon the Eternal and covet perpetuity for any of his undertakings. Yet we who concern ourselves with wilderness preservation are compelled to assume this boldness and with the courage of this peculiar undertaking of ours so to order our enterprise as to direct our efforts toward the perpetual—to project into the eternity of the future some of that precious unspoiled ecological inheritance that has come to us out of the eternity of the past."[41]

Linda Graber has stated the case for wilderness in more explicitly religious terms: "Wilderness has become a contemporary form of sacred space, valued as a symbol of geopiety and as a focus for religious feeling."[42]

Joseph Sax not only defends continued federal land ownership of wilderness and other unusual areas, but also defends such ownership of all land now in federal ownership.[43] Indeed, he argues that there are important "collective values" in federal land ownership and that a much expanded federal ownership, or some form of public control over private land which would shift the decision-making from private to public hands, is highly desirable.

Though all of these persons quoted above support continued federal land ownership as basic to the preservation of wilderness areas, their positions with respect to the economics of wilderness range widely. Krutilla would argue that, if all factors and outputs were properly valued, many, if not all, wilderness areas now established or under serious consideration for inclusion in the wilderness system would find their highest economic use in that characterization. (I would agree with him in general, although we might differ as to specific areas.) Thoreau never dreamed of economic tests; for him, wilderness was its own excuse for being. Zahniser would have rejected economic analysis as a reasonable test. Sax almost totally ignores costs, at least in a monetary sense, just as he does benefits or gains in a monetary sense. Graber would consider economic tests as profane.

Equity for future generations

One of the arguments against private ownership of the land and its associated resources, which runs through much of the literature, is that private ownership is concerned primarily or wholly with present profit and disregards the needs of future generations. It is argued that private owners have short time horizons—in effect, their own lifetimes—with limited consideration for their own descendants and none at all for those unrelated to them. "What has posterity ever done for me?" they ask. Those who take this position often cite the example of forest exploitation during the nineteenth and early twentieth centuries—the cut-and-get-out philosophy which I have noted elsewhere. Other examples include the exploitation of richer mineral deposits leaving larger volumes of lower-grade ores untouched; the utilization of groundwater far beyond the recharge capacity of the acquifers; and the plowing of virgin sod and exploitation of its stored fertility before land abandonment.

Because future generations cannot today make their wishes or needs apparent through either the economic or the political process—unborn persons do not buy, save, invest, or vote—decisions made by living persons are invariably biased toward the present, with inadequate consideration for the future.

One who has dealt with intergenerational analyses of natural resources is Talbot Page. While advancing these intergenerational arguments, he is most careful to analyze what the market can and cannot do. He recognizes that a profit-seeking person or firm, with no special or ethical concern for the future, may nevertheless decide to forgo exploitation of some natural resource today if they have confidence that its value or price will be higher tomorrow—that is, higher by enough to earn a reasonable interest return on the present value of the resource. His analysis—while more explicitly concerned about the intergenerational problem than any other experts on the subject—is carefully stated and avoids the conceptual and analytical errors of many other writers on this subject.

According to Page:

Markets can be expected to allocate resources more or less efficiently relative to a given distribution of wealth or market power (a hypothetical ideal market would actually achieve efficiency). But markets cannot be expected to solve the problem of what is a fair or equitable distribution of wealth, either among different people at a point in time (intratemporally) or among different generations (intertemporally).... Sometimes these distributional aspects of resource use are obscured by the assertion that depletion resulting from market forces will automatically benefit the future as well as the present. Resources in the ground are sterile, the argument goes, and the future will be better off if resources are extracted so that they can be turned into productive capital. The obscuration arises because "can be benefitted" is different from "will automatically be benefitted." Market forces channel most material, perhaps 90 percent of it, into short-lived consumer goods rather than productive capital. If iron ore is taken from the ground, mixed with tin, and then made into soft drink cans that are used once and scattered along the roadside, the future is not benefitted.[44]

In applying his analysis explicitly to federal lands, Page writes:

On public land in our own country mineral rights are acquired upon the discovery of the mineral in the same way that fish become owned upon their capture. This rule of capture, stemming from the 1872 mining law, tends to promote more mineral exploration and exploitation than the efficiency standard calls for, just as does the rule of capture in ocean fishing. For minerals on public lands, exploration may be undertaken on a preemptive basis in order to prevent a competitor from obtaining a claim first. Once the claim is established, mineral exploitation may have a higher priority than other uses of public land.[45]

Page's primary concern here is with mineral resources, and he does not cite examples from forestry, agricultural land use, or most other uses of land. However, one may reasonably assume that, if he had addressed these other uses of land, his analysis and his conclusions would have been similar.

Summary of the case for retention

From the literature explicitly cited in this chapter and other sources, the positive case for retention in federal ownership of the lands presently owned by the federal government can be summarized as follows:

Those who administer the federal lands can better consider the national— as opposed to regional or local—interest. Their concern is geared to the public welfare rather than to that of special interest groups. Not only are these lands publicly owned, they are federally owned; there exists a national interest in them, which should be paramount. Private profit and local economic advantage are all very well, but not at the cost of the national interest. Persons living far from the large tracts of federal land nevertheless have an interest in them. The laws concerning these lands are made in the national political arena—by the Congress and the president—and the appropriations for their administration are paid out of the federal Treasury.

Public ownership of land and its associated resources requires a longer view of resource management and resource needs than does private ownership. Generally, public agencies operate on a longer time horizon for their planning, and the needs of future generations in particular can be more fully considered under public than under private ownership. The economists holding to this view might say that the discount rate was lower for public than for private owners and that future benefits need not be so severely discounted to present values under public ownership. The noneconomist might reject this language, yet argue for essentially the same asserted value of public land ownership—the ability and the willingness of the public, acting through government, to consider the needs of future generations.

Conservation methods of resource development and use are more likely to be executed under public ownership than under private ownership. The methodology often requires research and testing, as well as thoughtful and timely applications, but the retentionists argue that they are far more probable under public than under private ownership. Harvesting of mature trees in such a way as to protect the young growth, grazing of livestock well within the long-term carrying capacity of the land, and similar conservation measures are far more likely to occur on federally owned lands.

The multiple uses of land can be achieved more easily under federal than under private land ownership. The Forest Service and the Bureau of Land Management have greater capacity to protect the wildlife or to develop more fully the recreational potential of the land, than would a private landowner, who is more likely to have a single purpose in his management of the land to the detriment of other values. The whole concept of multiple use thrives under federal land ownership.

The protection and use of the intrinsic but nonmarketed outputs and values of the land is greater under federal than under private land ownership, argue the retentionists. Wilderness areas can be preserved, managed, and used under federal ownership while under private ownership they are more likely to be sacrificed the minute there arose the prospect of a profit from the exploitation of timber, mineral, or other marketable products. If we are going to have wilderness areas, they must be under federal (or state) ownership. The same is largely true for aesthetic, wildlife, and even watershed values. The public land manager will take into account many values, various ways of using the land, and conservation measures which private owners would reject or ignore. Many of these values are among those most highly regarded by the people of the United States, and if we are to have such values in reasonable proportion, then federal land ownership is a necessity.

The values arising from land use, but accruing to persons and groups not resident on the land, can be more readily realized under federal than under private land ownership. The existence of external positive values and of external costs, each arising out of actions on the land, are values or costs which do not accrue to the landowner. When the federal government is landowner, "externalities" in one sense disappear— the land belongs to everyone, the values and the costs thus accrue to the landowner. All the costs and all the values of any method of land management are taken into account when the land is federally owned, but not when it is privately owned. The costs and the values are thus fully "internalized"—a relationship which economists view with approval.

The Retentionists' Case in Perspective

Up to this point I have made an effort to state the *retentionists' case* as I think they would do. No doubt some retentionists will feel I have not put their case strongly enough; nonetheless, I hope they will credit me with good intentions. In this concluding section of the chapter, I resume my role of objective researcher and look briefly at some aspects of the retentionists' case as I see it.

Support for retention in federal ownership of all or essentially all the land now federally owned is consistent with demands for improvement in management of those lands. The retentionists as a group have been among the most vocal and active of all interest groups in their demands that the federal lands be managed better than they have been managed in the past. Naturally enough, their concepts of "better management" include more consideration of their goals and objectives for these lands, but they surely accept efficiency in meeting these goals as being important. I interpret the legislation of the past decade—RPA, NFMA, FLPMA, and others described in chapter 2—as embodying these objectives of retention and of improved management of the federal lands.

While a demand for improved management of the federal lands is consistent with the position for their retention in federal ownership, improved management does not seem to be essential to that position. That is, as far as I can judge, the retentionists as a group would support continued federal land ownership even if no improvement in the management of these lands were achieved. They regard improved management as desirable but not necessary.

Some retentionists, such as Joseph Sax, argue for retention of *all* the present lands in federal ownership. My judgment is that other advocates of retention reluctantly would accept something considerably less. Many retentionists have agreed that some carefully selected disposal of federal lands would be permissible, provided that the lands are not needed for public purposes or that it is impossible to manage them efficiently because of their location or small size. If a specific proposal for disposition of a quarter or a half the present federal land estate were to be pushed strongly by the administration, the retentionists would surely make themselves heard; but even that might be grudgingly acceptable if the wilderness and other unique areas were excluded from disposition and if sufficient safeguards were placed on the uses that could be made of the lands so disposed. These are my interpretations of the retentionists' position under a scenario not yet played out; they would almost certainly disavow such a position, for bargaining purposes alone if for no other reason. Until a specific proposal has been made that seems likely to be approved, no one can know what position would be accepted.

I find it noteworthy that the retentionists state their case in words, with an almost total absence of numbers, and with an almost complete disregard of costs. The issue of who gains from federal land ownership and who pays the costs is rarely raised in retentionist literature. No mention is made of the fact that the national forests run an annual cash deficit of nearly $1 billion, and that the Forest Service plans that such deficits will continue more or less indefinitely. The BLM does proportionately as poorly on its grazing operations, but its very large revenues from mineral leasing overwhelm its deficits from grazing management.

Who pays these costs, and what do they get in return? It has been estimated that as much as half of all federal taxes are paid from the New York metropolitan region, in part because so many corporations are headquartered there and because it is a major port for imports. What do the residents of this region gain for the nearly $500 million they contribute annually to the management of the national forests, all of which are remote from this metropolis? Would the governor of New York state, the mayor of New York City, other appropriate local officials, and the various activist groups in the metropolis choose to spend this sum of money in this way, had they any real choice in the matter? Supporters of the Forest Service and BLM often bemoan the fact that the general electorate of the United States does not understand the value and the nature of these lands; perhaps such supporters should be thankful that most voters are so ill-informed, for if they really appreciated what these federal lands cost and how little they benefited from them, opposition to federal appropriations for management of these lands might be a great deal more forceful than it now is.

Even the most dedicated retentionists would agree that serious questions now exist for the federal lands and that policy issues are likely to persist and to grow more serious in the next few decades. Chapter 1 offers a general classification of federal land policy issues which I think represents the past and will fit the future. While retentionists would probably phrase the federal land policy issues differently, I believe that as a group they could accept my list as a reasonable one. I argue that the retentionists' specific federal land policy issues will fit into my general classification.

Thus, as I understand it, they believe that continued retention in federal ownership of all present federal lands is essential, but that, as a policy position, it alone is an inadequate measure—other features of federal land policy are important also.

Notes

1. Joseph J. Malone, *Pine Trees and Politics: The Naval Stores and Forest Policy in Colonial New England, 1691–1775* (New York, Arno Press, 1979).

2. Clarence P. Gould, *The Land System of Maryland, 1720–1765* (New York, Arno Press, 1979).

3. Charles J. Bayard, *The Development of Public Land Policy, 1783–1820, With Special Reference to Indiana* (New York, Arno Press, 1979).

4. Samuel T. Dana, *Forest and Range Policy: Its Development in the United States* (1 ed., New York, McGraw–Hill, 1956). The first edition is much superior to the second edition on this point.

5. Henry Clepper, *Professional Forestry in the United States* (Baltimore, Md., Johns Hopkins University Press for Resources for the Future, 1971).

6. Roy M. Robbins, *Our Landed Heritage: The Public Domain, 1776–1936* (Princeton, N.J., Princeton University Press, 1942). The first and second editions are identical on this subject.

7. Paul W. Gates, *History of Public Land Law Development* (Washington, D.C., Government Printing Office, November 1968) p. 478.

8. Dana, *Forest and Range Policy,* pp. 126–130.

9. S. A. D. Puter, *Looters of the Public Domain* (Portland, Ore., Portland Printing House, 1908).

10. Gates, *History of Public Land Law,* p. 488.

11. John Ise, *The United States Forest Policy* (New Haven, Conn., Yale University Press, 1924) p. 61.

12. Gifford Pinchot, *Breaking New Ground* (New York, Harcourt, Brace, 1947) p. 82.

13. Glen O. Robinson, *The Forest Service—A Study in Public Land Management* (Baltimore, Md., Johns Hopkins University Press for Resources for the Future, 1975) pp. 4–5.

14. William Voigt, Jr., *Public Grazing Lands: Use and Misuse by Industry and Government* (New Brunswick, N. J., Rutgers University Press, 1976) p. ix.

15. George Perkins Marsh, *Man and Nature; or Physical Geography as Modified by Human Action* (New York, Charles Scribner, 1865). A modern version is available: David Lowenthal, ed., *The Earth As Modified By Man's Action* (Cambridge, Mass., Harvard University Press, 1965).

16. Robbins, *Our Landed Heritage,* p. 314.

17. Richard G. Lillard, *The Great Forest* (New York, Alfred A. Knopf, 1947).

18. Samuel P. Hays, *Conservation and the Gospel of Efficiency: The Progressive Conservation Movement, 1890–1920* (Cambridge, Mass., Harvard University Press, 1959) p. 27.

19. *A National Plan for American Forestry,* originally published as Senate Document no. 12, 73 Cong., 1 sess., *Letter* from the Secretary of Agriculture Transmitting in Response to S. Res. 175 (Seventy-second Congress) the Report of the Forest Service of the Agriculture Department on the Forest Problem of the United States (Washington, D.C., Government Printing Office, 1933); republished verbatim by the Arno Press, New York, in 1979.

20. Hays, *Conservation,* p. 50.

21. Robbins, *Our Landed Heritage,* p. 251.

22. *The Western Range,* originally published as Senate Document no. 199, 74 Cong., 2 sess., *Letter* from the Secretary of Agriculture Transmitting in Response to S. Res. 289 a Report on the Western Range—A Great But Neglected Natural Resource (Washington, D.C., Government Printing Office, 1936); republished verbatim by the Arno Press, New York, 1979.

23. This material is discussed and additional references are found in Henry C. and Anne Dewees Taylor, *The Story of Agricultural Economics in the United States, 1840–1932—Men–Services–Ideas* (Ames, Iowa State College Press, 1952), see especially chap. 13.

24. Dana, *Forest and Range Policy,* pp. 191–194.

25. Hays, *Conservation,* see especially chap. VII.

26. John Ise, *Our National Park Policy: A Critical History* (Baltimore, Md., Johns Hopkins University Press for Resources for the Future, 1961) p. 20.

27. Dana, *Forest and Range Policy*, see pp. 115–117; also see Hays, *Conservation*, p. 72.

28. Hays, ibid., especially chap. VII, VIII, and IX. See also Pinchot, *Breaking New Ground*, especially sect. 41–53.

29. Pinchot, ibid., p. 261.

30. Aldo Leopold, "The Wilderness and Its Place in Forest Recreation Policy," *Journal of Forestry* vol. 19 (1921); and also Leopold, "Wilderness as a Form of Land Use," *Journal of Land and Public Utility Economics* (October 1925).

31. Hays, *Conservation*, especially chap. VII.

32. Henry Clepper, personal communication, August 1982.

33. M. M. Kelso, "Current Issues in Federal Land Management in the Western United States," *Journal of Farm Economics* vol. 29, no. 4, pt. II (1947).

34. Ayers Brinser, "Standards and Techniques of Evaluating Economic Choices in Environmental Resource Development," in F. Fraser Darling and John P. Milton, eds., *Future Environments of North America: Transformation of a Continent* (Garden City, N.Y., The Natural History Press, 1966).

35. Ise, *Our National Park Policy*.

36. William E. Shands and Robert G. Healy, *The Lands Nobody Wanted* (Washington, D.C., The Conservation Foundation, 1977).

37. *Environmental Law* vol. 8, no. 2 (Winter) 1978. A publication of the Lewis and Clark Law School–Northwestern School of Law, this issue reports a Symposium on Federal Lands Forest Policy.

38. *Arizona Law Review* vol. 21, no. 2 (1979), reports a Symposium on The Federal Land Policy and Management Act of 1976.

39. John V. Krutilla, "Conservation Reconsidered," *American Economic Review* (September) 1967. This is also RFF Reprint 67. See also John V. Krutilla and Anthony C. Fisher, *The Economics of Natural Environments: Studies in the Valuation of Commodity and Amenity Resources* (Baltimore, Md., Johns Hopkins University Press for Resources for the Future, 1975).

40. The words of Henry David Thoreau are quoted by Sigurd F. Olson, "The Spiritual Aspects of Wilderness," in David Brower, ed., *Wilderness—America's Living Heritage* (San Francisco, Sierra Club, 1961).

41. Howard Zahniser, "Wilderness Forever," in Brower, ibid.

42. Linda H. Graber, *Wilderness as Sacred Space*, Eighth in the Monograph Series (Washington, D.C., Association of American Geographers, 1976).

43. Joseph L. Sax, "For Sale: A Sign of the Times on the Public Domain," a paper prepared for a Resources for the Future National Workshop on Rethinking the Federal Lands, held in Portland, Ore., September 1982.

44. Talbot Page, *Conservation and Economic Efficiency—An Approach to Materials Policy* (Baltimore, Md., Johns Hopkins University Press for Resources for the Future, 1977) p. 9.

45. Ibid., p. 8.

5

The Federal Lands—The Disposers' Case

In this chapter I will present the case for the disposers, who would choose to transfer most of the federal lands to private ownership. As in chapter 4, I will be a self-appointed advocate, striving to present forcefully and effectively a position which I do not necessarily hold.

The disposers, like the retentionists, argue in favor of their position as well as criticizing their opponents' case. In this chapter, I will first offer the positive case for disposal and proceed from that to a criticism of the retentionists' position. The positive case for disposal proceeds in a stepwise fashion: the general case for private property and private initiative; the application of these ideas to the land; and, finally, the application of such ideas to the land now federally owned.

The General Case for Private Property and Individual Enterprise

Over the years, numerous economists (and others) have argued the advantages of private property and of individual enterprise for economic activities of all kinds. More than 200 years ago, Adam Smith published his famous *Wealth of Nations*, in which he argued at length about the productivity and general desirability of private property and individual economic enterprise. He was rebelling against the widespread mercantilist philosophy of the day which sought, through government action and detailed supervision of private action,

149

to direct the national economy in desired directions. The mercantilists were particularly concerned with the balance of trade, especially with the necessity of having a net inflow of gold, silver, and other money, which required a net outflow of goods. Smith argued persuasively that most of the mercantilist actions were counterproductive to their own ends.

Smith was followed by a succession of other outstanding British economists—Mill, Marshall, Pigou, and others—who developed Smith's ideas more fully, made them more precise, often gave them mathematical expression, and, in general, refined and developed concepts relating to private property and to individual economic enterprise. During the same decades, various European economists—Pareto and Walras, particularly—also developed economic theory substantially from the base Smith had laid.

The United States in more modern times has seen many economists who have proceeded in the tradition of these Classical and Neoclassical economists, for example, Hayek, Friedman, Samuelson, Baumol, and others. Most of these writers defended or proclaimed the virtues of private property and individual economic initiative, not merely because they could demonstrate its economic efficiency, but for philosophical reasons as well. There is no need to summarize the immense volume of modern economic literature on this general subject. One can simply say that a thoroughly respectable professional case has been made for private property and individual economic enterprise.

Most writers will acknowledge that no economy in the world today is wholly private—that government everywhere plays a larger or smaller role in the national economic life. Some would regard this as necessary, others would accept it as an undesirable fact. Most writers would agree that in the world today the economy of the United States is about as free of governmental regulation, interference, and control as is the economy of any country. Some would go further to point out that the United States is the world's richest country (even though on a per capita basis we have yielded first place to some smaller, often oil-rich, countries), and others would go still further and assert that the combination of relative freedom and great national wealth was not a coincidence but rather a cause-and-effect situation.

These general economists typically considered land as one factor in production, along with capital, labor, and entrepreneurship, but did not focus on land. Other economists did, as noted below. Virtually none of these general economists was aware of the existence of vast areas of publicly owned land in the United States, and for the most part they paid scant attention to the problems and opportunities of land.

The Economic Case for Private Property and Individual Enterprise

Though a full review of economic literature seems unnecessary in this book, a very brief and rather general summary of the content of much of that literature may provide a starting point for this chapter.

One spends one's income as one chooses, given individual wants and desires, until the satisfaction or pleasure from the last dollar spent for each kind of good or service brings the same amount of satisfaction or pleasure. With income limited in relation to wants, choices must be made among various goods and services in order to buy the combination which gives the greatest satisfaction within one's means. The expenditure of money cannot be shifted from one use to another without in some degree diminishing total satisfactions and pleasures. When all consumers follow this principle in open and competitive markets, they establish a system of prices for consumer goods and services; and these prices then become basic data for the individual consumer, to guide future choices in making expenditures.

A generally similar or analogous situation exists for producers of every good and service. Each producer buys or uses inputs of every kind, until for the last dollar of expenditure the gain is equal in every use. This applies alike to purchase or rental of capital, purchase or use of owned natural resources, hire of labor or use of one's own labor, and to entrepreneurial input. On this basis, not a dollar of expenditure can be shifted from one input to another without diminishing in some degree the return to the enterprise as a whole. If each kind of input is available at the going price, without limitation as to quantity, then resources will be used to the point of maximum net return and cannot be withheld or added without loss of income. When producers as a group follow these principles in open and competitive markets, they establish a system of prices for the inputs and outputs; and these prices then become data to guide the individual decisions.

At the producer level, this process necessarily includes some inputed prices for labor, capital, resources, or entrepreneurship owned by the decision maker. The possibility of disposing of some of these inputs always establishes a floor price for each. The imputed value cannot be less than the price if the good or service is disposed of, and may be greater.

At both the consumer and producer levels, this process involves a balancing of present gains against estimated future ones. One does not eat the pie today if one will want it more tomorrow, and one does not use up today a resource input if one estimates its production value will be greater tomorrow. There are obviously uncertainties about the future. Partly because of the element of uncertainty and partly because a satisfaction or reward today is valued more highly than one tomorrow, all else being equal, future gains and future costs are always discounted to arrive at a present value figure.

These decision systems enlist the intellectual and professional powers of millions of consumers and producers. In a society like that of the United States, where everyone is literate and most people are highly educated, and are likely to be widely traveled and experienced, there is an enormous reservoir of knowledge, ingenuity, and resourcefulness. The individual may make a mistake in some consumption or production decision, but that individual bears the cost; and the individual who makes wise decisions gains the benefits thereof. Although the individual may make mistakes, the collective judgment of all individuals is likely to be very sound. A private market can never go totally astray as can happen in an economy planned by a dictator or a central planning organization. The collective pursuit of private gain secures the broad public good in a way that no direct pursuit of the public good by a central authority could ever do. This is the "unseen hand" noted by earlier economists.

Even the most dedicated advocate of private enterprise will concede some role for a central government—national defense, preservation of law and order, establishment and maintenance of a system of courts wherein disputes among individuals may be argued, measures to ensure the performance and enforcement of contracts, and the like. Many, perhaps most, private enterprise advocates in the United States would also concede to the federal government a major role in transportation and communication—roads and highways, airports and air safety control, laws under which private firms can provide telephone and television services, a postal system, and the like. Nonetheless, some would dissent even on some of these, for example, the postal service. Most private enterprise advocates would also concede a role to government for the establishment and enforcement of a system of weights and measures, and for at least some of the nation's basic research programs. But the really dedicated would deny a role for federal or other governmental ownership of land beyond the minimum necessary for the performance of these accepted governmental functions.

Even the most dedicated advocate of private property will acknowledge that in practice the system does not work perfectly. There is often a serious lack of knowledge on the part of both consumers and producers, who sometimes make decisions which, if they had been better informed, would not have been made. There is always a cost factor in getting more information, including a cost measured in time, and there are always costs involved in changes and adjustments. Some consumers and producers therefore may decide to stick with whatever they have, as being slightly, but only slightly, less than ideal and with adjustment costs not worth the effort. Moreover, monopoly, monopsony, oligopoly, oligopsony, collusion, and fraud exist in the real world, so that the individual choice mechanism is not allowed to work as smoothly and as perfectly as theory predicts. Nevertheless, despite these flaws in the mechanism, the private choice process works better than does collective decision making. Public ownership of the factors of production, including land, and public management of the production process is no cure for the admitted deficiencies in private ownership.

Economics applied specifically to land

All economists give some attention to land, but some economists have made land the center of their concern and of their analysis. Approximately contemporaneous with Adam Smith was David Ricardo, whose development of the concept of rent still dominates this part of economics. Since the turn of the century, several notable American economists have paid major attention to land—Richard T. Ely, Henry C. Taylor, George Wehrwein, and others for rural land use, and Homer Hoyt and many others for urban land uses. Raleigh Barlowe has very well described the content of modern land economics:

> Land economics deals with the economic relationship between man and land. Much of its emphasis is on the application of strictly economic principles to land resources. But it also involves the workings of many other factors which affect our social conduct concerning the development and use of the natural and man-made resources people control through their possesssion of certain portions of the earth's surface.
> The broad scope of land economics makes it a subject of interest to many groups. It has particular significance for economists, geographers, planners, political scientists, real estate operators, and many others who work with land resource problems.[1]

Barlowe cites many other authors and surveys much of the professional literature up until 1958. Barlowe and those he cites deal with any type of land for any use; but, in general, they dwell only incidentally with the public lands, public domain, national forests, national parks, and the rest of the federally owned land. Most of them would, I think, argue that their general analysis would apply equally to public as well as to private land; but I think most of them would agree that the economics of the market place have to be modified or supplemented by other considerations in the politics of public management.

Land economists as a group have considered numerous aspects of land use. One group of considerations is strictly economic—amounts of other inputs into productive processes, production functions from land and associated inputs, intensive and extensive margins of operation, marginal value product, and the like. Another group of considerations may be described as institutional—land tenure, property rights, credit, taxation, and the like. The literature on land economics describes such institutions and analyzes the economic consequences of various institutions. For instance, literature exists on farm tenancy, including the most desirable terms for farmland leases (a literature which will be drawn on in chapter 6). Some, perhaps most, land economists would agree that institutions may be invented or modified by innovative thought. Indeed, much of current farm, residential, and other financial arrangements have been devised in the past by such innovative thinking.

Land economics applied to the federal lands

There has been some application of land economics to the problems and opportunities of federal land management. Until fairly recently, however, there was comparatively little such professional writing, and much of it was descriptive rather than analytical. During the last two decades of the nineteenth century and the first decade of the twentieth century, when the reservation process for federal lands was in full swing, economics entered hardly at all. Pinchot and other advocates of permanent federal land retention were innocent of economics; if economic considerations had been brought to their attention, they probably would have swept them aside, asserting that federal land reservation and retention were socially desirable and that precise calculations of economic costs and benefits were irrelevant. As far as I have ever been able to learn, no professional economist paid any attention to the federal land reservation process of this period. In fact, few American economists had attained much professional stature by this period in history. Richard T. Ely was beginning his career as a land economist but focused his attention elsewhere. The Forest Reserve Act of 1891, and the executive actions taken under it, stopped the process of disposal of federal lands for the areas included in the reserves; and had it not been for those withdrawals, the process would have continued rapidly despite laws whose terms were unsuited to such disposals. But economists did not play a major role in these essentially political decisions.

Likewise, when the Taylor Grazing Act was passed in 1934, further wholesale disposal of public domain ceased. Had it not been for that act, disposal would have continued until today—again, despite laws unsuited to the disposal process—and the public domain would have been greatly reduced. Far more and far abler land economists existed in 1934 than in 1891, but generally, they did not play a major role in passage of the act. L. C. Gray and other agricultural economists had been arguing for the closing of the public domain for several years, but my judgment is that their voices were not the major forces behind the act.[2]

In the years from 1934 until the early 1970s, land economists wrote at times about federal lands but, in general, without questioning the social wisdom of retaining these lands in federal ownership. I regard my earlier book written during this period, *Uncle Sam's Acres*, as being more descriptive of the policy issues than it is analytical.[3] Foss and Calef wrote explicitly about the administration of the federal lands; but since neither is an economist, the focus of their analysis is not economics, nor have they explicitly considered whether the federal land in the grazing districts should remain in federal ownership or should be disposed of.[4] As I noted in chapter 4, Kelso considered multiple-use management of federal lands, but he did not consider the issue of their retention or disposal.[5]

Much of this lack of explicit consideration of retention versus disposal of federal lands during these decades stemmed from a general feeling that the policy issues had been settled. If federal land ownership was going to continue, why argue whether it was wise or unwise?

This disregard has changed in very recent years, as Baden, Stroup, Hanke, and Tullock have come on the scene.[6]

Stroup graphically has stated the general case for private land ownership, which he applies to the federal lands as well:

. . . The resourcefulness of profit-seeking entrepreneurs is continually underrated. . . . Market failures clearly do exist, and many of them are important. Nearly all of these stem from the fact that easily enforced and transferable property rights to the resource in question are held *in common* [Stroup's italics] or do not exist. Grizzly bears and blue whales are in danger precisely because, unlike exotic animals on Texas game ranches, they are unowned. To take this as a signal to automatically make all property rights communal is simply absurd. . . .

> Probably the gravest error . . . is the asumption that short-sightedness
> will dominate in market situations, relative to government. A strong,
> logical arguement can be made that precisely the reverse is true. . . . In
> the market, one's charitable instincts toward the future are reinforced
> by market incentives and signals. Not so in government, where only
> charitable instincts help future generations.
> Who will own a piece of land? The high bidder (or the owner who
> rejects the high bid) values the property most. That is, it is the person
> or group who places the highest estimate on what the present discounted
> value of *all future services* [Stroup's italics] from that land will be.[7]

Baden, in addition to presenting the case for the disposal of federal
forest and grazing lands, has argued that wilderness areas might also
be privately owned and managed,[8] and at the same conference Hanke,
spoke particularly to the privatization of the federal grazing lands.[9]
Tullock argues for the sale of all of what he calls "the national
domain," by which he apparently means all the land administered by
the Forest Service and BLM, but apparently not the national parks
and wildlife refuges.[10] His analysis is unique in its explicit linkage of
the sale of such land with the retirement of the national debt. Despite
some uncertainties, he concludes that sale of these lands, if pushed
vigorously but not so precipitously as to force down land prices,
would produce enough revenue to substantially lower the federal
debt.

The writings and speeches of these men and others are important
in themselves, but they are more important as indications of a new
public interest in the whole matter of the optimum amount of public
land ownership. It will be recalled from chapter 1 that the first of
the federal land policy issues I raised was how much land the federal
government should acquire, and that the second issue was how much
of the federal land should be disposed of. For several decades debate
on these two policy issues was at a very low level, but in the past few
years that debate has become active again.

Summary of the disposers' case

The policy position taken by those advocating disposal of the
present federal lands to the private sector is based on the considerations listed below:

- Private ownership and management of natural resources generally is efficient, not wasteful, and would be for the land now
  federally owned. According to those advocating disposal, in the
  attainment of efficiency there exists no substitute for the private

profit motive. Many private landowners possess the expertise and are resourceful and alert to opportunity in ways that no bureaucracy could ever hope to achieve. The gap in efficiency between private and public ownership-management is great— too great for the costs of inefficiency to be borne by the general public.

- Private ownership and management leads to a careful balancing of benefits and costs, say the disposers. This balancing extends to the present-future relationships of cost and benefit; the private owner is alert to the real, as contrasted to the merely asserted, values of the future. The private owner-manager will reject unproductive uses and methods of management, whereas a bureaucracy will be under political and other pressures to make economically inefficient decisions. Avoidance of error is as important as choice of wise action.

- Advocates also argue that if any use of any tract of land produces real—as contrasted with imaginary—values from any land use, then the private owner will be alert to produce those values. He will balance the values created by one use of land against the values that might be created by a different use of the same land, and choose that use which maximized the net values. His decisions would not necessarily be all or nothing; if there were genuine net gains from multiple-use management, he would be alert to obtain them.

- When individuals each maximize their net gains from the use of their land, then the total social net product has also been maximized, assert the disposers. The individual, pursuing his own ends in the use of his land, at the same time produces the maximum gain for the whole society.

The Disposers' Case Against Retention

Some of the disposers' case against federal land retention is ideological and some is specific to the federal lands. Indeed, many Americans believe that the role the federal government plays in their lives has expanded too much and should be reduced. "Get the Government Off Our Backs," a slogan of the 1980 elections, appealed to many voters. There is no need in this book to explore the subject further; every informed person is aware that such an attitude exists currently.

It carries over into the matter of federal land ownership: People ask, Why should the federal government own so much land, or why should it own specific tracts?[11] Many advocates, uninformed about U.S. land history, seem to think that extensive federal land ownership is a comparatively recent phenomenon. But even those most dedicated to continued federal land ownership generally will agree that it is hard to make a case for federal ownership of many tracts. Sax is an exception, as noted in chapter 4, in that he argues for the retention of *all* lands currently under federal ownership.[12]

The disposers claim that federal land ownership is not only wasteful but unduly costly. In part, because all government operations lack the spur of personal profit and personal gain, all too often, they contend, it is easier to follow an inefficient or costly process than it is to expend the necessary effort and to incur the necessary costs to improve operations. They point out that every governmental activity is under constant bureaucratic pressure to expand the scope of that activity and to make the processes more formal and more ritualistic. As a consequence, federal bureaucrats are inevitably exposed to political pressures that lead them to make inefficient decisions. According to the disposers, federal land-managing agencies may be relatively efficient, as federal agencies go, nevertheless the inefficiencies of the federal government are so great and so pervasive that no agency can be truly efficient in natural resource management.

The costs and inefficiencies of federal land ownership may have been tolerable for custodial management of the land and resources, when the demands for these resources and the costs of their management were not, in any case, very great. But now that the demands for these resources have risen so much, and for so many kinds of uses, and the value of the federal lands has increased so much, the capacity of government to manage intensively is simply too inadequate to be tolerated. Advocates of disposal point out that the greater costs of federal management are bad enough, but the government's failure to secure the maximum efficiency of output of these lands is far more serious.

A number of studies have explored these inefficiencies and attempted to place monetary values of the costs so involved. Hirshleifer, in 1974, developed the analysis and data to show that the Forest Service management of timber production and harvest on the national forests was economically irrational.[13] And in 1976, I developed additional analysis and more data, which reached the same general conclusion.[14] I showed that the national forests operated at a small cash deficit in 1974; but when all outputs and all costs (including noncash as well as cash) are included, there is a large deficit. In particular, I concluded that too much money was spent in management of sites with low inherent productivity while, at the same time, full advantage was not taken of the productive capacity of the most productive sites. Lenard also supports the same general conclusion.[15] Analysts at the Wilderness Society repeatedly have documented that many of the timber sales from the national forests cost more to make than they bring in returns, as well as often having serious adverse environmental consequences.[16]

A strong attack on the inefficient administration of the grazing on the public domain and of the grazing districts by the Department of the Interior has been made by Libecap,[17] who concludes, "Bureaucratically assigned use rights . . . encourage inefficient land use for a number of reasons: First, since bureaucrats do not hold property rights to the range resource, they do not bear the costs nor receive the benefits of their actions and, hence, can ignore market signals and engage in socially wasteful land management policies. Second, the rights assigned are inherently tenuous since bureaucrats reallocate rangeland and readjust use privileges to meet changing political conditions." Libecap feels that destruction of vegetation on the virgin range has been greatly exaggerated, but nevertheless there has been a serious deterioration of that plant cover, primarily because the land has been publicly rather than privately owned. He develops the "commons" argument in some detail, pointing out that each user felt compelled to overgraze the range because, if he did not, someone else would. Libecap strongly recommends disposal of the federal grazing lands to the ranchers who are using them, believing that the latter will manage to restore the land's productivity and to make more efficient use of these natural resources.

Where the costs of federal land management are much greater than the values produced—as they are on extensive areas of land presently in federal ownership—the Treasury would be better off if the lands were simply given away. This does not mean that such lands should not be sold for all they will bring, if or when a program of large-scale federal land disposal is decided upon. But it does mean that the costs of continued federal land management must be considered in any economic analysis of the comparative advantages of federal and of private ownership.

One of the most serious inefficiencies arises from delays in federal action. The necessity for review and approval at several stages or levels in an agency takes time. The requirement for providing the opportunity for public comment (see chapter 8) also unavoidably delays the procedure. The possibility of a private lawsuit or of adverse congressional review also leads the federal bureaucrat to be excessively cautious—when in doubt, stall, or at least ask for approval from a higher level in the agency. Such foot-dragging is costly in terms of time and money.

These higher costs of federal land ownership and management are inherent in the federal governmental processes, but if they could somehow miraculously be cured, so that the federal management of any land was as efficient as private management of the same land, this would not really bolster the case for federal land ownership in the eyes of the disposers. If federal land ownership just might, in some instances, achieve the efficiency of private ownership, why not go to private ownership?

According to advocates of disposal, any talk of a longer planning horizon for federal than for private land is sheer bunk. The government of the United States will endure for centuries, if not forever. But the operators of this governmental system change—two years is the term for the congressman, four years for the president, and six years for the senator. The president appoints, with Senate confirmation in some cases, secretaries, under secretaries, and assistant secretaries of the departments, and many agency heads and board or commission members as well. Each of these persons in the legislative and executive branches enlists a corps of assistants, sometimes numbered in the hundreds. All of these people have the same time horizon as their political mentors. The career civil servants necessarily must accept, or pretend to accept, the policy guidance of this host of political figures, while at the same time often holding on to ideologies at variance with the official position. Thus, it is claimed, they perform with an inevitable resistance or foot-dragging—while waiting out the present crop of political leaders—to continue as best they can their own conceptions of how federal lands and resources should be managed. This situation may be inevitable in a democracy, but it is wholly incompatible with efficient natural resource management; it is particularly deficient in its adoption and adherence to programs of long-range resource management. One cynical federal policymaker said not long ago, anything over ninety days is long range.

The 1974 Forest and Rangeland Renewable Resource Planning Act (RPA), the 1976 National Forest Management Act (NFMA), and the 1976 Federal Land Policy Management Act (FLPMA) include efforts to divorce annual appropriations for federal land management from the urgencies of the current budget, but so far none has been successful and it may be that none ever will be. Presidents and budget specialists strongly oppose such efforts. The large private firm, whether forest industry, oil and gas producer, mining company, or rancher is better able to make investments in land for long-range productivity than is the federal land-managing agency; the limitations on private investment funds are less than the limitations in appropriation of federal investment funds. The larger private firms and the conservation organizations are better able to make and to follow long-range resource management programs than are the federal agencies, subject as the latter are to the winds of annual budgets and the whims of changing political leadership.

The so-called public participation in federal land management, required by recent legislation, does not truly involve the general public, claim the disposers. Rather, in practice it proves to be a means whereby various specialized interests can pressure the federal agencies into courses of action which the interest group would never think of taking with its own land and its own capital. Public participation is seen by its critics to be, to a large extent, a farce. Many of the groups seeking to influence federal land management are irresponsible in the sense that they know they will not have to bear the costs of what they urge upon the agencies, so that the sky becomes the limit. According to the disposers, the private landowner has to bear the consequences of his decisions for land management, but the special interest group does not have to accept the costs or the consequences of its proposals.

The alleged values of many nonmarket outputs of the federal lands, such as wilderness and wildlife, are grossly exaggerated, say advocates of disposal. In large part this is because those alleging such values do not have to pay directly for the values obtained; their share of the costs of providing these services, paid by their income taxes, is miniscule and unrelated to the values obtained. Thus, they can exaggerate to their heart's content or to their imagination's limit without assuming any real costs in return. If there are any genuine values from any use of land now federally owned, a private owner would be eager to secure such values and to manage the land to produce the values in question. And he or she would do so more efficiently than the federal agency.

The so-called option demand is a fraud, conceived by intellectuals to present their pet theories and, claim the disposers, is wholly nonoperative in practice. In particular, to designate it as a "demand" is misleading, for the demand by nonusers of a resource is never put to the test of their willingness to pay. Many persons, when interviewed, will say that they support the use of public funds to provide a wilderness area that they never plan to use; but they do not have to put their money where their mouth is. Let the proponent of option demand canvass average persons on the street or in their homes, asking each to donate $5, $10, or $25 annually to the maintenance costs or to offset the forgone income from a remote wilderness area, and he or she will quickly learn how empty is the concept of option demand. The disposers claim that even the device of checking off a box on the annual income tax return, if it involved an extra charge upon the taxpayer, would produce virtually no revenue. Option demand is easy to assert, but nearly impossible to use to produce revenue, and has no useful place, its critics contend, in real-world management of federal land.

The argument that special concern must be given to intergenerational demands and needs for natural resources is, at best, an exaggeration. There are so many uncertainties in resource supply, resource demand, and resource technology that postponing use of resources today on the basis of some estimated or assumed future condition is simply unwise, claim advocates of disposal. Had the intergenerational argument been applied to American natural resource use in the past, the present economic development of this country would not have occurred. One might make considerable sacrifices today, only to discover in the next generation that they were unnecessary. Indeed, say its critics, even if one accepts the intergenerational argument, there is no reason to think that the welfare of the next generations will be better protected by actions of public agencies than would arise through the operations of the private market. The present price of every natural resource reflects the consensus of judgment as to its future value and the private market will preserve real, as contrasted with asserted, future values.

In this regard, Wolf says, "There is no reason to believe, given the record, that the public use and administration of land in America is more exemplary than its treatment by the private sector. At times, land has been systematically abused as a resource and systematically exploited as a commodity by both."[18]

The Disposers' Case in Perspective

As I did in chapter 4, I will step out of the role of an advocate of disposal and return to my role as the impartial researcher, to offer a few comments about the disposers' case from the perspective of this book as a whole.

There are undoubtedly great advantages to an economic system based on private property and on relatively unhindered private initiative in economic affairs. Though many persons are critical of what they consider excessive governmental roles in this country, yet we have one of the freest economies in the world today. One who has lived, as I have, in other countries where the governmental role is much greater, or as one who was an adult during World War II, when rationing and other governmental controls were in effect that are not found today in this country, or in normal peacetime, I can personally attest to the great advantages of our relatively free economic system. When there are governmental controls, much private initiative is directed at circumventing the control; when there is relative freedom, that same initiative can be directed in more productive directions. So I, at least, and most informed persons, accept much of the argument of the private enterprisers.

But do they exaggerate, especially as they direct their analysis to natural resources? The free enterprise advocates—the disposers, as far as federal land is concerned—do not really explain the serious resource depletion and the undesirable social conditions associated with wholesale federal land disposal, which were noted in chapter 4. Can one really argue that all the undesirable effects were caused by ignorance? Can one reasonably argue that all such ignorance was in the past, that none exists today, and that none will exist in the future? In short, have the disposers quoted earlier in this chapter somewhat overstated their case?

Likewise, anyone who has been a member of the federal land-managing bureaucracy, as I have, or one who has observed rather closely the operations of the federal land-managing agencies, as I have, can agree with much of the criticism regarding inefficiency in the federal agencies. There are indeed many pressures that result in inefficiency, and few rewards for efficiency. But, again, do the disposers exaggerate? Libecap, for instance, blames the condition of the federal range on the fact that its use is governed by the federal agencies; but the 1936 Forest Service report on the range held that the condition of the privately owned range was little better than that of the public domain range.[19] The agency may have exaggerated the extent of the depletion on each but perhaps not more on one than on the other. Perhaps factors other than ownership were largely responsible for the results Libecap notes for the federal range.

The disposers make their case primarily on the basis of comparative efficiency. It may also be pointed out that the case for greater private than public efficency is more asserted that it has proved to be. I, too, value efficiency in resource use highly, and I think that for many operations private actions are more efficient than public ones. But we should recognize that many advocates of federal land ownership base their argument on equity—on who gets the benefits—not on how great or how costly those benefits are. Regardless of one's personal position on the equity issue, one must recognize that this is one basis for support for federal land ownership and thus one should face this point in arguing for disposal. The disposers, for the most part, do not.

If there were effective national agreement that most or all of the present federal lands should be disposed of to private ownership, or even to state ownership, it is doubtful that this could be accomplished quickly or that it could be accomplished totally, regardless of time. The history of land disposal during the many decades it was national policy suggests this conclusion. Ignoring all other factors, disposal would take time—time almost surely measured in decades, not time measured in a few months. During this lengthy period, federal agency management of the dwindling federal lands would continue.

Even if there were a strong national sentiment to dispose of the federal lands, many important policy issues would still remain. To whom should disposals be made? Industrial firms, conservation organizations, others? Would the federal agencies decide which lands they chose to dispose of, or would applicants make the choices? The results would differ greatly, I would judge, depending on who was doing the choosing. How would the particular purchasers of the lands be chosen? By competitive bid, by some type of qualifying characteristics, by lottery, or by some other method? On what terms would the lands be transferred? By competitive bid, by appraisal (and who would be the appraiser?), by terms spelled out in law, or by other means? Would the terms be the same for all applicants? For instance, could the Wilderness Society buy a tract of virgin timber for less than what a forest industry firm must pay? How much pressure would be exerted for rapid disposal? Would the disposal program seek to get rid of all the federal lands, or only some of them? If the latter, which will be disposed of and which retained, and who makes the choices? Should the disposal be unconditional, in the sense that the new private owner would have no obligations about land use other than those he would face on any other privately owned land, or should there be some restriction on use running with the title to the land? One could think of other questions, many of which have been raised previously during the long disposal process, and the record of that period hardly inspires confidence in a new disposal process.

It is apparent, at least to me, that a general decision to dispose of federal lands might establish a national policy but that its implementation would involve many difficult questions. One can be fairly sure that a disposal policy, if accepted by a majority of the Congress, by the president, and by a majority of the public, would leave many persons unconvinced of the wisdom of such a policy. Further, one can be fairly sure that many of its opponents would offer all manner of criticisms and objections, including probably lawsuits to the way the disposal process was carried out. Thus, any idea that a law authorizing disposal of federal lands would be the last word, even if it tried to answer the policy issues raised above and would dispose of all political struggles over the federal land, is clearly a mirage.

The Sagebrush Rebellion

The Sagebrush Rebellion has attracted a considerable amount of publicity in newspapers as well as in the publications of the conservationists or retentionists. Nevada and Arizona had tried in 1970 to persuade the Public Land Law Review Commission to include a recommendation giving each of them a new grant of 6 million acres of land.[20] The commission rejected this proposal. In 1975 the Nevada legislature passed a resolution proposing new grants of federal land to the state; in 1978 the Western Conference of the Council of State Governments agreed to form a coalition on public lands; and, about the same time the Nevada legislature enacted a statute laying claim to the public domain within the state. Other western states have followed Nevada's example, more or less, while still others have rejected similar moves.

Several factors seem responsible for the Sagebrush Rebellion. The long decline in authorized grazing use of the national forests and the grazing districts (see figure 3-1), affecting many old families in every western state, occurred at the same time that many other uses of the federal lands which more favorably affected persons from outside of the state than they benefited residents (for example, recreation and oil development) were on the increase. The 1974 court decision, in *NRDC* v. *Morton,* which forced the BLM to furnish Environmental Impact Statements on grazing operations that had existed for many decades, was a considerable further factor—it convinced many Westerners that decisions over the use of "their" federal lands were made predominantly in the East. The 1976 Federal Land Policy and Management Act (see chapter 2)—with its policy declaration that federal land should remain permanently in federal ownership—was still a further factor.

The Sagebrush Rebellion has been primarily an expression of discontent with federal land ownership and management and, as such, is significant. Regional discontent with actions or legislation of the federal government are an old story, as was noted in chapter 1. The positive proposals of the Sagebrush Rebellion have been unclear. Bills have been introduced in the Congress which would turn over some or all of the federal lands in each state to the ownership of that state, without cost to the state. Some of the bills have included restrictions on what the states might do with the land, others have not; and the states in various ways have described their intended management of the lands. If all the federal lands are turned over to the states, the state will incur a deficit in managing the lands, if something like the present system of management is followed. This is true even if the state receives all the mineral leasing revenues, and more so if it does not.

> The Sagebrush Rebellion is a political phenomenon—a marriage of diverse interests in political and economic struggle for control of federal lands and the subsidy those lands provide. . . . The legal underpinnings of the Sagebrush Rebellion are tenuous at best, but they are apparently perceived by proponents as having some value. . . . The victory sought by the Sagebrush Rebellion will not be realized in the courts. If realized at all, it will be in Congress or in the federal agencies charged with administering the public lands. . . . Most probably the Reagan administration will soften, if not silence, the angry voices in the West at least for a time. The push for a new approach to federal land management likewise may abate. But the nature of the federal system and the extent of federal landholdings in the West make it probable that intergovernmental conflict will reemerge to become another version of the current edition of the conflict—the Sagebrush Rebellion.[21]

In the terms of chapters 4 and 5, the Sagebrush Rebellion as it originally appeared is a substitution—that is, neither a retention nor yet a full disposal. If a successful Sagebrush Rebellion transferred some or all of the federal lands out of federal ownership and management and into state ownership and management, this would be a substitution of one kind of public land management for another. Many of the advocates of the Sagebrush Rebellion have emphasized that the states will not dispose of much or any of the land to private ownership; rather, the state will manage the lands for the same purposes as now, with many of the same personnel working now for the state rather than for the federal agencies, but all of the management to be more efficient and more responsive to the needs of citizens. On the other hand, Hanke, in September 1981, argued for privatization of the federal lands and the States Right Coordinating Council adopted a resolution endorsing that position in December 1981.[22] If this were done, it would be a disposal.

A cynic might argue that, as originally formulated, the Sagebrush Rebellion proposed to incorporate the worst of both worlds—to continue public ownership rather than to promote private ownership, but to substitute states for federal agencies, with a substantial loss in expertise and in objective management for broad social purposes. Baden, who has repeatedly urged sale of the federal lands, says, "We have consistently argued that a transfer to the states would represent the worst of both worlds."[23] He is a disposer, not a substituter. Some other advocates of the Rebellion might dispute his position.

As Mollison suggests, most of the steam has gone out of the Sagebrush Rebellion, and its promise or its threat—depending on how you view its possibilities—seems remote in 1983. But if wholly new policies for the federal land are to be considered, as I will discuss in chapter 6, then state ownership, or state management of some functions on federal land, are surely alternatives to be considered seriously.

Notes

1. Raleigh Barlowe, *Land Resource Economics—The Political Economy of Rural and Urban Land Resource Use* (Englewood Cliffs, N.J., Prentice–Hall, 1958) p. vii.

2. National Resources Board, *A Report on National Planning and Public Works in Relation to Natural Resources and Including Land Use and Water and Mineral Resources, with Findings and Recommendations* (Washington, D.C., Government Printing Office, 1934). This report has a long section on land, prepared under the direction of L. C. Gray, which summarizes better than any other single document the thinking of land economists about land problems generally and about the federal lands at that time.

3. Marion Clawson, *Uncle Sam's Acres* (New York, Dodd, Mead, 1951).

4. Phillip Foss, *Politics and Grass* (Seattle, University of Washington Press, 1960); and Wesley Calef, *Private Grazing and Public Lands* (Chicago, Ill., University of Chicago Press, 1960).

5. M. M. Kelso, "Current Issues in Federal Land Management in the Western United States," *Journal of Farm Economics* vol. 24, no. 4, pt. II (1947).

6. John Baden and Richard Stroup, eds., *Bureaucracy vs. Environment: The Environmental Costs of Bureaucratic Governance* (Ann Arbor, University of Michigan Press, 1981); John Baden, Richard Stroup, and Walter Thurman, "Myths, Admonitions and Rationality: The American Indian as a Resource Manager," *Economic Inquiry* vol. 19, no. 1; G. Hardin and John Baden, eds., *Managing the Commons* (San Francisco, Calif., W. H. Freeman, 1977); Richard Stroup, "Some Land Use Concepts: Comments," Discussion presented at The Conference on Forest Land Management, Resources for the Future, Washington, D.C., March 1981; and Richard Stroup and John Baden, "Property Rights and Natural Resource Management," *Literature of Liberty* vol. 2, no. 4 (1979). The Hardin–Baden book includes five chapters by Baden or by Baden and coauthors. Steven Hanke is a professor of economics at The Johns Hopkins University who served on the staff of the Council of Economic Advisers in 1981 and 1982; while there, speaking in a private rather than an official capacity, he made a number of speeches in Washington, D.C., and elsewhere, arguing the case for privatization of the public lands. While those speeches attracted considerable attention in the press and in trade publications interested in such matters, there is no professional journal article or book to be found in any library. Gordon Tullock, director of the Center for the Study of Public Choice, Virginia Polytechnic Institute and State University, gave a presentation at the Workshop on Rethinking the Federal Lands, sponsored by RFF, that was held in Portland, Oregon, in September 1982.

7. Stroup, "Some Land Use Concepts."

8. John Baden, "Private Rights and Public Lands," Paper presented at a conference sponsored by the Heritage Foundation, held in Washington, D.C., June 21, 1982.

9. Steven Hanke, remarks during a radio interview on "Privatizing Public Lands: The Ecological and Economic Case for Private Ownership of Federal Lands," as reported in the *Manhattan Report on Economic Policy,* Manhattan Institute for Policy Research, New York, vol. II, no. 3 (May) 1982.

10. Tullock, presentation at Workshop on Rethinking the Federal Lands.

11. *Time* Magazine, August 23, 1982, had an excellent story, with striking illustrations, of tracts of land the federal government owns but which now has been marked for disposal.

12. Joseph L. Sax, "The Claim for Retention of the Federal Lands," Paper presented at Workshop on Rethinking the Federal Lands, sponsored by RFF, that was held in Portland Oregon, in September 1982.

13. J. Hirshleifer, "Sustained Yield Versus Capital Theory," Paper presented at a symposium on The Economics of Sustained Yield Forestry, sponsored by the University of Washington, Seattle, in November 1974.

14. Marion Clawson, "The National Forests—A Great National Asset Is Poorly Managed and Unproductive," *Science* vol. 191, no. 4228 (Feb. 20, 1976). Also available as RFF Reprint 127; Marion Clawson, *The Economics of National Forest Management* (Washington, D.C., Resources for the Future, June 1976).

15. Thomas M. Lenard, "Wasting Our National Forests," *Regulation* (July–August) 1981.

16. Tom Barlow has made a number of statements, some published, others not, on this point; and Gloria Helfand has made a detailed analysis of timber sales from national forests, to document this point.

17. Gary D. Libecap, *Locking Up the Range—Federal Land Controls and Grazing* (San Francisco, Pacific Institute for Public Policy Research, 1981) pp. 100–101.

18. Peter Wolf, *Land in America: Its Value, Use and Control* (New York, Pantheon, 1981) p. 536.

19. U.S. Congress. House. *Letters* from the Secretary of Agriculture Transmitting in Response to Senate Resolution No. 289, a report on The Western Range—A Great but Neglected Natural Resource, 74th Cong. 2nd sess., 1936. Republished verbatim in *The Western Range* (New York, Arno Press, 1979).

20. For an excellent, lucid, informative, and well-balanced discussion of the Sagebrush Rebellion, see Richard M. Mollison, "The Sagebrush Rebellion: Its Causes and Effects," *Environmental Comment*, Urban Land Institute, Washington, D.C. (June) 1981.

21. Ibid., p. 11.

22. Personal communication from Steve H. Hanke, March 1, 1982. At the time, Hanke was a staff economist of the Council of Economic Advisers, on leave from The Johns Hopkins University, but he spoke as an individual, not as a representative of the council.

23. Personal communication from John Baden, Political Economy Research Center, Bozeman, Montana, February 1982.

6

The Federal Lands—
Future Directions

In view of the intensity of use and rising economic value, which have increased the importance of the lands now federally owned; the increasing dissatisfaction with the present management of these lands, expressed by many user groups and others; and the emerging debate over their continued federal ownership, it is time to consider the major alternatives for the use of these lands in the future.

Clearly, there are now, as in the past, major uncertainties about the future. I will attempt neither to forecast what is most likely to happen nor to project what might happen under any assumptions. Rather, I would like to outline alternatives in a way that will help various interest groups reach policy decisions and formulate the kind of compromises on public affairs which are essential. I have tried to present each alternative in an unbiased manner. It is true that I outline one alternative more fully than others, but this is because I think that such detail is necessary for full understanding, and not because I necessarily advocate that alternative.

An assumption basic to this chapter is that methods of managing these lands, which differ from the methods presently employed by the agencies, will be seriously considered and perhaps adopted. It might reasonably be argued that in the future the most likely system

Author's Note: This chapter draws heavily on a paper I presented to the RFF-sponsored Workshop "Rethinking the Federal Lands," held in Portland, Oregon, in September 1982; and also on a paper I presented to the U.S Senate Subcommittee on Public Lands and Reserved Water, of the Committee on Energy and Natural Resources, *Workshop on Public Land Acquisition and Alternatives,* June 1982.

of management will be a continuance of the present one because the bureaucratic and other obstacles to change will be too great to overcome. Without expressing a judgment on this point, alternatives may well be considered.

Management Versus Income

In considering alternatives for the federal lands, it is essential to distinguish between who has the power to manage lands and who receives the income from their use. As it now stands, the Forest Service and the Bureau of Land Management (BLM) have the legal power and responsibility to manage the federal lands under their respective jurisdictions, subject to pertinent laws. They are required by their major legislation to consult with the public (a matter which will be considered in more detail in chapter 8), but the ultimate responsibility for management decisions rests with the agencies. However, states and counties receive a major part of the revenues resulting from private use of the onshore public land. A multiplicity of complex relationships govern the division of gross income between the federal government and the states and counties (table 6-1). Table 6-1 shows that under some current laws 100 percent of revenues go to the federal Treasury with none going to states; while in other cases, the Lower 48 States and counties receive as much as 75 percent of the receipts, and Alaska as much as 90 percent. Table 6-1 shows the disposition of receipts from BLM operations only; receipts from the National Forest System are distributed according to their own laws, but in general 25 percent of such receipts go to the states and counties. For the big revenue producers of onshore land uses— mineral leases and timber sales—the states and counties receive large percentages of the receipts which amount to very significant sums. In fiscal 1979 the states and counties received nearly $330 million from the BLM, and in fiscal 1980 they received $280 million from the Forest Service.[1] The states and counties do not yet, however, share in the revenues from mineral leasing on the Outer Continental Shelf; and, as was shown in table 3-2, more than two-thirds of the BLM's receipts come from this source. The diverse laws relating to revenue sharing can be explained only on the basis of historical developments—the rationale for such diverse arrangements is difficult to determine.

But the data in table 6-1 raise a number of questions: If the management (that is, those empowered to make decisions) were in

TABLE 6-1. LEGAL ALLOCATION OF BLM RECEIPTS, FOR FISCAL YEAR 1980

Source of receipts	Authority	Disposition of gross receipts (%)				
		States and counties	General fund	Indian trust	Recla- mation	Range improve- ment[1]
Mineral leases and permits						
Public domain (except Alaska)	30 U.S.C. 191 and 286	50.0	10.0		40.0	
Public domain (Alaska)						
Oil and gas royalties	30 U.S.C. 191 as amended by Acts of July 7, 1958, and December 18, 1971 (Statehood Act and Alaska Native Claims Act)	75.6	8.4	[2]16.0		
All other mineral rents and bonuses		88.2	9.8	[2]2.0		
Oregon and California grant lands	43 U.S.C. 1181f	[3]75.0	25.0			
Coos Bay Wagon Road grant lands	Act of May 24, 1939	[4]75.0	25.0			
Choctaw Chickasaw lands, Oklahoma	58 Stat. 484–5			100.0		
LU lands (Section 3)	Executive Orders 10046, 10234, 10322; Comptroller General Decisions 102563	12.5	37.5			50.0
LU lands (Section 15)	Executive Orders 10046, 10234, 10322; Comptroller General Decisions 102563	50.0				50.0
LU lands (Section 3)	Executive Orders 10787, 10890; Solicitor's Opinion March 11, 1971	25.0	25.0			50.0
LU lands (Section 15)	Executive Orders 10787, 10890; Solicitor's Opinion March 11, 1971	25.0	25.0			50.0

Category	Authority					
Shoshone-Arapahoe tribes, Wyoming	25 U.S.C. 611					
Naval petroleum and oil shale reserves	30 U.S.C. 191			100.0		
Acquired lands	30 U.S.C. 355	(5)	100.0			
Outer Continental Shelf	43 U.S.C. 1338		100.0			
State selected lands (except Alaska)	Act of September 14, 1960	90.0	10.0			
South half of Red River	Act of June 12, 1926	37.5		62.5		
Land and materials (including timber)						
Oregon and California grant lands	43 U.S.C. 1181f	[3]75.0	25.0			
Coos Bay Wagon Road grant lands	Act of May 24, 1939	[3]75.0	25.0			
Public domain and acquired lands in "Reclamation States"6	43 U.S.C. 391 and 30 U.S.C. 601	[7]4.0	20.0		76.0	
Public domain and acquired lands outside "Reclamation States"6						
LU lands	31 U.S.C. 711 (17)	[7]4.0	96.0			
	Executive Orders 10046, 10234, 10322; Comptroller General Decisions 102563; Executive Orders 10787, 10890; Solicitor's Opinion March 11, 1971					
Reclamation lands (within Reclamation project)	43 U.S.C. 394 and Cooperative Agreement March 8, 1972	(8)			[9]100.0	
Townsites in Reclamation project	34 Stat. 116; 20 C.G. 365	5.0			[10]95.0	
Naval petroleum and oil shale reserves	10 U.S.C. 7431		100.0			
Grazing (Section 3)						
Public domain lands (grazing fee only)	43 U.S.C. 315i	12.5	37.5			50.0
LU lands (grazing fee only)	Executive Orders 10046, 10234, 10322; Comptroller General Decisions 102563	12.5	37.5			50.0

TABLE 6-1 (*continued*).

Source of receipts	Authority	Disposition of gross receipts (%)				
		States and counties	General fund	Indian trust	Recla-mation	Range improve-ment[1]
LU lands (grazing fee only)	Executive Orders 10787, 10890, Solicitor's Opinion March 11, 1971	25.0	25.0			50.0
Public domain and LU lands (range improvement fee)	Same as public domain and LU lands					100.0
Public domain (Alaska)	43 U.S.C. 316h	(11)				
Reclamation lands (within Reclamation project)	43 U.S.C. 394 and Cooperative Agreement March 8, 1972				100.0	
Leased lands	43 U.S.C. 315m-4		[12]100.0			
Grazing (Section 15)						
Public domain lands (total receipts)[6]	43 U.S.C. 315i	50.0				50.0
LU lands (total receipts)	Executive Orders 10046, 10234, 10322; Comptroller General Decisions 102563	50.0				50.0

	Legal authority			
LU lands (total grazing receipts)	Executive Orders 10787, 10890, Solicitor's Opinion March 11, 1971	25.0	25.0	50.0
O & C and Coos Bay Wagon Road grant lands	43 U.S.C. 1181d	75.0	25.0	
Reclamation lands (within Reclamation project)	43 U.S.C. 394 and Cooperative Agreement March 8, 1972		100.0	
Other receipts	Not specifically designated by law	100.0	100.0	

Source: Department of the Interior, Bureau of Land Management, *Public Land Statistics* (Washington, D.C., Government Printing Office, 1980) pp. 172–173.

[1] Range improvement fees are appropriated and available to Bureau of Land Management for the construction, purchase, or maintenance of range improvements.

[2] Amount to Indian trust is for Alaska Native Fund. Commitment fulfilled as of March 31, 1980.

[3] One-third of this amount is to reimburse Treasury for moneys appropriated for access roads and reforestation; counties receive at least 50% of gross receipts.

[4] Amount to counties is available for payment upon receipt of tax bills. Any surplus after each 10-year period is paid into the general fund.

[5] Distributed by the Agency having jurisdiction over the lands in the same manner as prescribed for other receipts from the same lands.

[6] Includes revenues from Reclamation lands outside Reclamation projects per Cooperative Agreement of March 8, 1972.

[7] Payment to States represents 5 percent of net receipts.

[8] Distribution same as LU mineral leases and permits.

[9] Payment to Reclamation Fund is made after deducting costs of sale, or 10% of revenue, whichever is less, to reimburse Bureau of Land Management for sale expenses.

[10] Bureau of Reclamation may pay costs of sale from Reclamation Fund, or expenses may be paid and deducted by Bureau of Land Management prior to transfer to Reclamation Fund.

[11] Payment to State represents receipts in excess of the actual cost of administration of the grazing program in Alaska.

[12] Appropriated and available to Bureau of Land Management for the leasing of lands for grazing purposes.

other hands, would the total receipts be different—would the pie be larger? Is the present division of receipts between levels of government fair and equitable? What justification can be advanced for the great variations in arrangements for division of the income? Is any change in present arrangements (other than more generous treatment of states and counties) politically feasible? Could states and counties who now get half or more of the total revenues manage the lands to receive any larger net revenue from these lands if ownership were transferred to them? Their present share is part of total or gross receipts; they do not share in management costs; hence their share of net receipts is much greater, sometimes more than 100 percent. Would states and counties prefer to manage some or all of the federal lands within their boundaries, even if their net revenues were no larger or perhaps even smaller?

There are two other aspects of the management-revenue relationships which merit brief discussion: the relationship between receipts and income taxes, and that between federal investments and the revenues received by states and counties. The federal government receives royalties from mineral leasing (and, in some cases, from rentals of mineral lands) and revenues from timber sales and grazing leases; to a large degree these are a sharing of gross revenue derived from the respective private productive enterprises. The federal government, and most states, levy income taxes—a sharing of net income from the private businesses. There is a relationship, albeit not a simple one, between royalties paid and income taxes paid by any lessee. A lessee is required to pay royalty even when its net income, and hence its income taxes, are zero. On the other hand, net income and income taxes might be high while royalties and other fees might be moderate. The income taxes depend upon the profitability of the private business—and upon the ingenuity of its tax consultant. If royalty rates were raised but all other factors remained the same, the net income of lessees would be lowered and, as a result, less income tax would be paid. Income to the federal Treasury from royalties, net of income tax deductions, is always less than gross royalties, by varying amounts and percentages. Indeed, there may be sound policy reasons for raising royalty rates, sale prices, or other charges, but the net gain in federal revenues will always be less than the amount of the increased charges.

When the federal government invests in the building and maintenance of roads, tree planting, range reseeding, and other improvements, presumably one consideration is that such activities will increase the income from the federal lands. But if so, that income must then be shared with the states and counties. Thus, although the federal government has borne all the costs of the investment, it gains only a part of the increased income. In fact, the states and counties have had a share of the federal appropriation for the investment. It is true that state and local governments levy a charge upon the net income of the private investor on his land, but a share of net income is quite different than a share of gross income. Numerous proposals have been made, and some devices for recoupment of investment costs on federal lands have been established before revenue sharing with states and counties has been calculated. On the O & C lands in Oregon, road costs and some other investment items are deducted from the 75 percent of the gross revenues that the counties would otherwise receive. Formerly, under the Knutson–Vandenburg Act, deposits on timber sales on national forests were used to make certain investments—such as restoration of the site after harvest—before receipts were divided with the states and counties. A road-building allowance in stumpage prices operates in somewhat the same way. However, a sharing of gross revenues with states and counties is a major obstacle to economic rationality in investments on federal lands.

In this chapter, our primary concern will be with the management of the land. The matter of distribution of gross or net income is not considered directly, although implicit in the management of the resources is some idea of income distribution. For instance, if the present federal lands were sold to private individuals, these persons would collect the income and be subject to real estate taxes levied by local governments. Or, if the lands were transferred to the states, then they would collect the income, unless some royalty interest were retained by the federal government. However, different arrangements for the sharing of income are possible, as is shown in the sections which follow.

Future Alternatives for the Federal Lands

If growing dissatisfaction with present federal public land management should lead to major changes, then it seems desirable to consider possible alternatives. As I contemplate the history of federal lands and speculate on their future, five broad alternatives for management of these lands seem possible:

1. All or most of the present federal lands could be retained in federal ownership, but strenuous efforts would have to be made

to improve their management, including more concern for the costs and returns from such ownership and management.

2. All, or a large part, of the present federal lands could be turned over to the states, free or on payment of some price, and the further management or disposal of the lands could be determined by the states.

3. All, or a major part, of the present federal lands could be sold to private individuals, corporations, and groups or associations, under terms which would be established in the enabling legislation.

4. All, or large parts, of the present federal land area could be transferred to public or mixed public-private corporations, to be managed as decided upon by those corporations, but according to terms of enabling legislation.

5. Long-term leasing of federal lands could be greatly extended, not only for mineral leasing as at present, but also for other commercial uses and for conservation or preservation purposes as well.

No one of these alternatives is likely to be the whole answer to the problems and dissatisfactions now apparent; a mixture of changes along the various lines seems more probable. However, the proportions of the mixture might vary greatly. Most of the land could remain in federal ownership as at present, with only modest disposals to states and to private parties and none at all to public or mixed public-private corporations. Or, at the other extreme, most could be sold to private parties with only a little remaining in federal ownership; or any one of many other intermediate admixtures might be put into effect. In the sections which follow, each major alternative is discussed as if it were the only line of change, but, in fact, each might be combined in almost any proportions with the others—except, of course, that the total federal land area sets an overall constraint on the acres of land allocated to any combination of management systems.

Each of these alternatives, if less than the total federal land area, would be selective in character. The disposal and reservation processes of the past were highly selective. Given their knowledge of land capabilities and the economic circumstances of the time, the private parties and federal agencies chose the best land available to them. This selectivity will continue, again within the limits of land availability, of knowledge, and of competition from other management systems. Even if all—or essentially all—the present federal land remains in federal ownership, the management practices applied to it will be selective—that is, more intense on some types of land and less so on others. Given the freedom to make choices, all individuals or groups or entities choosing federal land for purchase or lease will choose that best suited to their needs, rejecting other parcels.

Each of these major alternatives for future federal land management requires time to work out fully. An effort for more efficiency in federal land management will take some years to be effective. Any efforts at sale or lease disposal will take some years to be carried out. Even if there were a national commitment to sell all the federal lands and no significant opposition to such a policy—a most unlikely set of circumstances—it would take years for the disposal process to run its full course. The disposal process of the nineteenth century was rapid; nonetheless, much land remained in federal ownership over many decades. Thus, regardless of which major alternative or combination of alternatives may be chosen, and regardless of the vigor with which such lines of action are pushed, a considerable amount of land presently in federal ownership will remain under federal agency management for a good many years.

Retention with greatly improved management

Applying a standard of economic management. There are many ways in which the management of the federal lands might be "improved." But it is to be noted that specific measures constituting improvement to some users or some interest groups might not be considered improvements by others. The basic issue is to provide the maximum benefits on a long-term or continuing basis, in relation to the costs incurred. The ideal is that for every sensible management unit within the federal estate, the values or benefits, including those not customarily marketed for cash, should have the most favorable possible relationship to the costs—including interest or other capital charges on the value of the property—and that the resultant management system should preserve the productive capacity of the area indefinitely. If this ideal were achieved, then no management practice could be added, subtracted, or altered, without lowering the net total benefits. Application of this standard does not require an allocation of costs to each resulting output, nor does it require an exactly even flow each year, if annual changes in inventory values are properly evaluated.

Some aspects of this standard may require elaboration. The values or benefits should be the full value to society of the output. For those goods or services from the federal land which are sold for cash—timber, grazing, oil and gas, coal, and other minerals—the present prices are often below full competitive market prices and the best estimates of the latter are a more accurate reflection of value to society than are the prices actually received. For those goods and services from the federal land not ordinarily sold for cash—water, wildlife, recreation, wilderness, aesthetic values—some estimate of value produced by the provision of these goods and services is necessary, despite the difficulties of doing so. Even those persons who profess scorn for economic analysis choose some outputs, or some amounts of some outputs, more than they do others. Hence, they have made an economic comparison, however crude it may be. In some cases, ordinal as contrasted with cardinal values may be sufficient—a judgment that one value exceeds another without having specific numbers on either.

The costs must include all cash costs of management, of course, and also give some consideration to alternatives forgone by one method or objective of management as contrasted with another. If one system of management includes road building and another does not, then, obviously, total costs will be different. One need not make a cost allocation to each output to contrast the net results of one combination of outputs with another. The costs also must include reasonable charges for the use of the capital involved. The federal lands today have great capital value, as was noted earlier in chapter 3, and economic management of these lands must return reasonable interest on these capital values. Indeed, one of the best expressions of values forgone by any management program is the interest on the capital value that would exist from some other system of management.

This standard of economic management should be applied to sensible management units, as evident on the ground. Within a national forest or grazing district, one management regime might be followed on sites with high productivity, whether that productivity was for timber growing, wilderness, or any other purpose, and a different plan followed for sites of lower productivity. But there obviously would be spatial limits to such management differentiation—a tract 100 acres or more might be set aside for different management when a 1-acre tract could not reasonably be separated from the surrounding area, for instance.

Last, this standard of economic management should be applied with due consideration to cost of analysis, to ease of understanding by the users and by agency personnel, and to time required for the management analysis. If uncertainties about the future are great, a rough estimate may actually be as accurate as a finely tuned one.

Management planning involves costs, and those costs should be included in the management analysis.

There is good reason to believe that the Congress, in passing the 1974 Renewable Resources Planning Act (RPA), the 1976 National Forest Management Act (NFMA), and the 1976 Federal Land Policy and Management Act, was striving generally, but not precisely, for just the kind of standards described above.[2] This is the general conclusion of Krutilla and Haigh:

> The Renewable Resource Planning Act as amended by the National Forest Management Act can be looked upon as the culmination of a process of changing the congressional directives to the Forest Service from those consistent with an initial custodial role, to those of management—and indeed ultimately an intensive management—role in the administration of the national forests. . . . There appears to be little doubt that Congress has charged the Forest Service to manage the forest and rangeland resources in an economically efficient manner. . . . The objective of such a management approach is to maximize the aggregate value of the beneficial uses of all the resource services of the national forests without impairing the long-run productivity of the land.[3]

Improved planning.   All three acts stressed planning, including the objectives and methods to be used in the planning process, especially public involvement and interdisciplinary teams. The 1974 RPA, in language retained in the 1976 NFMA, requires, according to Section 4 (1): "Specific identification of Program outputs, results anticipated, and benefits associated with investments in such a manner that the anticipated costs can be directly compared with the total related benefits and direct and indirect returns to the Federal Government."

The 1976 NFMA, in Section 6 (g)(3)(A), added some sentences regarding planning: "Insure consideration of the economic and environmental aspects of various systems of renewable resource management, including the related systems of silviculture and protection of forest resources, to provide for outdoor recreation (including wilderness), range, timber, watershed, wildlife and fish." Other language in the act is consistent with these quoted objectives, while still other sections impose some constraints or restrictions on attainment of full economic management of the federal lands. It is true, however, that the 1974 and 1976 Acts, while requiring such balancing of costs and benefits in the *planning process,* only implicitly (not explicitly) require that the resultant plans shall govern the actual administrative actions of the Forest Service.

Each of these three acts embodied many compromises among interest groups, including the Forest Service and BLM as one interest group. The acts as passed were acceptable to interest groups only because of their vague language; more precise language would almost surely have been rejected by some group. In the end, of course, the acts will mean what the courts say they will mean, and this may take some time. It is sobering to remember that the full meaning of the 1897 Act providing (among other things) for timber sales from national forests was given final meaning by the courts only in 1974. It can be argued that each act would have been more statesmanlike and more constructive if passed many years earlier—the 1974 Renewable Resources Act in 1960 instead of the Multiple Use and Mangement Act of 1960, the Federal Land Policy and Management Act of 1976 instead of the Taylor Grazing Act of 1934, and so on. Congress normally responds only to an evident problem and a clearly felt need, and this is one of the most serious limitations of land management by a federal agency.

Establishment of a capital account. If the general direction toward more economic land management (in the broadest sense of that term) is accepted, consideration could well be directed to the establishment of a capital account for the federal lands, in total, or by agencies, or by administrative units (such as each national forest). Under present procedures, annual appropriations for capital investment are lumped with appropriations for current operations in a manner that no private firm would be allowed by law to follow. Investments which should be productive over a considerable period of years are treated as if they were operating costs for the year in which the expenditures were made. No account is taken, on the income side, for the increase in capital values that arise from these investments or from management practices. For instance, the national forests have been adding to their total volume of standing timber and at the same time have been slowly liquidating the largest of the old-growth timber. Is the value of all the standing timber rising or declining? No answer is readily available from agency records. The situation is enormously complicated by the very great changes in prices of timber which have taken place in recent years. Some of the investments are not from appropriated funds; that is, on national forests many roads are built by timber purchasers, and although the allowances for the cost of these roads are included in the timber sale provisions, they do not show up as cash receipts in the revenue account.

Many of those advocating a capital account for the federal lands assume that the purpose and the result would be to encourage larger appropriations for operations because elimination of capital investment from annual appropriations would make a more favorable contrast of appropriations with receipts. This is a totally erroneous view. A true capital account would require annual depreciation charges on past investments and annual interest charges on the value of the resources. An estimated annual interest charge on the value of the capital embodied in timber and other separable resources is a reasonable charge against the continued management of the federal lands. If such capital costs were included, the federal lands as a whole and the national forests in particular would make a much worse economic or financial showing than they do when current appropriations, including capital investments, are compared with current cash receipts.[4] Nevertheless, an accurate economic analysis of the management of federal lands must include separate treatment of investments, of changing capital values, and of reasonable charges for the use of the capital included.

Imposition of fees and charges. Another management practice facilitating more economic management of the federal lands would be the imposition of fees and charges for some services, notably outdoor recreation, with the resulting revenues plowed back into better management of the areas from which the revenue originated. There has been considerable public and political opposition to the imposition of charges and fees for outdoor recreation on federal lands, although such fees and charges produce a substantial part of the costs of administration on state and local parks.[5] One reason for the acceptance of such charges for the use of the public parks but not for the federal lands is that the revenues produced by the public parks have been used to provide necessary services. An earmarking of revenues for specific expenditure is often opposed by political scientists and public administrators on the grounds that this frees the agencies from legislative oversight through the appropriation process. This objection can be met easily by the device of depositing the revenues in a special account from which the accumulated revenue can be appropriated each year by legislative action, thus reassuring users that their money is being used for their benefit, giving administrators reasonable assurance of funds, and giving legislators periodic opportunity to control appropriations. If the cost of services provided bore some reasonable relationship to revenues generated, effective control on the level and suitability of federal management would be provided.

A more drastic step would be to limit cash operating expenditures on each unit of federal land (national forest, grazing district, and others) to total cash revenues collected from that area. While this would not meet the test of economic feasibility—since it would be only cash costs and cash revenues, rather than total costs and total revenues—it would make it difficult, if not impossible, to sell timber or other management practices at a loss. It also would reduce sharply the present intensity of management on less-productive federal areas but permit, if not encourage, more intensive management on more productive sites. If strictly applied, a requirement such as this would drastically alter the present situation in which a considerable part of the federal estate is managed at a loss.

Some use of revolving funds or of multiyear budgets for the federal land-managing agencies would provide the agencies with assured funds for longer-term management goals, thus reducing some of the uncertainties arising out of annual budgets. Aside from the political difficulties of getting legislative approval for multiyear budgets or revolving funds, there would be difficulties in anticipating needs for more than a year ahead, of having flexibility to meet disasters or other unusual situations, and of having funds available for meeting new conditions. Longer-term appropriations could reduce inefficiencies arising out of annual appropriations (which often are not made in timely fashion) but do little or nothing about other inefficiencies.

Little progress has been made toward more efficient management of the federal lands since passage of the 1974 and 1976 Acts, and what has been accomplished has come slowly.[6] The planning is under way, but thus far it has been a slow and costly process and has had dubious results. As a result of this planning, the appropriations to the Forest Service and to the BLM may have been larger than they otherwise would have been, as some persons in these agencies have argued; but this measure of success is more agreeable to the bureaucracy than to the taxpayer. The large deficits from national forest management have apparently grown, even in real terms. One defense of the 1974 and 1976 Acts is that it is still too soon to judge their results accurately. On the other hand, it may be argued that the goals of greater efficiency in federal land management are simply unrealistic. Perhaps the most accurate judgment in 1983 is that the jury is still out.

Efficiency. Those who advocate continued retention of lands in federal ownership but with a greatly improved efficiency in their management face a substantial dilemma. Unless efficiency is improved, public dissatisfactions with present management will continue to rise, and major changes will be proposed and perhaps effectuated. If greater efficiency is achieved so that federal management becomes as efficient as private management, what is the rationale for continued federal ownership? Why not sell the federal lands to private parties?

Finally, there is serious doubt that federal agencies, subject to the inevitable political pressures that affect public programs, who are caught up in the extensive bureaucratic and administrative web that seemingly unavoidably encompasses federal activities, can ever hope to manage extensive lands and associated resources intensively and economically. Perhaps federal agency management of land was suitable for the custodial era, but it is less suitable or completely unsuitable for the intensive and consultive-confrontational management of the same lands.

If all other alternatives were rejected, the acreage of land in federal ownership would remain essentially unchanged but the relationship of income to costs would be greatly improved. It is not possible to make firm and accurate estimates of the latter for future periods. There is a possibility that the federal lands as a whole could produce a net income above costs, even if mineral revenues were excluded. More probably, costs would be reduced sharply from present levels and income increased somewhat for a more favorable relationship without necessarily producing a net income.

Transfer to the states

A second direction for future management of the lands presently in federal ownership would be to transfer their titles to the states in which they lie, without charging a fee or on payment of specified, but presumably small, sums per acre. The states thereafter would manage the lands. Prior to 1970, Nevada and Idaho had proposed large-scale federal land grants to the Public Land Law Review Commission, but that body rejected their proposal.[7] One version advocated by the Sagebrush Rebels would also turn federal lands to state ownership.[8] The idea of transfer of federal lands to state ownership was voiced by several speakers, including Sen. Steven Symms (R–Idaho), at a conference on "Private Rights and Public Lands," sponsored by the Heritage Foundation and others on June 21, 1982, in Washington, D.C.

Historic perspective. Relations between the federal and state governments on land matters have a long and involved history.[9] There never was any acreage, or at least any significant acreage, of federal lands in the original thirteen colonies, or in the states formed from them (Maine, Vermont, West Virginia, Kentucky, and Tennessee);

or in the states which had been independent countries before their admission to the Union (Texas and Hawaii). The matter of federal land grants to the states was an important political issue in all other states formed out of federal land (or public domain, to use a common term applied to such states), beginning with Ohio in 1802 and continuing across the Mississippi and Missouri basins, the South, and the Rocky Mountain, Intermountain, and Pacific regions, to Alaska (which achieved statehood in 1958).

In general, the following arrangements arose and were followed for each state:

- The Congress insisted and the states, often under protest, accepted a disclaimer by which they relinquished all further claims to federal land. Some of the present advocates of federal land transfer to the states seem to believe that this disclaimer was forced only on the western states, the present-day public land states; in fact, from Ohio onward, every state formed from public domain has been admitted only under such a disclaimer.

- The new states agreed not to interfere with the disposition of the federal lands by the federal government and not to collect taxes on the federal land. Indeed, in some cases they agreed not to collect taxes for a few years after the lands passed from federal to private ownership.

- On admission, the new states were given specific grants of land, in place, particularly for common schools. Each state admitted to the Union prior to 1850 received one section (640 acres) of common school grant per township of thirty-six sections (23,040 acres); after 1850 this was increased to two sections per township and, beginning with Utah in 1896, to four sections per township. Nevada, which had received two sections upon its admittance in 1864, relinquished its grant (of about 4 million acres) and in return received a quantity grant for common schools of 2 million acres, the land to be selected where the state chose. In addition to the common school grants the new states upon admission were given quantity grants, to be selected where they chose, for land grant colleges and other public purposes.

- The new states were given 5 percent of the receipts from disposition of the federal lands within their borders, to be used for roads or other purposes.

- Beyond all this, at varying dates after admission, the states formed from the public domain were given other grants, notably of swamp and overflow lands. There was much fraud in the disposition of these lands, as has been noted in chapter 4. There was also much controversy between states and federal agencies over these grants. The swampland provision was especially important in Florida, where title to more than half of the total land area went to the state under this law. It was also important in Louisiana and Arkansas (each having received more than 7 million acres by this route), in Mississippi, in Michigan, Minnesota, and Wisconsin (where many millions of acres were involved); and also in California, where more than 2 million acres, including the most fertile parts of the Central Valley, were transferred to the state under this law.

Although the forgoing general provisions applied to all states formed from public domain, there were some variations in the exact terms of these general provisions. For example, in some states the common school grants were made to the states, to be administered as the state chose; where in others, the grants were made directly to the local township governments. Or, to use another example, the uses to which the 5 percent of federal revenues from public land disposal could be put varied somewhat from state to state.

The large areas of federal land granted to the states did not satisfy; indeed, those appetites may have been whetted for more. As Gates puts it, "The states were never to accept federal management of the lands and federal reduction of their power with equanimity and were to devote much time to considering plans for reversing the disclaimer provisions in their enabling acts and ordinances they were compelled to accept."[10]

When the public domain states of the Midwest and South were growing rapidly in population and their residents were fast converting federal land to private ownership, it was these states which were eager to change the disclaimer provisions in their enabling legislation. They found that they lacked the political power to make such changes. Today, these same states have nothing to gain from a change in their enabling acts, and there is little interest on their part in such changes. If some effort were made to revise the disclaimer clauses today, the public domain states would be more likely to line up with the older states in opposition to more favorable treatment for the western states. As John Francis of the Brookings Institution has pointed out, the western states are far from unanimity on the issue of federal land transfer to the states.[11]

Gates shows very clearly that the disclaimer provision in the state enabling acts was no barrier to further substantial federal land grants. Most of the swamp and overflow lands and the transportation grants given to the states (see table 2-1) were made after the disclaimer clauses had been imposed on the affected states. If now or in the future there were to be a substantial national consensus for major new federal land grants to the states, the disclaimer clauses in their enabling legislation would offer no barrier to the federal government's making further land grants. This is not to say, of course, that states outside of the West would generally support additional land grants.

How well have the states managed the federal lands granted to them? Gates, providing some sharp commentary, draws on the available record, "The early story of state management of public lands is not a pretty one."[12] Incompetence was mixed with fraud in most states, and money derived from the sale of grant lands was frittered away in many instances. Gates feels that state administration of grant lands has improved greatly in recent years, noting that "gradually an increasing sense of responsibility in public administration and a wider interest in the purposes for which the grants were given contributed to improved management of state lands."[13] Nonetheless, some of the sources he cites do not quite support his optimism. He does point to the very real accomplishments of New Mexico and Washington in retaining much or all of their grant lands and in making them yield substantial revenues for their respective school systems. He winds up on an optimistic note, saying, "In fact, one can say that the newer states have done as well as has the federal government in the management, sale, and leasing of public lands."[14] My own verdict, based on a considerable knowledge of state land administration over the past four decades, would not be so generous, although I do agree that major progress has been made.

Opposition to transfer. Regardless of the terms proposed for the transfer, if a major effort were mounted in the Congress or by any administration to allot additional areas of land to the states, almost certainly there would be major opposition from conservation and other groups in the West as well as elsewhere. Some of that opposition would be based upon fears of the states' incompetence or veniality based on many episodes of the past. Some would fear that the states would be more interested in cash returns and less interested in the preservation of resource productivity for the future, than would the federal agencies. The argument that a state administration would be closer to the users is an argument both for and against a larger state role. The opposition would also question the competence of the states, as compared with the competence of the federal agencies. Some opponents would be likely to say that substituting state for federal administration would be the worst of both worlds: that is, still public land, not private, and state-managed rather than federally managed. Of course, opposition almost surely will arise regarding any future management of the federal lands, including a policy of continuing the present arrangements (without improved efficiency), so that the probability of opposition should not be taken as definitive in arriving at decisions about future management of the lands now in federal ownership. For many western states, assumption of title to present federal lands would worsen the states' revenue-expenditure relationship, hence creating political and other problems in an era of tight budgets.

Disposal to private ownership

A third alternative for future management of the present federal lands administered by the BLM and the Forest Service would be their disposal, by sale or other means, to private individuals, corporations, and groups of all kinds.

History of land transfers. The virtues of private, as contrasted with public, ownership and management of land have been described in chapter 5 and need not be repeated here. There is, of course, a long history of land transfers from federal to private ownership. Over the years, the total land area of the public domain was 1,838 million acres; by 1980, 1,144 million acres, or 63 percent of the total, had been disposed of by one means or another, to some class of private recipients. This was in addition to the grants to states discussed earlier.[15] (See table 2-2 for details.) More than 800 million acres—or 35 percent of the total land area of the nation, or 45 percent of the area ever in the public domain, or 71 percent of all land transferred out of federal ownership—went directly to private ownership. The states sold or gave away to private parties much of the land that had been granted to them.

These figures substantially understate the importance of the past process of transfer of land from federal to private ownership. These transfers took place despite the fact that no legal means existed for the transfer of forested and grazing lands in economically sized units. This occurred particularly in the West, where the minimum size of economically viable ranch and forest enterprises was large. Moreover, they took place despite the substantial withdrawal of land, beginning in 1891, for the forest reserves and for other purposes. And contrary to a generally held belief that large-scale transfers of land *de facto* had come to an end by 1934, when the Taylor Grazing Act was passed and all remaining federal land was withdrawn from disposal to private ownership except upon classification and approval by the Department of the Interior, disposals had continued at a rather rapid pace all through the 1920s and early 1930s. It is true that all or virtually all land capable of cultivated crop agriculture had been homesteaded or otherwise disposed of by 1920, and in many areas much earlier. But total entries for federal land ranged from 3 to 5 million acres annually from 1923 (when the flush of homesteading for crop farming had ended) until 1934.[16] These disposals occurred despite laws particularly unsuited to the kinds of land involved and to the kinds of uses contemplated. But this rate of disposal, if it had continued unchanged for forty or fifty years, would have exhausted the unreserved public domain as it stood in 1934. One can only speculate, of course, as to the considerable acreage that might have been disposed of by now, had the Taylor Grazing Act (or some other legislation cutting off federal land disposal) not been passed. Likewise, had the national forests not been established when they were, substantial parts of them would have gone to private ownership, even under the ill-suited laws then existent.

Those who state that the federal lands—or the lands managed by the BLM and some of the national forests—are the scraps of the public domain and unsuitable for private ownership (the "lands nobody wanted") are implicitly accepting a totally static view of history and economic change. Land on the frontier always had a marginal value; that was one definition of the frontier. As settlement progressed and the economy developed, land which previously had had little or no value came to be more valuable. I have elsewhere described the disposal of the federal lands as a modern miracle of loaves and fishes—the more federal land that was given away, the more valuable became that which was left.[17] The same economic changes which have increased the total value of the federal lands more than twenty-fold since the 1920s (see table 3-4) have equally increased the values of the intermingled private lands and of the remaining federal lands. Railroad grant checkerboard lands in northeastern Nevada, which could have been bought from the railroad land company for $2.50 per acre as late as the end of World War II, are now selling for $50 an acre; and ranchers who earlier hesitated to make investments in grazing land are now convinced that they must own more of the lands on which their livestock graze. If these ranchers had the opportunity to buy the intermingled federal lands on terms and at prices they considered favorable, they would almost surely buy much of this federal land. Similarly, in the interwar years timber processors, who owned little forestland and bought their timber from public or private landowners, preferred to invest their limited capital in plant and equipment. Since World War II, they have actively sought to acquire some or all of the land privately owned from which their timber must come. Many small firms (and some large ones, too) have been consolidated into larger, vertically integrated forest firms in the last three decades. Had there existed a means whereby such firms could have acquired federally owned forestland, it seems clear that many would have done so, and for considerable acreage.

The economic "recession" or "depression" of the early 1980s has severely dampened the commercial demand for the land and its associated natural resources. The speculative bubble which pushed prices upward so fast in the 1970s has burst. Farmland prices are down in important agricultural areas, and net farm income in real terms is back to the level of the 1930s. Ranchers are unable or unwilling to buy large areas of grazing land, and many forest industry firms are seeking to sell their timbered lands and to become processors of timber bought from others. There is gloom in many industries, including the forest industry. The euphoria of the 1970s was un-realistic, but so is the gloom of the early 1980s. The real prices of outputs from land will rise in the future, albeit slowly; the profitability of land management will also rise; and the market for the land and its associated resources will become active and rising again. The timing and the rate of rise are problematical, but I judge that the longer-term outlook is not. If a large acreage of federal lands were actively pushed for sale at any time, it would have a depressing influence on the private land market. The depressing effect of public land sales would be especially great if federal land sales were actively pushed in times of general economic depression. If, as a national policy, the federal lands were sold on any significant scale, it should be done over a period of one to three decades, not during a president's four- or eight-year administration.

The conservation and preservation organizations have generally sought to use their economic and political strength to secure the establishment of national parks, monuments, wilderness areas, and other entities. But some of them also have acquired land by purchase or by gift from other private owners. For example, the Sierra Club and the Wilderness Society have not sought to be landowners, but the Audubon Society and the Nature Conservancy have acquired considerable areas by purchase, gift, or bequest.

Had laws existed by which such organizations could have secured federal land in units and at prices suitable for their use, they, too, might have acquired substantial areas of federal land in the past. Private ownership does, after all, more nearly guarantee security of land use than does any system of management of public lands.

My judgment is that over a considerable period of years substantial acreages of the present federal lands would be bought by ranchers, forest industry firms, mining and oil firms, and conservation groups, if they had the opportunity to do so. Much would depend, of course, on the terms of sale. Price per acre is not the only factor involved. The minimum and the maximum units of purchase, the constraints on future use of the land, the degree to which preference would be given to present users of the federal land or to owners of adjoining private land, and other factors would greatly influence the eagerness with which private parties would seek to buy federal land. Competitive sale is one obvious means of disposal, but so-called competitive sales may not be very competitive if there is only one potential buyer, as the sales of timber from national forests and O & C lands have long since demonstrated.

The Reagan administration through various public statements has announced its intention to sell "unneeded" federal lands and properties and to use the receipts from such sales to reduce the total federal debt. Some of the most valuable unneeded properties are urban or semiurban in character, but the BLM reportedly has identified 4.4 million acres of land that could be auctioned off in the near future.[18] It is estimated that these lands have a cash value of $2.4 billion, or about $550 per acre. This total includes about 590,000 acres lying in and around urban areas, with an estimated value of $1.7 billion, or about $2,900 per acre. The total also includes about 730,000 acres of "agricultural" land with an estimated value of $215 million or about $285 per acre. It is by no means clear that the areas the agency is willing to sell are the lands that potential buyers are most interested in buying. I intuitively judge that both the acreage and value figures are too high, at least for relatively immediate sale, but only experience with an accelerated and active sales program can test these or any other estimates. It should be pointed out, in passing, that the BLM has in effect "sold" much public land, including areas of the Outer Continental Shelf, when it entered into long-term oil and gas leases. While these leases are for periods of years, they remain in effect as long as oil and gas is produced in paying quantities. When a lease finally expires, there is little value remaining, especially in the Outer Continental Shelf areas; and although these leases are for only one use of the land, often that use constitutes by far the greater part of the total value of each tract. Indeed, other uses are less valuable or may not exist at all.

Reducing the federal debt. In the publicity about proposed early sales, much is made of the possibility of reducing the federal debt by use of the sale receipts. This may be good public relations to win over people to the idea of the land sales, but it has limited economic significance. If the BLM is successful in making the projected sales, and if such sales do, in fact, yield the estimated revenue, it only would come to little more than 2 percent of the total federal debt. Moreover, there is no assurance that the total debt will actually be lowered by receipts of this magnitude from federal land sales—the debt responds to many other economic and political factors and any revenues received from land sales, as announced in 1982, may be totally overwhelmed by other events.

My judgment is that the federal lands as a whole have great value and that a substantial private market potentially exists for them; but to realize any significant sums of money, the federal government would have to sell large areas of the most valuable forests and grazing and mineral lands. If debt reduction is a serious objective of federal land disposal, then such disposal must go far beyond any lands considered for sale in recent discussions.

The multipurpose federal lands (that is, those administered by the Forest Service and BLM) have a high value, as the data in table 3-4 show. An appraisal of these lands—no matter how detailed and competently done—is not a complete indicator as to the amount of revenues that could be realized from their sale. The latter would depend on the terms of sale (especially how far concessionary prices were offered to present users) and the speed with which the sales were made. If the sales were pushed rapidly, this would surely push prices down. Realizable receipts over a longer period of time would depend on future inflation and on future changes in property values of all kinds. In my judgment, if reduction of the federal debt were the dominant objective in a program of sales of federal land, this might yield as much as $300 billion, perhaps more, over a decade or two.

The usual statistics show the federal debt at about $1,100 billion. This figure is to a large extent misleading, for a substantial part of this debt is owed by the federal government to itself. Tullock has shown that the net federal debt owed to private parties is more in the order of $700 billion.[19] In view of the many uncertainties in any sale and in these figures particularly, one cannot make a precise estimate of how far sales of federal land, even if pushed to the extreme, could go in reducing the federal debt. I think, however, that active sales of the multiuse lands (excluding national parks, wilderness areas, Indian trust lands, and other areas generally excluded in any talk about selling federal lands) might make a substantial reduction in the net federal debt, over a period of years. To a major extent, this would simply be a rearrangement of the asset portfolio of the American people. That is, at present the average person has substantial capital in the federal lands and also substantial debt; after land sales, both capital value and debt would be lower.

To estimate that active sales of federal lands could be managed to make a significant reduction in the federal debt does not, of course, necessarily argue that such sales would be wise in any sense. The sales alternative does exist, and it is important, but it must be weighed against other alternatives for future management of the lands now federally owned.

It is true, however, that for much federal land—the national forests as a whole and most of the grazing land administered by BLM—the cash costs for current administration are considerably larger than the revenues received from sale of timber, forage, and other products except oil and gas, and from provision of services such as recreation, wildlife, watershed, and wilderness. The federal Treasury, and hence the average taxpayer, would thus be better off in terms of current cash flow if these lands were given away if they cannot be sold. At the least, in any analysis of the economics of proposed sale of particular tracts and areas of federal land, the relationship of current costs to current revenues should be a factor for consideration.

Which lands to sell? If the alternative of selling federal land to private parties were chosen, one important policy issue would be who decides which federal lands are to be sold, assuming some but not all lands are offered for sale. Even if all federal land ultimately were to be offered for sale, who decides which tracts to offer first? If the choice is left to the agencies, they will resist offering the best lands, so that what they offer may not be what potential buyers are most interested in buying. If private parties are given the option of proposing tracts for sale, who decides and how are choices made among rival claimants? There would be innumerable problems in the large-scale transfer of federal lands to private ownership which would have to be resolved in legislation, or by administrative action, or by private actions, or by some combination of these. Past experience and present economic values may show that there exists a substantial potential interest in such transfers but does not offer much in the way of guidance as to how a future disposal program might be best worked out.

Two conclusions do emerge from past experience, however: (1) any system of disposal from federal to private ownership, regardless of how widely accepted, would take considerable time to work out fully; my judgment is that the process at its most rapid rate would be measured in decades rather than in years; and (2) the disposal process would be selective as to the lands involved, however the process might be structured and managed. Some lands would be eagerly sought, but other areas would not be. Prices, whether administratively determined or arising out of competitive sale, would to some extent, but not fully, equalize the attraction of tracts of different capabilities. Much would depend on the concensus as to future costs of land ownership—local real estate taxes in particular. Given the structure of local government and the minimum real estate taxes almost certain to be levied, I do not see why anyone would be interested in buying the least productive federal lands, almost irrespective of their price and of their planned future use. A continuation of federal land ownership for many years and on many areas thus seems inescapable even if rapid and full-scale disposal of federal lands to private ownership were to become the national objective.

Management by public or mixed public-private corporations

A fourth alternative for the future management of the lands now federally owned would be to turn their management over to a federal corporation, corporations, or to mixed public-private corporations.

Public and mixed public-private corporations have been established for various purposes in the United States, but to date none have been established for federal land management. Where the functions to be performed are of a commercial or semicommercial nature, with substantial investments, expenditures, and revenues, and with substantial dealings with a user public which involve payments, a corporate form of organization may be quite appropriate. Some intergovernmental organizations (such as the New York Port Authority), having some attributes of a corporation, are one way of pooling governmental powers from separate units of government, such as states, local governments, or even the federal government. There is no need here to describe and analyze these various corporate or quasi corporate arrangements, except to note that some do exist but not for federal lands.

Because there has been no direct experience with public or public-private corporations in the management of federal lands, it is impossible to draw guidance from past experience. Reliance must be placed on analysis and description of proposals conceived by their proponents, perhaps as modified by the reactions of contemporaries. While such a course is inevitable if anything new is to be developed, there are clearly dangers that some important problem has been underestimated, that some feature will not work as estimated, or that in operation some problems will develop that were unforeseen in the planning process. A particular danger exists when an idealized innovation is being compared with actual operations which have easily observable imperfections. Nevertheless, some proposals have been made and this is one alternative for future federal land management which should be explored.

Structuring a federal land management corporation. In 1957 Held and I outlined the possible structure and functioning of one of the first federal land management corporations ever proposed.[20] Our concern was to secure greater efficiency in federal land management, give greater incentives for efficiency on the part of the land managers, and to allow greater freedom for investing in federal lands when economic circumstances so warranted. As we said:

> From an economic viewpoint, the basic need for federal land management in the future is for a more careful appraisal of expenditures and revenues; for larger appropriations, especially for investment, in order to make the lands fully productive; and for generally less restrictive methods of resource management. At the same time that these basic needs are met, the methods of land administration must preserve the nonmonetary values of the federal lands, and must also be compatible with the American system of government. The administration of these lands must be not only responsible but also responsive to the wishes of the public.[21]

We envisioned one large federal corporation, encompassing all lands managed by the Forest Service, the Bureau of Land Management, the National Park Service, and the Fish and Wildlife Service. We believed that a corporation managed by professional career employees would deal more generously with outdoor recreation, wildlife, and other nonmonetary values than the Congress and the

Executive budget process had dealt with them in recent decades. There was much less concern then over wilderness areas, and we did not explore wilderness designation and management as fully as other aspects of federal land management. At that time, the national parks had suffered a period of serious neglect, and as a result many facilities were sadly run down.

Very little of an explicit nature resulted from our suggestion. In 1958 the Senate Interior and Insular Affairs Committee (as it was then known) made a tentative move toward requiring the federal agencies to provide a consolidated annual investment, income, and expense statement, such as a private corporation normally provides, but this tentative move was never fully followed up and came to naught. Our proposal may have had some influence on later legislation, but this would be difficult to prove. Now, some twenty-five years after making our proposal, I judge it to have been rather naive. The interagency rivalries in such an all-encompassing federal corporation would have been very great. At the time, we gave little consideration to the possibility of substantially different management programs for highly productive and poorly productive lands, though that might have been worked out later. However, we were struggling to describe problems then existent and to suggest major alternatives for dealing with them, and the legislation of 1974 and 1976 clearly was aimed at the same problems.

In 1981 Nelson outlined a program for management of all the federal lands in the future,[22] which is notable for its differentiation of types of land and its expected uses. He envisages only modest changes for the National Park System and for the Wildlife Preserve System. He would transfer large areas of recreation lands of primarily state and local interest to the states but does not specifically say whether by sale or by gift. For the recreation lands of national interest outside the national parks—the wilderness, conservation, and wild and scenic areas, particularly—he would have a Federal Recreation Service assume management. He thinks this might be created from the current Forest Service. He would lease grazing lands "to ranchers for grazing purposes for 50 to 100 years at a time, with the preferential option to renew."[23] He would turn leasable minerals to the states but leave the mining law more or less intact with its administration in the hands of the agency managing the surface resources of each area. This is a very brief and somewhat sketchy review of a carefully thought-out and crafted paper.

Attention should be focused on his proposal for the 40 million acres of national forests and the 2 million acres of O & C lands which he designates as "prime." This is a slightly larger area than what I have classified as "commercial Class A" forest.[24] Whatever the exact acreage may be, we agree that only a part of what the Forest Service statistics show as "commercial forest" has truly economic possibilities for sustained forest management. As Nelson says:

> It is possible that the Forest Service could be transformed to show a much greater capacity for a business-like, efficient approach to timber management. . . . A much greater likelihood of introducing efficient timber management to a limited acreage of high quality timber stands is found in the creation of new timber management corporations. Initially, stock in such corporations could be distributed to match the current distribution of revenues from public timber operations. Local counties thus would receive 25 percent of the stock in timber corporations created from national forest lands, with the remaining 75 percent of the stock going to the Federal government. Federal shares would then be sold gradually over a transition period. At the end of the transition the ultimate objective would be a private timber corporation—although the local counties could of course retain their shares.[25]

Although Nelson speaks of "corporations," he provides no specific statement as to their number or their average acreage. Neither does he provide specific information about the probable length of the transition period or how the federal shares would be sold to private parties. Nor does he discuss in detail why he proposes the mixed public-private corporation when the ultimate goal is a private one. Despite this lack of detail, Nelson's proposal is clearly an imaginative and innovative one, and soundly based on differences in physical and economic characteristics of the land. The missing details can be developed from debate and further public consideration.

In 1982 Teeguarden proposed the creation of public corporations, apparently for any or all federal lands, although all his illustrations are for national forests.

> . . . I outline yet another alternative: the establishment of independent public corporations which could function like investor-owned public utilities. For example, each national forest could be chartered to operate as a public corporation, with a Board of Directors and administrative officers. Each unit would have the legal right to establish its own timber production and other resource output goals in response to the demand for its services and costs of producing them, just as do private investor-owned utilities. Operations would be self-financed through sales of products and services, and land-use leases. Investment capital would be obtained by the sale of tax exempt bonds or, as in the case of private corporations, by retained earnings. Services that would not voluntarily be provided because of lack of adequate profit margins or markets, but which were considered to yield significant public benefits, could be

assured through contractual arrangements in which agencies of the Federal or State governments pay the National Forest Corporation for specified kinds of quantities of such services.[26]

Teeguarden goes on to outline other provisions of his proposal: a Public Corporations Board, for general oversight; charters of limited duration, say, ten to fifteen years, which would not be renewed if the corporation could not earn sufficient profit to maintain its operations; a requirement that the corporations earn 11 percent return on their assets; requirements for reporting financial operations annually; and suggestions for splitting of profits (if any!). He concludes: "A system of public corporations, operating under the supervision of a Public Corporations Board, is one of several alternatives to the present method for managing the federal lands. Obviously many more details need to be developed before the proposal can be fully evaluated. My intent here is merely to stimulate serious study of what seems to be a potentially promising way of achieving more effective management of federal lands."[27]

He goes on to suggest that "consideration . . . be given to designating a portion of the federal lands, say, 25 percent, including national forests, for management by public corporations."[28]

As many other observers of current federal land management, Teeguarden was concerned with certain basic problems: the need to simplify a system of land management which has grown burdensomely detailed and complex; a need to impose some system of economic accountability of the federal land managers; and the need to devise a system more locally adaptable than a national management system. His proposal, tentative as it is, is unclear on several points: Are the national forests, as now delineated, too small for the kind of efficiency he strives for? How will mineral leasing and mineral disposal be handled? Is the rate of return he postulated for capital unrealistically high? If there are extensive areas of federal land which cannot be self-sustaining, let alone return 11 percent on their capital value (as I strongly suspect may be the case), how would these be handled? But these specific questions are not meant to detract from the value of this imaginative and innovative proposal.

For any of the proposals described in this section, or for those that might grow out of them, new legislation would be required. Its specific terms and limitations clearly would be critical. Even if agreement could be reached for a trial program or for a program of general applicability, and even if corporations could be established which initally were quite successful, would this really be a long-term solution to the problems of efficiency in federal land management? I am reminded of the enthusiasm with which the Tennessee Valley Authority and the Bonneville Power Authority were created in the 1930s. I recall also their rather successful operations for some years, and their increasing bureaucratization and inertia to meet changing times. A new broom sweeps clean, but will it last?

Large-scale, long-term leasing

The fifth and final alternative for future management of the federal lands is large-scale, long-term leasing of these lands for conservation and preservation purposes, as well as for commercial uses.

The lease.   Leasing, as contrasted to ownership, of land and associated resources is a time-circumscribed transfer of control to the lessee of some parts of the bundle of rights which go with land ownership, for a specified period of time and for agreed-upon uses and methods of management. Leasing is very common for privately owned land and associated resources. More than one-third of all houses and apartments in the United States are occupied by renters, for instance. Farmland is also rented, as whole farms or as additional acreage to supplement the land of an established farmer. Likewise, much office and commercial space is rented. But renting extends also to mineral development—a considerable part of all oil and gas development is under lease, by one private party from another. Some forestland is leased from private landowners, often small ones, by forest industry firms. Leasing of private land by private parties has been common in the United States for a very long time.

Long experience with private leasing of many kinds of property, in the United States and in other countries, has established certain principles governing leases that lead to efficient use of the property and that are equitable as between lessor and lessee. First of all, the lease should be written, not oral. While it may seem inconceivable that a federal official and a private party would enter into an oral lease for federal land, it is not inconceivable that one or the other might make some verbal statements that lead the other to expect some performance which will not be forthcoming. If disputes should arise, the written lease will govern. The lease should be specific on every important point that occurs to either lessor or lessee, yet at the same time it should preserve as much flexibility as possible for the lessee to make economically efficient use of the property. The lease should spell out what can, and what cannot, be done with the property;

and it should provide the lessor for reasonable opportunity for inspection but without undue inconvenience to the lessee. It should, of course, specify the length of the lease term.

Renewal of the lease. Well-drawn leases provide for consideration of their renewal. In general, renewal negotiations should be consumated when about a quarter of the original lease term yet remains— for example, three months before the end of an annual lease, two or three years before the end of a decade-long lease, and twenty or twenty-five years before the end of a ninety-nine-year lease. This gives both lessee and lessor time in which to work out other arrangements, if they cannot agree on an extension. The lessee should agree either to pay for specified improvements on the property when the lease period begins or to maintain improvements at a specified level, or both. The lease might well include penalties for degradation of the property, as well as a performance bond, to ensure that the lessee lives up to the terms of the lease. The performance bond for leases on federal land could take the form of Treasury notes (suitably rolled over, as they matured) from which the lessee could collect the interest, thus substantially reducing the annual cost while at the same time leaving the government adequately protected. The performance bond obviously should be large enough to guarantee performance in the event of failure of the lessee to carry out some agreed-upon action.

Cancellation of the lease. The lease should also spell out the circumstances, if any, on which either the lessor or the lessee could cancel the lease before the end of the term, and the penalties that should be exacted for cancellation. The lessor should agree to compensate the lessee for the unexhausted or undepreciated value of the improvements at the end of the lease period. This provision, plus the provision for negotiation over renewal well before the lease period ended should make unnecessary any neglect of maintenance of the property which otherwise might occur near the end of a lease period.

Last, the well-drawn private lease provides for the time and form of payment of rent—cash, share, or cash-share. It should also provide for the sharing, if any, in cost items.

All these features are found in well-drawn private leases for all kinds of property in many parts of the world. All have proved by experience to be workable, efficient, and equitable.

Leases for use of the federal lands. As applied to federal land, the term *lease* has a specific legal meaning; in addition to specific lease arrangements, there are other authorized temporary uses of federal land such as permits, licenses, or some other form. For the discussion which follows, I use lease to include all such arrangements whereby individuals, corporations, or groups are allowed to make some time-limited use of federal land for some defined purpose under specified conditions or terms, with the lessee having substantial discretionary power over the actual use and management of the land.

As thus defined, leasing of federal land is much more common than often is realized. The family which picnics at a national forest or BLM site has exclusive use of a small area, for a specific purpose, for a limited time; they are not permitted to cut down trees, drill for oil, graze cattle or sheep, or do any of many other things permitted on some federal land under some conditions. When this family has finished its picnic, it yields its site to some other group for the same purpose. For the person or group who camps for one or more nights on federal land, the use is similar except that it is a little longer and they are permitted a somewhat wider range of activities. The rancher who has a ten-year permit to graze livestock has a longer tenure, subject to rules and regulations of the federal agency, but again for a specified purpose. Although his permit is for ten years, in practice most such permits are renewed so that ranchers have longer tenures in practice, but not in law. Because of the possibility that their permits may not be extended, and because in practice the number of animals or season of use may be changed by the federal agency, their tenure is limited and insecure. The oil and gas lease is initially for a specified number of years but if a discovery is made, the lease continues as long as oil and gas is produced in paying quantities, which may mean for many years. The purchaser of timber from the federal lands has a defined time in which to remove the timber and to perform any site restoration specified in the sale agreement.

In considering temporary but often exclusive use of federal lands by some person, group, or corporation, the wilderness areas occupy a special situation. Wilderness areas are not reserved for individual users in the sense that campgrounds and picnic areas are reserved to individual users. But wilderness areas are by law largely reserved to a particular use and thus to one class of users. While in theory a wilderness area might some day be declassified and returned to a wider multiple-use status, in practice this is most improbable. Many wilderness advocates have emphasized the permanency of the wilderness designation.[29]

When this inclusive definition of "leasing" is used, it is apparent that nearly all the federal land is under some form of lease for some activity and that the number of lessees is very large, approximating one-fourth or more of the total population of the country. By far, the greatest numbers of leases (in the sense of the word used here) are for recreation use. What is envisaged in this section is a major expansion of leasing in the more formal sense of the term, for much longer time periods, and under terms for the various uses which are at one time more nearly uniform from use to use but at the same time flexible enough to meet the needs of lessees for different uses.

Leasing, or the temporary occupancy of federal land by private parties, could be greatly extended in area and in time and regularized in form. It could be extended to all physical types of land and to all land users. For instance, there is no logical reason why recreation and wilderness areas could not be leased to some groups, or other lands to wildlife groups. There have been some, but only a very few instances where municipal watersheds on federal land have been leased to the cities whose water supply originated there. Leasing for all these and for many kinds of commercial uses could be extended greatly, and the terms and conditions of all leases might be more carefully designed to meet the objectives of the user groups interested in such lands.

In the leasing of federal lands to private groups, companies, or individuals, all of the general strictures about good private leases also apply. That is to say, the written lease should be explicit, with no understandings (or misunderstandings) based on conversations; length of lease should be stated; permissible and impermissible uses of the property should be spelled out; provisions should be made for negotiating its renewal; payment for existing renewable resources (trees and grass, particularly) by the lessee at the beginning of the lessee period, for their maintenance during the lease period, and for the compensation to the lessee for unexhausted improvements at the end of the lease should be provided for; performance bonds should be specified; and the methods and timing of rent payments should be stated clearly.

In addition to these general strictures, there are some other points which should govern leasing of federal land. The leasing should not exacerbate the problems of intermingled federal and nonfederal land ownership; it would, on the contrary, be helpful if those problems could in some degree be reduced by the leasing. If the owner(s) of intermingled checkerboard land were given preferential rights in leasing of federal land, the whole area could be blocked up into more efficient management units. The lessee should be held to the same environmental controls over the leased land that would apply if the land were privately owned, although the actual issuance of the lease might be excluded from the necessity of an environmental impact report. It should also be made clear that the leasing of federal land to a private group did not in any way affect the state's legal authority over any game animals on the land.

The basic goal in formulating terms for private leasing of federal land would be to harness the self-interests of the lessee to the social goals of the national government as landowner. To the extent that the terms of the lease could harness those self-interests, the ingenuity and ability of the private lessees would be enlisted and the supervisory problems of the federal agencies would be reduced. Violations of the terms of the leases would also be reduced, and the lessees would surely find many ways of managing the land resources more effectively.

Clearly, the terms on which leases of federal land would be available would have to be attractive to the prospective lessees, otherwise they would be unwilling to enter into a lease. Similarly, the terms would have to be acceptable to the federal agencies, if they had discretion in granting or refusing lease applications, and would have to be acceptable to the total electorate as well. Present laws would have to be amended in various ways if leasing were to increase. Policy issues would include such matters as to what degree the terms of leases would be spelled out in the legislation and how much discretionary decision-making power would be granted to the agencies. For instance, at present both the Forest Service and BLM are required (with limited exceptions) to offer timber at "competitive sale," but the specific decisions about the area of land and the volume of timber in the sale are left to the agencies. Or, as another example, the royalty rate for oil and gas leases is specified in law but the decision to offer a specific tract on the Outer Continental Shelf resides with the secretary of the interior. At one extreme, prospective lessees could be given the right to demand a lease under terms specified in law, without the agencies having power either to refuse the lease or to modify its terms; at the other extreme, the federal agencies could be given nearly total discretionary power over leasing; and, of course, innumerable intermediate alternatives exist. If the idea of more extensive and more regularized leasing of federal lands is taken seriously, one can be sure the specific terms of the law will be debated at length.

Long-term leasing of federal lands, as outlined here, would give lessees many of the advantages of full ownership of the land and its resources. For a defined time, subject to defined and agreed-upon conditions, the lessee would have the opportunity to manage the land

and resources as the lessee chose—for profit, if a commercial use, or for other objectives as well. Federal expenditures for land management could be drastically reduced, nearly to zero, for the leased land; when the lease period was approaching termination, the federal government would have the option for renewal of the lease, for other disposal, or for resumption of federal administration.

An Illustrative Proposal

The forgoing section of this chapter has described in general terms the possibility of an augmented, regularized, and extensive system of long-term leasing of federal lands. As is often the case, it is only when general terms are reduced to specifics and when numbers are added to words that the full meaning of an idea is evident and a basis for criticism and judgment is provided. Therefore, in this section an illustrative proposal is outlined in some detail, in the expectation that this will add significantly to the understanding of the general idea.

Although the proposal in this section is illustrative, it does rest upon my extensive personal knowledge and judgment about the federal lands. I have chosen proposed terms of leases and proposed numbers (for acreages, rentals, and so forth) which, I believe, are practical for administration and attractive to at least some potential lessees, including groups interested in conservation and preservation, as well as to some commercial users. I also believe that the terms are equitable for users, nonusers, and the general public. Although I believe that the numbers used in this illustration are generally reasonable, I do admit that they are somewhat arbitrary. For instance, I use 90,000 acres as the minimum acreage per unit of lease for the highly productive forestlands. I could hardly assert that 85,000 acres or 95,000 acres would be impractical, but I do say that 10,000 acres would defeat the purposes of this part of my proposal.

Each part of this proposal is essential to the whole; some parts will be acceptable to rival user groups, the general public, and the Congress only because other parts also are included. In my judgment, these specific terms make the proposal economically and politically realistic.

Other illustrative proposals could be devised, of course, and my proposal could be modified in various ways, if not too drastically so, without basically changing it.

Before getting into specifics, a few general comments may reduce misconceptions about what is being suggested here. First of all, all leases issued under this proposal would be subject to all the general terms described on page 203.

Second, leasing by the group, company, individual, or unit of local government would, under this proposal, be voluntary. Such leases would be sought only when the prospective lessee felt that the lease would improve his or its position; this might include an estimate of a positive benefit from leasing, or it might be a means whereby the prospective lessee thought his or its position could better be protected against rival forces or interests. Groups, companies, individuals, and units of local government might indeed feel some pressure to secure a lease on some tract of federal land in order to protect their economic position, but would try to do so only if they felt their position was stronger with a lease than without one. If the federal lands not selected for long-term leases continued under present federal management, then all present, laws, regulations, and procedures applying to those lands also would continue. If they were offered for sale or transferred to states, then applicable laws would govern their management.

These suggested leasing terms have been carefully chosen to make only the most productive federal lands attractive for leasing—whether productivity is measured in terms of ability to produce wood or grass or oil or to provide recreation, wilderness, or wildlife values. The leasing process here described, if implemented, in its way will be as selective as the disposal and reservation processes of earlier decades.

Lessees operating under the terms of this specific proposal would not be limited to a single lease. Even at present, oil and gas and other minerals-extracting companies often have more than one lease, and timber buyers often have more than one purchase unit under contract at any date. The possibility of multiple leases would be extended to any and all lessees for all kinds of land and for all uses. Minimum acreages per lease for each kind of land use are specified later for this illustrative proposal; each has been chosen as large enough to be significant for any prospective lessee but not so large as to exclude smaller but economically viable operations. There is no connotation that the minimum acreages are in all cases economically optimum by themselves alone. They are units of practical size in the same sense that units now offered for oil and gas leasing on the Outer Continental Shelf or units now offered for timber sale are practical. Minimum acreages have been chosen to discourage nuisance filings and to avoid undesired fragmentation of the federal land. There would be no maximum acreage for a single lease under any of the uses outlined here, nor any limit on the number of leases any person, corporation, or group could hold. The costs of the leases and of the management of the leased area would, in practice, constitute flexible but significant barriers to large-scale leasing by any lessee.

This proposal includes no specific terms for new forms of mineral development leases. Unless changed in law, present leasing and mining laws would apply to all federal lands whose surface was not leased by some party under the terms of this illustrative proposal. Thus, oil, gas, coal, and other mineral development could proceed, onshore and offshore, under present law unless the surface was leased by some interest under one of the provisions outlined below. Mineral development leases could also be issued by new lessees of the surface. Leases of the surface would be possible when leases for mineral development had previously been issued for the same area, but in this case the lessee of the surface would be subject to conditions in the mineral leases. That is, a rancher might lease an area already included in an oil and gas lease, but in that case his rights to use the land would be subject to the rights of the oil and gas lessee to use the area for his purpose.

Basic tenents

Surface leasing of all federal lands now under the management of the Forest Service and the Bureau of Land Management. If included in long-term leases of the land surface, the land would then be open for mineral development (including coal, oil, gas, and other energy minerals) by other lessees, operating under mineral leases provided by the lessees of the surface. Since the surface of existing or proposed wilderness areas would be eligible for long-term leases for reservation or conservation purposes, mineral exploration and development would be extended to leased wilderness areas. Wilderness and other preservation areas not so leased would be subject to the present law governing such areas. Lessees of the surface resources for any purpose would have the power to establish controls over methods of access, proper site use, and proper site restoration by lessees of the mineral interest, but would not have the power wholly to refuse mineral development. Royalties might be at 12.5 percent for oil and gas and 5 percent of gross output for metals. One-fourth of the royalties would go to the holder of the lease for the land surface and the rest to the federal Treasury for distribution to states and counties in accordance with present law. This division of the royalties would provide an incentive to the surface lessee to permit mineral development under carefully controlled conditions.

The lessee of the surface could permit the use of the surface for outdoor recreation or could close it to such use. Fees or charges for recreation use could be levied, if the surface lessee so decided, and would accrue to the lessee of the surface. Specific conditions about outdoor recreation would not be included in the leases. Leases specifically for outdoor recreation are provided for on page 211, and persons or groups desirous of obtaining federal lands specifically for recreation could obtain land under lease as provided below. The probabilities are large that most lessees of the surface would tolerate recreation use but would not attempt to collect fees; the experience of the larger forest industry firms on their own land confirms that judgment. Simple public relations dictate making the land available for public use, but the poor income prospects of charging fees, collecting them, and excluding people who do not pay them lead to the judgment that no effort would be made to collect such fees.

Forestlands capable of producing 85 cubic feet or more of wood per acre annually under good natural (but not intensive) forestry would be available for lease by forest industry firms, wilderness preservation groups, or any other interest groups. They would be subject to *all* the following conditions:

- The lease period would be for one hundred years—long enough for two or more complete rotations under intensive forestry, even in the Douglas fir area.
- The lessee would buy and pay immediately for all the standing merchantable timber on the tract, at prices reflecting present stumpage prices for sawtimber and pulpwood.
- The lessee would pay a continuing annual rent for the site and for the immature timber, for the whole period of the lease, at a rate of 5 percent annually on the estimated value of the site and immature timber, adjusted annually in proportion to the implicit price deflator for the GNP.
- The lessee would be free to harvest standing merchantable timber on a schedule of his own choosing, including never harvesting it if he chose; but the lessee would be bound for the whole period of the lease and would be subject to forfeiture of performance bond if payments for the lease were not kept up.
- The minimum acreage per lease application, under this provision, would be 90,000 acres. In order to get leases of this size in reasonably compact blocks, it might be necessary to allow the inclusion of a small proportion (say, 10 percent) of the land to

have a lower timber-producing capacity. The 90,000-acre figure has been chosen to provide something like a minimum efficient forest management unit; large firms would almost surely seek more than one lease and would be likely to own other forests.

- The lessee would assume all costs of management of the leased area, including the provision of roads and the control of fires. No specific management requirements, such as reforestation or other timber management practices, would be imposed in the lease; but the compensation for improvements at the end of the lease would provide strong financial incentive for maintenance of the forest stand. The costs of such leases would be bearable by the lessee only if efficient and relatively intensive forestry were practiced.

Conservation groups traditionally critical of the forest industry may attack these conditions as being unreasonably generous. Several points should be made. In the first place, most of this timber would ultimately be sold to the same or a similar forest industry firm under existing federal land administration if there is no leasing; under my proposal, the lessee would get the timber on leased lands sooner and would more quickly move the forestland into productive new forests. In either case, the firm would pay for the timber at the estimated market price. Wilderness lovers and other conservationists would have the option under the pull-back provision (discussed on page 216) of taking a lease on as much as one-third of the area proposed for any long-term lease by a timber processor, if in their judgment the value of the site for wilderness, recreation, wildlife, or other uses were sufficient so that they would be willing to pay as much for the timber and the site as the timber processor would pay. This would give the advocates of these uses an opportunity to place their own value on use of highly productive forest areas for wilderness or recreation purposes. Since leases of this kind would be open to any lessee prepared to pay the price, wholly new timber-processing firms might be able to enter the business by means of such leases. While established timber processors would have many advantages, they would fall far short of a monopoly position on either obtaining such leases or on the prices paid for them. Firms now regularly buying federal timber would be under considerable pressure to lease forests, lest they lose their source of supply. This type of lease would not be available on the extensive areas of "commercial" forests where productivity did not reach the annual level of 85 cubic feet of timber per acre. Timber on such less-productive sites would be sold, if at all, under present federal land laws.

Forests owned by federal, state, and local governments in the United States have not customarily been leased for long periods, yet this practice is common in many countries. In particular, long-term leasing of publicly owned forests is common in British Columbia and Alberta.[30] Some American forest industry firms have long-term leases for forestland in other countries. Long-term leases have their critics and their defenders; there is no reason to enter into an extensive inquiry into this method of forest management at this point. However, the practice is neither novel nor untested.

Established public-land-using ranchers or associations of such ranchers could lease tracts of grazing land on which they now have grazing permits. The lease term would be fifty years, with a minimum area per lease of 5,000 acres. The annual cash rental per acre would be equal to the U.S. average farm value of one pound of beef. The lessee would assume all costs of management, including roads, fencing, water development, and fire control.

Data on beef prices at the farm have been collected by the U.S. Department of Agriculture for many decades, hence the data necessary for calculating the rental are readily available. The present formula for establishing grazing fees on national forests and grazing districts includes, as one item, the average farm price of beef (see chapter 3), hence the idea of gearing grazing rentals to beef prices is not new or novel. If continuing inflation cheapens the value of the dollar, presumably this leads to higher beef prices and to greater value of the forage from the grazing land. Thus there would be an automatic adjustment in grazing fee lease rates, as inflation or other factors pushed up the price of the beef produced from such land.

A rental of this size can economically be paid only on rangelands producing 1 animal-unit-month (AUM) of forage per 4 acres or less (hence the higher output per acre). For land producing 1 AUM from 4 acres results in a cost in 1980 dollars more than twice as high per animal-unit-month as current grazing fees on national forests and BLM lands. Ranchers would seek to lease federal lands on these terms only if they were convinced they could make the rangelands more productive than they now are or if they feared loss of the unleased land to other user groups. Only comparatively small parts of the Forest Service and BLM grazing lands can produce 1 AUM from 4 acres or less. These lessees would have no specific grazing management restrictions in their leases, but the lessee would be bound for the full period of the lease and also be subject to the performance bond and to a degradation penalty. Under these conditions, no rancher could afford to lease public lands without careful and relatively intensive conservation management. Short-term exploitation would be too costly, as would low-producing rangelands. Because ranchers typically have less investment in relation to output than do timber processors, and because grass grows on shorter rotations than does a tree, the length of the leases here could be shorter than those for timber-growing lands. Because the use of federal lands for livestock grazing is intimately interrelated with the use of private lands for livestock production, and because such relationships have developed over many years, it would be inappropriate to allow outsiders to bid for this type of lease. To avoid any temptation for misuse of this type of lease on lands not intended for this type of land use, the lessee should be forbidden to cut or sell timber from the land, but leasing for mineral development would not only be permitted but encouraged.

Private persons, groups, or associations, including conservation, preservation, wildlife, and similar groups, would be eligible to lease any public lands, for a lease term of fifty years, up to a total of all such leases (including any on established wilderness areas) of 60 million acres. If the lands chosen could qualify for either of the two preceding categories, the lessee would have to pay the same price as the timber firm or rancher who leased these productive forested or range lands. If the sites did not qualify for these timber or grazing leases, leases would require no cash down payment and the annual rental would be only $1.00 per acre. But in this case, the lessees would be prohibited from harvesting timber. Established wilderness areas would be available for this type of lease and, if leased, would then be open to subleasing for mineral development, as outlined above. If wilderness areas were not leased, they would continue to be managed under existing law.

In any case, the lessee would pay all management costs for roads, fire control, and exclusion of trespassers. As noted earlier, these lessees would get one-fourth of any mineral royalties if they subleased their area for mineral development. No requirements for management of the area would be imposed in the leases, but these leases might be subject to the same degradation penalties as are grazing leases. The fact that this type of lease would be available to any interested group, plus the provision for leases by units of local government, described below, make it unnecessary to require access to the leased area by the general public. The minimum area for leases of this kind would be 7,500 acres.

States and units of local government may select for lease up to 15 percent of the land within their boundaries, or may select for lease all of the federal land if the total federal land is less than 15 percent of the total land area in the jurisdiction. If the land is forested with a productivity under good natural forestry of 85 cubic feet or more wood annually, state and local governments would have to meet the same terms as other lessees of this type of land. For all other land, the leases would be for fifty years on payment of annual rental of $1.00 per acre. The local government would have to assume management costs for all lands, including roads, fire control, provision of recreation facilities (if any), and so on. Where the area of federal land within the jurisdiction exceeds 10,000 acres, the minimum area for lease would be 10,000 acres. As surface lessees, such local governments would secure one-fourth of the royalties from mineral development, plus any amounts accruing to them under legislation now applicable to this kind of mineral development. These lessees would be forbidden to sell timber from forests incapable of annually producing 85 cubic feet of wood per acre.

All leases under any of the forgoing arrangements would contain a provision against subleasing to other parties for the same uses of the land. For instance, no unit of local government could lease an area and then sublease all or part of it to some other interest. However, leasing for mineral development would be encouraged. My experience in federal land management has taught me that subleasing (other than for minerals development) is nearly always a subterfuge to enable some party to gain something not directly available under existing law. With all of the forgoing provisions in operation, the need or the temptation for subleasing would be at a minimum, since any person or group desiring a lease could get it directly from the federal government. Leases could be assigned to a new lessee, when there was a genuine succession of interest group activity. When there was doubt as to the genuineness of the transfer, the federal agency involved could require forfeiture of the lease, making the land available for a new lease.

The forgoing illustrative proposal is a package deal, in the sense that every part of it is essential. Economically, some parts are defensible only because of other parts; politically, some proposals will be acceptable, if at all, only because of the other parts. The various proposed lease forms are possible only because of the suggested terms for each, and only because some interest groups will find other aspects of the whole proposal acceptable to them.

For instance, industry, government, and many other groups will find the proposal that conservationists and preservationists be allowed to lease as much as 60 million acres for forty years at a nominal rental acceptable only because (1) other leases are available to them, and (2) the leased lands will be open to mineral development. Or, to take another example, the proposal to lease large blocks of the most productive forestland for long periods to forest industry firms will be acceptable only because (1) conservationists and others will have the opportunity to lease large areas of such land or of other land themselves, and (2) the forest industry firms will be paying for the merchantable timber and for the opportunity to grow more timber.

How Much Leasing?

If the illustrative proposal for augmented long-term leasing of federal lands were placed in operation, as described, how much federal land would actually be taken into such leases by individuals, corporations, and groups operating in their own self-interests? With leasing as with sales, much will depend on general economic conditions and also upon the rate at which the federal lands are pushed into leases. Until such a proposal is available under law, no one can know with certainty what will happen, but some estimates may be made.

For the productive forestlands, I would judge that the maximum possible acreage is about 32 million acres—an area equal to less than half of the acreage of forestland now owned by forest industry firms. This estimate is based on the published inventories of national forest and other federal forest productivity made by the Forest Service. These productive forestlands would be available for lease by wilderness and other preservation groups and by wildlife groups, and by local government, but the initial capital required to buy standing merchantable timber and the continuing annual rental costs would be so high that it seems unlikely that a large area of this kind of land will be leased for such uses. Some forest industry firms will no doubt welcome the opportunity to add to their forestland holdings; some of them have made purchases of large tracts of private forestland in recent years. But the necessity to buy the merchantable timber and to pay for it all at once will surely be a sobering factor in their leasing of such forests. The annual rental on such lands will force lessees to manage the lands and forests carefully and intensively—anything else would be prohibitively costly. Since such leases would be available to any interested party, large corporations (such as oil companies) might secure such leases and subsequently acquire timber-processing facilities, as a more economical means of entering the forest-processing industry than buying an established firm. As an initial estimate, I would judge that not more than half of the land potentially subject to this kind of lease will be chosen for lease during a ten-year period.

For the grazing lands, it is only the most productive lands that any economically rational rancher would choose. I would estimate that less than 20 million acres would actually be sought under this form of lease. Under the terms proposed, a rancher would have the opportunity to practice good range management over a long span of years, and substantial financial incentive to do so.

Both forest and grazing lands, tracts of potential productive capacity but not now in very productive condition might well be chosen by a lessee. Thus depleted timber stands would be built up over time, one of the outcomes much to be desired.

How much acreage wilderness, conservation, wildlife, recreation, and environmental groups or individuals might choose is unknown. Some highly valued and strategic tracts might be chosen from areas proposed for forestry or grazing leases, but the costs would be high. For other kinds of areas, there would be no capital cost and annual costs would be low. Some groups might be greatly interested in leasing present wilderness or proposed wilderness areas, on the grounds that they trust their own management more than they do that of the federal agencies. They would, of course, have the option of not leasing tracts of federal land, relying on present management practices of the federal agencies and gambling that no rival interest group would seek to lease areas of their greatest interest. Because the annual rentals are low and because there is no initial capital cost, small groups of wealthy persons might choose to rent and to use areas (mimimum 7,500 acres or more subject to pullbacks exercised by others) that did not meet forestry or grazing lease standards to establish private wilderness or primitive areas. The need to assume the management costs would be a sobering influence.

On the other hand, the possibility of revenues from mineral development would offer further opportunities. While the preservationists have generally opposed mineral development on public lands, the fact is that some land-owning preservationist groups have been willing to accept some mineral development, under carefully controlled conditions, on their own lands. It is conceivable that some areas might be leased by such organizations at no net cost—the low rentals and modest management cost being fully offset by royalties from mineral development. Leasing as here described might appeal to the Nature Conservancy or to the Izaak Walton League, because each has acquired some land in the past. Utilization of this leasing program would require substantial change in the operations of the Wilderness Society and the Sierra Club, but would offer them advantages as well. My guess is that less than 30 to 40 million acres might be leased under this general part of the suggested proposal.

State and local governments could choose to acquire some federal lands, but on the whole the incentives for doing so will be small. Interested private groups could apply for leases directly, hence there would be little reason for them to try to go through local government to get the land they want, and the provisions against subleasing and timber sales from less productive forests would greatly reduce the incentives to do so. The local governments will get some of the mineral royalties in any case, but their share of such royalties may not be high enough, if they lease directly, to offset the costs and bother of such leasing. The fact that state and local government leasing is possible will surely dampen any proposal for disposition of federal land to local government. My guess is that no more than 20 million acres, and possibly a good deal less, would actually be leased by state and local governments if the proposed alternative were translated into law.

On the basis of the forgoing rough estimates, it appears that something less than 100 million acres outside of Alaska would be sought under the long-term lease proposals, at least in a ten-year period. This contrasts with something over 360 million acres (outside of Alaska) that would remain under Forest Service and BLM administration. The federal agencies would lose some of the most productive lands from their administration, but they would continue to administer the larger part of the lands currently under their administration. Net revenues to the federal Treasury from the federal lands should increase. Revenues will be relatively high on the commercial leases, and federal administrative costs will be lower on all leased lands, some of which absorb considerable amounts of appropriated funds today. The unleased federal lands would be subject to the same laws and the same planning and management operations as apply to the federal lands today. The federal agencies could still practice multiple-use management. The leasing system would provide an escape route which substantially would reduce the pressures on the federal agencies and considerably would increase the alternatives available to potential users. The present federal land management system and the new long-term leasing system would operate side by side, with perhaps major benefit to each.

Pullback: An Innovative Proposal

Pullback is a new idea which could significantly affect future federal land use and management. It is most directly applicable to long-term leasing of federal lands, and the discussion which follows is largely in terms of its use in federal land leasing. However, the idea could also be applied to the sale of federal lands, or transfer of federal lands to states or to public corporations, if any one of any combination of those major alternatives should be chosen.

Who benefits from pullback? Under the pullback concept any person or group could apply, under applicable law, for a tract of federal land, for any use they chose; but any other person or group would have a limited time between the filing of the initial application and granting of the lease or the making of the sale in which to "pull back" a part of the area applied for. Pullback authority might be extended to local governments or even to a federal agency under the same terms as those being applied to private groups. The user of the pullback provision would become the applicant for the area pulled back, required to meet the same terms applicable to the original applicant and required to enter into the same kind of an arrangement on the pulled back area as the original applicant had applied for, but the use could be what the pullback applicant chose, not necessarily the use proposed by the original applicant. Competition would thus arise between users as well as between uses.

The right to pull back would be unconditional—that is, available to anyone, without the consent of the original applicant or of the federal land-administering agency. The right of pullback would have to be for a significant fraction of the area originally applied for, but far less than all of it—as much as the pullback applicant desired but not more than one-third, perhaps. The proportion available for pullback could not be too large, lest it jeopardize the whole lease proposal. Yet the user of the pullback authority should have the opportunity to take a significant share of the total, if he chose. The one-third limit is admittedly arbitrary, but it seems to meet these criteria. In practice, a user of the pullback authority might take as much as one-third or a smaller area, depending in large part upon his need for the land and his ability to pay for it. The minimum acreages per lease for different purposes in the specific leasing proposal were established on the assumption that as much as one-third of the area applied for might be pulled back; the remaining two-thirds or more would still meet the general criteria for each type of lease.

A few suggestions illustrate how this process would work. A forest industry firm could apply for a lease on a 90,000-acre or larger tract of federal forested land, for a period long enough to harvest the present standing timber and to grow at least one rotation. A group interested in wilderness, in developed outdoor recreation, or in wildlife, or in any other use of the land authorized under the law then would be permitted to file a pullback application for as much as but not more than one-third of the area applied for by the forest industry firm. The pullback applicant would have to meet the same terms as the original applicant, but otherwise its pullback application would not be subject to refusal by either the original applicant or the federal agency. Some limitations may have to be included in the law. A requirement that pullback applications be made only for reasonably contiguous lands might be needed. That is, there should be no pockmarking of the whole tract with scattered pullbacks of up to 40 acres in an effort to make the original application economically and operationally infeasible; and pulled-back areas should not be allowed to further complicate access to land. Some minimum acreage per pullback may have to be met so that no single acre could be pulled back in the midst of a large leased area, and probably some limits would have to be established as to the number (perhaps three) of pullbacks allowed per lease.

Although this example has been for a forest industry firm, the same provisions would apply to any pair of uses, in any sequence, or to rival parties who desire the area for the same use. A wilderness lease application would be subject to pullback from recreation groups, for instance; or an application by one forest industry firm for a heavily forested area would be subject to pullback from another forest industry firm.

At present, an individual, a corporation, or a group can seek the use of some tract or area of federal land, for some desired use, under applicable law. If some other person, corporation, or group seeks use of part or all of the same area, for the same or other uses, or if it simply opposes the use sought by the applicant without necessarily wanting to use the area itself, it brings all the pressures it can muster to bear on the federal agency concerned (the Forest Service or BLM). It uses its power in the courts, with elected governmental bodies, with politicians and political parties, and seeks by means of suits or legislation or administrative action to thwart the original applicant. The process is typically an adversarial confrontation, similar to a court suit. There is often no direct bargaining between rival applicants and no means of enforcing bargains if any are reached. Often there is no solution possible except a full victory by one party and a complete loss by the other. Intermediate or compromise solutions which would largely meet the needs of each and thus give both a partial victory are difficult, if not impossible, to arrive at or to enforce.

The pullback would work differently. Under the pullback procedure as outlined above, different groups interested in the use of federal lands would be forced to compete against each other and to bargain with one another. While the form of this bargaining would differ from the customary competitive bidding, the substance would be very similar to competitive bidding. The relationship would not be the perfectly competitive market of the economists (large numbers of buyers and sellers, each operating wholly independently of all others), but it would closely approximate competition of the business world. Every applicant would be vulnerable to the pullback application of every other potential user, and hence would be in competition with the other. This would force a substantial consideration of public or social values by each original applicant, because otherwise he would be subjected to pullback discipline applied by other groups. At the same time, the requirement that the user of the pullback authority had to meet the terms of the original applicant would largely or wholly eliminate nuisance or deliberately obstructive actions. Obstruction would be too costly. Competitive bargains among rival interests would be necessary: you stay out of my area of interest, and I will stay out of your area; you try to impede my use of federal lands and I will retaliate when you try to obtain some use of federal land; you concede something to me, and I will concede something to you. The competitive bargains would involve different prospective users of each specific area of federal land, different areas, and differing kinds of uses.

Effect on collusion.   Use of the pullback provision might regrettably lead to collusive action among applicants for federal land. The present

men now instead of gu

of, A-frame vacation house he
nts on a cliff above the beach,
astora congratulates himself for
t having been "devoured" and
not having said "yes to the
nericans."

He details military schemes and
litical plots he says stole away
right to fight. He fumes that
war in his country is "domi-
ed by Washington and not by
Nicaraguan people."

astora first won fame in 1978
n he and 24 other Sandinista
els stormed Nicaragua's Na-
al Palace in Managua and
the congress hostage. They
anded and won the release of
andinista prisoners from the

jails of dictator Anastasio Somoza
and were allowed to leave the
country by plane.

After Somoza's fall in 1979,
Pastora grew disenchanted with the
leftward drift of the new Sandinista government. In 1983 he
took up arms against his former
colleagues.

But Pastora quit the war on May
16, 1986, and asked for political
asylum in neutral Costa Rica, saying "We have been shot down by
the CIA, but never defeated."

He was referring to a Central Intelligence Agency decision in 1984
to cut off his U.S. aid unless he
cooperated with the Nicaraguan
Democratic Force, the largest an-

ti-Sa
Pa
sayin
"ge
Som
But
tired
resou
early
U.S.-

No
follow
fightin
sharks

"W
Pasto
guerri
are gl

THE B

Keeping trivial issu

CHEYENNE — The Department of Administration and Fiscal Control will begin screening items of business to come before the Capitol Building Commission.

The idea is great. But if history repeats, the mundane, the picayune, the minor, will creep back into CBC meetings.

The CBC, comprised of the

Joan
Barron

Star-Tribune

governor and the other four elected state officials, decide about capital construction, leased office space for state agencies, tree planting, parking and assorted other problems of the day that beset every property owner.

The CBC hasn't met often lately because there's no money for capital construction

But the minor questions persist. The officials spent considerable time recently discussing a movie company's request to rip a hole in a security wall at the old s penitentiary.

The City of Rawlins, which inherit the prison, always wa access to the exercise yard be the wall, anyway. Unlike o prison structures, the wall ha historical value.

No one objected to the poking. Movie-making is ecor ic development and should n discouraged.

The issue was which state b has jurisdiction over the old — the Board of Charities Reform which administers sta stitutions, the State Land B or the Capitol Building Co sion.

It really shouldn't make a difference since the five elect ficials are on all those boards.

Moreover, the officials, as the Board of Charitie Reform the day before, ha proved the hole.

But government being wh and to keep things tidy, Gov Sullivan called an impr meeting of the State Land The five officials put on the land board hats and approv hole-in-the-wall.

This business took abou an-hour.

s out of government

Displays in the Capitol Building also got a good working over.

State Superintendent of Public Instruction Lynn Simons noted that the Archives, Museums and Historical Dept. was folding a display in the capitol on Wyoming oil and planned to substitute a display of Wyoming diamonds.

The implication, she said, is that diamonds might replace the economic contribution of oil and gas. That notion, Simons said, is "absurd."

Robert Bush, AMH director, said frankly the oil display is "tacky" and should be removed.

Bush assured, however, that the dismantling was not intended to be a slap in face of the oil and gas industry.

Bush said his department could develop a better oil and gas display if that's what everyone wants.

Simons said the CBC should adopt a policy to be sure the displays in the capitol are uniform.

She cited one of the more famous capitol displays. Simons said it nearly provoked another Johnson County cattle war.

She referred to the display of sheep promoted by State Treasurer Stan Smith, a former sheep rancher.

Former Gov. Ed Herschler, a cattleman, responded with a mounted coyote behind glass directly facing Smith's woollies on the first floor of the capitol.

Bush said the coyote was not his idea.

Simons said the capitol displays should be brought before the CBC to be sure they are appropriate and not embarrassing.

Although it was entertaining and enlightening, the CBC meeting was time-consuming for the five elected state officials.

If DAFC can weed out the insignificant items it will help.

But it seems to me this has been tried before.

An independent, unpopular decision by DAFC tended to prompt phone calls to Wyoming's accessible and usually responsive elected officials.

As a result, the official brought up the business at the next meeting. Singed DAFC officials shied and henceforth dragged back before the CBC the minor, the trivial, and the picayune.

Maybe this time it will be different.

Pastora leads fisher

SAN JUANILLO, Costa Rica (AP) — Eden Pastora, the former Commander Zero, steps ashore from his boat, dressed in sunny-yellow swimwear and carrying a bulgy-eyed fish.

"It's a beautiful life at sea," says Pastora, gazing off at the last, dim light of a Pacific Ocean sunset.

Nicaragua's most famous guerrilla leader is bringing in the day's catch at his new fishing cooperative, which employs 40 of his former fighters and military gear left over from the war he was forced to abandon.

Pastora, now 50, looks fit and tanned. He has just put in a 14-hour day on the ocean in what says is a "completely absorbing profession and good therapy."

"All you have to think about out there is the poor little cabrilla," he says, drawing out the last three words in a mock-sympathetic voice.

And then, seriously: "You don't have to think about politics or intrigues or all the barbarity of men who devour other men like wolves."

But almost a year after quitting his jungle command in the war against Nicaragua's leftist Sandinista government, Pastora still thinks a lot about those things.

Sitting later in the thatched-

SPARKLING
DIAMOND
LOOK-A-LIKES
BY TACOA

competitive bidding process, where it is applied for any use of federal land, has not been wholly free of collusive actions. Leasing or sale without competitive bidding is always under suspicion that "sweetheart" deals have been made between a federal agency and a private party. Collusion is surely possible when "competitive bidding" is employed. Collusion is not unknown in wholly private transactions, of course. Collusion in the use of pullback would be as subject to legal action as it is in competitive bidding for federal timber or oil. However, it is highly probable that the pullback in operation would lead to less, not more, collusion than now exists, since the pullback would be available to any interested party without consent of the original applicant, the first person to pull back, or the federal agency. To a substantial extent, the pullback provisions would be self-policing.

Effect on competition. The pullback provision would also provide a mechanism for guaranteeing adherence by each party to any bargains reached. Today bargaining among rival interests in federal land is not common, but it is not unknown. One obstacle to the greater use of bargaining among competing interest groups has been that each mistrusted the other, and no adequate mechanism exists for enforcing agreements. Under the pullback provision, any party to a bargain might go back on one deal but would almost certainly face disciplinary or retaliatory action in some other situation.

The pullback authority would direct the energies of all claimants or aspirants for federal land against other claimants or aspirants, in a manner closely comparable to the operation of a competitive market. The use of the pullback provision would substitute bargaining and competition among claimants and aspirants for the established political process of trying to influence actions of the federal agencies. It would, to a substantial degree, replace administrative action of public agencies by bargaining among individuals and groups, and the strength of the private market in reaching bargains among rivals would be substituted for governmental decision making.

Effect on delaying tactics. The pullback provision would substantially reduce the incentive to delay. Today, any group which prefers the present use of federal land to any proposed different use has a substantial incentive to undertake stalling actions, including filing of lawsuits. This is a natural enough tactic, given the present administrative and management structures for making decisions about federal land use. But it can also be a costly one to society as a whole, especially if in the end the same decision is reached which could have been reached earlier. The possibility of disciplinary or retaliatory pullback action by other interest groups would make the rewards of stalling more dubious. Laws establishing the pullback authority might also provide for time limits within which actions had to be taken—a year between filing and granting of the original action, during which the pullback authority could be exercised by any claimant, for example; or six months for the pullback applicant to meet the terms of the original applicant.

The pullback provision would provide substantial help to politically weak contenders for the federal lands, to local and special interests. As it is now, persons or groups with relatively weak or limited political powers on the national or regional scene often suffer total defeat when they wish to influence federal land policy or to secure use of some area for their particular needs. The availability of pullback, without consent by either the original applicant or the federal agency, would greatly improve the competitive position of these special interests and not interpose a serious or fatal barrier to the original applicant.

If the pullback concept were to be applied to any of the alternative forms of future federal land management that have been described, new legislation would have to be passed, and this would, of course, stir up a debate over specific points. One would hope that the law would resolve many of the issues, or at least provide guidance to the federal land-administering agencies. There would remain, however, many practical issues to be worked out upon application of the law. Many of these may be unforeseen so there is little point in trying to suggest possible solutions to them here. I firmly believe that, given the will to do so, a way to solve such problems can be found.

Future outlook. The future is likely to see a continuation of the rising competition for the use of the federal lands, and pressures will be exerted on every user group on the federal lands to consolidate and strengthen its position. Long-term leasing offers a major avenue for such improvement of position by user groups; but so does the pullback provision. For instance, at present the wilderness groups have placed their faith in their political strength not unlike the ranchers of a generation ago who today have lost out seriously. A long-term lease might provide more assurance for the future than reliance on continual political strife; use of pullback might be a more effective way of limiting the inroads of rivals seeking use of federal land than by fighting in the courts, administrative halls, or legislative committee rooms. The various interest groups concerned with their long-term future would do well, I think, to ponder their future security under each of the major alternatives for future federal land management and particularly to estimate how they might use long-term leasing and pullback to their own interests and security.

Potential effects of pullback

The pullback idea has been described for augmented long-term leasing of federal lands, but it also could be applied to the sale of federal lands to private parties, to transfers of federal land to the states, and to the establishment of public or mixed public-private corporations for these programs, either singly or in any combination.

For instance, a proposal to establish a public corporation to manage one or several national forests could be met by a pullback proposal from some conservation or preservationist group to purchase or lease over a long term up to one-third of the area. Or one timber firm might apply to buy an area of highly productive forestland on which some other firm could exercise its pullback rights to purchase up to one-third of the same area. For any original application, by any party, the pullback provision might be exercised by any other party under the same or any other provision of law for securing the use of the federal lands.

There would be substantial national gains, both economic and political, from the general availability of pullback provision. The extent to which such potential gains will be realized in practice can be determined only by experience, but analysis and judgment provide a basis for estimating what might be expected.

The potential national *economic* advantages of the pullback provision include the following gains.

Private initiative and private skills would be harnessed to the public good, not arrayed against each other and the government agencies, as they so often are today. The results would be difficult to evaluate in advance, but one may reasonably expect they would be very great. The resourcefulness of American entrepreneurs should never be underestimated.

The long-term conservation output from the lands now federally administered would be greatly increased above present levels or above levels that would likely prevail in the absence of such a program. The effects can be measured most easily, perhaps, for timber growing. The forest industry firms have always achieved from 50 to 100 percent more wood growth per acre than have the national forests of the same productive capacity, and within twenty years one might reasonably expect that such firms would greatly increase the wood growth per acre on lands under long-term leases or under purchase. The first step in achievement of such greater wood growth would be to harvest existing stands and replace them with new and faster-growing stands. Ranchers would have incentives to invest in better range management, and thus to achieve greater grass production per acre. But wilderness lessees or purchasers would also have the opportunity to increase the quantity or the quality of the output of wilderness areas and at the same time preserve their basic characteristics.

The management of the lands under long-term lease, private purchase, or public corporation would be economically more efficient. Private parties would have the incentive to invest in greater outputs where these would be economic, and they would be less restrained by limitations of capital availability than the federal agencies, who are restrained by limitations of appropriated funds. But more economic management would also arise from screening out investment and management programs which did not promise returns commensurate with costs. The lease proposal would take into long-term leases only the most productive lands, whether "productive" be measured in ability to produce timber, grass, wilderness experience, outdoor recreation opportunity, minerals, or anything else; and sales likely would be limited largely to productive lands. The direct economic effects would be evident on the lands whose management was transferred to private hands, but some indirect economic effects would also be felt on lands remaining under federal management. If no group were willing to assume the costs of managing some proposed outdoor recreation area, for instance, the federal agency should consider carefully whether its development for outdoor recreation in the same or similar areas was really worthwhile.

Each of the proposed alternatives would reduce considerably public expenditures for these areas. Collection of lease rentals and royalties and any other necessary actions would require only small federal expenditures. While lessees would have to pay federal and state income taxes, they would not share their gross revenues with these taxing units of government, hence the inhibiting effect of revenue-sharing would be removed from their investment decision making. States and local governments could still be given the present share of lease revenues paid to the federal Treasury. Federal expenditures would be eliminated on lands sold or transferred to states.

The pullback provision would have substantial *political* advantages as well.

The pullback arrangement would provide a better mechanism for negotiation among rival private interest groups than is now available. Instead of forest industry firms and wilderness-preservation groups feuding with each other over some area, with each trying to direct the public agencies and the political process to its advantage, the basis for meaningful negotiation between them would exist. Adjustments in boundaries of a particular area or tradeoffs of one area for another would then be possible by means that are unavailable today. The wilderness group could propose to lease or purchase an area, and the forest industry firm could threaten to pull back as much as one-third of it, strategically chosen to inflict maximum damage to the wilderness proposal. Or the reverse could happen—the forest industry firm could propose a long-term lease or a purchase, and the wilderness group could threaten to pull back as much as one-third of the land, again chosen for maximum disruption. This process could be followed for every pair of uses of federal land, and the threats would not necessarily be confined to the particular area under consideration, but might include other areas as well. Concerned individuals or small groups could exercise their pullback rights against any applicant for any purpose, if they were prepared to meet the costs, and thereby could exercise an effective control over federal land use which is unavailable to them today. Intricate negotiations, with direct moves, feints, red herrings, bluffs, and all other aspects of gamesmanship, common in competitive markets for private property, would almost certainly result. The end product would almost certainly be a greater total social product than the zero-sum struggle the administrative-political arena typically provides today.

Closely allied to the forgoing, pullback would direct private initiative and private energy toward social gains, not away from them. Among other results, it would provide a private yardstick by which to judge federal agency administration. (Shades of the public power struggle of the past, by which public yardsticks to judge private actions were proposed!) Precise comparability between the more productive lands disposed of and the less productive land remaining under federal administration would be lacking, but nevertheless some broad valid comparisons could be made. The public-private interrelationships on federal land would enter a new phase.

The pullback provision for all forms of federal land management would lessen the pressures on the executive and legislative branches. Instead of prolonged public hearings, committee and congressional actions, administrative agency expenditures, and the like, the interest group seeking its own purposes and gains could choose one of the alternatives described in this chapter. Even when some alternative was not chosen, its existence would be a significant political factor. If the advocates of some wilderness area were unwilling to assume the costs of administration and the nominal lease costs, either by direct application or by pullback, this would provide unequivocal evidence of the area's actual worth for this purpose. And, similarly, if a forest industry firm were demanding increased harvest of national forest timber, the alternative of long-term leases or of land purchase would be a powerful measure of the values involved. Instead of oratory and political pressures, economic measures imposed by the applicants themselves would provide the standards now lacking.

Citizen energies would be redirected, from attempts to influence public action, to the attainment of positive goals chosen by themselves. Instead of public hearings, lawsuits, letter-writing campaigns, and all the other paraphernalia of the present federal land-management process, we would substitute positive planning, meaningful negotiation with rival claimants, and constructive actions in the field.

The Future of the Federal Lands

It is always difficult and hazardous to predict future changes in any field of human activity, as I have pointed out in the Preface. As time goes on, I am more cautious in the kinds of statements I make about the probable future. My reflections on the future of the federal lands are discussed below.

- That space on the earth's surface which is now the federal lands will remain there in perpetuity, judged on the scale of human lifetimes; its mountains, deserts, soils, climate, and other features will be little changed over any reasonable future. If the earth is to undergo a significant climatic change (a general warming up) as many persons argue, this will, of course, affect the federal lands similarly to the effect on intermingled and adjacent non-federal lands. Most of the plant cover on the federal lands will remain unchanged: forage plants will be consumed by domestic livestock, trees will be cut by timber harvesters, shrubs will be trampled by recreationists, and so forth, but all of these forms of plant life have enormous capacity for renewal. If they did not have such capacity, they long since would have vanished. There will be some changes in all these factors, even if we cannot now foresee just what will occur, but there will be relatively little that is specific to the federal lands, as contrasted with intermingled and adjacent nonfederal lands.

- But the *resources* of the lands now in federal ownership will differ greatly within several decades or a generation from now. As Zimmermann so graphically and clearly pointed out thirty years ago, resources are created by Man's activities.[31] Barnett and Morse pointed out that the basic resource is human intelligence and ingenuity.[32] Resources are as much a function of technology and of human desires or demands as they are of any characteristics inherent in the land and its attributes. By application of science, technology, capital, and entrepreneurship, human beings can create new resources out of what would otherwise be useless rocks, soil, topography, and biomass. There is every reason to believe that all of these human components of natural resources will change greatly over the next few decades or next generation, even if today we cannot be sure what those changes will be or how they will come about. So the resources of the present federal lands will change, probably greatly and in unexpected ways, and I now expect they will become more, not less, productive.

- The demands for the goods and services that can be produced from the present federal lands will almost surely continue to rise for the next several decades. We have shown, especially in chapter 3, how the outputs of these lands have increased in the past several years in response to greater demand. The same factors which have been operative in the past will continue, at least to a considerable degree, and new forces will likely arise also. There are some gains from trying to estimate future demand (in a schedule sense) but without such specific estimates we can be fairly sure that the trend in demand will be up.

- The problems of resource management on the lands now federally owned will continue, somewhat changed from the present, during the next few decades, if not indefinitely. There is little reason to believe that any of the important resource-management problems of today will go away. The probable increased demand will mean increased management problems, but increased opportunities as well. The management problem will become greater but not, I think, overwhelming. Young people contem-

plating a career as natural resource managers need not fear
there will be nothing left for them to do. Nor should they be
discouraged that the problems they are likely to encounter will
be truly insurmountable. Challenging, yes, but they should
welcome challenge. The same technology that will create new
resources will provide new tools for their management.

Each of the above general statements applies equally well to the
present federal lands, whether they remain in federal ownership or
whether they are disposed of to the states or to private owners or are
included in public corporations or are leased out on long-term leases.
The physical characteristics of the land, its potential for creating
resources, the demands for the outputs of these resources, and the
management problems are all to a large extent irrespective of who
owns the land. But there are some other aspects of the future for
which the ownership may be decisive.

- If most of the lands now in federal ownership remain in federal
  ownership indefinitely, then some special problems arise. In
  particular, the problems of achieving economically optimal
  management of these lands will become greater. In a United
  States where the demands on the total output of goods and
  services and upon the federal Treasury are likely to grow in the
  future, questions are likely to be raised about the national gains
  from management of federal lands where these result in substantial annual cash deficits. The greatest unresolved question at
  the end of 1982 is, Can the Forest Service and BLM master their
  own planning processes, to produce economically rational, politically acceptable, and operationally practical plans for the
  resources under each agency?
- If most of the present federal lands were disposed of to private
  owners or to the states, major questions will arise—To whom?
  How much? At what price? With what restrictions, if any, on
  land use after sale? The big question for the future would then
  become, How will the management of these lands and resources
  differ in a new ownership as contrasted with a continued federal
  ownership? Will there be more efficiency in producing goods
  and services at less cost per unit of output? Will the presently
  nonmarketed outputs be given proper consideration? Is there
  real danger that new ownership will be a major disaster, in a
  national social sense, because the new owners lack sensitivity

about some values or because they lack expertise in the management of what are often ecologically fragile lands? Or will the new owners, whoever they may be, do a much better job than is likely to be forthcoming from the federal agences? Clearly, it is easier to ask questions of this kind than it is to answer them. The most realistic answer is: only time will tell.

● Is there any real prospect for the long-term leasing of federal lands? Any such program would require new legislation and a substantial public commitment to this course, and these may not be forthcoming. If a major, long-term leasing system were established for the federal lands, would it work as described? Would the pullback provisions really result in a bargaining among rival contenders for use of the federal lands, in a manner similar to the way the competitive market works at its best? Would the presently nonmarketed outputs of the federal lands still be achieved, to the extent they were economically rational, either by commercial lessees or by the leasing of these lands by groups committed to the production of the nonmarketed outputs?

Notes

1. Bureau of Land Management, U.S. Department of the Interior, *Public Land Statistics 1979* (Washington, D.C., Government Printing Office, 1979); and Forest Service, United States Department of Agriculture, *Report of the Forest Service, Fiscal Year 1980* (Washington, D.C., Feb. 15, 1981) processed.

2. An excellent reference, which shows the language of the 1974 Act, what was stricken in the 1976 Amendment, and what was added by the latter is discussed in Dennis C. LeMaster, "The Resources Planning Act as Amended by the National Forest Management Act," *Journal of Forestry* vol. 74, no. 12 (December) 1976. For a good discussion of the 1976 Federal Land Policy and Management Act, see *Arizona Law Review* vol. 21, no. 2 (1979), which consists of a large number of articles specifically focused on this act.

3. John V. Krutilla and John A. Haigh, "An Integrated Approach to National Forest Management," *Environmental Law* (Lewis and Clark Law School–Northwestern School of Law) vol. 8, no. 2 (Winter 1978) p. 413.

4. Marion Clawson, *The Economics of National Forest Management* (Washington, D.C., Resources for the Future, 1976).

5. Barry S. Tindall, "Fees and Charges in Recreation and Parks—A Review of State and Local Government Actions," A Statement Presented to the Subcommittee on Public Lands and Reserved Water, of the Committee on Energy and Natural Resources, U.S. Senate, June 15, 1982.

6. John L. Walker, "National Forest Planning: An Economic Critique;" Douglas R. Leisz, "The Impacts of the RPA/NFMA Process Upon Management and Planning in the Forest Service;" and John V. Krutilla, Michael D. Bowes, and Elizabeth A. Wilman,

"National Forest System Planning and Management: An Analytical Review and Suggested Approach," in Roger A. Sedjo, ed., *Governmental Interventions, Social Needs, and the Management of U.S. Forests* (Washington, D.C., Resources for the Future, 1983). Richard W. Behan, "RPA/NFMA—Time to Punt," *Journal of Forestry* (December) 1981. I attended a meeting of the Western Forest Economists at Wemme, Oregon, in May of 1981, at which time there was much criticism and no open defense " of the Forest Service planning process under these acts. Nelson (see footnote 25, below) has pointed to the great costs and generally indecisive results of BLM planning under its acts and in response to court decisions.

7. Richard M. Mollison, "The Sagebrush Rebellion: Its Causes and Effects," *Environmental Comment* (June) 1981. This journal is published by the Urban Institute, Washington, D.C.

8. Ibid.

9. Paul W. Gates, *History of Public Land Law Development,* written for the Public Land Law Review Commission (Washington, D.C., Government Printing Office, November 1968). See particularly chapters XII and XIII.

10. Ibid., p. 317.

11. John G. Francis, "The West and Prospects for Rebellion: An Analysis of State Legislation Responses to the Public Lands Question, 1979–1981" (Washington, D.C., Brookings Institution, 1982).

12. Gates, *History,* pp. 336–339.

13. Ibid.

14. Ibid.

15. Bureau of Land Management, U.S. Department of the Interior, *Public Land Statistics 1980* (Washington, D.C. 1980) pp. 3 and 5.

16. Bureau of the Census, U.S. Department of Commerce, *Historial Statistics of the United States, Colonial times to 1970* (Washington, D.C., Government Printing Office, 1975) p. 429.

17. Marion Clawson, *Uncle Sam's Acres* (New York, Dodd, Mead Co., 1951) pp. 86–89.

18. See *Federal Lands,* June 21, 1981, p. 3. *Federal Lands* is a publication of McGraw–Hill, New York City.

19. Gordon Tullock, director of the Center for the Study of Public Choice, Virginia Polytechnic Institute and State University, prepared a paper for RFF's Workshop on "Rethinking the Federal Lands," held in Portland, Oregon, in September 1982, from which this figure is taken.

20. Marion Clawson and Burnell Held, *The Federal Lands: Their Use and Management* (Baltimore, Md., Johns Hopkins University Press for Resources for the Future, 1957). See chap. 6. And on p. 348 in a footnote, we refer to a proposal for a federal forestland corporation made by the Forest Products Industry of Oregon, a committee sponsored by Lewis and Clark College and Reed College in Portland, in 1956.

21. Ibid., p. 347.

22. Robert H. Nelson, "Making Sense of the Sagebrush Rebellion: A Long Term Strategy for the Public Lands," A Paper Prepared for the Third Annual Conference of the Association for Public Policy Analysis and Management, held in Washington, D.C., on October 23–25, 1981. Nelson made it clear that he was speaking as an individual, not as a representative of the Department of the Interior.

23. Ibid.

24. Marion Clawson, "An Economic Classification of U.S. 'Commercial' Forests," *Journal of Forestry* vol. 79, no. 11 (November) 1981.

25. Nelson, "Making Sense."

26. Dennis E. Teeguarden, "A Public Corporation Model for Public Land Management," A Paper Presented at the Conference on Politics Vs. Policy: The Public Lands Dilemma, Utah State University, Logan, Utah, on April 23, 1982.

27. Ibid.

28. Ibid.

29. Promotional literature from the Wilderness Society, received in the fall of 1981, states the case for the Society as follows: "We led the monumental struggle during the last Congress to save Alaska. There and in other states more than 62 million acres were placed in the National Wilderness Preservation System, *protected forever*, thanks to the efforts of The Wilderness Society" (*Italics* added for emphasis).

30. Peter Pearse, *Timber Appraisal: Policies and Procedures for Evaluating Crown Timber in British Columbia*, Second Report, British Columbia Task Force on Crown Timber Disposal (Queens Printer, 1974); and David H. Jackson and Kathleen O. Jackson, "National Versus Regional Control of Natural Resources Policy: A Comparative Study of the United States and Canada," *Public Land Law Review* vol. 2, 1981.

31. Erich W. Zimmermann, *World Resources and Industries: A Functional Appraisal of the Availability of Agricultural and Industrial Materials* (rev. ed., New York, Harper & Row, 1951).

32. Harold J. Barnett, and Chandler Morse, *Scarcity and Growth: The Economics of Natural Resources Availability* (Baltimore, Md., Johns Hopkins University Press for Resources for the Future, 1963).

7

Special Problems of Intermingled Federal– Private Land Ownership

The fact that federal and private lands are intermingled throughout the United States on both macro and micro spatial scales has led to many difficulties.[1] The intermingled and adjacent private lands create problems for both the users and managers of the public lands. And, perhaps equally so, the federal lands create problems for the owners, managers, and users of intermingled and adjacent private lands. In this chapter I will explore these problems and suggest the comparatively few practical actions that might reduce their severity.

All federal land ownership today is affected by the selective character of the process of public land disposal to private and state ownership, and of the early federal land reservations and the later federal land acquisitions. When the national forests were first set up, they tended to be located largely in the mountains and not in the valleys, especially in the West where the largest of the national forests are located. This occurred because the valleys always had been more attractive to private parties seeking public domain, whether by purchase or by homesteading. The railroads crossing mountain ranges nevertheless had followed the valleys so that the railroad grant lands were often located there. As a result, less public domain was available in the valleys and more in the mountains, as selections were made for national forests.

The lands under BLM control today tend to be the desert and semidesert areas, whether plains or mountains, because these are the lands least attractive for private purchase or homesteading. There

230

are many exceptions to these generalizations and, in any case, there are many small tracts of land within each broad category which are of different ownership than the adjacent or surrounding area.

The land disposal process was a selective one on a spatially fine-grained scale. While there were a few disposals of large contiguous blocks of federal land (especially in Ohio in the very early days), for the most part the disposals were in units of 640 acres or less. Even the railroad grants, which totaled large acreages, were made up of individual 640-acre tracts. The original Homestead Act provided for 160-acre units, the Enlarged Homesteads for 320 acres, and the Stock-Raising Homesteads for 640 acres. Sales of public domain were normally for units of 640 acres or less, and many purchases (as well as some homesteads) were for units as small as 40 acres.

The rectangular cadastral survey established boundary lines for land titles on cardinal directions, the lines running up and down hill with no recognition of the natural features of the land (except where steep topography or other conditions led the surveyor to stray from the lines he should have established). It is difficult to see how land surveyors, working in largely unknown and unexplored territory, could possibly have given any consideration to the natural features of the landscape which we today are able to perceive, and thus cadastral survey on more nearly natural lines was impractical.

Had the early land-disposal process ultimately disposed of all public land to private ownership, the fragmentation of the land ownership during the active disposal process would have caused boundary problems for private owners but no problem of intermingled federal–private lands. This essentially happened in such states as Ohio and Iowa, in the Corn Belt as a whole, in many areas of the South, and in some areas of the West, where all of the land is now nonfederally owned. In other areas—for instance, some of the Great Plains, or the foothill areas around some western valleys—nearly all of the land was disposed of, with only scattered tracts remaining in federal ownership. Without ever examining such tracts on the ground, one can be fairly sure the land is steep, the soils thin and rocky, or that the land is a local swamp, or otherwise not worth the small costs of acquisition from federal ownership for farming or grazing use. In still other areas, especially within the checkerboard railroad grant areas, nearly half the land is in federal ownership today and the rest is privately owned. This happens in cases where the railroad grant lands have remained privately owned by heirs of the original or successive owners, and most of the other land is in federal ownership, perhaps within a national forest. But in the case of the O & C lands, the roles are reversed—it is the original railroad grant lands which have been "revested and reconveyed" to federal ownership, while the interspersed tracts, originally federally owned, are now largely in private hands.

There are still other areas where most of the land is federal, with only limited acreages of intermingled private land. In the eastern national forests, where the federally owned land was acquired by purchase from private owners, the acquisition process was incomplete so that some privately owned land is interspersed with the federal lands. At the extreme are federal areas containing little or no private land, because the federal reservation was established before disposal to private ownership occurred. The classic example of this is Yellowstone National Park, which was established in 1872 before any disposal of the land within its boundaries to private ownership had occurred. Some national forests are similar in having nearly all of their area in federal ownership.

Of the total area within boundaries of national forests (and other designated areas under Forest Service administration), about 17 percent is not under Forest Service administration.[2] This ranges from less than 5 percent of the area for the Tongass, Chugach, Beaverhead, Bitterroot, Clearwater, Nezperce, Bighorn, Grand Mesa, Samuel R. McKelvie, Shoshone, Apache, Coronado, Gila, Kaibab, Tonto, Ashley, Bridger, Challis, Dixie, Salmon, Targhee, Teton, Mount Baker, Mount Hood, Okonogan, Umpqua, Whitman, and Winema National Forests to more than 50 percent of the total area in the Angelina, Bienville, Caribbean, Chattahooche, Conecuh, Daniel Boone, Davy Crockett, Jefferson, Nantahala, Oconee, Pisgah, Sabine, Sam Houston, Sumter, Uwharrie, Chippewa, Hoosier, Manistee, Mark Twain, and Wayne National Forests. It is noteworthy that all those in the first group of forests are in the West and that all the second group are in the South and East. But there are also forests in the West with large tracts of nonfederal land—the Cache, Shasta, and Fremont, for example, which have nearly one-third of their total area in nonfederal ownership. And, since these data were published, the Cache National Forest has been merged into the Wasatch National Forest. Clearly, the intermingled land problem is magnified when there is more intermingled land than when there is but little of it.

Partly because they were established so much later, and partly because the boundaries were set to include widely scattered areas of federal land, the grazing districts present a considerably different picture, with more than 40 percent of the total area within their boundaries not under BLM control. The latter include some relatively small acreages (4.4 million acres) of privately owned land on which the BLM administers the grazing by agreement with the landowners. Land ownership situations vary greatly among different grazing districts and among different areas within each district. In some districts nearly all the land is federally owned; in other parts, a substantial portion of the area is privately owned; and elsewhere there are but scattered tracts of federal land. Outside of the grazing districts, the BLM generally controls only a small part of the total acreage although there are exceptions—in the Mohave Desert of southeastern California the BLM administers most of the land, but it is not in a grazing district.

These data for acreages of private land within boundaries of federal land units substantially understate the seriousness of the problem. Data on miles of common boundary lines between federal and nonfederal lands would be much more revealing. Many of the problems arising out of intermingled ownership exist because of land of different ownership boundaries. Private land to the extent of 10 percent, 20 percent, or larger percentages of the total area would be easier to manage if it were in a reasonably contiguous area in one part of a federal unit than if it were spread widely in relatively small tracts throughout the federal area. The converse is true also for areas mostly privately owned but with some intermingled public lands. The acreage of the intermingled lands is but part of the problem; the spatial scale of the units presents problems as well.

But the data on acreages of intermingled ownership, based as they are on titles to the land surface, understate the problems caused by the separation of titles to surface and subsurface resources. The land title situations for coal-bearing lands were outlined in table 3-2, but even there the seriousness of the problem is understated because the scale on which the intermingling of ownership occurs is not considered.

Private land within or adjacent to federal lands may create serious problems for the users and the managers of the federal land, as Shands has described.[3] Many are of an environmental nature: the use of the private land often creates an air or water quality problem on the federal land; or the commercial developments on the private land may impair the attractiveness of the adjacent federal land; or timber harvest on the private land may impair the visual amenities of the federal land; or in other ways the use and developments of the private land may impinge on the federal land. One of the most intrusive activities on private land that is intermingled with or nearby to federal land is subdivision for private vacation, retirement, or other residential purposes, which may create septic tank or other drainage problems on the federal lands. Uses of various kinds on private land may stimulate trespass on the federal lands. And there are other adverse effects that some federal land managers attribute to the existence of nearby private lands.

At the same time, the public lands create problems for the owners, users, and managers of intermingled or adjacent private lands. Shands discusses some of these but his survey apparently did not include sending questionnaires to or interviews with commercial users and developers of private land and, as a consequence, he may have underestimated the number and the importance of these effects on private land. He does mention a number of effects of essentially environmental nature—the protection of predators and other wildlife on federal lands, which kill domestic animals on private land; the possibility of fires being allowed to burn on federal land but spreading to private land; and others. If the units of land in an intermingled federal–private landownership situation were each economic units for development and use, the problems of intermingled ownership would be lessened. There would still be some externality effects, as use of one tract in some degree impinged on the use of nearby tracts, just as there are some externality effects among tracts in wholly private districts or localities. But, in fact, the relatively small size of the federal and of the private ownership tracts in many situations means that neither is a reasonable economic unit alone. An efficient coal mine may require more land than is available in the privately owned tracts or in the federal tracts; or the road to permit timber harvest on either federal or private forest may have to cross land of the other ownership; or the small tracts of federal grazing land interspersed on a large, privately owned ranch may have little economic value when taken alone; and many other examples could be cited. The economic inadequacy of existing federal and intermingled private tracts is far more common than the adequacy of such units.

While economic use of land and resources is generally impeded by the spatial scale of the intermingling of federal and private lands, yet it must be recognized that some private landowners gain an advantage in the use of federal lands by reason of their ownership of intermingled private lands. For example, the owner of a dude ranch on a relatively small area of private land within a national forest may have major competitive advantage over his rivals because he can have easier use of the extensive federal lands adjacent to his holding. Or the owner of the private timber may have better access to the federal timber than any competitor; again, because of his ownership of private land. Such examples could be multiplied. It is a mistake to assume that every private owner would like to simplify the land ownership pattern.

Access

The intermingled land ownership problem is greatly exacerbated by the need for access to each ownership unit. The owner or user of land must have access to it, to enjoy there the services which must be consumed on the site or to remove from the land those products which must be marketed elsewhere. During the long disposal period access over the federal lands was encouraged in practice, and was simple and relatively easy for the kinds of uses and kinds of equipment then current. As the land passed into private ownership, the owners of land typically dedicated to public ownership and use the rights of way located along section lines, on which roads were constructed. The roads were crucial in the development of the great farming regions. As the ownership pattern grew more complicated in many areas, some owners of private land, as well as some managers of public land, saw advantages in denying access to some of the inter-mingled private and public lands. Shands cites cases where private timber land is rendered worthless because access across a wilderness has been denied.[4] In fact, mining interests often complain bitterly about being denied access via federal lands.

Ideally, full and easy access should be available to every tract of land, regardless of its ownership, but, in fact, the situation is often not quite this simple. If there is one 40-acre tract of public land sitting in the midst of several thousand acres of private land, should every deer hunter be allowed to cross the private land to get to that one small tract of public land? Many of them probably could not identify the boundaries of the public land and, even if they could find it, many would be unlikely to stay on it for their hunting. If any considerable number crossed the private land, they might well damage it, in terms of increased erosion caused by their vehicles, leaving gates open for livestock to get out, and the like. But should the owner of the private land, whose key location allows him to prevent access to large areas of public land, be allowed to deny access to the public land for recreation or for the harvesting of timber? Or should the owner of a valid mining claim within a wilderness area be allowed the kind of access which would seriously damage the wilderness character of the area?

States vary in how they handle access from one private tract of land to other privately owned areas. Laws and practices vary among federal areas for access across public land to private land and for the securing of access across private land to permit use of publicly owned areas. This is a complex set of relationships, not easily summarized, especially as to how laws and practices actually work out on the ground. If any program of large-scale disposal of public land or of large-scale leasing were undertaken (see chapters 5 and 6), care should be taken that the access problem is not thereby worsened.

Provision should be made in law and practice for relatively free access to both public and private land but with some regard for the costs involved to the owners of the land crossed over. There should be some room for negotiation between parties and interests, with perhaps a provision for arbitration if negotiations bog down. Solution of the access problem would mitigate the intermingled ownership problem, but not fully solve it.

Land Exchanges

Faced with the complex and unsatisfactory nature of the intermingled federal, state, and private lands, many observers have proposed land exchanges as a means of simplifying the land ownership situation. By trading federal land for private land, the scale of intermingling can be reduced even though the total acreages in each ownership remain unchanged. A number of official reports over many years, as well as many private analyses, have suggested increased land exchanges as a solution to the problems described above. Laws in effect for many decades have provided for such exchanges, yet progress has been very slow and shows little evidence of increasing. There are a number of reasons why this is so.

First of all, a land exchange is a form of barter—one tract of land for another—and under the law tracts must have equal value (or approximately so). Alfred Marshall, in his *Principles of Economics*, describes the problems of barter; as an example, he uses a man with surplus shoes and another with surplus hats. The problems were enormous in finding an interested other party, in finding hats or shoes that fit, in getting the desired colors and styles, and in agreeing on terms, as Marshall describes them. He demonstrated the great productivity of money as a medium of exchange. Nonetheless, he never tackled the problems of exchanging land for land. How can two owners of somewhat similar land in the same general region each benefit from an exchange—and unless each feels he benefits, the exchange will not go forward—where the commodities offered are so similar? There are indeed situations in which each can benefit, but they are not common.

Owners of private land are often loath to propose an exchange with a federal agency. They know years, not months, will be required to consumate the exchange, and that during that time some uncertainty exists as to the continued status of their land. They know the exchange proposal will be published, and that objectors will be given a hearing, and that perhaps they will be subjected to public criticism. There are always some groups suspicious of every proposed exchange, which they tend to call a "giveaway." Often the gains from an exchange, even if one could be worked out quickly and easily, would not be large. Indeed, many owners of intermingled tracts gain because of the intermingled situation. Moreover, many private owners have sentimental attachments, beyond sheer monetary value, to their land. For these and perhaps other reasons, owners of intermingled lands often will not initiate an exchange of land with a federal agency.

The federal agencies, too, are disinclined to do so. The federal land managers must make detailed land appraisals to justify the exchange, and they, too, face the possibility of public criticism. Unless there are major management advantages, the federal agencies may prefer to let sleeping dogs lie. As one who has been involved in several such exchanges, I know that the costs incurred by the federal agency (in addition to the costs of the land offered) are often greater than would have been involved in outright land purchase, had funds been available and had that course been politically acceptable. When there is an urgent need to acquire a piece of private or state land by exchange, the same circumstances that create the urgency often make difficult the reaching of an agreement. The federal agency seeking an exchange faces all the difficulties of finding a receptive trader with desired land, and must offer land in exchange which will appeal to the private owner. This requires reaching an agreement on values, as well as on other conditions governing the exchange.

How Have Past Federal Land Exchanges Worked?

At two recent workshops held under the auspices of the U.S. Senate Committee on Energy and Natural Resources, the experiences of federal and state agencies and private parties with federal land exchanges were described in some detail.[5] Numerous statements made at the time generally confirm the forgoing analysis and detail how the exchange process works out in practice. From the experiences related at these workshops, a few general conclusions can be stated:

- Land exhanges are desirable and beneficial, at least under many conditions.

- All the parties to an exchange must benefit from it, since the exchanges are voluntary and no one will participate unless some gain is foreseen.

- The general public interest must be served by any exchange which a federal agency initiates, approves, or accepts.

- There are many difficulties, including delays, inherent in the land exchange process.

From statements made at the 1982 workshop, as well as those documented in other sources, it is possible to assemble some quantitative data to support these general points (table 7-1). It is clear that, over a considerable period of years, each of the four main federal land-managing agencies has made substantial use of their land-exchange authority. The agencies and others have described specific case studies where land exchanges had been very helpful in dealing with difficult land management problems. But it is also clear from these data that, from the perspective of the total intermingled land ownership problem, the progress has been small. Even if the absolute rate of exchanges could be maintained indefinitely—and one must assume that the easiest exchanges already have been made, so that progress will be slower on the remaining, more difficult ones— it would take more than five hundred years for both the Forest Service and BLM to eliminate the intermingled land problem. In reality, this means that land exchanges, while important, can never completely solve the problems which stem from intermingled land ownership. Even if such exchanges could be made, the administrative costs would be considerable. The Forest Service representative at the second workshop stated that in the three preceding fiscal years the administrative costs of making the exchanges averaged $83 for each acre acquired. The necessity of appraisal of both offered and selected tracts, the costs of advertising, public hearings, and other necessary costs are considerable. If the costs for the BLM were the same as those for the Forest Service, and if costs per acre remained the same

TABLE 7-1. SUMMARY OF FEDERAL AGENCY EXPERIENCE WITH LAND EXCHANGES

Item	Forest Service 1970–80	Bureau of Land Management		National Park Service 1913–82	Fish and Wildlife Service 1966–81
		1970–82	1941–65		
Total number of exchanges in period					
Successfully completed	1,492	317	2,801	471	160[a]
Failed	108	120	—	—	97[a]
Pending at end of period	—	141	—	—	69[a]
Area transferred *from* federal ownership (1,000 acres)	510	—	4,146	—	34
Area transferred *to* federal ownership (1,000 acres)	805	—	3,954	555	45
Value of federal lands traded (million $)	330	—	—	—	—
Value of lands received by federal government (million $)	330	—	—	—	—
Total area of nonfederal land within exterior boundaries (million acres)	39	94	—	—	—
Years required to eliminate all nonfederal lands[b]	535	—	594	—	—

Note: There may be a small degree of double counting in some of these figures, to the extent that an exchange may have been reported by BLM as the agency providing the federal lands and the National Park Service or another agency also reported the same exchange as the recipient of the acquired land. Dashes (—) indicate that data are not readily available.

Sources: Statements presented to Workshop on Land Protection and Management, Subcommittee on Public Lands, Senate Committee on Energy and Natural Resources, June 15, 1982, by Vernon V. Lindholm, Dean Bibles, Willis P. Kriz, and Walter R. McAllester, respectively. Also, BLM figures for 1941–65 are from Marion Clawson, *The Federal Lands Since 1956* (Washington, D.C., Resources for the Future, 1967) pp. 80 and 81, excluding exchanges involving forest lands and timber. Data for the Forest Service's total area of nonfederal land within exterior boundaries are from Forest Service, United States Department of Agriculture, *Land Areas of the National Forest System, as of September 30, 1980,* FS-360 (Washington, D.C., 1981); for the BLM 1970–82, data are from area of nonfederal land within grazing districts, 1980; Bureau of Land Management, U.S. Department of the Interior, *Public Land Statistics 1980* (Washington, D.C., 1981) p. 77.

[a]These cover 1970–81 only.

[b]Assuming that the same acreage could be added annually as was added in the period of record.

in 1982 dollars—and it is more likely that they would rise than fall, as more difficult exchanges were made—the total administrative cost to eliminate the nonfederal inholdings would be $3.2 billion for the Forest Service and $7.8 billion for BLM.

How Can the Land Exchange Process Be Improved?

Some improvements to the land exchange process, while leaving that process basically intact, have been suggested and a few have been made.[6] Exchanges might be limited to the same kinds of land—grazing land for grazing land, forested land for forested land, mineral-bearing land for mineral-bearing land, and recreation land for recreation land. While this might seem to reduce the prospects for successful exchanges because it would narrow the alternatives, it, in fact, could make them easier. It would lessen the difficulty of evaluating each tract of land since comparisons could be made more nearly on an acreage basis with equal uncertainties about future trends in value of each type of land. Some of the political obstacles to land exchange might be lessened also—exchanges would be less likely to upset the overall balance of federal–nonfederal land ownership within a state or county. This type of restriction could be made by administrative action within the federal agencies by announcing that exchanges would be considered only when the types of land were closely similar.

Another option would be to place the receipts from federal land sales in a special account, which could then be used to purchase other desired lands. This would require finding an interested buyer and an interested seller, but buyer and seller would not have to be the same individual, as is the case for an exchange. Moreover, some semblance of a competitive market might exist for the tracts offered for sale and the tracts purchased. This proposal responds to Marshall's defense of the productivity of money as a medium of exchange—a recognition that barter was not the only way to make exchanges. There almost surely would be some political opposition to giving such authority to federal agencies unless it were carefully circumscribed in the law.

A modest step in this direction was taken in the Federal Land Policy and Management Act of 1976 where, in Section 206, exchanges are authorized if the values can be equalized by a lump-sum payment of not more than 25 percent of the estimated land value. While this will slightly reduce the problem of finding lands of nearly equal value, it does nothing about the problems of finding a person both willing to "sell" his land and to "buy" the federal land.

It is possible that various improvements could be made in the land exchange process, to reduce the time and effort now involved, but candor compels me to admit that changes in the process more likely will increase than decrease the administrative problems. Simplification of federal administrative procedures is a wonderful goal but usually an illusion, and is likely to prove so here.

One improvement, if it could be made in some way, would be to require that third-party objectors to land exchanges would assume some financial responsibility for their actions. As it stands now, any person or group may object to an exchange, tying up for months or years the completion of the exchange, and at no cost to the objector. Clearly, this is an invitation to obstruction. If, in some way, the objector could be required to assume some financial responsibility in those cases where the objection was finally overruled, this obstacle to federal–nonfederal land exchanges would be reduced. But it would scarcely result in a revolution in the making of such exchanges.

A Wholly New Approach to Land Exchanges

Perhaps a wholly new approach to land exchanges is needed; perhaps a quasi independent board could be established. It probably would have to be federally funded, but its members might be chosen by states, conservation organizations, and industry, as well as by federal agencies. The board would operate outside the control of any federal land agency. It would propose large areas or localities within which relatively large-scale exchanges of land of similar types could be effected, and could go as far as to indicate the general boundaries of federal land and nonfederal tracts. At this point the owner(s) of the nonfederal land or the federal agency could exercise their right to pull back, as has been described in chapter 6, and withdraw from the exchange as much as one-third of the area (which would be matched by an equal withdrawal on the part of the other party). Subject to this provision, the exchange would be formalized and, although subject to public comment, the whole exchange process might be shortened, perhaps to the extent of doing away with the attempt to arrive at a detailed appraisal of values, tract by tract—a process which is inexact, time-consuming, and costly at best.

If it were approved by law, this substantial departure from present practice would upset many. But it would have substantial values as well. It would eliminate the burden of initiating a land-exchange proposal from both the federal agency and the nonfederal land owners—each could say that the board required this step, thus lessening their responsibility and diminishing public objections to the exchange. The inclusion of fairly large areas of generally similar lands might well iron out differences in values attributable to smaller tracts. The possibility of the pullback provision would give each party an opportunity to modify the exchange without completely killing it. In other words, a new, rather bold, and untried approach might move the land-exchange process from dead center where it now seems to be stuck.

For example, take large areas of the West, where scattered state-owned lands, having no forest values, little if any recreation values, or no known or suspected mineral values, have been ignored by private developers. The lands are suitable only for grazing—often low-grade grazing—and, in units of 640 acres, they have little value for that purpose. They are surrounded by federal lands, mostly under BLM administration, of essentially similar types. The land-exchange board might designate large areas, perhaps 50 miles on a side, within which all state lands would be exchanged for an equal area of federal lands in one block, the location of which the board could specify or which might be chosen in some other way, perhaps by lottery. The state and BLM could exercise their right to pullback, which would enable each of them to bargain in their best interests. This would result in blocking up a substantial amount of both state and federal land. These state lands would have more value to ranchers than scattered sections currently have.

The board, the federal and state agencies, and private parties would know of areas where the chances of making an exchange were best, and if attention were focused there, it would be possible to make a limited, but still significant, number of exchanges. The more difficult situations would be postponed for later attention or simply passed over as possible exchange areas. Thus, by focusing on the most likely areas and rejecting, at least temporarily, the idea of a complete resolution of the intermingled land problem, some progress might be made.

Use agreements for grazing lands should also be mentioned, which at one time were used by the Forest Service in national forests. The carrying capacity of the private land was estimated, and the rancher was given a free use permit to use a corresponding amount of national forest land for grazing his and other ranchers' livestock. This kind of arrangement obviates trespass by either party. The BLM uses a similar arrangement for some lands within its grazing districts. Pooling of oil and gas or of coal deposits, partly on federal land and partly on nonfederal land, is at least theoretically possible, but practically it is difficult to arrange in an equitable and satisfactory way.

Both the Forest Service and BLM (for the O & C lands) have legal authority to enter into cooperative or pooling agreements with owners of private forestland that combines the private and the federal timber into one large sustained-yield operation. The Forest Service has entered into one such agreement with a private firm, but the BLM has made no such agreements. The working out of an agreement that will be equitable for fifty years or longer offers a great many difficulties, and it seems that this approach to forestland management will not be pursued in the future.

Land Acquisitions

Shands notes, "Acquisition is the most direct method of preventing land adjacent to federal units from being used in ways that damage the public resources."[7] Land acquisition has long been used by the National Park Service, but here I am not considering the land-management activities of this federal agency. The Forest Service has had land-acquisition authority since the Weeks Act was passed in 1911 and was followed by other legislation for specific situations, and over the years the agency has acquired significant acreages of land. The BLM lacked general land-acquisition authority until the Federal Land Policy and Management Act of 1976.

But having the legal authority to acquire private land is not enough; money is required, and, in fact, appropriations for this purpose have been very small when compared with the value of all the intermingled land. There are serious political and social obstacles to much federal land acquisition, even when legal authority and funds are amply available. Many owners of intermingled and adjacent private lands do not want to sell; they have emotional attachments to their land or they gain substantially in economic terms from the proximity of their lands to the federal land. Even when owners are willing to consider selling, it may be very difficult to reach agreement on prices. Above all, the amount of intermingled and adjacent lands that conceivably could be purchased is so great, and the probable value is so large, that it is politically unthinkable that the necessary funds will be available. This has been true for many years, and the Reagan administration clearly will not support large-scale federal land purchase. Even beyond these practical monetary considerations, there would be great opposition both locally and nationally to extensive federal acquisition of private land.

On the other hand, because some federal land acquisition in limited circumstances is desirable from many points of view, it would have local and national political support and could even be funded. Even persons generally opposed to federal land ownership often concede this. There are a number of special land use situations where federal acquisition of very limited areas of land would meet rather restrictive criteria. But federal acquisition of private land is not likely to be an important means of meeting the intermingled land problem in the future. The sale-and-buy suggestion made earlier would facilitate land acquisitions, but not on a large enough scale to solve completely the problem of intermingled landownership.

Is Long-Term Leasing a Solution?

If the alternative of long-term leasing of federal lands, as described in chapter 6, were adopted, this could reduce the problems of intermingled federal–private land ownership. The various private owners could lease adjacent or intermingled federal lands, subject to the laws permitting long-term leasing, and thus resolve, at least for some decades, the problems arising out of the present ownership pattern. If the leasing of federal lands were to proceed actively, this might have a considerable effect on reducing the intermingled land ownership problem; but it could hardly be expected to solve all such problems, in part because many private owners would have little, if any, incentive to incur additional costs merely to simplify the land ownership pattern.

Land Planning and Zoning

If it is difficult or impossible to greatly change the ownership pattern of intermingled federal, state, and private lands, would it be possible by land use planning and zoning to reduce the conflicts between landowners? It is at least conceptually possible to develop a land use plan for all the land, regardless of ownership, to zone each part for the planned use, and thus obtain compatible land uses within each planning zone and between them. On this basis, the conflicts between federal and nonfederal lands would be reduced to those conflicts which occur among privately owned tracts where there is no public land.

But who would do the planning, enact the zoning regulations, and enforce them? It is most unlikely that state and local governments would accept plans made by a federal agency, and surely they would rebel against any compulsory land use zoning or other plan emanating from a federal agency. In fact, the federal government lacks the legal power to enact and enforce general land use regulations on private land. On the other hand, the federal agencies and the Congress almost surely would be unwilling to grant zoning power over federal lands to local governments.

The Public Land Law Review Commission made a strong recommendation on this matter in 1970: "State and local governments should be given an effective role in Federal agency land use planning. Federal land use plans should be developed in consultation with these governments, circulated to them for comments, and should conform to state or local zoning to the maximum extent feasible. As a general rule, no use of public land should be permitted which is prohibited by state or local zoning."[8]

In general, this recommendation has not been followed although joint planning has taken place in a number of local situations.[9] Joint planning of a large area, and separate but compatible actions on the lands of each ownership category may be possible when direct control over land use by units of one government, as against lands under the jurisdiction of the other, is not likely. Given goodwill on both sides and a genuine interest in the welfare of a community or local region, considerable gains might be achieved by joint planning.

No Easy Solution

There exists no easy solution to the problems arising out of the extensive intermingling of federal and nonfederal lands. The problem is an old one that has evolved over many decades. If there had been an easy solution, it would have been found long ago and the problem would not exist today.

There well may be no effective solution. Significant progress is unlikely as long as present arrangements continue essentially unchanged. One bold and different approach has been suggested, and perhaps others could be devised. Quite possibly none of them will really deal effectively with the problems of intermingled ownership, and, in their absence, little progress is likely. But, then, perhaps not much more could be achieved with any new approach.

At the same time, the increasing demands for federal and nonfederal land will add to the seriousness of the problems of intermingled land ownership. What has been inconvenient in the past may become well nigh intolerable in the future. But federal agencies, states, and private parties must learn how to live in some way with intermingled land ownership.

Notes

1. William E. Shands, *Federal Resource Lands and Their Neighbors*, An Issue Report (The Conservation Foundation, Washington, D.C., 1979).

2. U.S. Department of Agriculture, the Forest Service, *Land Areas of the National Forest System as of September 30, 1980*, FS-360 (Washington, D.C., 1980).

3. Shands, *Federal Resource Lands*.

4. Ibid.

5. The problems of slow and cumbersome exchanges and some suggestions for improvement were discussed at two recent congressional workshops; see *Workshop on Public Land Acquisition and Alternatives*, Committee Print, Committee on Energy and Natural Resources, United States Senate, 97th Cong., 1st sess., Publication No. 97-34, October 1981; see also *Workshop on Land Protection and Management*, Committee Print, Committee on Energy and Natural Resources, United States Senate, 97th Cong., 2nd sess., Publication No. 97-101, June 1982.

6. Frank Gregg, in *Federal Land Transfers: A Westwide Program Based on the Federal Land Policy and Management Act*, Issue Paper (Washington, D.C., Conservation Foundation, 1982), makes a number of such suggestions. In brief, he proposes a greatly increased scale of land classification by the BLM, by which the agency would classify the tracts of federal land it thought should be retained permanently in federal ownership and the tracts which it thought should be disposed of, and that the latter should be offered for exchanges. He would institute a planning process involving substantial public participation, to consider proposed exchanges. While his proposals would surely facilitate some exchanges, it may be doubted that the areas would be large. The land classification of the federal agency might not agree with the judgments of private citizens or of state governments as to the suitability of lands for exchange; and in any case the difficulties of exchange, noted above, would remain.

7. Shands, *Federal Resource Lands*, p. 45.

8. Public Land Law Review Commission, *One Third of the Nation's Land* (Washington, D.C., Government Printing Office, June 1970) p. 61.

9. William E. Shands and Robert G. Healy, *The Lands Nobody Wanted* (Washington, D.C., The Conservation Foundation, 1977); see particularly chapter V.

8

Public Participation—
By Whom, How,
and When?

As we noted in chapter 1, the crux of federal land management is the federal ownership of the land and its private use. Out of this interrelationship come all of the specific problems of federal land management. The public—however it is defined—naturally enough wants a voice in how its lands are managed, in much the same way that the stockholders in a corporation want a voice in how the company they own is run. No one really challenges this viewpoint today, but the hard questions are: Who is the public? How can it be involved most productively and satisfactorily? And when should the involvement take place? These are the issues I will consider briefly in this chapter.

Public participation in federal land management takes many forms, of which the most important, by all odds, is the use citizens seek to make of the federal lands. Imagine, if you can, a world in which no one wanted to partake of outdoor recreation on any federally owned land—not a soul ever visited a national park, national forest, or BLM district; a world in which no one sought timber from federal land, by purchase or by trespass, and not a stick of timber was harvested; a world in which no individual or corporation sought to extract metals, oil and gas, or coal, where not a shovelful of earth was turned; or no one cared about wildlife. In such a world, clearly there would be no public participation in federal land management. Such a world does not exist today and never has, nor will it ever exist in the future. But by imagining such a world, we may come to realize how important are the desires of the public for federal land use.

247

One might reject this unreal model, even for analytical purposes, and yet realize that the demand for public participation is a function of the level of public use. Of course, as the data in chapter 3 have shown, public use of federal lands for almost every purpose was at a lower level two decades or more ago. Fewer persons sought outdoor recreation from federal lands, timber harvest was less, and minerals development proceeded at a slower pace. Public participation presented problems even then as I will show later, but by comparison with today, these were relatively slight. When use was less, the agencies needed smaller staffs, they spent less money in management, and they took in less revenue. While there were inevitable conflicts among competing user groups, none were as serious as those we face today.

With increased usage of the federal lands, pressures also have increased on the agencies, who have had to contend with new or unresolved problems of the past. In addition, they have faced a public clamor for a larger role in federal land management. The changing attitudes of the public and the increasing competence of all user groups have greatly changed the focus of federal land management (see chapter 2). The highly vocal calls for an increased role in federal land management today rest basically on this greater use of the federal lands for nearly every purpose. Literally millions of private decisions underlie that increased use. The demand for increased public participation in federal land management arises only in part from the actions or inactions of the federal agencies. By and large, the latter have not been the initiators of increased public participation—indeed, many of the older public land managers would like to shut the public out, at least to a large extent, from actual participation in planning and management of the public lands.

The problems and the opportunities of public participation in management of the lands presently in federal ownership will continue indefinitely and probably intensify in the future. Many people, operating chiefly through groups and organizations to which they belong, will insist on playing a role in the management of these lands, no matter which alternative for future land management (see chapter 6) is chosen and irrespective of the approaches adopted. The public will insist on participating in hearings on proposed legislation, when regulations are being written, and when plans are made; and they will scrutinize and comment upon the results of whatever programs are adopted and placed into operation. Public participation is thus a feature common to all conceivable forms of future federal land management. The extent of the public's involvement will depend upon the direction taken by future management of the present federal lands.

Public Participation Prior to 1960

Although the oldtime federal land manager did not encourage large-scale public participation in the planning and decision-making process, he did seek public approval of his decisions and actions—and enhanced the prospect for greater appropriations. In addition, he actively sought the participation of his professional peers, when he could see the value of their advice.

From its earliest days, the Forest Service put a good deal of emphasis on Information and Education—I and E. Agency personnel sought to tell the public what had been decided upon, in order to obtain their informed approval and support in political struggles. The Forest Service long used advisory boards, especially on grazing matters, whose members were selected by the Forest Service, not elected by the stockmen. In general, the boards were little more than an interested and concerned audience whose approval of Forest Service actions was sought. The men of the Forest Service did, however, interact with others in their profession, especially with other foresters and professional forestry organizations. The Forest Service, which had largely created the profession of forestry, had been for many years the chief employer of forestry school graduates. Foresters both inside and outside of the Forest Service shared a common professional training and generally endorsed a similar ideology about forest management. Consultation with such peers was not only natural but surely helpful to the Forest Service, as it sought to develop new and better ways of managing the forests.

During the days of the General Land Office, there were few contacts with users of its land. Indeed, their most frequent contacts were with the oil and gas industry. The Grazing Service, on the other hand, established an intimate relationship with its grazing advisory boards— too intimate, in the view of many critics. Shortly after the Taylor Grazing Act was passed, these boards, which were required by law, were indispensable in providing information about the ranges and their use. As I look back on it, I do not see how the Taylor Grazing Act could ever have been put into operation without the use of these advisory boards. Some boards indeed may have stepped over the line dividing advice from direct decision making, but on the whole the boards performed an indispensable function. Their members were elected by the stockmen within each district; spirited elections were not uncommon, and, at times, members were defeated. As a result, these boards had much greater standing with other stockmen and exercised more influence on the Grazing Service and on BLM management of federal land than that which the boards composed of livestockmen exercised on the national forests.

Those who made up the advisory boards for the grazing districts were strictly grazing people. In most districts, the board consisted of an equal number of cattlemen and of sheepmen elected by their fellows, along with one representative of wildlife interests appointed by the agency, ordinarily on recommendation of local sportsmen groups. In addition, for the O & C areas, the BLM appointed members of multiple-interest groups, attempting to include every important user group.

Prior to 1960, both the Forest Service and BLM would have been hard pressed to stir up active participation on the part of the general public in planning and management of the federal lands. The situation changed gradually between the end of World War II and 1960, but after that date it changed greatly. Earlier, I noted that essentially no public pressure was exerted for the Multiple Use Act of 1960, which the Forest Service sought and obtained; and that interest was slight in the Classification and Multiple Use Act of 1964, which the BLM sought and obtained. Today, it may be hard for some of the activist conservation groups to realize that their organizations—or other earlier groups—paid very little attention to federal lands more than twenty years ago.

After 1960

Clearly, historical changes do not begin at a precise date, but gradually evolve. Dana and Fairfax report, "The Multiple Use Act (1960) was an appropriate culmination of the transition taking place in the postwar years. While it recognized new uses and new pressures, it did so in a traditional way."[1] This act was devised and pushed by the Forest Service without much active participation by interest groups regarding the actual framing of the legislation. Frequently it has been criticized as providing, at best, only some general guides to the management of the national forests. It does not explicitly call for public participation in planning for multiple use, although it could be argued that the concern for all uses of the national forests would require a comparable involvement of all interest groups. The Classification and Multiple Use Act of 1964 also lacks specific provisions for public participation, although it does speak more explicitly to the matter of planning for BLM lands than the earlier act provides for the national forest. Under it the BLM held some public hearings in the West.

These acts and the public endorsement for their enactment gradually led to increased demand for more "public participation" in federal lands planning and decision making. These demands came primarily from the conservation, preservation, wilderness, and environmental activist groups. As they became increasingly interested in the use of federal lands, they demanded a greater say. The groups who had historically been concerned—the commercial firms who were interested in forest harvest, range use, and oil and gas development; and the professional groups, such as the foresters—initially expressed little interest in having greater involvement in federal policymaking. For some years, "public participation" really meant "conservationists' participation." And until the conservationist groups became both active and successful, the groups who earlier had been most involved were generally content with their relationship to the federal agencies.

The National Environmental Policy Act of 1969 did not explicitly require public participation in federal land planning and decision making. However, its requirement that an Environmental Impact Statement be filed, coupled with a changing attitude on the part of the courts, gave the conservationists a legal weapon for bringing their ideas to the attention of the federal agencies. It was easier to develop an Environmental Impact Statement if it rested on a plan, and, indeed, the statement itself was a plan. Having been ignored earlier when they knocked politely at the door, the conservation groups were now able to hammer it down and force their way into the planning and decision-making process. The results were often traumatic to the federal agencies and to the historic users of the federal land. The agencies gradually learned that sooner or later many interest groups had to be involved; and that although involvement during the process of planning took time and effort, it took less of each if invested initially than it did when public participation was postponed until after the agency had made its studies and its plans. The other user groups shortly woke up to the fact that, if they were to protect their interests, they had to become much more active, to the extent of filing lawsuits, when this was in their interest.

The Renewable Resources Planning Act of 1974 began making explicit in law the requirement for public participation in planning and decision making for federal lands, although the act in itself was more implicit than explicit on this point. Meeting the requirements of that act surely called for a greater degree of public participation than had ever been known. The 1974 Act was supplemented in only two years by the National Forest Management Act of 1976, and in it the requirement for public participation is quite explicit:

> Section 6 (d): The Secretary shall provide for public participation in the development, review, and revision of land management plans including, but not limited to, making the plans or revision available to the public at convenient locations in the vicinity of the affected unit for a period of at least three months before final adoption, during which period the Secretary shall publicize and hold public meetings or comparable processes at locations that foster public participation in the review of such plans or revisions.
>
> Section 14. Public Participation and Advisory Boards—(a) In exercising his authorities under this Act and other laws applicable to the Forest Service, the Secretary, by regulation, shall establish procedures, including public hearings where appropriate, to give the federal, state, and local governments and the public adequate notice and an opportunity to comment upon the formulation of standards, criteria, and guidelines applicable to Forest Service programs.
>
> (b) In providing for public participation in the planning for and management of the National Forest System, the Secretary, pursuant to the Federal Advisory Committee Act (86 Stat. 770) and other applicable law, shall establish and consult such advisory boards as he deems necessary to secure full information and advice on the execution of his responsibilities. The membership of such boards shall be representative of a cross section of groups interested in the planning for and management of the National Forest System and the various types of use and enjoyment of the lands thereof.[2]

In addition to the sections of the act which explicitly direct the secretary to seek public participation, other sections clearly imply that such participation is to be sought and taken seriously.

The Federal Land Policy and Management Act, the BLM "Organic Act," was passed also in 1976. Achterman and Fairfax have made a detailed analysis of the public participation aspects of this act.[3] As described by these two authors, a few excerpts from their article may be helpful in showing the manifold implications of this act.

First of all, it defined "public participation" more explicitly than did the NFMA, but in terms consistent with that act.

> Congress included many references to public participation in FLPMA ranging from broad policy statements and directives to specific requirements for certain procedures [p. 517].

BLM'S historic reliance on grazing advisory boards has been criticized, yet the multiple use advisory board system established in the wake of the Federal Advisory Committee Act (FACA) was working well enough for Congress to direct that it be continued and expanded [p. 518].

Congress also directed that traditional APA (Administrative Procedures Act) rulemaking procedures should be followed in adopting rules and regulations to implement FLPMA and other laws applicable to the public lands [p. 519].

The specific requirements of FLPMA pertaining to advisory committees and rulemaking do not mark any change in past objectives or procedures [p. 519].

Thus, Congress has given the BLM a broad new mandate, but without giving it any new tools or even suggesting tools to use [p. 521].[4]

A consideration of the Achterman and Fairfax article shows, explicitly and implicitly, that certain requirements for public participation are required of the Forest Service and for BLM. They are as follows:

- The public must be given an opportunity to participate throughout the planning and decision-making process; allowing comments only after plans have been largely formulated is not enough.

- Information must be dispersed in readily understandable language and must be easily available to all interested groups.

- Discussions of plans and other proposed actions by the agencies must be held at convenient times and locations for the users as a whole.

- There must be ample opportunity for user groups and other interested parties to react to proposed plans, both during the period the plans are being formulated and at the time they are announced—often in a formal public hearing. The agencies must so organize their operations that such public comments and reactions will be considered seriously.

- An effort must be made to obtain public participation from *all* affected persons or groups. This is not easy to achieve; more consideration will be given to this point later. The agencies must not only make a conscientious effort, but they must be able to prove that they have done so.

- Agencies must live up to their own regulations and rules, or be made to do so.

Problems with Public Participation

The idea that the people who own and who use the federal lands should participate in the management planning and decision making for these lands is a deceptively simple and attractive one. Who could reasonably oppose allowing owners and users to have a word about how their property is managed? As is so often the case with apparently simple and noncontroversial ideas, it is the implementation—not the concept itself—which raises the serious questions.

Almost everyone will agree that, if there is to be any public participation in federal land management, then all interests and all user groups should have an equal opportunity to be heard. Persons or groups with an interest in the use of federal lands fall into three general groups:

- The actual users—the picnicker and camper, the wilderness hiker, the hunter, the timber harvester, the rancher, the oil and gas developer, and others—who go on the land for shorter or longer periods and make direct use of some feature of the land
- Those whose economic welfare to some significant degree depends upon providing services to the actual users—the service station, store, and restaurant serving the recreationist, the outfitter for wilderness travel, the manufacturer of logging trucks, the manufacturer and dealer in well casing, and others—located both near the area of actual use and located more distantly but providing goods and services used by the actual user of the federal lands
- Concerned citizens, perhaps resident relatively nearby, perhaps resident hundreds or thousands of miles away, who are concerned that the federal lands be managed well, in a conservation manner, and with concern for all users and potential users. To some degree, this is "the general public" to which reference is often made in discussions of public policy issues. These persons may or may not be organized into associations capable of representing their interests.

Much is made by some writers of "option demand" for wilderness—a desire to know that wilderness exists even if one never visits it and even if one would not really care to visit a wilderness area if given the chance. Much less attention had focused on the implicit demand of the poorly housed large numbers of people, who would have most to gain were the total supply of houses to be greatly increased, even when they could never afford to buy a new house. Their needs would best be met by ample supplies of forest products at low or reasonable prices.

It is certainly arguable that the third group, by far more numerous than either of the two previous groups, has both a legitimate and a less selfish interest in the federal lands. The practical problem is to inspire this group to action, especially at the efficient stage of planning, before final decisions are made. All too often, so-called concerned citizens sleep until they are awakened by some impending development of which they disapprove. Once awake, they demand to have the final word about the plans. This situation arises frequently in urban planning as well as in planning for federal lands. Comparatively few people are willing to invest the time to study a public planning issue carefully, to sort out relevant fact from the obfuscating arguments, to reach a policy position that is rational by their own standards, and to take the time and effort to make their views known to the planning bodies. Yet these people, who have a right to be heard, are a serious threat to the planning organization that intentionally or inadvertently ignores them.

The basic difficulty is that a fundamental conflict exists between economic efficiency and public participation. Economic efficiency requires a balancing of costs and returns, each in monetary units—a voting by dollar power, as it were. Persons or groups have power in proportion to their economic strength, that is, their wealth or capital and their income. Public participation requires a balancing of views among persons, on a somewhat vague but essentially one-person–one-vote basis. This distribution of power to affect public decisions is different than the economic power reflected in prices. Krutilla and Haigh, who have explored this issue at some length, report:

> . . . The prices and costs used are a product of the existing distribution of income among individuals having widely different preferences for both public and private goods. The configuration of relative prices that emerges, therefore, is dependent on the existing distribution of income, and any significantly different distribution will give rise to a different set of prices and costs throughout the economy. . . . Submitting such plans to the general public for approval, where every participant's view is weighted by his vote and not by his purchasing power, is equivalent to having an expression of preferences for resource services unconstrained by any income consideration. This is equivalent to changing the distribution of income which undergirded the price and benefit estimates for the formulation of land use plans.[5]

Decisions on federal land management by competitive bidding or by the competition of the pullback arrangement (see chapter 6) operates, at best, for economic efficiency; decisions based on attitudes expressed by the public in the public participation process provide, at best, a degree of economic equity based on individuals rather than upon their economic strength. Which of these two approaches is deemed preferable depends to a major degree upon the ideological and attitudinal convictions of the observer or critic.

One of the truly difficult problems in public participation, both for the planner and for the serious and responsible private group, is to find some means of screening out the obviously stupid, naive, and self-serving suggestions of some members of the public, without at the same time discouraging genuine and sensible participation by the concerned public. Any public enterprise seems to attract a share of irresponsible self-appointed intervenors, whose major interest is entertainment and self-aggrandizement. Such people cannot reject any opportunity to speak in public and to sieze, if only for a moment, a degree of public attention—like the naughty boy at the party who would rather be noticed and despised than be ignored. Although their numbers may be small and they are not invariably present, a few persistent and vocal ones can make a mishmash of sensible public participation.

Falling short of such extremism are those persons and groups who seek to delay an action with which they disagree, but for which they know they cannot overcome public support or agency approval. Such objections often entail great costs: In terms of money spent on collecting and analyzing facts to meet their objections; in terms of personnel from agencies and other user groups that are marshaled to speak to their objections; and especially in terms of time, which is costly to everyone. Sometimes critics propose alternatives knowing they will be unacceptable, which, in fact, they would not adopt if the responsibility were theirs to decide and to act. Sincerity and great conviction may characterize those who object, but they do nothing to avoid the consequences of such objections. If one is convinced that some proposed line of action on federal lands is bad, then one naturally enough—from his own point of view—seeks by all means at his command to prevent that action, but the cost to society as a whole may be large, especially if in the end the same actions are taken which had initially been proposed.

All of this leads to a major question, How can the whole process of public participation in federal land management be made more efficient, so that, in regard to public participation, the terms of the acts are honestly met and delays are kept to a minimum? There is no simple answer. One component of a more efficient system of public participation is to require more responsibility on the part of critics and others who object, while at the same time taking care not to stifle their positive contributions to the process. Some of the ideas advanced in chapter 6 about long-term leasing and pullback arrangements might have possibilities here in that they offer some means to enable each group to force other groups to live up to the bargains that have been reached.

Public Participation and the Resource Manager

Public participation in planning and decision making for federal lands is often thought to diminish the role of the resource manager— forester, range-management specialist, wildlife specialist, and other professionals. In the "good old days" of truly long ago, the district manager could make a timber sale, issue a grazing permit, build a fire-control line, engage in some controlled burning, or carry out other resource management actions on the land, using his best professional judgment and the best facts available to him. Many such men, with the encouragement of their agency, would explain to the public why they had done what they had done, but usually after the action was taken. The public might be well-informed but not really consulted. The resource manager could act quickly to meet situations since there was no reason to consult the public.

That day of federal land management has passed, and today's resource managers realize that user groups must be consulted, listened to, and followed if their advice and criticisms are sound. The real challenge to the modern resource manager is to accept the fact that times have changed, and to use public participation to his or her advantage. He or she must find ways to enlist the interest and the participation of all user groups from the very beginning of the process, to carry their interest throughout, and to fully inform them as to the final result. In the process, each user group will, to a substantial extent, inform and discipline every other user group. The attacks upon specific proposals can be diverted away from the resource manager and toward the user groups which propose something else. User groups can be taught that multiple use often means less than complete acceptance of one viewpoint and requires some compromise from all groups. The small child who goes to nursery school or kindergarten learns more about accommodation to peers than is ever learned at home from parents, and the same relationship exists for user groups interested in the federal lands.

Culhane has well documented how this process can be made to work in hands of alert and imaginative federal land managers at the local level.[6] By involving all user groups, and by letting them discipline each other, the resource manager in the end can find a solution which meets his professional standards and is accepted by all interest groups as better than any other alternative. The resource manager's position can thus be strengthened, not weakened. The problems of delay and cost, noted earlier, still remain and often are serious, but the astute manager plans his actions far enough ahead so that delays are part of the act.

> The Forest Service and the Bureau of Land Management thus find themselves in the fortuitous position in which all criteria of administrative responsibility converge. They have so arranged matters that the political necessity of responding to their multiple clienteles reinforces the dictates of their professional expertise and statutory mandates. Most agencies in the federal bureaucracy are not so fortunate. The service's and the bureau's strong positions have been immeasurably aided by the access to the agency decision making granted to environmentalists and other new clients by the much criticized NEPA and public participation programs. Public participation enabled the agencies to pursue a multiple-clientele strategy and thereby buttress their professional commitment to conformity and avoidance of capture. While the benefits accruing to the agencies from public participation and NEPA were only partially anticipated by the environmentalist advocates of public participation, they vindicate those procedural reforms of the 1970s.[7]

It should be pointed out that the long-term lease and pullback suggestions of chapter 6 have direct applicability here. Any user group or other interested party, dissatisfied with the decision for management of the federal lands, would have the alternative of applying for a long-term lease under laws governing such leases; and any other party would have the alternative of pulling back up to one-third of the area applied for. As pointed out in chapter 6, this would not only permit, but would force, contending user groups to bargain among themselves, rather than to spend their energies attacking the federal agencies, and would force the user groups to honor all bargains so reached. This would be public participation with real responsibility. If the area selected for long-term leases were one-fourth or less of the total federal land area, as suggested in chapter 6 might be the case, then the direct effect of the long-term leasing would be exercised only on a relatively small part of the total federal area, but indirectly the effect might be felt on the remainder of the area. If certain arrangements were hammered out where the user groups bargained among themselves, this might have implications for reasonable arrangements on the lands which no applicant deemed suitable for long-term leasing.

Public Participation in Actual Resource Management

The discussion in this chapter has been about public participation in planning and decision making for federal lands. Two major points have been made and should be reemphasized: public participation is desirable in spite of some serious weaknesses; and the processes of public participation can be improved. All of the discussion thus far assumes that the role of the user groups is to provide information, to react and criticize, and to offer advice, but that the actual final decision and its implementation is to rest in the hands of the federal employees charged with the responsibility of actual management of the federal lands. A user may accept or be forced to accept responsibility for actions on leased lands, under the terms of the lease. But otherwise, the public cannot assume responsibility for actual decisions and actions; in only rare cases could the public be held accountable for the results of actions.

I have frequently observed that one reason both the Forest Service and BLM were effective in carrying out agreed upon policies and decisions was that each had been forced to fight forest and range fires. One does not fight a fire by a committee or by public participation; there must be one officer in charge, who knows he has the responsibility to put it out, along with others who receive their orders from him. The person in charge may seek advice and help from within or from outside the agency, but this does not relieve him of the ultimate responsibility. Most other resource actions on federal land do not have the same time-scale urgency as fire fighting, but there can be no dilution of responsibility for action. Otherwise accountability for results is destroyed, which affects everyone in an undesirable way, including the interest group which sought to insert itself into the management process.

One only can hope that this distinction between participation in planning and in decision making on the one hand, and actual action on the other hand, is understood and will be observed by all user groups interested in the federal lands. As noted earlier in this chapter,

Section 24 (b) of the National Forest Management Act of 1976 refers to "public participation in the planning for and *management of*" the National Forest System. Some user group may take this as an invitation for actual participation in field-level actions, which would be disastrous if the Forest Service agreed to let them do so. Fortunately for the general public, the agency's sense of pride and of possessiveness is likely to resist any such interpretation.

Notes

1. Samuel T. Dana and Sally K. Fairfax, *Forest and Range Policy* (2 ed., New York, McGraw–Hill, 1980) p. 204.

2. Dennis C. LeMaster, in "The Resources Planning Act as Amended by the National Forest Management Act," *Journal of Forestry* (December) 1976, has provided a very useful complete reproduction of the 1974 Act, the changes made by amendment, and the 1976 Act.

3. Gail L. Achterman and Sally K. Fairfax, "The Public Participation Requirements of the Federal Land Policy and Management Act," *Arizona Law Review* vol. 21, no. 2, 1979.

4. Ibid.

5. John V. Krutilla and John A. Haigh, "An Integrated Approach to National Forest Management," *Environmental Law* vol. 8, no. 2 (Winter) 1978, pp. 402–403. This journal is published by the Lewis & Clark Law School–Northwestern School of Law, Portland, Oregon.

6. Paul J. Culhane, *Public Lands Politics—Interest Group Influence on the Forest Service and the Bureau of Land Management* (Baltimore, Md., Johns Hopkins University Press for Resources for the Future, 1981).

7. Ibid., p. 341.

9

The Need for
Further Research

There is an old joke to the effect that the one result of any piece of research is a call for further research on the same topic. Surely, a great deal of research does end with such a plea, and very properly so—the researcher would be negligent if he or she did not communicate what had been learned about what he or she had not known. Good research pushes back the frontier of ignorance and spreads the territory of knowledge, but progress is measured in millimeters along a road which is kilometers long. The research reveals "truth" as defined and measured in some way, but it also reveals ignorance, some of which was unexpected when the research began. As the researcher pushes out across the plains and mountains, one ridge or mountain is climbed, only to reveal more ahead. It would be highly irresponsible of any researcher not to point out what he or she now thinks still remains to be learned, as well as to relate accurately what had been learned by the research.

It is in this spirit that this chapter is written. What lines of research should be pursued for the best management of the federal lands to meet the needs of Americans, now and for generations ahead, are briefly described in general terms. Obviously, the suggestions made here will have to be spelled out in specific terms, and funds will have to be obtained before actual research can begin. And as this research progresses, it will doubtless have to be redefined and redirected as our knowledge expands.

Physical and Biological Research

The federal lands respond to the same physical and biological processes and forces as do the intermingled and adjacent nonfederal lands, so that research which serves one ownership class serves the other. In proposing some lines of needed research, one must realize that a great deal is known about each of the subjects, largely as a result of past research; but the need remains for further research. In a great many instances, the greatest need today is for a careful weighing and synthesis of the large body of specialized research already done, and for research and planning on how best to integrate and apply past findings to the land management process.

Grazing. For the federal grazing lands under Forest Service and BLM management, it is necessary to develop management systems which will yield the maximum forage for livestock on a sustained and continuous basis. It well may be argued that this problem has not been satisfactorily resolved anywhere in the world, even over the centuries that domestic livestock has been grazed. The range areas of the United States and throughout the world are relatively fragile ecosystems that can be degraded easily by overuse. Such ecosystems recover slowly from destruction or deterioration. The temptation always exists to use native grazing areas more intensively than they can withstand for the long pull. Yet is is also true that wise use often is essential to maintenance of their full productivity. There are opportunities for increasing the usable productivity of natural range systems by reseeding with adapted species and by various improvements to make livestock management easier and more purposeful; but these also may have counterproductive results, by merely providing the opportunity for new rounds of exploitation. The grazing areas of the world, including those of the United States, are typically desert or semidesert and have highly variable climates—severe droughts alternate with years which are relatively wet for those climates. How can livestockmen take maximum economic advantage of a highly variable forage supply? This, too, is largely unresolved worldwide. Is extremely conservative stocking, based on feed supply in prolonged drought periods, the best grazing management system? Or is adjustment in livestock numbers to the actual forage supply in the particular season a better answer? And, if so, how can it be brought about in timely and economic fashion? Many tough problems exist here, to which ultimate answers may not be possible but on which much additional light might be shed.

Forests. There are also many unresolved problems for the best management of the federal and intermingled or adjacent forests of the country. For those forests that produce wood fiber for human use, the matter of when to cut, how to cut, how to insure regeneration, and what species or strains to use for such regeneration are basic. One cannot expect to grow wood in the forest unless one is willing to harvest what grows; and as a matter of practical fact, the most pressing problem on most federal forest land is to cut the present stand of timber, so that more can be grown. There are also many problems of management of growing stands— fertilization, thinning, disease and insect control, optimum use of fire as a management tool, and others. By intensive management, annual wood production may be more than doubled. For those forests which are not to be cut, or for which production of wood is not the primary purpose, there are also many difficult problems in management—how to determine the physical carrying capacity of recreation and wilderness areas, how to increase that capacity, and how to manage the use of such areas to preserve their productive capacity for these uses. Similar problems exist for the wildlife and watershed aspects of forests. There are difficult problems to be solved in road design and construction, especially how to keep erosion within tolerable limits. Our present knowledge is limited, and although some research is under way, more is needed—most probably, continuously into the future, because the problems are never solved once and for all.

Minerals development. In the case of mineral development on the federal lands (including coal, oil, and gas) the greatest problems are how to secure the maximum economic yield from a given deposit and how to keep the environmental damage to a practical minimum. The first is primarily a problem for the lessee, but it is of a general public interest as well, both in terms of revenues from the land but also in optimum use of a depletable natural resource. Minimizing of environmental impact is a major concern for the federal agencies, although one should not assume that the lessees are indifferent to it. In particular, the restoration of areas mined by surface mining methods is a major physical and biological problem, especially in the drier western areas where much of the federal coal is located. The present law specifies certain goals, methods, and standards, but it is generally agreed that the law is not perfect nor is its implementation.

Tradeoffs. Perhaps the most neglected of all areas of physical and biological science as applied to the federal lands is the matter of physical tradeoffs among different outputs and inputs, and between inputs and outputs. For instance, what are the tradeoffs between domestic livestock and game animals on particular grazing areas? If grazing by domestic animals is decreased, will numbers of game animals increase to harvest the same amount of forage so that there has been no conservation gain? Or what are the tradeoffs between outdoor recreational activity and game numbers and species? Or between timber growth and water yield from specific forested watersheds? Or between intensive timber management on the best sites and reduced, postponed, or prohibited timber harvest on the least productive sites? All of these tradeoffs and other issues involve economic and social issues, but they each involve many physicobiological relationships which are basic to any management programs. There is little to be gained and often much to be lost if the management program proposed or implemented is simply biologically infeasible: it will not achieve the desired goals, and its untimely use may discredit the agency and the proponents.

Economic Research

The forgoing brief listing of some of the major areas where physicobiological research is needed implies the need for matching economic research. If there is a biological tradeoff between game and domestic livestock in some area, there is also an economic tradeoff. Is a 1 percent increase in domestic livestock grazing as valuable as a 1 percent decrease in grazing by game animals, or as valuable as a 10 percent decrease in the latter? Is the use of a specified amount of fertilizer to obtain a specified increased growth of wood economically sound? This type of question could be multiplied many times in the management of the federal lands.

The answers to such questions depend, in part, upon the local demand for the various goods and services that might be produced and upon the local costs of the various goods and services that might be used. National studies of prospective future demand may be helpful—although their record of accuracy is distressingly poor—but the local situation may differ considerably from the average national situation. Estimation of future local demands is, by and large, more difficult and subject to more error than is the estimation of national demands. This is so in part because we in the United States are highly mobile so that population trends in local areas are often quite unpredictable as people move in or out. But if the Forest Service or

BLM is to develop a particular recreation area, it needs the best possible estimate of the expected future demand for that class of recreation in that specific area. Likewise, if timber management for harvest is to be practiced, one needs demand estimates for that class of timber in that location. Such localized estimates may differ significantly from national estimates of demand. The local demand and supply estimates can and, in fact, must be translated into estimates of values, rentals, royalties, and the like.

One difficult aspect of estimating local demand for outputs from federal lands is the valuation of outputs which are not ordinarily sold in the market—outdoor recreation, wilderness, wildlife, watershed outputs, amenity or esthetic values, and the like. I think this issue has been exaggerated in much of the professional literature. Admittedly, there are difficult problems here; but there is typically an overestimate of the accuracy and reliability of data on the prices received for the timber, forage, and minerals products which are sold. The market for none of these products is fully competitive in the economist's sense of the term, and the prices obtained are often as much the result of arbitrary administrative action as are the "prices" of the nonmarketed services. The wary analyst or resource manager looks critically at all prices and estimated values. There is no doubt that more accurate and dependable estimates of values of the nonmarketed services, in local areas, are much to be desired. Certainly many federal resource managers feel that their decisions are seriously limited, if not impaired, by the present lack of such good local estimates.

How shall the optimum management intensity and the maximum economic investment be achieved on the federal lands under the management of the Forest Service and BLM? These are some of the basic problems with which the 1974 and 1976 legislation was trying to cope; the acts set out many directives—perhaps incomplete and surely somewhat internally inconsistent—in trying to meet these problems. To a substantial extent, Congress bucked the problem down to the federal agencies. Those agencies are now struggling to make the analyses required by the laws. Few observers are fully satisfied with agency performance to date; at best, one can hope that methods are being developed which in time will be more satisfactory in results. Surely there is a large and fertile field here for the best research anyone can devise.

Closely related to the forgoing is estimating the optimum mix of outputs from federal lands capable—as all of them are—of producing more than one kind of output. The agencies have sought to devise methods for estimating optimum mixes of outputs. But there has been much criticism that the methods devised to date are unreliable in results, too slow and costly in operation, not easily understood by the prospective users, and generally distrusted by the latter, as well as by the resource manager in the field.

Resolution of the retention–disposal issue will be affected in no small degree by the outcome of the efforts to devise methods of estimating economically optimum intensity and optimum mix management on federal lands quickly, easily, dependably, and understandably, and of translating those plans into practice. If the planning system, as it exists in 1982, cannot be greatly improved in all these ways, the clamor for disposal, whether by long-term lease or by sale, will surely grow. If the planning system is too complicated, too slow, too undependable, and too imperfectly understood, it may collapse under its own weight. And planning without subsequent implementation becomes only an intellectual exercise.

Organizational Research Needed

There is also need to conduct research on the organization and functioning of the Forest Service and BLM. While these agencies have many similarities with other federal agencies, they are also unique. Most other federal agencies do not manage productive resources, do not have significant revenue income, and do not face problems of optimum intensity and of optimum mix of outputs, as do the Forest Service and BLM. There are some similarities between these two federal land managing agencies and the largest private resource-owning and -managing corporations—Weyerhaeuser, Georgia-Pacific, Crown Zellerbach, and other forestry firms, and the major minerals development firms—but there are the important differences that always exist between a federal agency and a private firm. Both the Forest Service and BLM have problems of fire control, planting trees, reseeding rangelands, building roads, and other specific actions which are closely similar to the same problems on private land. And added to these, they have the problem of obtaining adequate appropriations rather than deciding how to use corporate income for investment on company lands.

Research on federal resource agency organization and functioning has been limited to but a few researchers.[1] Valuable as these substantive efforts have been, there have been too few of them. Of course, additional organizational research has been reported in professional journals, and a substantial literature exists on the organization and functioning of the federal land agencies. But this has been chiefly critical of the policies being followed. Many persons in the agencies, in the private sector, and in conservation organizations are dubious about what organization *research* can accomplish. They may see the need for consideration, debate, and decision making in such matters, but they do not see how it is possible to conduct useful research. I do not agree, although, clearly, there are problems with conducting such research. It can best be done by someone outside of the agency, who is not personally committed to a specific organization chart or operating procedure. On the other hand, the outsider may also lack insight into what really happened or precisely why things are done as they are. But I am convinced that thoughtful and well-organized research is always helpful, and I think this is as true here as elsewhere.

One of the specific topics within the general field of research on organization is how best to make information flow in the agency— from the top down to the field level, from lower levels up to the top, and among personnel at every level—and how to get persons at every level to pay attention to the information that is available to them. If any large organization, whether public agency or private firm, is to function effectively as an organization and not merely as a collection of individuals, there must be adequate communication among its parts. At the same time, the communication should not demand extra time and energy at every level. The Forest Service and BLM seek to have good internal communication and each agency might well argue that it has done its best to achieve such communication adequately and with minimum effort. Outsiders may doubt that the results to date have been as good as they could be. For example, it is not always clear to those in the field just what management in Washington has in mind for conforming to the planning requirements of the 1976 Acts. There is a vast difference between real communication from the top down and a flow of paper. The fact that staff at the top propose actions which field people believe are impractical or impossible is evidence that communication from the bottom up is inadequate at present. The sheer volume of manuals, directives, instructions, and memoranda is to a considerable degree self-defeating—with so much paper, why pay any attention to any of it? Communication is a perennial problem, not to be solved once and for all, but to be striven for, tested, and reformulated continuously. Research can help one to accomplish this.

Another specific topic for research is concerned with how the agency can best reach its own policy decisions. This process is often unclear, and outsiders may suspect that policies are often determined without explicit or adequate consideration. Ideally, every employee should have the opportunity for input into the policy process; practically, this is not possible because of the large numbers of employees and the sheer difficulty of communicating with all of them. Moreover, it can be argued that persons of longer experience and greater commitment to the agency should have a larger role in policy formation than the less-experienced or short-term employees. Policymaking processes can be studied, described, analyzed, and evaluated. The results of such research, if heeded by top officials, should lead to better policymaking processes.

A perennial problem in every large public and private organization is how best to stimulate independent thinking, exercise of initiative, and maximum resourcefulness at every level, while at the same time operating within the general organization and policy framework of the organization. No one wants zombies who merely follow directions at the lower and intermediate levels, but an organization ceases to be an organization unless it is based on central control and a central policy which is adhered to at all levels of the organization. Individuals cannot be allowed to strike out independently of organizational policy. By and large, the federal land management agencies have done well in this respect, compared with government agencies generally. The necessity for fighting forest and range fires and for taking other specific actions quickly has surely driven home the need for independent, responsible, and innovative action in the field. But we should not be satisfied that the ultimate has been achieved, and further research should be able to help here.

From time to time the news media have a field day with some instance of "whistle blowing." An employee, outraged by some action taken by the agency which he or she thinks is illegal, improper, or unwise, makes a public protest, either to the media, or to some members of Congress, or both. Often because of deeply held convictions, the employee does so at substantial risk of reprisal, including loss of job. This has occurred less frequently in the federal resource-managing agencies than in other kinds of federal agencies. Even if they are largely vindicated, the agency and its top officials always emerge somewhat scarred from such incidents. And while I would agree that "whistle blowing" can be commended, the emphasis is often on the wrong aspect of the situation. Instead of admiring the employee for high moral standards, attention might well be focused on the question, How did this situation arise anyway? In general, a situation where whistle-blowing arises represents a failure of real

communication within the agency. Had there been adequate information, fully disseminated and generally understood, the situation
which led to the opportunity for the whistle blower would not have
arisen. The agency head who is embarrassed by the public furor
kicked up by a whistle blower might ponder that incisive research
into the operations of the agency could have prevented the incident.

In changing times, it is essential that every large public or private
organization challenge the old ideas which have governed its operations in the past, while at the same time it should not hastily abandon
the past merely because it is the past. In every large organization,
the natural response to every problem is, "How did we handle it the
last time this problem arose?" The "last time" syndrome extends very
much to public agency budgets and appropriations. There is, of
course, much to be learned from the past, and previous experience
should never be ignored. However, there is also a need to think
critically and to consider wholly new approaches to problems. It is
here that the outside researcher may be most useful. Not bound by
present organization and procedures, without personal rewards or
position at stake, he or she can suggest new methods and procedures
which persons within the organization would be unlikely to devise.
The insiders' initial reaction to the suggestions of the outsiders often
will be, "He or she does not understand us, those ideas are impractical
and will never work." Often the insider will be right, but sometimes
he or she will be wrong, and the outsiders' suggestions may be highly
important.

Research on Relations with the Public

As pointed out in chapter 8, new laws have provided new directives
for the Forest Service and the BLM, as far as relations with the public
are concerned, and these new directives constitute new burdens as
well as new opportunities for the agencies. It is also true that
bureaucratic self-interest is likely to push these (and other federal)
agencies into closer and more effective relationships with their publics.
The competition for federal appropriations is likely to grow keener
and the agency poorly regarded by its public has a difficult hurdle
to overcome in its pursuit of funding. This has always been true, of
course, but the cost of poor public relations may be rising.

It is generally recognized that many natural resource managers are
not well trained—in fact, many have had no formal training—in

public relations. At one time, foresters, range managers, wildlife managers, and other natural resource managers never would have taken any college courses that were connected to the field of public relations; however, this is changing now in many schools and with many graduates. One must recognize that some of the oldtimers in both the Forest Service and BLM, while lacking any formal training, were highly sensitive to how people reacted, based on their own experience and observations.

The experience of other public agencies at federal, state, and local levels in dealing with the public may be helpful to the Forest Service and BLM. The resource manager often faces problems which differ, as far as relations with the public are concerned, from those faced by public servants in other fields. For one thing, natural resource management faces inexorable laws of nature which no amount of good public relations can repeal. The publics for a welfare program, for example, may propose solutions to some problem which can be achieved simply by greater appropriations; for some natural resource management problems, no amount of appropriations can modify the climate or the growth habits of some species. While some members of the public propose phony or impossible "solutions" in regard to natural resources, such proposals are more likely to be shot down by someone on purely scientific or practical grounds. But the resource manager may still have trouble in making this clear to some part of the public, in a way which destroys the phony proposal while leaving intact the dignity of the proposer.

Research into relations with the public in federal land management could be very helpful to personnel in the agencies. In particular, what has really "worked" elsewhere in the agency? And how, indeed, does one define worked? Federal resource managers might understandably be dubious about experiences in relations with the public in other fields, but they would have a direct interest in careful, objective analyses of experiences in their own or closely similar agencies. Such studies may well consider what changes, if any, seem necessary or desirable for the future, given any social or demographic changes which seem likely in the relevant publics. When some procedure seems to have produced good results, to what was this due—sheer luck, good planning, the personality of the agency employee, or something else? And how far can methods successful in a specific instance be translated into generalities or be transferred elsewhere? And how different is the future likely to be? Will the local influx of new types of federal land users greatly modify the practices of good public relations?

Research on Overall Policy for Federal Lands

The processes by which overall policies are formed for the federal lands are imperfect in many ways, in no small part because of the considerable number of actors involved—the federal bureaus, their respective departments, the Office of Management and Budget as well as other agencies or departments from the Executive Branch, congressional committees, and numerous interest groups from business and conservationists. At the best, responsibility for final decision is diffused. There is good reason to believe that alternative policies are imperfectly understood and incompletely analyzed. One can make this statement without implying that economic analysis and economic efficiency are the chief objectives of all actors in the decision process. Even when some group has other criteria for judging policy for federal lands, it still may be true that alternatives are imperfectly understood and incompletely analyzed. And if imperfectly understood, then the basic policy questions are likely not to be raised at all or are likely to be improperly phrased.

For instance, the concepts of sustained yield and, to a lesser extent, of even flow are enshrined in Forest Service ideology, with rarely any major examination or serious consideration given to some major alternative. Or the idea that oil, gas, coal, and other energy resources on federal lands should be developed actively in response to market demands is rarely challenged or seriously examined. Likewise, the whole idea of continued federal ownership of the present federal lands has rarely been seriously reexamined in recent years (see chapters 4, 5, and 6). Many other examples could be cited. A major challenge or serious examination could result in reaffirmation of present policy or in basic changes, but presumably the choice would then be a reasoned one.

Research on the processes of overall federal land policy is especially important despite the difficulties which it entails. If it were easy to devise and conduct such research, it likely would have been done long ago. Difficulties in understanding the past and projecting what should be done in the future stem from the multiplicity of actors and their numerous objectives and standards. Much of the most significant decision making in the past has not been done openly, nor has it been recorded in accessible documents. Some of the major actors would be reluctant to speak frankly, because their ability to influence what actions are taken is derived in part from their work behind the scenes. The ostensible and the real reasons may differ; indeed, the reported actions and the real actions also may be different.

This is further complicated by the fact that no researcher, however brilliant, diligent, and well-trained, can fully grasp all the manifold issues and points of view. The complexity of the process and the multiplicity of the actors make any individual somewhat inadequate to deal with the situation as a whole. Any researcher is dealing with actors, some of whom are at least as able as he, and some of whom will not be frankly forthcoming.

But, as noted in earlier chapters, the federal lands today are a matter of economic, social, and political concern and too important for anyone to be satisfied with less than the best effort that can be made to illuminate the policymaking process. It is my strong conviction that research here is both desirable and likely to yield socially useful results—not necessarily from every project, but in total.

Social Invention in Federal Land Management

The need for social invention in federal land management is greater than the need for more research, important as research is. Social invention for the federal lands has brought the cadastral survey, competitive land sales, land grants for various purposes, homesteads, national forests, sustained yield, and many other entities. Whether one regards each of these ideas as "good" or as "bad" by some standard, the fact is that each one has significantly affected the management of the federal lands.

Inventions, whether social or mechanical, almost always involve certain characteristics:

- Many persons are almost sure to have contributed to the final successful invention, and the person whose name is most closely identified with an invention is very likely to have been the person who took the final successful step rather than the person or persons who first had the idea.

- Many false starts and many failures are likely to have been involved, from the first articulated idea to the first sufficiently practical invention put into operation.

- Many further refinements on the first practical model are almost sure to be made, often changing it greatly, sometimes changing it rapidly. One can easily think of the development of the airplane, the computer, and even of printing itself, for illustrations of these general ideas. They apply equally to social inventions.

Research is frequently backward looking or concerned primarily with the present. The researcher seeks to know and to understand what exists. Even when the researcher explicitly extends ideas into the future, past experience and present problems are likely to dominate the consideration of the future. Research can contribute significantly to invention, especially by analysis of causal relationships, but in my understanding of the terms there is significant difference between research and invention. Both are needed for federal land management.

Some of the proposals in chapter 6 are the first step in social invention. Nelson's proposal for a mixed public-private corporation to manage the more productive forests now included in the national forests, Teeguarden's proposal for public corporations for each national forest, and my proposal for pullback are each suggestions for a social invention for federal land management. At this stage, each is an idea, not a blueprint. Each will have to be debated extensively before its adoption into law, and each will likely undergo considerable change from the present proposal to a final adoption, assuming that the latter takes place at some date. And it is highly probable that each would almost certainly encounter some problems in operation and, as a result, would require further changes.

The proposals found in chapter 6, while representing some interesting and rather novel ideas for future federal land management, do not, in my judgment, include all the possibilities for social invention for federal land management. I cannot now specify what additional ideas may develop, but I am confident that not all social inventions lie in our past. I think that researchers, land managers, and the intellectual community generally should be encouraged to propose social inventions for federal land management. Most of the proposals will prove somewhat impractical, but on the whole, they may prove highly useful. Let us try.

Note

1. Herbert Kaufman, *The Forest Ranger* (Baltimore, Md., Johns Hopkins University Press for Resources for the Future, 1960); Paul J. Culhane, *Public Lands Politics— Interest Group Influence on the Forest Service and the Bureau of Land Management* (Baltimore, Md., Johns Hopkins University Press for Resources for the Future, 1981); Philip Foss, *Politics and Grass* (Seattle, University of Washington Press, 1960); Wesley Calef, *Private Grazing and Public Lands: Local Management of the Taylor Grazing Act* (Chicago, Ill., University of Chicago Press, 1960); Aaron Wildavsky, *The Politics of the Budgetary Process* (Boston, Little Brown, 1974); and Glen O. Robinson, *The Forest Service—A Study in Public Land Management* (Baltimore, Md., Johns Hopkins University Press for Resources for the Future, 1975).

A Chronological List of Publications Concerning the Public Lands by Marion Clawson

1936   (With R. T. Burdick) *Economic Considerations Affecting Permit Distribution on Public Range Lands, Yampa River Drainage, Colorado. III. The Agricultural Situation—an Economic Survey*, submitted to U.S. Forest Service (Fort Collins, Department of Economics and Sociology, Colorado Agricultural College in cooperation with the Division of Farm Management and Costs, Bureau of Agricultural Economics).

1938   "Determination of Sales and Lease Values of Private and Public Range Lands," *Journal of Farm Economics* vol. 20, no. 3 (August).

       (With Cruz Venstrom and T. Dean Phinney) *Range Lands of Northeastern Nevada: Their Proper and Profitable Use* (Washington, D.C., Bureau of Agricultural Economics and Forest Service).

1939   *Effect of Changing Prices Upon Income to Land from Cattle and Sheep Ranching, As Illustrated by Data for Montana, 1910 to 1936* (Washington, D.C., Bureau of Agricultural Economics).

       "The Administration of Federal Range Lands," *Quarterly Journal of Economics* vol. 53, no. 3 (May).

1941   (With G. Alvin Carpenter and C. E. Fleming) *Ranch Organization and Operation in Northeastern Nevada*, Bulletin 156 (Reno, University of Nevada Agricultural Experiment Station).

Author's Note: This bibliography omits testimony to congressional committees, speeches (unless they were published in a professional journal), book reviews, introductions to books written by others, and most reports about government activities.

1942   (With H. R. Hochmuth and Earl R. Franklin) *Sheep Migration in the Intermountain Region,* Circular no. 624 (Washington, D.C., U.S. Department of Agriculture).

"The Range Livestock Industry of the Western United States," Ph.D. thesis, Harvard University.

1950   *The Western Range Livestock Industry* (New York, McGraw-Hill).

1951   *Uncle Sam's Acres* (New York, Dodd, Mead).

"Administration of Federal Lands In the Public Interest," *Journal of Politics* vol. 13, no. 3 (August).

"The Principles of Public Land Management in the United States," in Kenneth H. Parsons, Raymond J. Penn, and Philip M. Raup, eds., *Land Tenure: Proceedings of the International Conference on Land Tenure and Related Problems in World Agriculture Held at Madison, Wisconsin, 1951* (Madison, University of Wisconsin Press).

1952   "The Role of the Public Domain in the Economy of the West" (Western Farm Economics Association, Flagstaff, Ariz.).

1953   (With J. Russell Penny) "Administration of Grazing Districts," *Land Economics* vol. 29, no. 1 (February).

"Economic Possibilities of the Public Domain," *Land Economics* vol. 29, no. 3 (August).

1957   "Federal Forest Land: How Much or How Intensively Managed?" *American Forests* (September).

(With R. Burnell Held) *The Federal Lands: Their Use and Management* (Baltimore, Md., Johns Hopkins University Press for Resources for the Future).

Your Land and Mine (Washington, D.C., National Wildlife Federation). This was revised and reissued in 1969.

1959   "Reminiscences of the Bureau of Land Management, 1947–1948," *Agricultural History* vol. 33, no. 1. Reprinted in Vernon Carstensen, ed., *The Public Lands—Studies in the History of the Public Domain* (Madison, University of Wisconsin Press, 1963).

"Our National Parks in Year 2000," *National Parks Magazine* vol. 33, no. 142.

1960   "Public Land Administration for the Next Generation," *The Northeastern Logger* (October).

1963 "Public and Private Interest in Public Land," in Howard W. Ottoson, *Land Use Policy and Problems in the United States* (Lincoln, University of Nebraska Press).

1964 *Man and Land in the United States* (Lincoln, University of Nebraska Press).

1965 Six articles in *American Forests:* "Should the Public Lands Pay Taxes?" (March); "How Much Should Users Pay?" (April); "Do We Want More Efficiency?" (May); "What Can Land Exchanges Accomplish?" (June); "Is Reorganization a Mirage?" (July); and "What is the Future of Public Lands?" (August).

1966 "Future Problems of Mining and Other Uses of the Public Lands," in J.C. Dotson, ed., *Symposium on American Mineral Law Relating to Public Land Use* (Tucson, College of Mines, University of Arizona).

1967 "The Federal Lands as Big Business," *Natural Resources Journal* vol. 7, no. 2 (April).

The Federal Lands Since 1956—Recent Trends in Use and Management (Baltimore, Md., Johns Hopkins University Press for Resources for the Future).

1968 "Philmont Scout Ranch: An Intensively Managed Wilderness," *American Forests* vol. 74, no. 5 (May).

The Land System of the United States—An Introduction to the History and Practice of Land Use and Land Tenure (Lincoln, University of Nebraska Press).

1970 "New Towns and Federal Land," in *Probable Future Demands on the Public Lands: New Cities and Urban Expansion* (Washington, D.C., Public Land Law Review Commission).

1971 "Conflicting Pressures on Forest-Resource Managers and the Role of the Public in Management Decisions," in Silas Little, ed., *Proceedings of Winter Meetings, Allegheny Section, Society of American Foresters* (Upper Darby, Pa., U.S. Forest Service Northeastern Forest Experiment Station).

Bureau of Land Management (New York, Frederick A. Praeger).

1972 "Range Management in the United States for the Next One to Three Generations," *Journal of Range Management* vol. 25, no. 5.

"Economic Aspects of Public Lands," in Harriet Nathan, *America's Public Lands: Politics, Economics, and Administration* (Berkeley, Institute of Government Studies, University of California).

1973 *Report of the President's Advisory Panel on Timber and the Environment* (Washington, D.C., Government Printing Office).

1974 "How Much Economics in National Forest Management?" *Journal of Forestry* vol. 72, no. 1 (January).

"Economic Trade-Offs in Multiple-Use Management of Forest Lands," *American Journal of Agricultural Economics* vol. 56, no. 5 (December).

"Conflicts, Strategies, and Possibilities for Concensus in Forest Land Use and Management," in *Forest Policy for the Future: Conflict, Compromise, Consensus* (Washington, D.C., Resources for the Future).

1975 *Forests for Whom and for What?* (Baltimore, Md., Johns Hopkins University Press for Resources for the Future).

1976 "The National Forests," *Science* vol. 191 (Feb. 20). This has been reissued as RFF Reprint no. 127.

The Economics of National Forest Management (Washington, D.C., Resources for the Future).

1977 *Man, Land, and the Forest Environment* (Seattle, University of Washington Press).

Decision Making in Timber Production, Harvest, and Marketing (Washington, D.C., Resources for the Future).

Research in Forest Economics and Forest Policy (Washington, D.C., Resources for the Future).

1978 "What's Ahead for the Forest Service," *American Forests* vol. 84, no. 1 (January).

"Public Log Markets as a Tool in Forest Management," *Land Economics* vol. 54, no. 1 (February). This has been reissued as RFF Reprint no. 151.

"Will There Be Enough Timber?" *Journal of Forestry* vol. 76, no. 5 (May).

"The Concept of Multiple Use Forestry," *Environmental Law* vol. 8, no. 2.

1979 "The Federal Land Policy and Management Act of 1976 in a Broad Historical Perspective," *Arizona Law Review* vol. 21, no. 2.

1980 "Wilderness as One of Many Land Uses," *Idaho Law Review* vol. 16, no. 3 (Summer). This has been reissued as RFF Reprint no. 191.

Appendix

TABLE A-1.　GRAZING OF DOMESTIC LIVESTOCK ON THE NATIONAL FORESTS, FOR 1960–80
(in 1,000 AUM)

| Year | No. of livestock | | Amount of grazing by domestic livestock | | Receipts from grazing | |
	Cattle, horses, and swine	Sheep and goats	National forests	National Forest System	Total ($1,000)	$ per AUM[a]
1960	1,307	2,574	8,359.6	9,783.0	4,507	.46
1961	1,293	2,491	8,131.0	9,529.8	3,899	.41
1962	1,307	2,367	8,098.2	9,411.2	3,806	.40
1963	1,339	2,280	7,992.4	9,373.5	4,023	.43
1964	1,360	2,204	7,977.2	9,340.4	3,790	.41
1965	1,376	2,112	7,996.2	9,341.0	3,521	.38
1966	1,476	2,309	8,054.9	9,432.3	3,861	.41
1967	1,521	2,264	8,044.2	9,441.0	4,184	.44
1968	1,531	2,210	8,065.4	9,484.1	4,083	.43
1969	1,577	2,162	7,926.8	9,367.8	4,438	.47
1970	1,607	2,105	7,840.1	9,284.5	4,371	.47
1971	1,606	2,051	7,835.4	9,292.6	5,413	.58
1972	1,633	2,049	7,681.1	9,126.3	5,515	.61
1973	1,571	1,598	7,612.4	9,105.7	6,196	.68
1974	1,580	1,470	7,637.9	9,093.6	7,796	.86
1975	1,626	1,549	7,394.5	8,838.3	7,665	.87
1976	1,690	1,750	7,514.1	8,987.5	10,909	1.21
1977	1,735	2,093	8,411.8	9,872.4	11,443	1.16
1978	1,728	2,006	8,314.5	9,894.0	11,037	1.11
1979	1,733	1,946	8,315.4	9,821.5	—	—
1980	1,894	1,709	8,284.2	9,756.6	—	—

Sources: Numbers of livestock are from *Agricultural Statistics*, various years, and from annual reports of Forest Service, 1978–80; amounts of grazing for 1960–65: AUM = ((Animal unit-months for sheep and goats divided by 5) plus animal unit-months for horses and cattle) times 1.2. For 1966–76: AUM = AUM × 1.2. For 1977–80: AUM as reported. Figures for 1960–76 are on a calendar year basis; for 1977–80 they are on a fiscal year basis. Other data are from the USDA Forest Service, *Annual Grazing Statistical Reports*, for various years. Data on receipts are from *Agricultural Statistics*, for various years.

[a]Calculated by dividing receipts by amount of grazing on the National Forest System.

TABLE A-2. AMOUNT OF GRAZING, GRAZING RECEIPTS, AND GRAZING FEES IN GRAZING DISTRICTS; AND GRAZING BY BIG-GAME ANIMALS IN THE NATIONAL FORESTS, FOR 1960–80

	Grazing districts			National forests		
Year	Authorized grazing use by domestic livestock 1,000 AUM	Receipts from licenses and permits (Sec. 3) $1,000	Grazing fee per AUM $	No. of big game (in thousands) Deer	Others[a]	Estimated AUM equivalent for game (in thousands)[b]
1960	12,454	2,729	0.22	3,620	540	6,650
1961	12,097	2,311	0.19	3,840	561	7,030
1962	12,000	2,190	0.18	4,018	582	7,350
1963	12,052	3,355	0.28	3,930	590	7,230
1964	11,861	3,611	0.30	3,965	593	7,290
1965	11,773	3,467	0.29	4,023	623	7,390
1966	11,801	3,817	0.32	3,800	618	7,020
1967	11,635	3,718	9.32	3,996	634	7,360
1968	11,665	3,788	0.32	3,839	596	7,050
1969	11,238	4,663	0.41	3,691	599	6,820
1970	10,981	4,647	0.42	3,609	601	6,690
1971	10,287	6,223	0.61	3,467	602	6,470
1972	10,410	6,576	0.63	3,292	608	6,200
1973	10,383	7,680	0.74	3,065	610	5,840
1974	10,393	9,671	0.93	2,992	636	5,770
1975	10,239	9,585	0.94	2,809	647	5,500
1976	10,228	13,511	1.32	2,698	652	5,330
1977	9,094	14,300	1.57	2,723	686	5,420
1978	9,385	13,246	1.41	2,778	682	5,550
1979	9,173	16,190	1.77	2,667	668	5,300
1980	8,875	20,035	2.26	—	—	—

Sources: BLM data come from Public Land Statistics, for various years; and big-game grazing statistics are based on inventory numbers as of April 30 each year; and data are taken from Agricultural Statistics, for various years.

[a]Includes antelope, elk, bears, lions, moose, mountain goats, big horn sheep, peccaries, and wild boar; population data also include alligators, beginning in 1973.

[b]Calculated by assuming that each game animal will consume 1.59 AUM per year. Data on animal-unit-months of grazing by game animals for 1960 to 1964 are taken from Marion Clawson, The Federal Lands Since 1956 (Baltimore, Md., Johns Hopkins University Press, 1967); during those years, the ratio between game numbers and animal-unit-months was 1.59. Figures are rounded to nearest 10 AUM.

TABLE A-3. NUMBER OF TIMBER SALES, VOLUME, VALUE, AND STUMPAGE PRICE OF TIMBER CUT AND SOLD FROM THE NATIONAL FORESTS, FOR 1960–80

Fiscal year	No. of timber sales	Timber sold			Timber harvested		
		Volume of timber sold (million bd-ft)	Value of timber sold (millions of $)	Average stumpage price ($ per 1,000 bd-ft)	Volume of timber cut (million bd-ft)	Value of timber cut (millions of $)	Average stumpage price ($ per 1,000 bd-ft)
1960	—	—	—	—	9,367	156.4	16.70
1961	—	—	—	—	8,381	124.5	14.85
1962	—	—	—	—	9,032	128.9	14.27
1963	—	—	—	—	10,026	134.4	13.41
1964	—	—	—	—	10,954	151.1	13.79
1965	—	—	—	—	11,244	161.1	14.33
1966	23,923	11,383	226.0	19.86	12,138	195.6	16.11
1967	23,266	11,655	208.6	17.90	10,851	188.7	17.39
1968	22,479	11,652	274.3	23.54	12,128	239.3	19.73
1969	23,418	18,931	502.1	26.52	11,783	327.0	27.75
1970	26,610	13,382	317.3	23.71	11,527	307.6	26.69
1971	23,243	10,636	215.3	20.24	10,341	257.0	24.85
1972	25,419	10,339	328.4	31.77	11,700	382.0	32.64
1973	28,851	10,199	636.2	62.37	12,357	479.2	38.78
1974	—	10,160	890.8	87.67	10,950	507.8	46.37
1975	35,977	10,824	657.2	60.72	9,174	366.0	39.89
1976	43,012	10,287	707.8	68.81	9,575	492.0	51.38
1977	44,466	9,920	987.4	99.54	10,462	732.5	69.89
1978	54,373	10,996	1,328.4	120.81	10,080	854.7	84.79
1979	64,135	11,330	1,962.6	173.22	10,377	968.0	93.29
1980	89,337	11,399	1,968.7	172.71	9,148	730.2	79.82

Source: Annual reports of the Chief of the Forest Service, for various years. Data for timber sales during 1960–65 are not available.

TABLE A-4.   NUMBER OF SALES, VOLUME, VALUE, AND AVERAGE STUMP-AGE PRICE FOR TIMBER SOLD FROM O & C LANDS, FOR 1960–80

Fiscal year	No. of timber sales	Volume of timber sold (million bd-ft)	Value of timber sold (million $)	Average stumpage price ($ per 1,000 bd-ft)
1960	115	1,006	34.4	34.19
1961	775	992	26.3	26.48
1962	780	918	22.7	24.72
1963	1,438	1,567	36.0	22.96
1964	1,653	1,569	41.6	26.42
1965	1,449	1,226	42.1	34.31
1966	1,666	1,224	44.5	36.35
1967	1,698	1,353	50.9	37.60
1968	1,592	1,347	51.6	38.29
1969	1,549	1,093	79.4	72.65
1970	2,048	1,662	82.1	49.39
1971	1,876	1,235	51.9	42.02
1972	1,886	1,179	65.6	55.60
1973	1,112	1,224	129.5	105.70
1974	1,281	1,233	212.6	172.41
1975	1,199	1,159	185.6	160.14
1976	1,288	1,122	170.9	152.33
1977	1,360	1,160	204.8	176.59
1978	1,594	1,141	217.1	190.36
1979	1,777	1,017	302.5	275.79
1980	1,845	1,121	365.7	326.33

Note: O & C lands are the Oregon and California railroad revested lands and the Coos Bay Wagon Road reconveyed lands.
Source: Public Lands Statistics, for various years.

TABLE A-5. NUMBER AND ACREAGE OF OIL AND GAS LEASES UNDER USGS SUPERVISION FOR THE PUBLIC DOMAIN AND THE OUTER CONTINENTAL SHELF, FOR 1960–80

Year	Public Domain		Outer Continental Shelf	
	No. of leases	Thousands of acres	No. of leases	Thousands of acres
1960	136,062	109,317.4	464	1,968.8
1961	133,805	101,382.4	457	1,924.8
1962	124,803	87,193.1	846	3,685.5
1963	110,107	72,424.1	881	3,880.6
1964	103,027	67,140.3	975	4,365.9
1965	98,999	62,685.3	931	4,120.4
1966	95,501	58,009.5	927	4,024.2
1967	90,797	53,597.3	842	3,544.8
1968	95,506	59,281.8	1,006	4,329.4
1969	99,047	63,341.4	1,004	4,287.0
1970	97,464	61,334.7	1,005	4,261.7
1971	94,092	61,244.4	1,072	4,584.7
1972	94,221	65,662.7	1,014	4,323.0
1973	94,954	68,587.2	1,258	5,600.2
1974	101,207	78,247.1	1,582	7,233.0
1975	102,102	81,318.4	1,784	8,307.0
1976	101,368	79,048.5	1,993	9,425.2
1977	103,053	85,799.0	2,146	10,230.5
1978	104,385	90,711.2	2,096	9,993.7
1979	105,135	94,670.2	2,161	10,337.5
1980	105,196	100,116.5	2,254	10,729.8

Sources: U.S. Department of the Interior, Geological Survey, Conservation Division, *Federal and Indian Lands Oil and Gas Production, Royalty Income, and Related Statistics* (Reston, Va., USGS, June 1981) pp. 13–16. Data for 1961–63 are from U.S. Department of the Interior, Geological Survey, Conservation Division, *Annual and Accrued Mineral Production, Royalty Income, and Related Statistics* (Oil and Gas). For calendar years 1958–63, published in 1964 in-house; for 1961, ibid., p. 235; for 1962, ibid., p. 229; for 1963, ibid., p. 223.

TABLE A-6. OIL, GAS, AND GASOLINE PRODUCTION FROM THE PUBLIC DOMAIN, FOR 1960–80

Year	Oil and condensate (million barrels)	Natural gas Production (billion cubic feet)	Natural gas Oil equivalent (million barrels)[a]	Gasoline and LPG Production (million gallons)	Gasoline and LPG Oil equivalent (million barrels)[b]	Total oil equivalent (million barrels)[c]
1960	155.6	513.5	85.6	343.7	8.2	249.4
1961	169.0	538.8	89.8	401.0	9.5	268.3
1962	171.1	518.1	86.4	436.1	10.4	267.9
1963	178.3	537.7	98.0	414.4	9.9	286.2
1964	179.5	664.9	110.8	457.1	10.9	301.2
1965	181.4	710.6	118.4	438.0	10.4	310.2
1966	186.6	807.0	134.5	493.5	11.8	332.9
1967	193.4	975.5	162.6	711.6	16.9	372.9
1968	201.0	942.2	157.0	470.1	11.2	369.2
1969	201.5	902.9	150.5	513.4	12.2	364.2
1970	196.1	933.9	155.7	541.8	12.9	364.7
1971	183.7	978.5	163.1	616.6	14.7	361.5
1972	175.6	927.3	154.6	555.3	13.2	343.4
1973	170.3	961.6	160.3	573.0	13.6	344.2
1974	168.3	1,049.7	175.0	487.1	11.6	355.4
1975	163.1	942.4	157.1	435.8	10.4	330.6
1976	160.9	1,027.0	171.2	388.2	9.2	341.3
1977	158.6	995.6	165.9	251.8	6.0	330.5
1978	154.8	1,010.8	168.5	234.4	5.6	328.9
1979	146.4	1,032.8	172.1	356.1	8.5	327.0
1980	142.3	993.4	165.6	225.2	5.4	313.3

Note: Public domain here means federal lands which have never been out of federal ownership, excluding acquired lands, state lands, and the Outer Continental Shelf.

Sources: Column 2 is from U.S. Department of the Interior, Geological Survey, Conservation Division, *Federal and Indian Lands Oil and Gas Production, Royalty Income, and Related Statistics* (Reston, Va., USGS, June 1981) p. 83; Column 3, ibid., p. 92; and Column 5 is from ibid., p. 99.

[a]6,000 cubic feet of natural gas equivalent to 1.0 barrel of oil.

[b]42 gallons of gasoline is equivalent to 1.0 barrel of oil.

[c]Total oil equivalent is equal to the sum of Columns 2, 4, and 6.

TABLE A-7. PRODUCTION VALUE AND ROYALTY VALUE FOR OIL, GAS, AND GASOLINE PRODUCTION FROM THE PUBLIC DOMAIN, FOR 1960–80

(in millions of $)

Year	Production values Oil and condensate	Natural gas	Gasoline and LPG	Total[a]	Royalty values Oil and condensate	Natural gas	Gasoline and LPG	Total[b]	Per barrel of oil equivalent $[c]
1960	402.1	66.4	17.1	485.6	51.5	8.1	0.9	60.5	0.24
1961	440.8	71.4	20.0	532.2	59.0	8.5	1.0	68.5	0.26
1962	448.5	71.3	20.1	539.9	57.5	8.9	0.9	67.3	0.25
1963	467.9	83.5	19.0	570.4	60.6	10.0	0.8	71.4	0.25
1964	471.7	95.0	21.4	588.1	60.7	11.6	0.9	73.2	0.24
1965	489.9	118.3	21.9	630.1	60.9	12.6	0.9	74.4	0.24
1966	511.3	126.2	25.4	662.9	62.6	14.2	1.1	77.9	0.23
1967	514.8	126.2	27.7	668.7	66.8	15.0	1.2	83.0	0.22
1968	528.5	136.9	25.5	690.9	68.0	16.6	1.2	85.8	0.23
1969	566.1	135.8	22.8	724.7	71.9	16.5	1.0	89.4	0.25
1970	564.5	144.1	26.9	735.5	71.5	17.8	1.2	90.5	0.25
1971	568.7	154.2	31.3	754.2	71.2	19.0	1.4	91.6	0.25
1972	543.3	169.7	28.6	741.6	69.5	20.9	1.3	91.7	0.27
1973	640.6	205.9	36.6	833.1	81.7	25.4	1.8	108.9	0.32
1974	1,099.9	264.8	54.5	1,419.2	141.5	33.0	2.5	177.0	0.50
1975	1,178.2	317.0	66.5	1,561.7	153.6	39.4	3.0	196.0	0.59
1976	1,221.1	497.3	46.3	1,764.7	159.7	61.4	2.3	223.4	0.65
1977	1,242.0	742.0	66.7	2,050.7	162.6	91.8	3.2	257.6	0.78
1978	1,359.9	938.7	51.1	2,349.7	178.2	116.0	2.1	296.3	0.90
1979	1,809.7	1,314.5	61.8	3,186.0	231.4	162.6	3.2	397.2	1.21
1980	3,099.8	1,671.5	110.2	4,881.5	392.6	207.3	5.4	605.3	1.93

Note: The public domain here means federal lands which have always been in federal ownership.

Sources: From U.S. Department of the Interior, Geological Survey, Conservation Division, *Federal and Indian Lands Oil and Gas Production, Royalty Income, and Related Statistics* (Reston, Va., USGS, June 1981) p. 83. Column 3, ibid., p. 92; Column 4, ibid., p. 99; Column 6, ibid., p. 83; Column 7, ibid., p. 92; Column 8, ibid., p. 99.

[a] Total production values are a sum of Columns 2, 3, and 4.

[b] Total royalty values are a sum of Columns 6, 7, and 8.

[c] Dollars divided by total oil equivalent equal price per barrel.

TABLE A-8. OIL, GAS, AND GASOLINE PRODUCTION FROM THE OUTER CONTINENTAL SHELF, FOR 1960–80

| Year | Oil and condensate (million barrels) | Natural gas | | Gasoline and LPG | | Total oil equivalent (million barrels)[c] |
		Production (billion cubic feet)	Oil equivalent (million barrels)[a]	Production (million gallons)	Oil equivalent (million barrels)[b]	
1960	49.7	273.0	45.5	—	—	95.2
1961	64.3	318.3	53.1	—	—	117.4
1962	89.7	452.0	75.3	—	—	165.0
1963	104.6	564.4	94.1	—	—	198.7
1964	122.5	621.7	103.6	—	—	226.1
1965	145.0	645.6	107.6	—	—	252.6
1966	188.7	1,007.4	167.9	—	—	356.6
1967	221.9	1,187.2	197.9	—	—	419.8
1968	269.0	1,524.2	254.0	—	—	523.0
1969	312.9	1,954.5	325.8	222.4	5.3	644.0
1970	360.6	2,418.7	403.1	1,075.4	25.6	789.3
1971	418.5	2,777.0	462.8	1,550.7	36.9	918.2
1972	411.9	3,038.6	506.4	1,737.2	41.4	959.7
1973	394.7	3,211.6	535.3	1,634.8	38.9	968.9
1974	360.6	3,514.7	585.8	2,031.5	48.4	994.8
1975	330.2	3,458.7	576.5	1,983.2	47.2	953.9
1976	316.9	3,595.9	599.3	1,923.7	45.8	962.0
1977	303.9	3,737.7	623.0	2,054.6	48.9	975.8
1978	292.3	4,385.1	730.9	718.8	17.1	1,040.3
1979	285.6	4,673.0	778.8	(4.9)	(0.1)	1,064.3
1980	277.4	4,641.5	773.6	2.5	0.1	1,051.1

Note: Data for gasoline and LPG are not available for 1960–68.

Sources: Column 1, from U.S. Department of the Interior, Geological Survey, Conservation Division, *Federal and Indian Lands Oil and Gas Production, Royalty Income, and Related Statistics* (Reston, Va., USGS, June 1981) pp. 84–85; Column 2, ibid., p. 93; Column 4, ibid., p. 100.

[a]6,000 cubic feet of natural gas is equivalent to 1 barrel of oil.

[b]42 gallons of gasoline is equivalent to 1 barrel of oil.

[c]Total oil equivalent is equal to the sum of Columns 1, 3, and 5.

TABLE A-9. PRODUCTION VALUES AND ROYALTY VALUES FOR OIL, GAS, AND GASOLINE FROM THE OUTER CONTINENTAL SHELF, FOR 1960–80
(in millions of $)

Year	Production values				Royalty values				
	Oil and condensate	Natural gas	Gasoline and LPG	Total[a]	Oil and condensate	Natural gas	Gasoline and LPG	Total[b]	Per barrel of oil equivalent[c]
1960	146.4	52.8	—	199.2	29.2	7.6	—	36.8	0.39
1961	201.7	64.6	—	266.3	37.3	9.5	—	46.8	0.40
1962	278.9	92.2	—	371.1	51.5	13.7	—	65.2	0.40
1963	333.0	106.8	—	439.8	59.2	16.1	—	75.3	0.38
1964	375.6	118.4	—	494.0	68.6	17.9	—	86.5	0.38
1965	443.8	127.0	—	570.8	80.4	19.2	—	99.6	0.39
1966	579.7	189.4	—	769.1	103.7	29.1	—	132.8	0.37
1967	682.2	227.7	—	909.9	121.4	32.0	—	153.4	0.37
1968	835.3	291.3	—	1,126.6	148.0	48.5	—	196.5	0.38
1969	1,019.1	365.8	9.8	1,394.7	178.3	57.4	0.7	236.4	0.37
1970	1,193.6	438.1	51.2	1,682.9	207.1	69.4	3.7	280.2	0.35
1971	1,481.7	549.6	80.6	2,111.9	253.2	87.4	5.9	346.5	0.38
1972	1,454.0	663.6	89.2	2,206.8	247.7	105.9	6.5	360.1	0.38
1973	1,620.7	736.9	105.4	2,463.0	271.5	118.2	7.8	397.5	0.41
1974	2,398.8	877.7	254.7	3,531.2	394.4	141.7	19.8	555.9	0.56
1975	2,428.8	1,205.7	216.0	3,850.5	399.5	195.2	16.4	611.1	0.64
1976	2,533.4	1,652.8	246.4	4,432.6	412.3	268.1	19.7	700.1	0.73
1977	2,683.6	2,766.4	314.6	5,764.6	441.1	449.3	27.7	918.1	0.94
1978	2,854.3	4,135.2	85.7	7,075.2	466.6	672.6	7.7	1,146.9	1.10
1979	3,127.6	6,125.5	(0.6)	9,252.5	509.3	1,002.7	0.0	1,512.0	1.42
1980	5,143.1	7,885.2	3.3	13,031.6	837.2	1,295.3	0.3	2,132.8	2.03

Note: Data for gasoline production and royalties are not available for 1960–68.

Sources: Column 1 from U.S. Department of the Interior, Geological Survey, Conservation Division, *Federal and Indian Lands Oil and Gas Production, Royalty Income, and Related Statistics* (Reston, Va., USGS, June 1981) pp. 84–85; Column 2, ibid., p. 93; Column 3, ibid., p. 100; Column 5, ibid., pp. 84–85; Column 6, ibid., p. 93; and Column 7, ibid., p. 100.

[a]Total production values are equal to the sum of Columns 1, 2, and 3.

[b]Total royalty values are equal to the sum of Columns 5, 6, and 7.

[c]Dollars divided by total.

TABLE A-10. COAL LEASES ON PUBLIC LANDS (EXCLUDING ACQUIRED AND INDIAN LANDS), FOR 1960–80

Year	No. of coal leases	Acreage of coal leases (thousands of acres)	Receipts from coal leases, licenses, and permits ($1,000)	No. of producing mines	Quality of coal produced (1,000 tons)	Production value ($1,000)	Royalties value ($1,000)	Royalties per ton coal produced ($)
1960	514	551.1	746.2	138	5,091.0	31,265.6	616.5	0.12
1961	—	—	827.8	—	5,131.6	31,818.3	642.5	0.13
1962	—	—	1,013.1	—	5,733.2	31,077.6	737.8	0.13
1963	—	—	908.2	—	4,936.1	25,467.9	630.2	0.13
1964	626	761.1	985.3	113	5,408.7	27,870.7	704.3	0.13
1965	675	872.1	1,118.9	101	5,480.6	27,260.9	741.3	0.14
1966	659	861.3	1,918.3	93	6,079.3	32,704.5	813.3	0.13
1967	704	1,103.5	2,148.0	102	6,985.9	40,091.6	913.8	0.13
1968	679	1,162.4	3,987.0	79	6,698.4	33,983.8	911.3	0.14
1969	697	1,223.4	2,041.1	71	7,481.7	34,902.2	1,079.0	0.14
1970	789	1,497.4	2,096.4	67	7,444.6	36,815.9	1,069.9	0.14
1971	840	1,662.7	9,799.7	70	9,917.5	51,679.1	1,466.1	0.15
1972	807	1,533.9	—	66	9,882.5	53,315.7	1,515.4	0.15
1973	767	1,419.2	2,724.4	63	13,592.3	62,471.6	2,088.6	0.15
1974	763	1,394.7	4,083.5	65	20,178.2	102,824.0	3,245.3	0.16
1975	765	1,393.4	5,050.9	64	26,655.0	165,561.0	4,730.8	0.18
1976	749	1,375.4	7,184.1	70	54,464.5	438,354.2	10,761.0	0.20
1977	682	1,245.5	10,122.7	76	51,864.1	457,808.2	9,799.5	0.19
1978	570	917.4	11,908.9	81	60,168.7	583,865.3	13,374.0	0.22
1979	593	961.5	16,320.1	88	60,227.2	746,466.5	17,353.1	0.29
1980	587	978.5	—	103	69,089.5	854,809.4	32,251.8	0.47

Note: Data for 1961–63 are not available for coal leases, acreage of coal leases, and number of producing mines.

Sources: For Columns 1, 2, and 4 (1960, and 1964–80) are from U.S. Department of the Interior, Geological Survey, Conservation Division, *Federal and Indian Lands Coal, Phosphate, Potash, Sodium, and Other Mineral Production, Royalty Income, and Related Statistics, 1920 Through 1980* (Reston, Va., June 1981) pp. 10–15. Note that figures are as of June 30 of the year stated through 1975, and as of December 31 of the year stated for 1976 through 1980. For Column 3, data are from *Public Lands Statistics,* for various years. For Columns 5, 6, and 7, data are from ibid., p. 36. Due to the change in fiscal year, 1976 data consist of an eighteen-month period (July 1975 through December 1976). Subsequently, all data will be on a calendar year basis.

TABLE A-11. RECREATION ON FOREST SERVICE LANDS AND ALL LANDS ADMINISTERED BY THE BLM, FOR 1960–80

(millions)

Year	Forest Service lands		BLM lands	
	Recreation visits	Recreation visitor-days[a]	Recreation visits	Recreation visitor-days
1960	92.6	101.8	N.A.	N.A.
1961	101.9	109.9	N.A.	N.A.
1962	112.8	119.4	N.A.	N.A.
1963	122.6	126.5	N.A.	N.A.
1964	133.8	135.0	14.5	N.A.
1965	N.A.	N.A.	27.2	N.A.
1966	N.A.	150.7	37.8	N.A.
1967	N.A.	149.6	48.5	19.1
1968	N.A.	156.7	56.9	24.1
1969	N.A.	162.8	64.8	38.8
1970	N.A.	172.6	67.2	38.7
1971	N.A.	180.6[b]	69.2	31.8
1972	N.A.	184.0	52.3	31.2
1973	N.A.	188.2	90.0	41.6
1974	N.A.	192.9	78.0	48.6
1975	N.A.	199.2	61.1	33.0
1976	N.A.	199.9	149.9	58.3
1977	N.A.	204.8	144.5	91.5
1978	N.A.	218.5	196.0	58.2
1979	N.A.	220.2	146.3	64.7
1980	N.A.	233.5	107.9	69.5

Note: N.A., no data are available. One recreation visitor-day is the recreation use of land or water that aggregates twelve visitor-hours.

Source: Man days, 1960–64, Marion Clawson, *The Federal Lands Since 1956: Recent Trends in Use and Management* (Washington, D.C., Resources for the Future, 1967); other data are from annual reports of the Forest Service and from *Public Land Statistics,* for various years.

[a]For 1960–64, man-days were used rather than visitor-days.

[b]For 1971, includes an estimate of 50 million visitor-days in California.

TABLE A-12. RECEIPTS OF THE BLM, FOR 1960–80
(in millions of dollars)

Fiscal Year	Sales of public lands	Sales of timber	Fees and com-missions	Mineral leases[a]			Total[b]
				Onshore	Outer Continental Shelf	Other	
1960	5.1	36.4	1.8	94.6	229.5	3.8	371.1
1961	4.2	32.1	2.5	109.7	7.3	3.4	159.2
1962	3.6	34.7	2.8	117.1	11.6	3.7	173.5
1963	3.4	33.6	3.0	118.6	366.8	5.3	530.7
1964	3.2	47.2	3.7	122.2	16.5	6.2	199.1
1965	3.1	44.9	3.8	123.3	53.5	5.9	234.4
1966	2.3	47.6	3.9	125.3	248.3	6.3	433.7
1967	2.6	47.1	3.3	124.9	637.3	6.3	821.5
1968	2.5	56.2	3.9	128.6	961.3	6.5	1,158.9
1969	1.8	69.7	4.9	138.6	428.3	7.9	651.1
1970	2.1	65.4	4.5	141.2	186.9	7.3	407.4
1971	2.0	70.7	4.1	151.3	1,050.5	9.2	1,287.9
1972	1.9	83.5	5.4	145.1	279.4	9.8	525.1
1973	1.8	104.6	6.8	149.3	3,955.6	12.0	4,230.1
1974	2.1	127.8	12.5	271.7	6,148.4	15.3	7,177.7
1975	20.3	108.2	18.3	329.7	2,427.9	15.3	2,919.6
1976[c]	5.8	130.8	19.4	347.7	2,662.4	25.8	3,191.9
1976[c]	1.5	67.0	6.2	63.1	1,311.1	11.3	1,460.2
1977	2.8	235.3	26.8	344.5	2,373.0	25.6	3,008.1
1978	1.6	195.4	31.8	402.3	2,259.3	33.5	2,923.9
1979	9.2	218.2	39.7	486.5	3,267.4	30.9	4,051.9
1980	7.8	216.1	28.6	682.1	4,100.9	43.8	5,079.3

Source: Public Lands Statistics, for various years.

[a]Including permits.

[b]Totals may not equal sum of columns due to rounding.

[c]Until 1976 the fiscal year for U.S. government operations ran from July 1 to June 30; in 1976 this was changed to October 1–September 30. The first line of figures are for the period July 1, 1975–June 30, 1976, and thus are comparable with fiscal year data for prior years; the second line of figures is for the transition period, July 1, 1976–September 30, 1976. Shift of dates for fiscal years does not significantly affect comparisons between fiscal years before 1976 and for years thereafter.

TABLE A-13. FOREST SERVICE CASH RECEIPTS AND OTHER INCOME, FOR 1960–80

(in millions of dollars)

Fiscal year	Cash receipts from deposits for expenditure on national forests	Estimated value of roads built by timber purchasers	Collections by Department of the Interior for mineral leases, licenses, and permits on public domain national forests[a]	Cash receipts from all goods and services sold[b]	Total[c]
1960	23.6	47.4	d	149.1	220.1[e]
1961	22.2	44.2	d	107.4	173.8[e]
1962	24.5	48.9	11.3	115.6	200.3
1963	28.2	54.5	11.4	127.7	222.1
1964	30.3	51.0	15.7	138.8	235.9
1965	32.0	56.7	17.8	149.2	257.5
1966	34.6	56.0	19.4	177.2	287.3
1967	38.2	50.7	21.9	186.3	297.3
1968	38.6	71.2	24.8	220.1	355.0
1969	49.2	93.8	28.6	323.3	495.0
1970	48.0	51.9	28.8	302.2	431.1
1971	50.0	49.4	32.9	237.6	370.1
1972	67.1	52.3	31.6	352.3	503.5
1973	80.8	67.9	33.9	473.4	656.3
1974	89.3	66.1	61.8	489.5	706.9
1975	79.2	97.6	75.0	376.1	628.1
1976[f]	97.9	112.7	79.3	457.3	747.4
1976[f]	32.9	33.0	33.8	206.0	305.7
1977	165.3	123.3	79.3	693.6	1,061.7
1978	134.8	124.2	87.2	769.4	1,116.0
1979	193.7	154.7	162.2	889.9	1,401.2
1980	203.7	164.2	219.3	700.6	1,287.8

Source: Unpublished data from the Forest Service.

[a]These receipts are also included in BLM receipts.

[b]Including receipts from O & C lands administered by the Forest Service and receipts from national grasslands.

[c]Includes small sums for collections by Federal Power Commission for power licenses.

[d]Data unavailable.

[e]Excludes collections by Department of the Interior for mineral leases, licenses, and permits.

[f]Until 1976, the fiscal year for U.S. government operations ran from July 1 to June 30; in 1976 this was changed to October 1 to September 30. The first line of figures are for the period July 1, 1975–June 30, 1976, and thus are comparable with fiscal year data for prior years; the second line of figures is for the transition period, July 1, 1976–September 30, 1976. Shift of dates for fiscal years does not significantly affect comparisons between fiscal years before 1976 or for years thereafter.

TABLE A-14. EXPENDITURES OF THE FOREST SERVICE AND THE BLM, FOR 1960–80
(in millions of dollars)

| Year | Forest Service | | BLM | | | |
	National Forest System	Total	Appropriations to BLM for management of land and resources	Total appropria- tions to BLM	Appropriations transferred from other agencies to BLM	Total
1960	210.7	251.5	28.5	35.2	0.3	35.5
1961	310.9	354.4	32.5	42.6	0.3	42.9
1962	275.1	329.8	34.8	43.0	0.3	43.3
1963	329.5	385.5	43.8	53.7	7.0	60.7
1964	341.1	399.0	46.5	57.0	5.0	62.1
1965	358.7	453.6	50.7	68.6	4.8	73.5
1966	382.7	513.7	51.3	81.7	6.7	88.4
1967	407.8	543.8	59.1	76.0	6.4	82.4
1968	453.0	590.2	61.8	83.4	5.8	89.2
1969	451.7	592.4	68.0	86.2	5.0	91.2
1970	490.6	627.2	88.5	116.7	1.0	117.7
1971	572.1	719.0	88.5	114.9	1.0	115.9
1972	604.0	780.9	94.2	125.1	1.1	126.3
1973	626.6	806.8	102.1	131.6	1.2	132.8
1974	700.4	896.4	123.2	161.9	1.0	162.9
1975	841.5	1,071.5	181.4	226.9	1.3	228.2
1976[a]	899.6	1,156.6	205.0	250.8	2.6	253.4
1976[a]	329.0	400.5	b	b	b	b
1977	1,195.8	1,613.1	284.5	455.1	3.6	458.7
1978	1,298.5	1,635.6	288.8	459.0	1.5	460.5
1979	1,574.1	1,934.2	344.8	538.1	4.0	542.1
1980	1,709.4	2,071.5	357.3	584.2	4.8	589.0

Sources: Unpublished Forest Service data; and *Public Lands Statistics,* for various years.

[a]Until 1976 the fiscal year for U.S. government operations was July 1 to June 30; in 1976 this was changed to Octoer 1 to September 30. The first line of figures are for the period July 1, 1975 to June 30, 1976 and thus are comparable with fiscal year data for prior years; the second line of figures is for the transition period, July 1, 1976 to September 30, 1976. Shift of dates for fiscal years does not significantly affect comparisions between fiscal years before 1976 and for years thereafter.

[b]Not reported in *Public Land Statistics* for either 1976 or 1977.

Index

Achterman, Gail L., 113, 252, 253
Acquisition of federal lands, 1, 15–16
  fraud relating to, 17, 25
  Indians and, 17–19
  O & C area, 19–20
Alaska, 17, 41
American Forestry Association, 28, 139
Atomic waste disposal, 8

Baden, John, 156, 167
Barlowe, Raleigh, 153
Barnett, Harold J., 225
BLM. *See* Bureau of Land Management.
Brinser, Ayers, 138
Bureau of Corporations, 132
Bureau of Land Management (BLM),
    11, 47, 48, 145, 184
  formation, 31, 37
  grazing control policy, 68, 69
  land acquisition authority, 243
  land exchanges and, 238–239, 242–
    243
  management function, 118–20
    advisory boards for, 250
    O & C lands, 19, 20
    public participation in, 253, 269,
      270
    research on, 266–267
  oil and gas leases, 41, 87, 89, 192–193
  planning by, 113–118
  proposed long-term leases for lands
    of, 207, 210
  revenues
    expenditures versus, 38
    disposition of, 171, 172–175
  sale of public lands, 192
  visitor-days on lands of, 100, 101
Burr, Aaron, 6–7

Cadastral survey, 20–21, 231
Calef, Wesley, 155
Cameron, Jenks, 25, 27

Capital account, for federal lands, 182–
    183
Carhart, Arthur, 137
Carpenter, Farrington, 36
Church, Frank, 45
Civilian Conservation Corps, 37
Civil War, 7
Classification and Multiple Use Act, 47–
    48
Clawson, Marion, 10, 196
Clean Air Act, 52
Clean Water Act (1977), 52
Clepper, Henry, 137
Coal Leasing Amendments Act (1976),
    95
Coal resources
  leases for extracting, 42, 93–95
  national–regional differences over
    development, 8
  production, 38, 94
  state severance taxes on, 95–96
Conservation of federal lands, 12–13
  acquisition for, 191–192
  federal land retention and, 128–129,
    139, 143
  forestry and, 72
  grazing fees and, 70–71
  litigation over, 54, 55–56
  mining development and, 98
  proposed long-term leases for, 207,
    209, 213, 214–215
Corps of Engineers, 134
Counties, revenues from public lands,
    171, 172–175
Crowell, John B., 83
Culhane, Paul J., 39, 258

Dana, Samuel T., 56, 126, 132
Darling, F. Fraser, 138
De Voto, Bernard, 71
Department of the Interior, 31, 93, 126,
    135, 190
Disposal of federal lands, 2, 3, 9, 20, 41

Disposal of federal lands (*cont'd.*)
alternative for federal land
management, 178, 189
amount, 25, 26
arguments for, 157–162
choice of lands for, 194–195
debt reduction as objective of, 193–194
effects, 25, 27
fraud and trespass from, 124–128
history of, 21–24, 189–192
policy issues relating to, 10, 164
resource depletion from, 128–131, 163
selective, 145, 195, 230–231
social costs of, 131–132, 163
See also Land grants.
Dragoo, Denise A., 24–25

EIS. *See* Environmental Impact Statement.
Ely, Richard T., 154
Endangered Species Act (1973), 52
Enlarged Homestead Act (1909), 57
Environmental Impact Statement (EIS)
content, 51–52
on grazing operations, 166
public participation through, 251
Environmentalists, litigation over federal land management, 55–56
See also Conservation of federal lands.
Exploitation of federal lands, 25
forests, 129–131
grazing land, 131, 133
land disposal leading to, 129–131, 133
mineral deposits, 141, 142
Outer Continental Shelf, 40

Fairfax, Sally K., 44, 45–46, 56, 113, 252, 253
Farm tenancy, 132
Federal Land Policy and Management Act (1976), 10, 31, 47, 57, 139, 160, 166, 181, 243
changes in mining law from, 97
effect on planning processes, 113–117
provisions, 50–51, 239
Public participation and, 252–253

Federal lands
amount of, 4, 26
costs and inefficiencies relating to ownership, 158–160
future of, 224–227
land economics applied to 154–156
permanent, 4, 19
policy issues relating to, 2–3
public capital from, 11–12
revenues from, 11, 37, 171, 176–177
uses of, 11, 63, 106–107
value of
increase in capital, 110–112
methods of estimating, 108–110
See also Acquisition of federal lands;
Conservation of federal lands;
Disposal of federal lands;
Exploitation of federal lands;
Management of federal lands;
Planning, federal lands; Public participation in federal lands;
Reservation, federal lands;
Retention of federal lands
Federal Water Pollution Control Act (1972), 52
FLPMA. *See* Federal Land Policy and Management Act.
Ford, Gerald, 48, 49
Forest and Rangeland Renewable Resources Act (1974), 10, 48, 54, 160
Forest Reserve Acts (1891 and 1897), 32, 135, 154
Forest resources. *See* National forests; Timber.
Forest Service, 9, 11, 33, 34, 48, 50, 59, 163, 184
appropriations to, 184
deficits, 145
functions, 33–35
grazing control policy, 30, 65, 68
land acquisition, 19, 243
land exchanges and, 238, 242–243
management process, 118–120
advisory boards for, 249, 250
public participation in, 253, 269, 270
planning by, 112
legislation of 1970s influencing, 113–118

Forest Service (cont'd.)
    proposed long-term leases for lands
        of, 207, 210
    research on organization and
        functions of, 266–267
    Roadless Area Review and Evaluation,
        I and II, 46
    report on forestland ownership, 130–
        131
    report on western rangelands (1936),
        131, 163
    revenues
        distribution of, 171
        expenditures versus, 37–38
    timber sales policy, 82–84
    wilderness areas and, 30, 44–45
Foss, Phillip, 155
Francis, John, 187

Gas. See Leases, oil and gas; Oil and gas.
Gates, Paul W., 126, 187
General Accounting Office, 82, 83
General Land Office, 19, 31, 135, 249
    efforts to prevent land frauds and
        trespass, 126
    management of forest reserves, 32–33
    management of public domain, 35
    mineral leasing by, 36
    See also Bureau of Land Management.
Gould, Clarence P., 58
Graber, Linda, 140, 141
Gray, L. C., 155
Grazing
    on federal lands
        big game versus domestic livestock
            on, 67–68
        conservation on, 129
        control of, 30–31
        controversy over, 34
        custodial management of, 31, 33–
            34
        inefficiencies in, 159
        permits for, 71–72
        proposed long-term leasing for,
            210–211
        research on management of, 262
    intermingled land for, 232–233
    private lands for, 65
        forage depletion from, 131, 133
    trends in, 63–68

Grazing Service, 31, 34, 37
Greeley, Horace, 21

Hagenstein, Perry R., 113
Haigh, John A., 114–115, 181, 255
Hall, John F., 49
Hanke, Steven, 156, 167
Hays, Samuel P., 130, 131, 132, 137
Healy, Robert G., 139
Held, Burnell, 10, 196
Hibbard, B. H., 27
Hirshleifer, J., 158
Homestead Act (1862), 23, 57, 231
Homesteading, 21, 23, 35, 231
Hot Springs National Park, Arkansas, 27

Ickes, Harold, 69
Individual initiative, 149–150
Interest groups
    compromise on federal land planning,
        181–182
    national versus regions, 6–9
    pullback procedures and, 231
Intergenerational analysis, 141–142, 162
Intermingled federal-private lands
    area of, 232–233
    factors leading to, 230–231
    ownership problems from, 233–235
        on access to units, 235–236
        future of, 245–246
        land acquisition to remedy, 243–
            244
        land exchanges to remedy, 236–243
        land planning and zoning for, 244–
            245
        long-term leasing to reduce, 244
Ise, John, 27, 28, 29, 127, 134, 138–139
Izaak Walton League, 215

Jackson, Andrew, 7
Jefferson, Thomas, 15–16, 20

Kelso, M. M., 137, 155
Knutson–Vandenburg Act, 177
Krutilla, John V., 114–115, 117, 139,
    140, 181, 255

Land economics, 153–154
    application to federal lands, 154–156

Land exchanges
  defined, 236
  federal and private reaction to, 237
  new approach to, 241–243
  past experiences with, 237–239, 240
  proposed improvements in, 239, 241
Land grants
  O & C area, 19–20
  railroad, 24
  state, 22, 23–25
  See also Disposal of federal lands.
Leases
  long-term, 205
    amount of land available for, 213–
      216
    terms of, 206–213
  oil and gas, 38
    legislation influencing, 84–85, 87
    number and acreage, 41, 86
    OCS, 89–91, 171
    production from, 88, 89
    revenues from, 84, 105
  proposed long-term, 200
    advantages of, 204–205
    cancellation or renewal of, 201
    for intermingled lands, 244
    licenses or permits as, 202–203
    public participation through, 258–
      259
    terms of, 203–204
    types of land covered by, 203
  See also Pullback procedures.
Legislation, federal land, 9–10, 30, 36
  environmental, 51–53
  grazing land, 9, 30, 35, 36, 67, 69,
    138, 155
  management, 13, 44, 47–49, 58–59,
    160–161
  mining, 84–85, 87, 89–91
  persons responsible for, 57–58
  planning, 48–49, 113–117, 181–182
  public participation resulting from,
    54, 250–253
  regulations to extend, 59
  response to crises with, 57–58
  wilderness areas, 44–47
Leisz, Douglas R., 116
Leman, Christopher K., 113
Lenard, Thomas M., 159
Leopold, Aldo, 137
Libecap, Gary D., 159, 163, 164

Lillard, Richard G., 129–130
Litigation
  Environmental Impact Statements
    and, 51–52, 166, 251
  land conservation, 54, 55–56
  Sagebrush Rebellion and, 7–8
  timber sales, 32
  withdrawal of public domain and, 85

McGuire, John, 48
Malone, Joseph J., 58, 72
Management of federal lands, 3, 4, 11,
    13
  acquisition era of, 15–20, 39, 40
  alternatives for future, 177–179
    capital account establishment, 182–
      183
    disposal to private ownership, 189–
      195
    imposition of fees and charges,
      183–184
    improved efficiency, 185–186
    improved planning, 181–182
    long-term leasing, 200–205
    management by corporations, 195–
      200
    setting of standards, 179–181
    transfer to states, 185–189
  complexity of, 13–14
  confrontation over, 55–56
  costs and inefficiencies in, 159–160
  custodial
    over forest resources, 31–33
    over grazing lands, 31, 34, 36–37
    over homesteading, 35
    over mineral resources, 36
  disposal era of, 20–27, 39
  expenditures for, 118–120
  income from lands versus, 171, 176–
    177
  intensive, 37–39, 118
  predicted problems in, 225–226
  public participation in, 161, 247
  reservation era of, 27–31, 39
  resource, 257–259
  staff for, 119
  See also Research, management.
Marsh, George Perkins, 128
Marshall, Alfred, 236
Materials Disposal Act (1955), 97
Mercantilism, 149–150

Milton, John P., 138
Mineral Leasing Act (1920), 85–86, 92–
        93, 96
Mineral resources
    expenditures versus revenues from,
        38–39
    exploration for, 96–98
    Outer Continental Shelf, 40
    proposed long-term leases for, 206–
        207, 212
    protection of, 29, 141–142
    research on development of, 263
    See also Coal resources; Leases, oil and
        gas.
Mining Laws (1866 and 1872), 84, 96–
        97
Mississippi Valley, 6–7
Mollison, Richard M., 167
Monongahela court decision, 32
Morse, Chandler, 225
Muir, John, 71, 135, 136
Multiple land use
    economic rationale for, 137–138
    explanation of, 136
    public ownership and, 138, 143
    value of lands for, 193
Multiple Use Act (1964), 137
Multiple Use–Sustained Yield Act
        (1960), 10, 44, 137

National Environmental Policy Act, 51–
        52, 55, 68, 251, 258
National Forest Management Act (1976),
        10, 32, 54, 57, 58, 83, 160
    effect on BLM and Forest Service,
        113–117
    objective, 81
    provisions, 49–50
National forests
    grazing in, 65–67
    intermingled land in, 232
    land acquisition for, 41
    land frauds in, 126–127
    land reservation for, 27–29
    management
        custodial, 31–32
        deficits from, 184
        NFMA and, 49–50
        research on, 263
    proposed long-term leases for, 205,
        208–210, 211, 212, 213–214

National forests (cont'd.)
    pullback process applied to, 217, 221–
        222
    resources from, 129, 130–131
    revenues from, 37–38, 171
    timber sales from, 42, 73–77
        Forest Service and, 82–84
        prices for, 77–80
    use and development, 136–137
    visitor-days on, 100, 101–102, 103
National Parks, 9
    land acquisition for, 41
    land reservation for, 27–28, 30
    visitor-days on, 100, 101–102, 103
National Park Service, 30, 243
National Research Council, 93
National Trails System Act (1968), 10,
        51
National Wild and Scenic Rivers Act
        (1968), 10, 51
Natural resources
    depletion, 128–131, 163
    development and use, 5–6, 8–9
    human component of, 225
    intergenerational analysis of, 141–
        142, 162
    option demand and value of, 139–140
    predicted demands upon, 225
Nature Conservancy, 215
Nelson, Robert H., 197–198
NFMA. See National Forest
        Management Act.
NRDC versus Morton, 166

O & C lands
    advisory board for, 250
    grants for, 19–20, 177
    timber sold from, 38, 74, 77–79, 108
OCS. See Outer Continental Shelf.
Office of Management and Budget, 82,
        83
Oil and gas, land use for, 84–91
    See also Leases, oil and gas.
Option demand, 139–140, 162, 254
Oregon, land frauds, 126
Outdoor recreation
    camping, 102–103
    economic importance of, 104
    features of, 98–99
    fees and charges for, 183
    increase in, 34, 38–39

Outdoor recreation (*cont'd.*)
land designation for, 41
proposed long-term leases for, 208
pullback procedure applied to, 222
usage, 99–102, 103, 105, 108
Outer Continental Shelf (OCS), 40
BLM responsibility for managing, 118
oil and gas leases, 89–91, 106, 171
sale of public land in, 194–195

Page, Talbot, 141–142
Pickett Act (1910), 84–85
Pinchot, Gifford
on forest reserve management, 32–33, 135
forest service and, 33
grazing concerns, 30, 64–65, 68
on resource depletion, 128
support for natural resources use and development, 135, 136–137
timber harvesting concerns, 72, 73
Planning, federal lands
Bureau of Land Management, 113
Forest Service, 112
intermingled lands, 244–245
legislative efforts to improve, 181
long-range, 160–161
PLLRC. *See* Public Land Law Review Commission.
Policy issues, federal land, 2–3
For disposal, 10, 164
interpretation of laws on, 3–4
research on, 271–272
Preemption Act (1841), 57
Preservation. *See* Conservation of federal lands.
Private land ownership, 4, 149
arguments for, 150, 155–157, 163
central government role in, 152
comparative efficiency of, 163–164
long-range plans for, 160–161
market decisions on, 151–152
Public domain. *See* Federal lands.
Public Land Law Commission, 10, 127
Public Land Law Review Commission, 25, 47, 51, 165, 245
Public Land Sale Act, 47
Public participation in federal lands, 53
in decision making, 259–260
through litigation for conservation, 54, 55–56, 251

Public participation in federal lands (*cont'd.*)
in management, 161, 247
through advisory boards, 249–250
delaying effects of, 256
economic efficiency versus, 255–256
groups involved with, 254–255
legislation influencing, 54, 250–253
research on, 269–270
resource management and, 257–259
by users, 247–248
Public Rangelands Improvement Act (1978), 69
Pullback procedures
applied to federal land sales, 221
benefits from, 216–217
collusion from, 218–219
competition from, 218, 219
economic advantages of, 221–224
effects of, 218–220
explanation of, 216–218
public participation through, 258–259

Railroad grant lands, 24, 230, 231, 232
RARE. *See* Roadless Area Review and Evaluation, I and II.
Reagan administration, and sale of federal lands, 192
Recreation. *See* Outdoor recreation.
Regions
federal government versus, 6–9
role in natural resource use and development, 5–6
Renewable Resources Planning Act (1974)
effect on BLM and Forest Service planning procedures, 113–117
objective, 181, 182
public participation and, 252
Research, management, 261
economic, 264–266
on forests, 263
on grazing areas, 262
on inventions, 272–273
on mineral resources development, 263
for organization and functioning, 266–269
on overall federal land policy, 271–272

Research, management (*cont'd.*)
  public relations, 269–270
  tradeoffs among land inputs and
    outputs, 263–264
Reservation, federal lands
  Forest Reserve Act and, 135
  forest resources protection and, 27–
    29, 30
  grazing rights and, 30–31
  land disposal versus, 134–136
  purpose, 29–30
Retention of federal lands
  arguments against, 157–162
  arguments for, 124–133, 142–144,
    164
  intergenerational arguments for, 141–
    142
  land management and, 144–145
  land values under, 137–138, 140, 144
  permanent, 123, 133
  popular and political support for,
    138–141
  varying policy positions relating to,
    145–146
Revenues, federal land, 11, 37, 171,
  176–177
Ricardo, David, 153
Roadless Area Review and Evaluation
  (RARE), I and II, 46, 117
Robbins, Roy M., 125, 129
Robinson, Glen O., 128
Rohrbough, Malcolm, 21
Roosevelt, Theodore, 29, 33, 72, 85,
  128, 132
RPA. *See* Forest and Rangeland
  Renewable Resource Planning
  Act.

"Sagebrush Rebellion," 23, 185
  factors responsible for, 68, 165–167
  regional antagonisms in, 7–8
Sax, Joseph, 140, 141, 145, 158
Shands, William E., 139, 233, 234, 243
Sierra Club, 215
Smith, Adam, 149–150
Society of American Foresters, 139
Society for Range Management, 139
South Carolina, 7
States
  claims to federal lands, 8, 165
  land grants to, 22, 23–25

States (*cont'd.*)
  land ownership, 1–2
  proposed long-term leasing of federal
    lands by, 212, 215
  pullback procedure and, 222
  revenues from public lands, 171
  transfer of federal land management
    to, 185–189
States Rights Coordinating Council, 167
Stock-Raising Homestead Act (1916), 23,
  57
Stroup, Richard, 155–156
Surface Mining Control and
  Reclamation Act (1977), 95
Surveys. *See* Cadastral survey.

Taft, William Howard, 84–85
Taylor Grazing Act (1934), 35, 48, 57,
  67
  administration, 36
  closing of public domain following, 9,
    30–31, 138, 155
Teeguarden, Dennis E., 198–199
Thoreau, Henry David, 140, 141
Timber
  appraisal process for, 80–82
  Forest Service sales policy for, 82–84
  illegal harvesting of, 72–73
  national forest sales, 73–77, 80
  prices, 77–80
  revenue from, 108
Trans-Alaska Pipeline Act (1973), 48
Tullock, Gordon, 156

United States v. *Midwest Oil Company,* 85
Uses, federal lands, 11, 63, 106–107
  See also Coal resources; Grazing;
    Mineral resources; Multiple
    land use; Oil and gas; Outdoor
    recreation; Timber

Voigt, William, Jr., 71, 128

Walker, John L., 116
Water resources
  management, 105
  federal versus Indian rights, 96
  regional–national differences, 8
Weeks Act (1911), 19, 30, 41, 243
Western Livestock Grazing Survey
  (1966), 69

"Whiskey Rebellion," 6
Wilderness Act (1964), 10, 44–47
Wilderness areas 11, 43
    areas qualifying as, 137
    characteristics, 104
    establishment, 35
    federal land ownership and, 140, 144
    leasing for reservation or
        conservation, 207, 209, 211
    pullback process applied to, 217
    value of nonmarket outputs of, 161
Wilderness Society, 215

Wildlife, 11
    outdoor recreation and, 105
    refuges, 9, 41
Wolf, Peter, 162
Works Progress Administration, 37

Yellowstone National Park, 28, 134, 232

Zahniser, Howard, 140, 141
Zimmerman, Erich W., 225
Zivnuska, John A., 73
Zoning, for intermingled lands, 244–
        245